ASCENDENT GOVERNMENT

ASCENDENT GOVERNMENT

ALBERT BRILL

ASCENDENCY FOUNDATION

NEW YORK

PRINTED IN THE UNITED STATES OF AMERICA
KINGSPORT PRESS, INC., KINGSPORT, TENNESSEE

3980

TABLE OF CONTENTS

v

CONTENTS

CONTENTS

ASCENDENT GOVERNMENT

I

INTRODUCTORY

ASCENDENT GOVERNMENT IS THE FINAL VOLUME OF A series of three. The first volume, INDIVIDUAL ASCENDENCY, introduces Ascendent Psychology and stresses the development of the individual. The second volume, COLLECTIVE ASCENDENCY, discusses collective activities of man other than government, which is being dealt with here. Throughout the entire series the development of the individual and his duty to himself and others are stressed. Reform of our political and social institutions must aim to improve society itself. Inasmuch as society is composed of many individuals, this improvement must be made through the individual. Further, it must come from within the individual himself, not be thrust upon him from outside sources. This is the theme that continually appears throughout this series. New words or expressions used in this volume are defined in the preceding volumes.

The unsatisfactory condition of affairs in our country today has been a development of many years. The evils existing in our social and political structures have not been pointed out to the public. All too often only those evils have been exposed that furthered political success. Capital, the wealthy, have been attacked and blamed for all existing evils. This has gone to such extremes, has created such harmful and erroneous beliefs throughout the nation, as to prevent proper reform. We must not attack capital or wealthy people because such attacks are popular. We must attack evil where we find it. The evils confronting us today that require the greatest of attention are the low standards of citizenship, poor standards of leadership, and the development of many selfish interest groups seeking to serve their own interests at the expense of the nation as a whole. None of these three glaring evils are primarily the fault of capital or wealthy people. They are the fault of our leaders and of the citizenship of the entire nation. If, instead of attacking others, each citizen will seek within himself for his own faults and perform his duties as a citizen, existing evils of all forms will be insignificant.

The object of this book primarily is to encourage thought, questioning of all existing political institutions, in order that harmful tendencies may be generally understood and corrected. The evils from which we are suffering have developed as the result of lack of understanding, lack of reflection. To correct social ills we must think long and constantly in order to locate the causes which are often obscured by numerous effects. Treating the effects aggravates the evils. If we seek the causes we may obtain sufficient understanding to eradicate the evils.

In previous writings I have attempted to avoid personalities, to avoid discussion of the acts of individuals when they were of a discreditable nature. However, in this volume I feel it necessary to discuss individuals. Our political standards are low because of poor standards of citizenship and poor leadership. In order to educate the public, in order to improve our present-day institutions, in order to point out the causes for this unfortunate condition to future generations, we must expose the men who are guilty. Unpleasant as the task is, it is a public duty. If a man is vicious, if he advocates vicious policies, if he is able to obtain public following and do great harm, we should carefully analyze the reason for his ability to do this. Let the public understand these reasons. Let future generations be able to see them. Then the public of today may be aroused to reform our institutions and future generations may be enabled to guard against a similar occurrence.

If evil men and evil women can be exposed and discredited, they should be so exposed, they should be so discredited. Writers in a position to do so, who fail to point out the causes of evil conditions, to point out evil men, are failing in their duty. If they do this in an earnest seeking for the truth, they should receive attention. However, when one does attack individuals he must guard against extremes, not falsely impute bad motives to them, not accuse them of things of which they are not guilty. Regardless of the men, their positions, their measures, we should seek for the truth. When they advance the truth, we should give them credit for doing so. When they violate the truth, we should expose them in a detached objective manner free of personal animus. This I have attempted to do.

My general rule is to say nothing that a hundred years hence will not be credible and creditable. I shall attack all evils in the most convincing way. Unless they be exposed, they will not be corrected. It is cowardly to pass viciousness by, leaving the unpleasant task for others. But when you attack viciousness and the vicious you must risk soiling your hands.

It is the duty of each citizen to contribute toward honest government. When the fulfillment of this task requires dealing with filth he should not hesitate. Each decent citizen should endeavor to clean up his country's institution just as the worthy home owner should clean up the filth in and around his home. They will then have the satisfaction of having done an excellent job and will have the reward of enjoying the beauty, the order, the cleanliness which has replaced the filth.

To understand disease we must investigate it. This requires close association. To understand vileness we must likewise associate with it, not to the extent of permitting it to corrupt us, but that we may understand its manifestations in order to protect ourselves from its onslaught. Denying vileness—wishing, hoping, saying that it does not exist—will not destroy it. Investigating vileness, finding out why it exists, placing the vile in the public eye that it may be recognized, is not a pleasing task but is necessary and sensible.

Many people and conditions are so despicable as to be unworthy of discussion. However unpleasant a task may be, one who endeavors to advance civilization must not shirk his duty in calling attention to and discussing the unworthy. However, calling names, even when speaking frankly about vicious people, detracts from high standards of thought. Denunciation will lessen the merit of a work. Nevertheless, we should denounce the vicious, the unworthy. Pursuing this view, some thoughts are expressed herein regarding people who are undeserving of consideration. The reader can profit from learning about them.

Education is both positive and negative. We should learn about that which is worthy of our attention by positive efforts. We should likewise learn about that which is unworthy of our attention in order that we may guard against it. It will frequently be found that unworthiness will be associated with virtue and good intentions just as touches of insanity may be associated with genius.

It becomes increasingly difficult to be generous to men who are breaking down the character of our citizenship at the same time claiming to serve noble and worthy causes. I have tried to avoid unfairness. I have, however, permitted much feeling to appear. This is sometimes expressed under the heading of "Gripes" and is sometimes incorporated in discussions of men and measures. In all cases it is based upon reasoned conclusions intensified by deep feelings of disgust and irritation, and sometimes shows traces of primitive savagery.

It is fatal to believe hopefully that because America has always overcome difficulties in the past she will do so in the future. America has not been threatened in the past by the same evils that are threatening her today. There was far greater strength of individual character in citizens of previous generations than in the citizens of today. We are undermining the character of our citizens. This is the greatest evil threatening us today. If we permit it to continue America will not survive and will be undeserving of survival. Let us be sensible. Let us not wishfully believe that we will overcome our difficulties. Let us actually face the problems, solve and overcome them by intelligent efforts. Let us raise the standards of citizenship. If we raise them sufficiently high they will insure the preservation of our nation.

The ability of Switzerland with three races and three languages to establish and maintain a good government over such a long period is very instructive. The country is small, and there is a sufficient community of interests and enough intelligence among the citizens to cause them to co-operate for the benefit of the nation. They have established an enlightened government by building up an intelligent citizenship which serves and receives service.

Civilizations perished because they failed to insure the intellectual and moral development of their citizens, to understand the principles of human nature, and to develop a sound religion that would teach them. Another great failure was living in the present, failing to plan for the future and solve the problems of future generations before they became impossible of solution.

The downfall of Rome and other nations was due to incompetence of the government, war, poor character of individual citizens, poor religion, poor educational system, vicious economic and social system, slavery, seeking for physical pleasure, lack of public spirit on the part of the citizens, and selfishness on the part of individuals. One can enumerate many causes that contributed to the downfall of nations. We should profit from their blunders and avoid having them occur in our own country. Unfortunately, but little effort is made to utilize this experience from the past, and the world is blundering on much as the Romans did and with as little intelligent control as they had in the last few centuries of the Empire. We are living from day to day, without real plan for the future or energetic efforts to elevate the intelligence and moral character of the citizens. We have much talk about education and moral character, but the talk is by impractical people.

We are attempting to carry out impractical measures intended to benefit the nation. These measures do much harm by requiring the deserving citizens to support the undeserving. Because of our scientific and industrial development, we are confronted with more difficult problems today than faced the ancient nations. Foolish acts are threatening our destruction in the future just as surely as they caused the destruction of nations in the past. It is not difficult to point out the evils that threaten us and correct them, but we are being governed by impractical people. They have many ideas to correct existing ills and are equally good at finding fault with all sound measures; therefore we drift with conditions steadily growing worse.

When our Constitution was adopted, we were put in possession of a government adequate to the needs of the times and superior to most governments then in existence. Under it our country has prospered and made greater progress than any nation in history in a like period of time.

A great contributing factor toward this development was that the government interfered as little as possible with the individuals, and each one was encouraged to his greatest efforts, knowing he would reap the full reward from them. We were favored by having large quantities of free land in the West, and by having our national development coincident with the many great discoveries of the industrial age. The steam engine, steamboat, and railroad inaugurated this era; and following them, further improvements and discoveries were made, all of which contributed toward increasing the wealth of the country, but brought with them additional problems for the government to solve.

Our leaders have been unable to solve these problems. In their efforts to do so they have blamed capital and big business, and created ill feeling among the citizens. We hear much denunciation of others, and in some cases have had resorts to violence.

Our situation in this respect is not unlike that of the Roman Republic during the era of Social Wars. The really fine qualities of the early Romans deteriorated under conditions of internal strife and their republic perished.

Let us all stop fighting among ourselves and work together for each others' benefit. All the virtue and right is not on our side. The other side may be as good or better. Since the dawn of man he has been fighting himself. What a waste of effort! If that effort spent in fighting among ourselves were used in strenuous efforts to further one another's interests, fighting would cease for the causes would have disappeared.

During the Great War Germany put up a magnificent fight for four years, holding back overwhelming numbers of foes. The German nation was welded into a strong aggregation of individuals fighting for what they believed to be right as the result of influences so molding their beliefs. We had in the United States a great number of Americans of German descent. When the United States entered the war many of these men entered the United States Army and fought just as strongly against Germany as Germans were fighting for their country. If we give this a little reflection we will see here individuals of the same race, the same characteristics, brought to an entirely different viewpoint because of circumstances, of different environment. In this particular case they were brought to fight and kill one another. Certain basic factors governing human nature brought about their acts. One cannot help but think of the vast results for good that could be accomplished if the forces causing these men of the same blood to kill each other were utilized to make them work together for the advance of man the world over. It is this which Ascendent Psychology attempts to do. If man is ever to solve his problems it will have to be based upon a sound understanding of human nature and the ability to employ the human mind for man's best good.

The reason our problems are not being solved is because

people are not thinking sufficiently about them. Those who are thinking either do not know how or else have solutions based upon inadequate knowledge or already formed opinions. With the development of Ascendent Psychology, with critical analysis of all suggested solutions, with much thought upon present-day problems, solutions could be found.

To solve man's problems, we must approach the individual through both duty and self-interest. Let each one solve his own problems, make his own way in the world, cease to be a burden to others, be an ascendent influence, and let those who live in accord therewith assist others in doing likewise. By such action each person will be advancing his own interests, doing his duty to himself, the future, and others.

"Right is right." That insane expression so often used, coined by politicians for its demagogic appeal to further their ends, of "human rights versus property rights," is an appeal to stimulate class hatred. What all should do is merely do right. If each person does so, the expressions "human" and "property" can both be omitted, and the implied conflict between them will disappear.

But few people think and conduct themselves in accordance with what is right. We have too much of a heritage from the past of ignorant superstition and false teaching. We are the victims of a religion that does not know how to promote good conduct or even know what good conduct is, of an education that does not educate, of a government that knows little of how government should be conducted, of nations crazy with nationalism, killing or threatening to kill the best manhood, of an economic system that fails to solve problems in the interest of all, of a legal system that gives not justice. We are what we have been made. Now let us be men as we should be, make ourselves what God intended man to be, dominate the evil, and not permit the evil to dominate and control us. When we reach that stage, then we may claim to be men, to be civilized. Instead of permitting ourselves to be controlled by the forces that now control us, let us control these forces for man's good.

My aim throughout this book is to present the facts regarding human welfare to the best of my ability. It is not my intention to attack individuals or groups. My research into the various problems culminating in Ascendent Psychology has caused me to realize that most individuals, such as demagogues, politicians, agitators, who do so much harm, are led by forces beyond their knowledge but which they fondly believe they are directing and leading. It does arouse a great feeling of resentment within me to see men, themselves unable to understand problems, attacking others and spreading ill will and class hatred throughout the land. Despite my desire to be generous to all, the conduct of most politicians inspires me with the utmost disgust. Appealing to the prejudice and ignorance of large masses of people, promising benefits impossible of fulfillment and eventually leading to disaster, is conduct which I cannot regard without a feeling of extreme revulsion. Our modern civilization has advanced but little in the way of developing sound thought and real moral character when we permit such miserable creatures as our existing politicians to conduct the affairs of our great nation. If our leaders were able, they would lead us forward to better things. Instead of doing this, they place the blame wherever it will do the least harm from a political standpoint, and follow the mob, trying to anticipate what the mob will think and flattering themselves that by so doing they are leading it.

This is not a pleasant picture to contemplate, nor are the statements pleasing to make. But they are substantially what my calm judgment dictates. No amount of eloquence or promises will correct existing evils. It will take intelligent action, having as its aim the promotion of sound thought, moral character, and work. The politicians flatter the populace and tell them that they are already intelligent and can think, tell them that their moral character is above reproach, tell them that they are being overworked, and promise to lighten the burden. The truth is that the mob is not intelligent, is not of high moral character, and from the standpoint of work would be better off if it did more honest work with less talk, denunciation, and belittling of others. But with all this, there is real virtue in the average citizen. He will respond to good leadership if it will but lead the way.

That our friends are often our worst enemies and that a mere desire to serve without intelligent control results in greater harm, is well shown by many classes having great influence upon our institutions. The politicians are ruining our government. The preachers are discrediting the religion. The lawyers are worshiping legal technicalities and have forgotten the purpose for which the law exists. The writers are obscuring thought. Our psychologists have discredited psychology, rendering understanding of human nature almost impossible for those desiring to obtain such understanding. We are certainly passing through an era but little removed from the antics of an insane asylum.

Our democratic form of government is being destroyed in our country: first, by incompetent leaders unequal to the task of conducting the government, and second, by the development of many strong interest groups who exist to browbeat politicians and obtain benefits for themselves. The bad feature about this for the future is that no one seems to point out the evils connected with interest groups, show how they originated, developed; no one points out the evils of our political system that prevents able leaders from getting in control. To insure an efficient government we must correct these two things. We must obtain able, honest men to conduct the affairs of the government. We must abolish the activities of interest groups in demanding benefits for themselves and require that all citizens work for one interest group, the nation.

The conspicuous failure of man is to establish an efficient form of government. Further progress in making this a better, happier world will be greatly retarded, almost impossible, unless we solve the problem of government. Throughout man's history he has endeavored to meet the problem of government, with but a moderate degree of success. Many different types of government have existed, but regardless of the particular form which the government takes, it is essential that it be conducted by able men with a broad viewpoint, a great understanding of the effect of their acts upon the future. To govern a nation efficiently requires a knowledge of all sciences affecting man's welfare. We have not as yet developed institutions capable of producing governments adequate to the complex conditions of modern civilization.

The object of government is to promote the present and future welfare of the people of a nation as a whole. Our government as at present constituted is but ill-adapted to perform this duty. Great progress has been made in all lines of human endeavor in the past hundred years, but the improvement of government has not kept abreast of this progress. The conditions of modern life are so complicated that the government must of necessity interfere more and more with the individual's freedom of action in order to regulate affairs requiring the intervention of an impartial outside agency for the general good.

The development of civilization has placed increasing burdens upon the government. In the simple forms of life, such as those of our frontier communities, but little government was necessary. In this modern age of industrialization, so many new problems have been brought about that the government is required to assume greater and greater burdens. With this increase in government activities, the need for a most efficient government becomes greater. Unwise policies will result in great distress to many citizens, and the problems are so numerous, so complex, as to tax the ability of the ablest.

Too much stress has been placed upon the industrial revolution and machine age in their effect upon man. He has always been faced by the problem, not yet solved, of a true religion, good government, sound social system. The machine has bearing on these problems, but much less than commonly accepted.

Able government will have just laws and insure compliance with them. When the laws are unjust, they encourage violations; if the government officials sworn to enforce these laws do not do so, the government is in danger of disintegrating. If groups within the nation can disregard laws, why cannot individuals? Thus a spirit of lawlessness and disregard of all laws is built up. When we see lawlessness it proves two things: first and foremost, incompetence of government officials; and secondly, usually the existence of unwise laws. We are today passing through a gradual stage of disintegration in our government in which our officials refuse to maintain law and order. This may be corrected before it goes too far if public opinion becomes aroused, but the very effort of our government officials to avoid using force at this time may require the use of far greater force at a later date. Our government has failed to solve the economic problems of the nation despite its many promises to do so. Its policy has contributed to ill-feeling and it is standing idly by while strikes and violations of the law are going on. Just what the future outcome will be remains to be seen. It should, however, impress upon all the need for having an honest government deserving of the respect of all citizens.

Orators, writers, those who have much to do with the creation of public opinion, should be fair, should present both sides of the question. Much of the existing feeling in the country on government policies and economic questions is one-sided, stimulated by the presentation of one side of the case, without recognizing that another side exists. Continual denunciation on the part of those who should contribute toward better understanding is bound to be reflected in the citizens of the country, resulting in ill-feeling, prejudice, and a tendency to use violence to obtain correction of evils that are being constantly brought to the attention of the public, and which are not being corrected. One cannot blame groups of citizens for becoming impatient when they are being continually told about grievances. They have their feelings unduly aroused and often decide to take action into their own hands. Such action is more likely to be cruel and

unjust than considerate and sensible. President Lincoln once
. pardoned a deserter from the Union Army during the Civil
War, and upon someone protesting to him for his action,
replied, "Why should I permit this poor boy to be hanged
when the wily agitator who induced him to desert goes un-
harmed?" The strikers committing offenses against the public are less to be censured than the agitators who stir them
up, and still less than a government that promises to improve conditions, fails to do so, and blames its failure upon
capital—upon anyone or anything but itself.

The development of man is greatly retarded by the general
inertia of the masses to respond to measures designed to advance man's affairs. The mass of citizens would be only too
willing to contribute toward the advance if they but understood and were sure of their actions. Thus when we see
inertia opposing progress we may attribute it more to lack of
intelligence, lack of understanding, than to any other quality.
Generally the more sound people are inclined to be conservative, to accept the familiar and known and oppose the unfamiliar and unknown. When the measures suggested to
advance progress conflict with established beliefs, it is first
necessary to correct the beliefs in order to obtain support.
This may be very difficult if the beliefs are deeply grounded.

We also find in large numbers of people a feeling of uncertainty when new ideas conflict with old. When this lack
of decision exists the natural tendency is to adhere to the old
and known rather than accept the new and unknown. There
are also many who are faint-hearted, who prefer to leave
things as they are rather than to try unknown measures. The
inertia of the masses may be overcome by an appeal to their
emotions, by existing conditions becoming so bad as to make
them impatient and demand action, without, oftentimes,
full consideration of the consequences.

The progress of man is sometimes a gradual growth, in
which advance is made under the leadership of able leaders
formulating wise measures and obtaining the support of the
masses. Progress is also often obtained by an emotional out-

burst, the French Revolution for instance, in which the masses pass from inertia to the opposite. Usually in these. revolutionary uprisings they go to extremes, employ violence, do much harm, and cause many to wish for a return to the old days of peace and quiet.

The true method for progress to overcome mass inertia is not by appeal to the emotions. This may be effective, but intelligence and judgment do not usually form a part of emotional action, with the result that much harm is done by unwise measures. The most sensible means of overcoming the inertia and advancing man's affairs is by the process of education and gradual growth. If the measures are sound, if they advance the intelligence and character of the individuals, they will gradually obtain increasing support and overcome the inertia to change if the proper leadership exists. The masses of people are helpless by themselves. They must act through leaders. If they have able leaders they are extremely fortunate, and if their leaders are unequal to the task they are unfortunate. The French Revolution, and in fact all revolutions of a similar kind, were the direct result of incompetent leaders.

Mass inertia is sometimes a good characteristic when we have, as today in our own country, many selfish interest groups striving for means to advance their own interests. These selfish measures will not overcome the inertia of the masses and their proponents find it necessary to ally themselves with other interest groups in an effort to obtain their ends. Thus we have many interest groups displaying great energy trying to obtain benefits for themselves and unable to overcome the inertia of the people as a whole. This is because they lack the confidence of the people and their measures are designed not to contribute to the interest of all but toward certain favored groups. Thus their measures fail to win popular support. To overcome the inertia of a large mass of people measures must be under consideration that affect the welfare of the nation generally, that are intended for that purpose, not for a particular group or as the result of compromises between many such groups.

Neither communism nor socialism without a spiritual motive will solve man's problems. When the have-nots get power, the abler ones among them will monopolize the benefits just as they now accuse the wealthy of doing under the capitalistic system. It is but a change of name and masters, with additional difficulties. Ascendency can be better advanced within a capitalistic system and the capitalists themselves enrolled in furthering it, thus lessening class feeling and prejudices.

Social institutions designed to insure the highest degree of Ascendency must be based upon two contradictory principles—individual liberty and co-operation. Each individual must be permitted the fullest expression, but this expression must have due regard for others. All members of a community must co-operate if high standards are to be preserved. It is not difficult to reconcile these two principles. The expression of the individual must be beneficial to himself and without harm to others. Co-operative action must be of such nature as not to limit individual expression of a beneficial nature. A society composed of intelligent and considerate members will have no difficulty in reconciling the need for individual freedom of expression with whole-hearted co-operation.

Co-operation itself may be divided into two classes: the voluntary co-operation of the individual himself, which comes from within him; and statutory co-operation, that co-operation required by the government under law. Successful social institutions will insure that individual voluntary co-operation is unrestricted, but they will limit statutory co-operation to essentials, to a minimum of interference with individual freedom of action. Statutory co-operation will strangle both individual expression and voluntary co-operation. This is exactly what our existing governmental policies and social reform measures are doing. They stress statutory co-operation. They do not stress individual expression or voluntary co-operation. As statutory co-operation increases, individual expression and voluntary co-operation will decrease.

We are attempting to accomplish by statute what we should accomplish by encouraging individual expression and voluntary co-operation. Were the latter to grow, the need for statutory co-operation would diminish and would be consistently lessened, thus permitting freer individual expression. We see this same blunder being made throughout the world today under both communist and fascist forms of government. All alike attempt to effect reforms by statute, which crushes the finer human qualities, prevents the freest individual expression, and prevents the development of the far more wholesome voluntary co-operation.

The government itself should encourage the development of voluntary co-operation. It has an excellent agency for this in the schools. As ascendent environment will contribute to a maximum of individual expression and voluntary co-operation. The government should promote an ascendent environment by encouraging all to strive for Ascendency by individual efforts. When the government promotes an ascendent environment it is lessening the need for statutory co-operation. One of the greatest criticisms we can apply to our government institutions today is that they are failing to build up an ascendent environment, failing to build up voluntary co-operation; in fact, our politicians encourage the opposite. They encourage the voters to expect benefits from the government, to expect assistance, to demand co-operation from others, but not voluntarily to co-operate themselves.

After our government inaugurated the policy of extensive relief measures, charitable agencies had more difficulty in obtaining contributions from private individuals. This to some extent was due to the business depression and to increased taxation, but it was also a direct result of the government's relief action. People who formerly gave much voluntarily to charity had their resentment aroused by government policies, and instead of contributing to charity as formerly, would say, "Let the government do it. They're running everything now. I pay heavy taxes, I'm called names, I have a difficult time making ends meet. These people running the government think they know it all. Let them take care of all the charity themselves." This is an excellent illustration of the fact that an increase in government activity lessens voluntary co-operative efforts.

Whatever statutory co-operation is employed should have, for its primary purpose, the object of encouraging voluntary co-operation. We should carry this same principle into our labor difficulties and crime prevention: use the minimum of statutory co-operation for the employer and let that be of such a nature as to encourage voluntary co-operation on his part. The statutory co-operation in the criminal code should have as its primary object the encouragement of voluntary co-operation: a minimum of prohibition, repression, regulation. Then, that statutory co-operation which is employed should have the primary object of promoting wholesome co-operation, a co-operation coming from within each individual, not a co-operation thrust upon him from the outside.

II

DEMOCRATIC INSTITUTIONS

THE DISCUSSION OF DEMOCRATIC INSTITUTIONS IN THIS CHAPTER is directed chiefly toward pointing out weaknesses, evils, and harmful tendencies. The merits of democratic institutions have been extolled so often by so many as to make it somewhat unnecessary to dwell upon them. To insure the success of our democratic institutions, we must preserve the merits and correct the faults. If we concentrate entirely upon the merits and fail to see the faults, we cannot correct the latter. Democratic institutions have been overthrown throughout many countries in the world. They are threatened with downfall in our own country today. The real friend of democracy is not he who continually extolls its merits and disregards its faults. The real friend of democracy is he who points out harmful tendencies, who seeks for the evils in democracy and for their correction. We must frankly admit the existence of evils, seek for them, and correct them in order to preserve the merits.

Present-day democracy is threatened because politicians desiring office continually promise benefits in order to obtain votes; this, with other influences, brings about an environment conducive to the development of poor citizenship. The average citizen, not being well informed or very intelligent, will naturally be influenced to support those measures that he supposes will benefit him. A successful democracy will require a more general striving toward Ascendency on the part of all citizens and the development of a citizenship higher than has yet existed in any nation. To bring this about, present-day politicians will have to be discarded. They are leading the citizenship downward. We must obtain men from some source capable of advancing Ascendency.

One of the great faults of democracy is concentration on present benefits to the neglect of future good. What we are pleased to call present benefits are often not productive of future good. When the two are in conflict in even a small degree, future benefits should be given preference. It is the duty of each generation to leave the following generation without burdens, and set a good example by solving present-day problems. Thrusting burdens upon future generations is starting them with too great a handicap. It is cowardly— unfair to them. What parent would willingly shirk his duty and require his children to start life under a handicap preventing them from achieving success in life, or would leave an example of neglected duty? This is what we, as citizens, do when we fail to solve the problems of the present and thrust them upon the future.

We are witnessing within our own country a very vicious development of democracy, in which the government is being controlled by those who are supported by it. True democracy demands that the government be supported by all the citizens and that it not support any group of citizens. This is where the threat to our democratic institutions exists, and the problem will some day have to be met. The people who are being supported by the government will become such a great burden that the government will be unable to continue this policy.

The revolutions that began with the French Revolution and extended to the Russian Revolution were a revolt of the masses against the abuse of privileged classes. Now the pendulum has swung the other way. The masses themselves are oppressing that element within the nation that supports the government and maintains itself by its own efforts. We are now seeing revolution within democracies in which the most desirable element of the population is revolting against the abuse of power by the undesirable portion which demands that they be supported.

The natural tendency of a democratic form of government is to abuse taxation. That is to say, those people paying no taxes directly are all too willing to support taxation of the wealthy or those possessing property. This is a tendency that can be corrected by high standards of citizenship and education. The man who has little does not usually realize that by supporting heavy government expenditures, he is creating unsound economic conditions that will eventually cause him to suffer.

Democracy is contributing toward the breakdown of high moral character in our people. The deserving are being penalized and plundered by the undeserving under the name of charity, relief, social welfare, and reform, thus putting a good appearance on an insidious canker that is growing and thriving in our midst. If man cannot have character the race had better perish. If democracy breaks down character it should perish. The evils within our government are not essentially evils of democracy; they are evils of man. If we can raise the standard of our citizens above these evils, we will at the same time be raising democracy and the standards of our government.

Among the finest examples of democracy in operation was that displayed by the settlers in opening up virgin territory. A small group would go to unoccupied land, assist one another in building roads, put up log cabins, clear the land, defend themselves against the attacks of Indians, perform all the duties of government, all the work. They asked for no benefits from any government except the right to be left alone and handle their own local affairs. We have indeed gone far from that stage to the present era of democracy in which practically every community has its hand out for federal largess in some form: benefits, public buildings, local improvements, any means by which they can get appropriations from the government. No government can endure under such a condition of affairs, nor is it fit to endure. The general object of government is to serve the people, but not to support them. The duty of the citizen is to support his government, not to be supported by it. A democratic form of government will be successful when the large mass of citizens serve it faithfully, giving of their best in its support. But it becomes as vicious a system of government as is possible to conceive when its institutions are controlled by politicians arousing class feeling, buying votes by promises of government benefits, and when large masses of citizens demand that they be supported and cared for by the government.

Our citizens are not thoughtful, not reflective, do not weigh what they read and hear upon its merit. The remarks of such a violent labor agitator as John L. Lewis would condemn him to thoughtful people. One can seek in vain in any of his statements for an understanding of the problems, a desire to co-operate and solve them. All his statements indicate that John L. Lewis is right and all who oppose him are wrong, that the union which he heads is without faults, and that the employers who oppose it are utterly vicious, without merit. Yet this man has attained a large following, is courted by the politicians. When we have a democracy that permits such a condition to exist, it is doomed to disaster and is deserving of it.

Our present political institutions have a bad effect upon the environment. When we have politicians denouncing each other, denouncing capital, denouncing worthy people, it cannot but have a bad effect upon the citizens, particularly young people. Able government will contribute toward the improvement of the environment; and we should endeavor to improve our democratic institutions so as to do this. This can best be done by raising the standards of the individual citizens both in their intelligence and character so they will see through the flimsy promises of agitators and will scorn men who do not possess good character. With this general feeling on the part of citizens, politicians would cease to make such vicious, unjust attacks because they would thereby be discrediting themselves.

A common weakness of democratic government is an unwillingness to face the facts, to face issues squarely. The general tendency of politicians dependent upon popular support for office is to avoid controversial issues. Thus the problems of primary importance are often avoided. Avoiding problems will not insure their solution.

When we critically examine the merits of democracy and its weaknesses, we must not overlook the fact that a large percentage of the inhabitants of our country are insane, criminal, feebleminded. The class of those mentally deficient will vary from one-fifth to one-third of the total population, depending upon how rigid are the standards one establishes. It is from this large group that most demands for relief come and it is to this group that politicians appeal for votes. Our efforts should be directed toward eliminating them, toward raising the standard of citizenship and with it the standards of democracy.

Democracy as now practiced in our country is opposed to science. The politicians control affairs through appeals to the most unintelligent element of the population by arousing prejudice and hatred; by appealing to man's most undesirable qualities; by appeals to those very things that science is striving to eliminate and which must be eliminated if man is to advance. We must eliminate the unintelligent, undesirable classes in our population, and we must eliminate the prejudices, hatreds, and undesirable qualities existing in human beings. Our much vaunted present-day democracy appeals to the worst in man, and endeavors to perpetuate it. True progress cannot be made in the solution of man's affairs unless democracy be overthrown or reformed, and science given full opportunity to control the affairs of man in such way as to bring out the best in him.

A most serious fault of democracy is opposition to and obstruction of sound far-reaching reform. A reform measure may be sound but difficult of execution, and require the support of all the people. When, instead of getting the wholehearted support of all, large numbers endeavor to discredit and oppose it, it may become impossible to carry it out. It may, in fact, be discredited by the vast amount of opposition. The evils of political parties are especially apparent in opposition to good measures. The party in control is subjected to criticism by the opposing party. Constructive criticism is helpful, obstructive criticism is harmful. Efficient government demands, first, that wise measures be inaugurated, and secondly, that their execution receive the support of all citizens.

Criticism and the abuse of the privilege of free speech may prevent the efficient functioning of democratic government. So many people have so many ideas as to what should or should not be done that any suggested measure, even if perfect, is criticized by many and harshly attacked. The very freedom granted by our democratic institutions prevents the conduct of sound government. The communists in Russia found that in order to carry out their measures they had to establish a ruthless dictatorship. It is very questionable whether we can correct our existing evils without a resort to some form of dictatorship.

Under a democratic form of government measures of vital import and offering great future good may be so difficult of enforcement that unless opposition ceases and all citizens support the measures to insure their success they will be harmful. Thus a minority can often obtain its will by continued opposition against the wish of the majority and the future good. To inaugurate far-reaching reforms, it may be necessary to prohibit harmful opposition. If so, such measures should be carefully considered before being put into practice. This is where there is great danger of democratic government breaking down. When measures that will solve vital problems are opposed by a minority, the future good demands that the minority be repressed. This will eventually result in abuse, the prohibition of free speech, the throttling of constructive criticism, which will be very harmful. Captious criticism and attack on measures that have been carefully considered before enactment is not a feature of good citizenship. When sound government policies have been established, all opposition should cease and all citizens should support the measures in order to make them a success. Opposition to them by even a small minority may prevent success.

The weakness of democracy as a form of government is exposed by labor disorders and strikes. A democratic government has a difficult problem in maintaining law and order for the reason that the politicians controlling the government depend upon votes to obtain office. When they employ the force of the government to suppress strikes, they are threatening political destruction to themselves. This for the reason that the working classes have a feeling against the wealthy, sympathize with the strikers, and while they would applaud the use of force against capital, they oppose the use of force to suppress lawbreakers disguised as labor organizations.

Both France and the United States have experienced increasing difficulty in this respect of late years. The politicians weakly follow the popular method of denouncing capital and avoid the use of force. In many cases strikes have been ended by the resentment of the public, not by the action of the government. This again illustrates the need for high standards of citizenship in a democracy; the citizens should appreciate the need for law and order; they should realize that it is the responsibility of the government to regulate disputes between all citizens and that when the government fails to do so it is incompetent; that strikes, riots, labor disorders generally are positive evidence of incompetent, inefficient government. No attempt is today being made to elevate the standards of citizenship. Many well-meaning people talk about it but nothing of a positive nature is done.

It will be interesting to see what the net result will be in the next few years. One cannot safely make predictions when so many complex factors are involved. The most likely result is that the more sensible respectable citizens will finally become disgusted with their government, politicians, and labor agitators; that they will then unite under some able leader, if such a leader can be found, and establish a form of government capable of maintaining law and order. When this happens, our democratic institutions will have perished not through the attacks of their enemies but through the incompetence of their leaders and defenders; through the efforts of politicians more concerned with their personal fortunes than public welfare.

I have sometimes compared the Scandinavian nations and other small countries possessing democratic institutions to our own nation, claiming in general that they were more successful than ourselves. Yet this morning (January 18, 1938) there is a notice in the paper about a strike in Swedish hotels, a general lockout of some twenty thousand workers demanding higher wages. This demand was refused by the employers who claimed inability to pay more because the government under a new administration of the liquor monopoly prevents the employer from profiting from the sale of liquor. These smaller countries are suffering in a less degree from the same evils that present day democracies promote. Democracies will yet have to profit from dictatorships, will have to seek energetically for, and correct, the inherent evils of democracy that threaten to destroy it.

Present-day democracy is developing to a far lower stage than the absolute monarchy it superseded. The absolute monarchies defended what they believed was right. Present-day democracy attacks the successful, glorifies the unsuccessful. Politicians in order to obtain votes continually promise, to those who have little or nothing, many benefits which of necessity must be taken from others. This is an entirely erroneous conception of government. What we should stress is character, ability, worth to the community, supporting those that contribute toward this and eliminating those that oppose it. Stress intelligence and moral worth—they of themselves will correct the economic evils existing. Our attempts are the opposite. We attempt to correct economic ills by attacking them, and the very ones who attack are often the most noisy, the most incompetent, the most undesirable elements in the community. Thus in effect democracy has resulted in government of the desirable element by the undesirable element. When we reverse this process, when we place the government in the control of the desirable elements and eliminate the undesirable, we will be approaching a scientific solution of the problems of both government and economics.

The primary reasons for the breakdown of democratic institutions are Descendent Groupo and the establishment of citizenship standards in which the citizen demands to be served instead of serving. This demand of the citizen to be served, to receive benefits, is in large part a development of intensified selfish Groupo. Of necessity in a democratic country, individuals having interests in common must band together to elect their representatives to office and to protect their interests. Interest groups have reached the stage of demanding benefits from politicians by virtue of their mass voting strength. Thus, while we have many extolling democratic institutions, democracy's privileges are being so generally abused as to break down the foundation upon which democracy itself rests: the character of its citizens. The liberty guaranteed by our constitution is being converted into license. Many groups demand benefits under the guise of helping others or obtaining justice. The weakness of our politicians encourages these groups. None are strong enough to expose or denounce them. Few men in the country even understand the insidious threats they contain to democratic institutions.

Now, as compared to this condition in our own country, let us consider conditions in Italy or Germany where dictatorships prevail. Much as we dislike some of their acts we must conclude that they maintain far higher standards of citizenship than a democracy. Neither country has intensified selfish groups within it demanding benefits from the government. Neither do the citizens of either country demand that they be served by the government. They almost unanimously serve. Thus the dictatorships which are commonly considered enemies of democracy are most successful in establishing the high standards of citizenship upon which a democracy must rest.

France is another example of democratic institutions rapidly deteriorating, an example of citizenship rapidly deteriorating, for much the same reason as in our own country. In Great Britain the evils are less manifest. The British have had more difficult problems to face than the Americans but they have faced them in a more courageous manner; their citizenship is of a higher type and their standards of government service are far superior to those we have in America.

One can trace this great difference in the development of the institutions of the two great English-speaking countries. Basically the people themselves are very similar. America, starting as a new nation without traditions and having more vociferous politicians, developed a form of constitutional government which more readily lent itself to political abuse. As a result, the democratic institutions deteriorated more rapidly than in Great Britain.

In Great Britain, on the other hand, higher standards of political leadership, greater regard for the welfare of the country, the influence of a great conservative body of upper and middle classes, has tended to prevent the demoralizing breakdown of their institutions. Many other contributing factors are involved. For instance, Great Britain was not divided into the North and South, does not have a negro question, did not within recent years have a vast civil war, and did not suffer thereafter from a vicious carpetbag government. Neither has Great Britain been demoralized to the extent that the United States was in the vast industrial development and opening up of new territory.

The Americans as a nation have drifted with the influences of the moment. Now they must face facts, profit by the blunders and mistakes of the past, and endeavor to improve their standards of citizenship, of leadership, in order that democracy may be preserved. In doing this we will do well to profit by the ability of Italy and Germany to maintain higher standards of citizenship than we. If we can establish as great a devotion to the nation, as great a willingness to serve as today exists in Italy and Germany our democratic institutions and our country will be preserved.

Democracy is being doomed to destruction in this country by its own defenders. We hear them denounce dictators abroad and extol at length the virtues of democracy. If they were sensible men, they would seek to correct the ills of democracy, thus saving it from dictators. By denouncing dictators harshly, by glorifying democracy without seeking to correct its faults, they are making future dictatorship in our own country inevitable, with the destruction of the democratic principles they vaunt so highly.

When we see a democratic form of government superseded by a dictatorship, we should not denounce the dictator; we should rather analyze the influences permitting democracy to fail and causing a nation to accept dictatorship as a lesser evil. The primary reason for the failure of democracy is incompetent leaders, demagogic politicians resorting to any means that will obtain votes. They themselves are but products of their times, of existing institutions. These institutions must be modified both to develop able leaders and to insure them support. Democracy, in order to assure success, requires a higher standard of intelligence and of moral character than any nation has yet possessed. Our efforts should be directed not toward denouncing dictators, but toward seeking the faults within democracy and correcting them to bring out the best in the human being and establish upon it a firm foundation of government.

Friends of democracy in our own country belittle and decry militarism in foreign nations and the institutions of dictatorships generally. While unquestionably there is much to criticize in these countries, there likewise is much to criticize in our own. If we seek carefully we will find in foreign nations elements of merit superior to our own. In the United States there is little recognition on the part of the average citizen of a sense of duty to his government. Everything he does for the government is paid for. Many foreign nations demand unquestioning service from their citizens, in the army and in many other ways. It is unfortunate if this service be put to bad use. What I wish to emphasize here is that it has strong virtuous features; it is service by the citizen to his country. If we can bring about in our own country equal willingness on the part of the citizens to serve their country, direct this effort into constructive channels for the solution of our own internal problems and eventually perhaps for the abolition of wars throughout the world, we will be putting this fine service to excellent use. What many of our well-meaning people fail to see is that the spirit of service in many countries is abused, is being put to bad use, but of itself is an excellent thing and only requires wise leadership to accomplish results of enduring value.

The utter incompetence of our politicians is well displayed by their denunciation of foreign dictatorships accompanied with extolment of democracy and American institutions generally. They also make threats that unless the people follow them democracy will be overthrown to be superseded by dictatorships or some form of government destructive of American liberties. Able men would not seek to solve the problems by defense of democracy on the one hand and abuse of dictatorships on the other. They would seek the shortcomings of democracy, tell the people about them, and endeavor to correct them. The policies of our politicians in extolling democracy are preventing correction of its manifest defects. Inevitably it will be overthrown. The politicians will be the ones responsible for this. They have proven incompetent to govern the country or make democracy a stable institution. They are perfectly willing to obtain office, power, through democratic institutions; in fact their personal interests and democracy are one in their eyes. The greatest argument in favor of overthrowing democracy in our country is the fact that by so doing our present-day politicians likewise will be overthrown and removed from office. One can contrast the denunciation of our politicians with the beneficent rule of a dictator who would put them to work and require them to keep their mouths shut. If we can find a dictator equal to the task, he would be a great improvement on our existing leaders.

Politicians thrive on stirring up class feeling. After the Civil War the northern politicians obtained support among their constituents by waving the bloody shirt and reviving war issues. True statesmanship demanded efforts to smooth over past difficulties and look to the future. We should condemn politicians who stir up class feeling. They do this because it is popular with the stupid, unthinking multitude to denounce those who have been successful in life and have achieved. True statesmanship would dictate not the fomenting of class hatred against the successful but against the bad individuals—whether they be rich or poor—and the protection of the good whether they be rich or poor. When we see a politician denouncing capital, we should be convinced that he is appealing to prejudice for purposes of getting votes, that he is inadequate to his task, and is a bad influence. The true statesman would find what the causes were that made capital such a bad influence, and instead of denouncing all capital and all successful people, would attempt to correct the evil influences. This continued stirring up of class feeling on the part of politicians, if permitted to continue, will gradually split the people of the country into classes, those who have been successful and are able to make their own way as opposed to those who are unsuccessful, who demand government benefits, who demand support by the government.

Our own Civil War was preceded by years of denunciation of the North and South by their politicians and agitators, and the ill feeling brought on four years of bloodshed. Sensible men should realize that in continually stirring up hatreds of this kind they are bringing about inevitable bloodshed. Do we see capital attacking anyone, causing ill feeling? No. Capitalists struggle on, trying to keep the industries of the country going. It is the politicians, radical labor leaders, agitators, and reformers generally who are continually attacking capital and creating ill feeling. The possibility of civil war in this country is not to be lightly disregarded. Decent people would be justified in resorting to arms to defend themselves against consistent abuse, taxation, regulation, being penalized by their very ability to solve their own problems to care for others.

The politicians do not realize it as yet, but they are very short-sighted and are sealing their own doom as well as that of democracy in this country. Popular measures and acts may maintain them in office for a time, but when the unsound effects become manifest to all, the politicians will be discredited and they will get little popular support against a really strong, able man aiming for the dictatorship.

The great threat to democratic institutions in all countries is the employment of violence by selfish interest groups within the nation to obtain their demands by intimidation. This is most commonly exhibited by labor unions, which resort to strikes to obtain high wages, shorter hours, benefits of some kind; which demand collective bargaining; or which sometimes go on strike because some agitator has been discharged by the employer. When this violence gets so bad as to arouse the resentment of the public generally, democratic institutions will be overthrown to be superseded by a stronger form of government. We have seen this very thing take place in several foreign nations.

Our labor unions fail to see that by resorting to violence, they are threatening democratic institutions. Not only this, but when the democratic form of government is superseded by dictatorship or some similar form, past abuses will also be remembered and labor unions will be so regulated, so repressed, as to prevent them from existing except in a very limited way. We have had in many cases, in the past year in our country, strikes which substantially amounted to civil war. Our weak government was unable to enforce the law, was too incompetent to correct existing injustices. If democracy is unable to enforce the law or establish laws worthy of respect; if it is unable to insure justice and fairness to all, it will perish and it should perish.

Before permitting democracy to perish by default, let us

make a final effort to improve our democratic institutions and perpetuate them. The unfortunate part about dictatorships which supersede democracies is that the dictators crush the initiative and liberty of the individual too much. Democracy in our country today permits the abuse of these liberties. If we can establish a democracy that will preserve the liberties but prevent the abuse, we may yet survive. This will not be accomplished by law. It must be accomplished by raising the standards of citizenship and the standards of leadership.

Thoughts

Democracy is fast becoming the worst tyrant of all time, creating class hatreds, perpetuating prejudices, penalizing industry, thrift, and merit to reward the vicious, worthless, and undeserving.

———

Our democratic institutions have degenerated into a means of pleasing and cajoling the masses instead of solving the real problems of government.

———

The universal breakdown of democracy is due to the abuse of its privileges by those who neglect its obligations.

———

Socialism, communism, and democracy generally tend to lower the ablest and best to the level of the inferior, the lower grade, rewarding the mediocre at the expense of the superior. Enlightened government would have the opposite aim.

———

It is easy to stir the masses with the trite and commonplace, if one but appeal to their emotions.

———

Our efforts should not be directed towards trying to sell democracy; they should be directed toward making it a superior product of such merit as to sell itself.

III

DEMOCRACY, CITIZENS

As one looks back on the past history of nations, one is impressed with the fact that they have all failed. Why have they failed? The great cause of their failure was inability to realize that the citizens of a nation must be raised to the highest intellectual and moral standards. Because of failure to recognize this need, study was not directed toward acquiring knowledge of the essentials of human nature in order to elevate the citizens.

Democracy and Ascendency go together and are essential to the success of the democratic form of government. Ascendency strives for the highest development of the individual and of man collectively, and it is these very things that democratic government should promote. If we have a citizenship throughout the nation all striving for Ascendency, of high character and intelligence, such evils in our government as patronage, appealing to interest groups, arousing passion and class feelings, would not exist. The low state of our political life is a reflection not only upon our politicians but upon the citizens. Our politicians flatter the citizens, tell them how good they are, but never point out their faults. The citizens have drifted into the support of this vicious institution, being brought constantly lower as the politicians talk more vociferously about their own virtues, the virtues of the people, and the good they intend to accomplish. When all the citizens strive for Ascendency they will seek for errors both in their political institutions and in themselves, and strive to correct them. A democratic form of government supported by a citizenship all of whom are striving for Ascendency, will be successful.

It has become popular of recent years to condemn rugged individualism as a thing of the past and unsuited for modern conditions. Many reformers consider it inconsistent with a government that is endeavoring to solve modern economic problems and bring about more uniform standards of living. When we condemn rugged individualism and demand reform, we are employing the wrong method. We are attempting to accomplish reform by forcing it upon people and crushing individual initiative. The true method is to encourage rugged indiviaualism to the utmost, give the individual the full benefit of his efforts and elevate all individuals to such a high standard that they will, of their own volition, mutually cooperate for the general welfare of all. Thus, instead of thrusting reforms upon them by governmental fiat, we will have the individual citizens themselves voluntarily accomplish the reforms. In great measure this will render governmental action unnecessary because the problems will have largely disappeared in the attainment of this universal high standard of individual citizenship.

A great cause for the success of democracy in our own country in the past was the fact that the people demanded the greatest of individual liberty and the least amount of government. They did not want the government to give them benefits or interfere with the management of their affairs. As a matter of fact, in the early days the country was so thinly populated and communications were so poor that no such effort could have been made. There was a great deal of excellent co-operative effort on the part of the small communities, but it was done by mutual voluntary effort.

The citizens of our early days were on the whole less intelligent and less well educated than the present citizens, but they were far better citizens because they demanded little from the government except freedom to conduct their own affairs. Today all too many citizens demand assistance, benefits, special legislation or action from the government to help them or their interest group. From the standpoint of citizenship the character of the individual citizen today is far less worthy than the character of the citizens of a hundred years ago. If we can return to the idea of government our forefathers had, that the government interfere as little as possible with their affairs and give the greatest of liberty to each individual, and if with this we conduct a campaign of education, create an ascendent environment and encourage each individual to achieve Ascendency, we may yet save our democratic institutions and modern civilization.

Character and intelligence are the two crying needs. If we can make these universal among our citizens it will be a relatively simple matter to solve the economic problems. The greater the character, the greater the intelligence, the less will the government have occasion to interfere with the daily life of the citizens. The fewer laws, the less regulation, the more efficient the government. No government can long exist that does not endeavor to develop the intelligent character of its citizens. The old Roman and Greek democracies proved this only too well, and our present civilization will become unworthy unless we profit from the past and strive to develop a worthy citizenship.

We will increase the efficiency of our government by simplifying it and reducing its task to the essential things, leaving the fullest liberty to the citizens. It should be the duty of all citizens to handle their own problems and care for themselves. The government should encourage all citizens to do this and avoid becoming an agency to care for those who wish to thrust their burdens upon others.

You as a citizen should realize that your interests will suffer in the end if you abuse your privileges by thrusting burdens upon others. Your own interest requires that your fellows' interests also be considered. Once this is universally lived up to throughout our country, we will have a worthy citizenship which will result in worthy institutions and a sensible economic system which will provide opportunity for all and prevent any deserving person from being in want.

A serious fault of our democratic government is the fact that citizens are unwilling to serve the government in any capacity without remuneration. There are many ways in which citizens can serve the community, not only by positive action but in refraining from action that increases government costs. Our citizens fail to realize that their government is their own and intended both to serve them and to be served. The average citizen feels that the government is some far-removed wealthy uncle from whom it is a fine thing to obtain gifts and benefits; he commonly neglects to think of the duties and obligations of citizenship. Our politicians never call attention to this; they flatter and cajole, extolling the merits of the American people, when as a matter of fact they have serious faults which, if unchecked, will make an advanced degree of civilization impossible.

The lack of a deep sense of duty on the part of average American citizens bodes ill for the future. They demand pay for all service to the government, demand that the government serve them, support them. They fail to recognize that all benefits given by the government must be obtained in some way by the government from some class of its citizens. By simple logical reasoning, a moderately intelligent person can see that when they obtain benefits from the government, someone else must pay for them. The general attitude of interest groups is to "let the other fellow worry about that; let's get what we can; everybody else is doing it, why shouldn't we?" Truly, such a sense of civic duty deserves the destruction of the institutions permitting it to exist.

The low standard of our citizenship both as to intelligence and civic understanding is illustrated by the fact that one of the presidential candidates, Mr. Roosevelt, in his endeavor to obtain office, promised upon election to make a twenty-five per cent reduction in government expenses. When Mr. Roosevelt obtained the presidency, instead of carrying out his promise to reduce government expenses, he greatly increased them. This aroused no great feeling on the part of the general public, no great wave of moral indignation. When a candidate for our highest office can pledge himself to do certain things, then upon election do the opposite and be applauded for such action, it shows a very low state of civic duty and understanding on the part of the citizens and very poor quality on the part of the man who is guilty of such treachery.

We have any number of highly moral people advocating measures to improve the character of the citizens who ignore this sort of conduct. We are being constantly led down by our politics, our writers, our thinkers. For this day and age, with so much facility of communication, the general ability to read and write, we are far below, in intelligence and moral conduct, the standards of the ancient Roman and Greek republics. We should recognize this fact and determine to do all possible to elevate the character and mentality of our citizens. If they are permitted to decline as present indications show, our country will perish, as did Greece and Rome.

Another example of lack of thought is shown by a sign of a picketer saying, "We strike for higher wages, not higher prices." Common sense would tell anyone that when you demand higher wages, production costs are increased, resulting in higher prices, unless the employer is willing to absorb the increased cost himself. If he does this and the wages are continually raised, eventually he will become bankrupt. This is the class of intelligence by which we are being controlled; ignorant, stupid pickets having no knowledge of the far-reaching causes of economic conditions, seeing solution only in higher wages for themselves.

The unfitness of our citizens is well displayed by the general ignorance regarding government taxation and budget deficits. The average citizen simply does not care a great deal how much money the government spends or how greatly it exceeds receipts. This situation could be corrected if our schools taught citizenship and if our politicians endeavored to enlighten our citizens to an understanding of sound government policies. Any sensible person can realize that a business concern that consistently spends more than it receives will eventually wind up in bankruptcy. The same thing is true of a government. Borrowing and spending today is merely putting off the day of reckoning to a future day. If high standards of citizenship prevailed in our country there would be a universal demand for government expenditures not to exceed receipts. Problems of money and finance become so involved as to be difficult of understanding but sensible educational methods would provide for the teaching of certain simple essentials to the citizens and one attribute of good citizenship is to keep out of debt. Do not spend more than you earn.

A majority of our citizens today support an increase in government functions. This belief has been established not by individual reasoning, but by environmental influences. But these same citizens entertain a very poor opinion of politicians. These two conflicting viewpoints illustrate the inability of the average citizen to reason logically on governmental policies. If he demands an extension of government functions, he should, to be consistent, demand that men of the greatest ability and character be entrusted with the conduct of government. He admits that his present leaders are of poor quality morally. He makes no attempt to remedy this condition but supports measures which increase their power and give them greater opportunity to serve their personal interests at the expense of the public.

The greatest threat to man's future is lack of Primo and Co in the individual and in all great interest groups, whether they be labor unions, nations, lobbies, or what-not. In this respect they are akin to criminals and the insane. It is in this direction that democracy is now leading. Both can be easily developed, but man is stupid and seems bent on destroying himself. While the destruction is going on he blames everyone except himself, which is where the blame should properly be placed. The individual citizen must be elevated to a higher standard of duty, knowledge, and character. Primo

and Co must be developed to a high degree and the individual
taught to raise himself.

Americans are being controlled by entirely too much
foolish sentiment. Our nation is very sick, has many serious
tumors that should be removed by heroic operations. Our
sentimental people refuse to inflict the pain necessary to
remove these tumors, but insist that they be allowed to grow
and receive sustenance in order to assist them in growing.
This policy will result in the destruction of the rest of the
body if it is permitted to continue.

All things considered, in civilized countries man is better
in Co than in understanding. Why? Because Co appeals,
whereas Primo and thought, which are essential to understanding, are too much obscured by other factors. Not the least,
sometimes, is a sentimental appeal to Co itself.

There is something wholesome about the American people despite many unwholesome influences. Witness the popularity of Lindbergh and his flight, showing a real liking
for courage. The same for any person who displays heroic
qualities. There is a vast power for good within the average
American if it can only be brought forth and harnessed.

The people are basically sound. It is the vicious social, economic, international, legal, governmental, educational, religious, and moral system and atmosphere in which they are
living that is at fault. They are bound to absorb their environment.

Democracy tends toward a weak form of government because the citizens are not able to master government problems
in addition to making a living. If the schools and other environmental influences worked toward that end, it would
be possible to cause them to select and support able men.
We should insure adequate training of the citizens to be
equal to the demands of democracy. This requires the combined efforts of schools, of religion, and of all publicity
agencies.

Merely saying that democracy is the best form of government does not make it so. This attitude prevents fulfillment

because it is not conducive to questioning the evils of democracy in order that they may be brought to light and corrected. For democracy to be a success, it must rest upon worthy citizens. Therefore let us strive to make our citizens worthy and assure its success. Democracy but reflects the citizens themselves, and will be as good as they. It is our duty as individuals to contribute toward a high standard of citizenship by setting an example of it. The more good citizens, the better the standard of citizenship. While every citizen cannot exercise great influence upon others, he can greatly influence and control himself, and his very effort to do so in setting an example will encourage others to do likewise.

The relative success of democratic institutions in the United States in the past can be contrasted with their failure in many Latin American countries. When these countries obtained their independence the standard of education was relatively low, they were unfamiliar with the processes of representative government, an enlightened unselfish middle class did not exist; as a result the government usually fell into the hands of leaders who governed without permitting the common people much voice in affairs.

The more primitive uncivilized people must be ruled by a superior class of rulers whom they respect and obey. The failure of the negroes to achieve a satisfactory form of government in Santo Domingo or Liberia well illustrates the inability of backward races to maintain democratic institutions. Backward races can be raised from this condition if they are fortunate in having wise rulers who will mold the institutions so as to create an enlightened citizenry. The attempts of many well-meaning friends of democracy to extend democratic institutions to all nations of the world regardless of their standards of education is more creditable to their good intentions than their judgment. When backward races are given the franchise and do not understand their duties as citizens they easily become the followers of politicians or leaders who will promise benefits from the government to obtain their support.

Democracy as well as any other form of government depends upon the ability and character of the men entrusted with conducting the affairs of the country. If they are incapable or unequal to the demands the government will be unsatisfactory, regardless of whether it be democratic or otherwise. Thus we must so remodel the institutions of democracy we now possess as to place the ablest leaders available in control of the affairs of the nation; to do this and insure the success of these leaders we must elevate our citizens to a higher degree of understanding and a greater willingness to serve and sacrifice for the nation at large, the direct opposite of the principles being promulgated throughout the nation today, in which many are demanding that the government support them or give them benefits of various kinds.

Democracy can function most satisfactorily in a small community under simple conditions with an intelligent citizenry. In a large community under complex conditions democracy becomes merely a name. Of necessity it results in government by professional politicians appealing to whatever will keep them in office. It is possible for democracy to be a success in a large complex community if the standard of citizenship is high; if the citizens are intelligent, self-sacrificing, understand the principles of government, and attend to their duties as citizens with more regard than for their privileges as such. The very high quality of such a citizenry will result in the leaders being of high quality.

We should endeavor to raise ourselves to that standard. We must provide some way whereby able, honest, sensible, leaders are put in charge of the government. We must also see that they do not have to obtain office by appealing to the most ignorant portion of the populace. We must eliminate hatreds, and the purchasing of votes by promises of government benefits, thus penalizing the fit for the unfit. The government should be conducted by the fit and the unfit eliminated either by direct means or education. We must raise the environment to such a high standard that it will not tolerate unfit individuals within it.

Democracy to be a success demands intelligent, loyal, thoughtful citizens. This truth is not fully recognized by many who extol the merits of democracy. They say in effect that the vast number of ignorant, stupid, and vicious are enlightened, intelligent and virtuous. The falsity of this assertion is well seen when you observe a large group of men who have achieved little success in life. Politicians and agitators speak to men like this, stir them up, dwell on their grievances and denounce those who have achieved some success in life. This group is then dominated more by grievance and envy than by intelligence.

They can easily be aroused to violence against the more successful when under the influence of envy, inferiority, grievances, and sometimes want. These men, in common with all other humans, are prone to see only faults in their enemies and only merit in themselves. They are but too willing to demand that the more successful share their success. Such an attitude is destructive of individual development and of high standards of citizenship. Successful democracies demand citizens who will serve, not citizens who demand that they be served. These unsuccessful men of themselves would not be bad influences. It is the fact that the politicians and agitators continually stir them up. If these men were subjected to the influence of able leaders, talkers and thinkers who would teach them to understand the duties of citizenship, to understand the harmful effects upon one's own character of envy and the harboring of grievances, many could be made desirable citizens. Yet this is not even being attempted in our country today. Those who claim to be serving the interests of democracy are the ones who are stirring up these poor deluded men, making undesirable citizens of them, fomenting class hatreds, threatening future civil war and the eventual downfall of our democratic institutions. Let us face the facts and correct this condition before it is too late. We have examples abroad of democracies having failed for this reason. Let us not have democracy fail in our own country. Let us rather show how it can be preserved and by our example cause other nations to return to democratic institutions of a higher type than have heretofore existed under this name.

It is possible under existing conditions for a man of little actual worth to build up a great reputation by skillful publicity. Generally a man who talks much will expose his ignorance, his incompetence, if he be ignorant or incompetent. This is true if thoughtful men analyze his words. The average citizen, however, is not very thoughtful. He does not analyze all things that are said. If they be pleasing, he usually is willing to follow. The cure for this is to raise the citizens to a higher degree of understanding, that they may be able to detect flaws in the arguments of their leaders, detect real merit when it exists.

The citizens must be able to look at both sides of questions on public policies. They must demand that their leaders present both sides to them. Our present-day politicians present their views on public questions too much after the manner of the attorney arguing before a court. The latter appeals to all human feelings, beliefs, anything he can to win his own case and present it in a favorable light. At the same time he resorts to all possible means to ridicule and discredit the other side of the case. Our politicians have inherited the attorney's methods of presenting public questions to the citizens. This attitude of mind prevents the politicians themselves from forming sound conclusions. Their mental processes are a regression to the most primitive thought. The untutored savage also would glorify himself, his tribe, and his beliefs, and discredit, belittle, and destroy any contradictions regardless of merit.

When we have statesmen of character and ability, they will endeavor to educate the public to an understanding of the difficulty of social problems, will impartially present the arguments for and against contemplated action, will arrive at a reasoned conclusion which to the best of their ability and based upon all facts available to them, will be sound. When our citizens demand statesmen of this nature, when they cease to heed the demagogue, the primitive savage glorifying

himself, crushing opposing thought, we will have a democracy that will endure, a democracy that will solve the problems
of the day, a democracy that will be worthy of the emulation
of future generations.

Thoughts

The destruction of democracy is threatened by the poor
quality of the citizens in combination with the incompetence
and poor character of its leaders.

The politicians succeed because they appeal to the unthinking approbation of the multitude. If the latter were
able to think, present-day politicians would not exist.

Democratic government to be successful must limit the
franchise to the desirable citizens. Morons, vicious, mentally
maladjusted, and undesirables generally should not be given
the franchise. When they possess it they are too easily controlled by any agitator who appeals to them.

We are being ruled by noisy people at the top and noisy
people at the bottom. The politicians at the top make much
noise to attract attention and obtain votes, and they make
promises of future grand achievements, always leading the
fight of the little fellow against the big capitalist. The politicians direct their attention to the ignorant noisy element
at the bottom; the people, for instance, who are wont to
write to their representatives, senators, and to the president
demanding benefits and special legislation. The sensible
level-headed people composing the vast majority of our citizens are between these two noisy elements. For the most
part they are busy making a living. When the noisy people
cause the sensible to suffer by unsound acts and policies,
the latter may be forced to resort to drastic action in self-
defense, suppressing both the noisy ones above and the noisy
ones below.

IV

CITIZENS, LEADERS

THE PROGRESS OF MAN HAS RESULTED FROM THE EFFORTS OF great leaders, thinkers, men who were far above the average and who by their efforts added to knowledge and led their less gifted fellows by superior ability. We today have able men in many walks of life who have contributed much to the advance of our times. Unfortunately, this advance has not been in improving our government. The very qualities necessary to be a successful politician are opposed to the qualities needed to be a great statesman. We have had some men who were both statesmen and politicians, but the development of modern times has reduced statesmanship, and increased demagoguery. Instead of our country being led by leaders, the "leaders" are looking toward the people, trying to flatter and please. This tends toward mediocrity. In any society, the average intelligence is not great, and when we permit the policies of government to be dictated by demagogic appeals to the masses, the government will be inefficient. If the masses are intelligent, understand and perform the duties of citizens well, they will not heed demagogues.

Our problem of improving the government is twofold. We must improve the citizens and improve the leaders. If the citizens are elevated to a higher degree of understanding, they will not be content with anything less than able leaders; and if we have able leaders, they will tend to elevate the citizens.

The people are helpless by themselves; they must have

able leaders, and it must be possible for the people to select able men. At present the selections are dominated by politicians who shop among themselves for support of their own interests. They claim to be serving the people, but are serving themselves.

In the long run the politicians will be as good as the people who put them in office. Our politicians do not reflect a high standard of intelligence or citizenship, but the people are confused, misled, have too many conflicting interests. Present the facts to them and they will respond to honest capable leadership.

Are not our political parties being short-sighted in appealing to the voter with promises of all things that will bring votes? Is there not in our American manhood much of the old solid American virtues: a desire to be men, to have freedom, to maintain themselves by their own efforts? There is nothing in the conduct of the politicians to encourage a man to be a good citizen. A feeling of disgust will some day be aroused against politicians, sentimental reformers, and labor agitators. American manhood will assert itself and relegate these persons to the background, bringing forth men of character and ability to control the affairs of our country. The American citizen cannot be forever imposed upon by promises, appeals to help the underdog, and constant talk of reform. This will reach a limit sometime; the more thoughtful will demand results, are demanding them now. What is needed to consolidate the manhood of America is able leadership appealing to man's better nature.

The natural tendency of men is to follow leaders, strong able men who are admired for their force, their character, their ability. Why, may we ask, is it possible for such leaders as we now have to obtain following? They are not leaders in the real sense. They lead by flattering the masses and obtain their support by doing what the masses think they would like to have done. This is a product of much social welfare talk, in which sentimental reformers have been the predominating influence. Virile manhood cannot be altered in such a brief period. It is still stirring beneath the surface and will respond to able leadership. One reason for the success of our politicians in getting control of the government has been lack of capable leadership opposing them. The public has taken for granted the domination of political institutions by politicians for so long that it has failed to realize that a respectable leader cannot be produced from our present politicians. If some outside leader appears capable of attracting a following, he will get the support of men who only need an able leader to assert their manhood.

Despite the ignorance of the average man, he is far less at fault than his leaders. He will follow in the right path if he but have the right men to lead. All man's history emphasizes the poor quality of leaders and the long-suffering patience of the common people. If they could only have leaders who fulfill their tasks as well as the scrubwoman and ditch-digger perform theirs, all would be well.

A country such as our own containing millions of voters cannot be governed by the voters directly. They must select men to conduct the government for them. If they seek for and select the best men in the community for this task, they will have an efficient government. To do this the citizens must be enlightened and be able to see real merit when it exists. They must be broadminded enough to realize that their own best interest is served in the long run by advancing the best interests of the entire nation. They should not support leaders who offer them benefits detrimental to others. We have permitted our politics to become so low as to keep desirable men from seeking government office. Our public affairs have drifted into the hands of demagogic politicians, appealing to the poorest element in the country to retain themselves in office. It is useless to trust reform measures to such hands. The first reform is to improve our political institutions and place worthy men in control. When this is accomplished we may undertake reforms and obtain satisfactory results.

The average citizen does not want to be bothered with

government affairs. He is too busy making a living, enjoying life. Only when it is to his interest, or when his interests are threatened, or because of party loyalty or the excitement which stirs emotional response around election, does he give it much thought. He would willingly turn over to experts the conduct of the government if they could be found and if they inspired sufficient confidence.

A democratic form of government appeals to the emotions of the citizens rather than to their intelligence. A skilled talker can obtain a greater following than a skilled thinker. This can be changed by educating the citizens to think for themselves, to discredit the man who talks well but thinks little and to elect the man who can think. The citizens must be made more discerning, more discriminating, able to select leaders capable of conducting the affairs of the government. Our schools could do a world of good in promoting this. They have young minds under their control who can have high ideals of citizenship impressed upon them. It is here where our schools are failing today and it is here where we must institute drastic reforms so as to have them assist in developing a citizenship deserving of our country.

The existence and natural development in man of the Leader-Follower psycha opposes democracy to some degree. It is self-evident that when men are assembled in large numbers the best results will be achieved if the best men assume control and dictate policies. Man in the simpler forms of society fumbled toward this by having his affairs directed by patriarchs, chieftains, or other forceful leaders who managed to be strong enough to obtain control; thence developed kings and emperors. In the small family groups the patriarchs were able to control affairs without difficulty. When the development proceeded to kings and emperors controlling vast empires the problems became vastly more difficult. The original king or emperor, who was often a forceful character, would die and be succeeded by his son. The son would commonly lack the vigorous qualities of his father, not have obstacles to overcome, be made much of, have luxuries, live a soft life. As a result he would further deteriorate and either he or his descendants would in time prove unequal to the task. Often the governing would be conducted by favorites or ministers. This is what is known as absolute monarchy and it eventually became discredited.

As a revulsion against this, democracy sprang into being, in which people selected their own leaders. As long as the people select wisely and well they will have a fairly satisfactory government. It is when they fail to select able leaders that their government deteriorates, and this is the general cause for the failure of democracy today. If democracy is intelligent enough to appreciate the fact that the Leader-Follower relationship is basic in human affairs, democracy may yet preserve itself. To do this the individual standard of citizenship must be raised very high, both from the standpoint of intelligence, character, and civic obligation. Select the ablest men as leaders and nobly support them. The serious threat to the success of democracy is when the people respond to demagogues who flatter, who appeal to their prejudices and who are selected as leaders not for ability as statesmen but for the ability to please.

The great amount of denunciation on the part of politicians and many others having much to say accustoms the people to such talk, and results in preventing those who really see the dangers of the course we are following from being heard. The average American citizen will not be aroused to the evils of our existing institutions until he begins to suffer from their ill effects. This is one of the inherent faults of democracy. Evils run their course until they are so bad as to be generally recognized and then some measures are taken to correct them. If we can educate our citizens to understand economic and governmental problems better, to analyze what they hear and see more, to seek able leaders and support them, future ills could be avoided. Anything that will elevate the citizenship should be encouraged. It is here that the solution to our problems of government lies.

The appeal of our politicians to the voting public is not

to their mental processes, nor to sound thinking or to stimulate them to think. It is to their emotions, to their feelings, to their previously established beliefs, to what they would like to hear, to about everything the opposite of sound thought and action. The remedy for this is clear. Our schools must modify their teachings so as to teach civil government and history, point out the dangers of democracy and the imperative need for each citizen to think; not to be guided by appeals to his emotions or any other feeling opposed to sound reasoning on public questions.

We have many people making noise; politicians, reformers, and labor agitators all demand reforms and denounce everybody else. The American public must rouse itself and cease to be controlled by those who make the most noise. We have more laws in existence now than ever before, are getting an increasing amount of discontent, and the prospect for the future indicates worse to come. Is it not plain common sense that if conditions are so bad the ones at fault are those in control of the government, those who condemn all but themselves? The very volume of noise they make in condemning others is their means of diverting attention from their own incompetence. Until we develop a citizenship capable of seeing incompetence even when surrounded by noise and promises, we will have an incompetent government and unsatisfactory economic conditions.

Governments the world over are controlled by public opinion. If the citizens are elevated to a high standard of intelligence and character, they will demand like conduct of their government. Public opinion is created by many individuals, and the effort to improve it must be started by improving the individual as such. We must encourage the individual citizen to be more critical of his leaders, to realize that his own character is reflected in them. If he has poor leaders controlling his government it is a reflection upon himself. We must teach our citizens not to be influenced by denunciation of wealth, by appeals to their prejudice and self-interest. We must teach them to think and to require of their leaders less denunciation but a real desire to solve the problems of the government and serve the people. Our present-day politicians do not inspire much respect on the part of the better class of citizens. The commonly heard expression "only a politician" does not show that they are regarded with any great degree of respect. Decent citizens feel helpless under existing conditions because the politicians appeal to the lowest element in the country and by numbers smother the wishes of the better element.

But among the decent citizens themselves there is so much conflict of opinion, so much impractical discussion, so much lack of fundamental understanding. The decent citizens of the country could control the undesirable element and put good officials in office if they would determine to do so, cease to disagree on nonessentials, and concentrate on essentials. The two vital things that are essential to the success of democratic institutions and to the survival of any nation are raising the standard of intelligence of the citizens and improving their moral character. Other things may be utterly neglected if these two be accomplished, because in their accomplishment the other problems will be solved with relative ease. The first essential in accomplishing this is the selection of able, honest men to conduct the affairs of the government and the creation of an ascendent environment. Neither of these things is difficult. It requires merely intelligent effort, which thus far has failed to develop.

The citizens are sound at heart and will follow wise leadership and a wise plan. The reason they do not do so today is because neither exists. Seek where you will throughout this land; where will you find a sound program for improvement of conditions? Where will you find a man or men to carry it out? Neither exists. But there is ability in the country. It can be harnessed for this effort, can work out a plan, and then the public will have something worth supporting. Anyone who believes the American people will support politicians fomenting class hatred and ill-feeling, instead of able and sincere men seeking the truth, is doing the people a grave injustice. They will support the latter.

Our politicians permit themselves to be controlled by the noisy element which thus controls the more sensible element among the citizens. The politicians do this because the noisy element, lacking intelligence and knowledge, makes more noise, which the politicians accept as being the voice of the people. The more stable element, having a greater understanding of the problem, is less sure, less certain that they have a solution. Therefore the mob governs.

You may yourself observe the means by which this is accomplished by observing the conduct of a mixed crowd at a motion-picture performance largely devoted to news events and occurrences of the day. The noisy unthinking people respond vigorously to all those who claim to be fighting for the underdog all over the world. They hiss those who represent fascism in any form. They applaud vigorously the activities of radical labor unions in our own country. One would, from a casual impression, get the belief that a vast majority were in sympathy with communism, radical labor unions, and in general inclined toward the left. But think a moment. Among this audience there are many sensible level-headed people guided more by their thoughts, by their minds, than by their emotions. They remain quiet during these performances. Occasionally when some particular thing appeals to them they may respond by demonstrations of approval, but this is relatively rare.

One can devote much thought to the task of evaluating public opinion and obtaining the support of the worthwhile citizens to worthwhile measures. If we give them proper leaders, if we give them a sound policy, we can obtain their support. We can get as much support and approval from the deserving elements among the citizens as the agitators are now receiving from the thoughtless. With this support it will be possible to effect far-reaching reforms within a brief period of time.

Furnish the leaders and the policy; adequate support will

be forthcoming. Both leaders and policies must not only appeal to the intellect but must appeal to the feelings, the emotions; but instead of arousing emotions by appeals to prejudice and hatreds, we must appeal to the finer feelings, to intelligence and to regard for the future. A plan that offers the abolition of poverty, of crime, of evil, of suffering throughout the world, has emotional appeal to the finest intellects and will arouse an intelligent, enthusiastic response if leadership adequate to the task appear.

Citizens, stop! Look over your country today. See what its condition is. Look over the world; see what its condition is. Are they not both in bad shape? Are they not both just blundering along without plan, without sensible control? Give this some consideration. See if you as private citizens cannot contribute toward the solution of these problems. Our present-day leaders are clearly inadequate to the task. The very reason they have failed is the reason why all should strive to do something to remedy the existing state of affairs. If all citizens will contribute their utmost to the solution of today's problems, they can be solved. We must disregard those who counsel violence, who agitate, who have panaceas without sufficient knowledge or reflection, and must find a solution based upon facts, upon human nature, something that will work, that will answer the problem.

The environment surrounding the individual is not conducive to the best citizenship. Little is heard about the duties of the citizen. The politicians and most reformers stress too much the rights and privileges of the citizen, the injustices done him, and the unfair treatment received by the weak. Unfairness, injustice, discrimination, have always existed in the world and will not be eradicated by mere denunciation. Their removal must delve deep into underlying factors, and is only handicapped by a spirit of hatred, prejudice, and class feeling. Thankfulness and appreciation for what we have now, a frank determination to do our duty, to criticize ourselves before criticizing others, would create a better atmosphere and accomplish more.

Our politicians are setting an awful example for leadership to the youth when they spend their time denouncing, belittling others, blaming everybody else for the ills of today. We should have men who admit their own faults but who strive to solve the problems and do so without denouncing all others; men ready and willing to take responsibility for their acts, men our youth can be proud of and can follow. If we permit this present era of domination by self-seeking politicians to continue indefinitely, the manhood of our nation will be destroyed. We will have a spineless, characterless race of humans not deserving of survival.

Our politicians are not so much at fault as the environment which creates them. They are responding to the influences of the moment, being no better and no worse. To improve the grade of our politicians we must improve the quality of our citizenship and elevate the environment. When this is done, a corresponding improvement will be shown in the politicians.

In order to become a leader in a democracy, one must be a good salesman, must be able to show the people how good one is. This very characteristic opposes the development of able leaders. Really able men do not extol their virtues, their merits, tell the rest of the world how good they are. They work and really do something. Our political leaders are mere talkers. We should modify our institutions so as to obtain doers and eliminate talkers.

How is it that radical labor agitators and demagogic politicians can so readily stir men up? The average man is basically good. He intends to do good, and resents unjust treatment, but is not always intelligent. The agitator, by appealing to the prejudices of his audience, dwelling on their grievances, denouncing those who have money or are successful, arouses envy and jealousy. The skilled agitator very often has a practical understanding of what appeals to human beings, and he uses this knowledge to attain his ends, appealing more to the emotions than to the mind. If the ablest thinkers of the day are unable to solve the problems or even understand them, how much less chance is there of the man in the street understanding them? There is a vast fund of common sense in the average working man, and he is able to see sound measures when presented, often more readily than the more educated but less practical men. But when no sound measures are presented to him, he can hardly be blamed for heeding agitators who do have a sympathetic understanding of the grievances from which he is suffering.

Oratory is not conducive to sound thought. The latter is best exhibited under conditions of solitude, quietness, where there is ample time for the individual to question his conclusions, to discover errors, and to correct them. When the orator endeavors to think while delivering an oration, he has two contradictory missions. One is to think and the other is to please the audience. If the audience is of a critical discerning type demanding the truth, the orator may be stimulated by this to seek consistently for the truth. Intelligent audiences of this kind, however, are rare.

Oratory by its very nature appeals more to the feelings, the emotions, than to cold ruthless logic. When the orator, however, has previously reached his conclusions by sound thought and then employs eloquence to convince others, his oration will be as sound as his established conclusions. One of the weaknesses of democracy is the employment of oratory of a type to please the feelings of the audience regardless of truth.

It should not be very difficult to educate citizens to a proper understanding of what to look for in their leaders. If we teach Ascendency to all citizens, they will develop the faculty of Primo in their own use. It should then be very easy to extend this faculty in analyzing their leaders. They should require them to point out their faults, show what is wrong, suggest means for correction, and under no consideration should they flatter, please, promise, or resort to the measures politicians now do to obtain votes. With the development of an enlightened citizenry of this nature, our present-day politicians could not exist. We could inaugurate this move by teaching citizenship of this nature in our public schools. It is true the politicians control the public schools, but the people control the politicians; they can be ruthlessly brushed aside and proper conceptions of citizenship taught our young people. Then they in their day will be able to select able leaders and not be misled by demagogues.

One good test each citizen could apply to his public leaders would be to ask himself, "Does this man contribute to arousing hate? Does he attack classes such as capital without pointing out specific individuals?" When the citizens thus ask this question, they will promptly repudiate and discredit all our existing politicians. It should be apparent to all that there are fine people among the wealthy just as there are vicious people among the poor, and that general attacks against the wealthy because they are wealthy, against capital because it is successful, is a means of arousing hate against the successful element in the country, making use of the natural envy of those who have little.

Capital is being so taxed, so abused, so regulated, so oppressed, as to be unable to adequately perform its duties. If it must support all the people in the country, pay the taxes, it must be assisted instead of attacked. The fact that our public men attack capital should alone be sufficient to discredit them. Men who consistently attack capital show their inability to control it. The citizen should now do some serious thinking. Attacking capital has been going on for many decades. This denunciation on the part of politicians shows their utter inability to deal with it. Let us just for a change put somebody in control of the government who will not attack capital but will co-operate with it, direct it into wise channels, protect it, and see if the results in a brief period are not far better than this present policy of continually attacking it.

When we have citizens of sufficient intelligence to recognize fools, we will cease to be governed by fools. A man who can see no fault in himself or his measures, with only selfish motives and viciousness in opposing measures, is a fool; and by this definition all politicians are fools. We as citizens must demand that our public men discuss both sides of the question, that they seek the facts, that they denounce less. We should realize that the more denunciation, the less certain that person is in the soundness of his own policies. It is so easy for one to make much noise to cover up his own shortcomings. A little thought will show that this is what our politicians are doing today. They govern the country. Why cannot they correct existing ills? They have been talking for generations, we still have the ills with us, and they are shouting more vociferously now than ever.

When you as a citizen decide to give your support to some leader, you should analyze his acts and words closely to see if he is worthy of your support. If he looks at one side of the question, denounces capital, belittles others, creates class hatred, you can well rate him as being unworthy. But if you were to apply this critical view to those in public life today, you would reject them all. The answer is simple. We have no one in public life deserving of support. We, as citizens, are permitting a vicious environment to place poor leaders in control of our government and render it impossible to produce good leaders. If we are to bring about any improvement in our institutions we must find good leaders and put them in control. This is the most essential reform to be made.

I happened to be in New York City during a recent mayoralty campaign. Whatever may be the merits of democracy, political campaigns as practiced in our country are a bad influence upon mental and moral development. I heard nothing constructive during this campaign. There was much denunciation by opposing candidates and their supporters, of each other; the imputation of vicious motives, attempts to mislead, discredit. The discussions of speakers were inane, trivial; showed little intelligence, no attempt to grapple with the problems facing the largest city in the country.

The intelligent citizen should condemn those who create catchwords to appeal to prejudice, who denounce others without justification. Democracy will fail if the standard of citizenship is so low as to permit leadership by demagogues. It will succeed if the standard of citizenship is so high as to demand leadership by men of character and ability.

The promises of our politicians in their endeavors to obtain votes are constantly increasing government expenses, making it a vast parasite, eating the very life of the deserving citizens of the nation. This is the fault of the citizens themselves. They should have common sense enough to realize that politicians who are continually promising benefits to voters are not desirable citizens, that the government should never be reduced to the status of paying benefits to large numbers of its citizens. It is there to serve them but not to support them. We, who have so much pride in our democratic institutions, permit our government to be conducted on principles that we, as business men, would never tolerate in the conduct of our own affairs.

The vicious denunciation which politicians indulge in is their means of discrediting others and attracting popular support. It is effective for a low type of men, but at what a cost! It would not be effective if we had an intelligent, moral citizenry. It is this very sort of conduct that prevents men of ability and character from entering politics. What chance would they have against vicious politicians who attack, ridicule, abuse in all ways possible? A decent man does not do that and cannot fight against such tactics; therefore he remains aloof and does not enter into such a disgusting calling. There should be character and intelligence enough in our country to support really able, honest men, but we have permitted our institutions to develop in such way that the abler honest men do not even make an attempt to enter politics.

Where will the people get able, honest leaders to conduct their governments? They do not seem to exist. We will have as difficult a time finding suitable leaders to direct the affairs of our government as President Lincoln had in finding generals to command the Union Army. The great dearth throughout all man's history has been able men. We have been successful in having some great men of science, great artists, great geniuses in many lines of activity, but man has yet to see a really able government administrator in all essentials. There have been many who have achieved a considerable success, but they failed to leave a guide for the conduct of government. They did not see the need for building up an intelligent moral citizenry, or if they saw such need, they failed to inaugurate measures that would bring it about. The conquest of vast territories, the building of great structures, efforts to improve economic conditions, are all desirable, but the main effort should be toward building up man, without which no other things are worthwhile.

We have many good citizens in the country, but we have no truly able leaders in public life. Able leaders will raise the citizens, and bad ones will tend to lower them. The large mass of people cannot act collectively except through leaders. Therefore the improvement of the nation and of its citizens demands able, honest leaders. To obtain leaders of this type requires a high grade of citizens capable of discrimination. It is easy to talk about elevating the standards of citizenship and selecting the best leaders to conduct the government; but it is extremely difficult to put this into practice, to suggest means to improve either citizens or leaders. The citizens are made as they are by their environment. Able leaders may, however, spring from the most undesirable environment.

The true method to bring about better leaders and better citizens is in concentrating on education that will contribute toward Ascendency, teaching each person the principles underlying human nature. Teach sound economic principles, create an environment that is ascendent in the highest sense. Any effort made that will encourage the citizens to think, to reflect, to strive to correct the errors in themselves and government, will contribute toward this. But when citizens delude themselves as individuals or submit to flattery from politicians and others, they are preventing the development of sound leaders, sound government, and sound citizens.

The answer to our national difficulties is: Develop the individual to his highest estate. Cause him to think and decide for himself. The nation is composed of many individuals, and if all are striving to do what is right, they will soon have a government worthy of their own high character.

V

LEADERS

JUST AS THE EXAMPLE OF THE PARENTS WILL UNCONSCIOUSLY influence the character and conduct of the children in an infinite number of ways without effort on their part or even knowledge of its occurrence, so will leaders affect the citizenship of a nation. If the leaders are able, conscientious, highly moral men, they tend unconsciously, by both example and influence, to improve the standards of conduct and citizenship. When the leaders are men of poor character who make promises impossible of fulfillment, who are herd reflectors, who denounce whatever the voters wish to hear denounced, they encourage similar conduct among the body of citizens.

What man is there in public life in any country in the world whose veracity is unquestioned, whose every statement is true and accepted as such? Not one. What miserable creatures are now directing man's affairs! There is little hope of decent government until we have men of character in control.

Whenever any man prominent in national or international affairs makes a statement or desires something, we can never believe just what he says. We must interpret. Often the man is lying, other times partially so. Rarely does a frank, truthful, sincere statement appear. I wonder if a truthful honest man could get a following? His very novelty would almost insure his success, if coupled with ability, understanding, and determination.

Our politicians are afraid to make frank statements on

61

major questions for fear of losing votes. Does this denote strength, character, leadership? Is this not an indication that the American people as a nation are becoming effeminate? The normal staunch man desires to follow strong, aggressive leaders. We are following men who are neither strong nor aggressive in promoting the welfare of the nation. They are aggressive in attacking and belittling opponents, but not in attacking the evils when such attacks would cause them to lose votes. They seek to evade essential public questions, avoid committing themselves, utter platitudes, attack wealth, attack anything that is unpopular with the masses, regardless of the amount of ill feeling it creates. And this is the kind of men whom we constantly elect and re-elect to office and to whom we entrust the affairs of our nation! We cannot hope for anything but disaster under such a ruinous system.

We, as individuals, have work demanding skill by specialists. Doctors, dentists, watchmakers, electricians, auto mechanics, civil engineers, do work of a specialized nature which they have spent years in mastering. We would not go to a bricklayer to have our teeth fixed. Why should we not therefore have government by specialists, by men chosen to conduct the affairs of the nation because of their ability to do so? Then and then only will we have a government that will prove equal to the demands of modern conditions and contribute toward Ascendency. At present we are calling upon the most incompetent people in our country to conduct our government. We select our leaders based upon their ability as flatterers, promisers, vote getters, on anything, in fact, but honesty and ability.

I have sought in vain in communists, socialists, labor leaders, preachers, reformers, writers, intelligentsia, Republicans, Democrats, orators, college professors, for sound knowledge of fundamental issues facing man today. Nowhere have I found evidence of sufficient knowledge to deal .adequately with them. We have the ability within the country to meet these problems, but those who possess the ability are workers, not talkers. The greatest judgment lies in those who are working, but they are too busy to devote the time necessary to mastering the problems of government. If they did, under existing conditions they would not be able to do much because our public is educated to listen only to those who talk, please, flatter, and promise.

The present low estate of our political life and our unsatisfactory economic condition has been brought about under the control of politicians. To correct these evils, the first step should be to remove all these politicians from office. They have been talking and promising long enough, and have shown that they are unfit to govern the country. If we can find able leaders to govern the country in their place, we might well declare a moratorium on all abuse for a period of five years and endeavor to educate the younger generation to a proper understanding of their responsibilities as citizens. By removing these politicians from office and preventing them from attacking sound measures, we will be creating an ascendent environment that will bring about a better spirit within the nation. This again is easy to say but difficult in its application. But our affairs are in bad condition and constantly getting worse. Drastic action must be taken if we are to improve them. It should be self-evident to even those of limited intelligence that the existing state of affairs has been brought about by incompetent leaders.

Most nations that perished have perished as the result of incompetent leaders. The world is in a sorry state today as the result of incompetent leaders. If the nations of the world permit themselves to be forever governed by incompetents, by politicians appealing to popular prejudice, the situation will constantly get worse. The solution to sound government, to world problems, demands able leaders of character in control of the affairs of the nations.

Present-day leaders of all nations, except perhaps some of the smaller ones such as the Scandinavian countries and Switzerland, have failed. The fact that they have failed should be sufficient justification for removing them from office and putting men in control who will succeed. We can profit from the example of successful business concerns who seek far and wide for able managers, men who can achieve success. Men who fail are instantly and quickly removed as soon as their failure becomes apparent, or they will bring failure upon the business.

We are being governed by nitwits. Men are more important than measures, the execution more important than the plan. The best of plans, institutions, are of no avail without men of ability, character, vision, performance. This is the crying need of the world, particularly as pertains to government and human welfare. Our much lauded democratic system has succeeded in bringing government down to the lowest level of mediocrity.

The essential of efficient government is institutions that encourage the ablest men to enter public life, thus insuring that the affairs of the nation will be conducted by the ablest men within it. This is not true of our political institutions today. Our politicians are far from being our ablest men. Our existing political institutions are not conducive to the development of able leaders in public affairs. Present-day politics is a profession which a self-respecting man will refrain from entering.

We are the victims of vicious politics. The politicians, by resorting to all devices that obtain votes, have discredited democratic government. The first and most essential measure of reform is so to modify our political institutions as to insure consideration of all questions with regard to promoting the welfare of all, not to obtaining votes or appeasing selfish interest groups. And further, no government, regardless of its form, can be any more respectable than the men who administer it. Our politicians may not be the worst men in the country, but they are far from respectable or able. They must be replaced by men adequate to the task.

Our politicians and agitators bring to my mind very vividly some of the boisterous noisy boys of my youth. These noisy fellows liked to make much noise around smaller boys whom they could intimidate, but when with fellows of their own or greater size, their boisterousness ceased. Somewhere in one of Mark Twain's books he describes very vividly and interestingly an incident of the same kind among adults. Several men were on a barge or similar structure floating down the Mississippi. Two of the men got into a controversy over some trifling affair and started making great threats against one another, with much noise and violent language. This continued for some time. Finally a quiet man had occasion to do something connected with the operation of the craft and made a quiet remark which reduced the two noisy fellows to instant obedience and silence. The quiet man knew his business, meant business, and did not have to make a lot of noise to accomplish results.

My observation has brought the same conclusion home very forcibly. It is not the loud-mouthed boisterous leader who is the efficient one usually. The able, quiet man devotes his effort to thinking and planning, forms a conclusion, and gives his orders in a quiet, unhurried, distinct manner that inspires confidence and obedience. The noisy man commonly gets excited, contradicts himself, creates confusion, and causes those under him to lose confidence in his ability and the possibility of success. The people have yet to learn this truth. When they cease to entrust their destinies to a leader who makes up for his lack of ability by noise, and place in his stead the noiseless man who knows, we will have efficient government.

We have placed our government in the hands of those who make the most noise, the most promises, flatter the public the most, and vote the most government benefits. If we want efficient government, we should seek for the thinkers, the able men, the practical doers. These very men do not enter into politics. They are exact opposites of the noisy ones. They go into business and professional life and quietly pursue their way. We are being governed by noisy people whom we could use if we wanted only noise. If we want sound action we will not obtain it from the noisy.

Up until recently our politicians were fairly practical men.

Their moral character in all cases was not of the best, but they were pretty shrewd judges of human nature and had a vast fund of common sense which enabled them to conduct the affairs of the country in a fairly satisfactory way. Some were even able men capable of carrying out great projects. The development more recently has been in the direction of liberalism, the labor movement, the social reform movement—trying to do something to better social conditions. This movement has been taken over by the politicians because popular and successful in obtaining votes. As a result they have become less practical. The present-day politicians are largely a product of our present-day reform madness, Wisho liberalism, and the capital complex. The more able practical ones have been outnumbered by the impractical ones.

In justice to the politicians, it is only fair to say that non-politicians have failed to produce measures that would solve the problems of the day and be sufficiently popular to receive public support. The problem is indeed complex and difficult. The politicians have a certain ability in knowing what the voters will support. We have some able thinkers well versed in economics, government, and related topics, who have a sound understanding of conditions, and can suggest sound measures to meet the problems. Unfortunately these men lack popular appeal or do not court it, and are therefore unable to make their influence felt. Despite all this, among our ablest writers, who have full freedom to express themselves, there is a dearth of constructive thought. All alike are bewildered and unable to meet the demands of the problems they discuss.

The prevailing beliefs in our country are caused by theorists, not the practical men. A minister, for instance, who spends much time studying the Bible preparing for his religious life, develops a theoretical mind. He is not a practical doer. He can find much to criticize, much to say about evil but is unable to suggest measures to correct, or to carry them out. He is a theorist by specialized adaptation. The same is true of the great mass of our writers who wish to be liberal and solve social problems but who are mere theorists specialized in writing, having much to say but lacking ability to do. This is true of most of the sources from which our public opinion is formed.

The practical men capable of doing things are too busy doing them to talk and write; too busy minding their own affairs, tending to their own business, to try to direct the business of others or conduct affairs with which they are not familiar. It is the meddling theorist who is all too willing to tackle all the problems and solve them to his satisfaction. In theory he can read the facts about as he wishes and make them work out, but theory and practice are two entirely different things. Theory will very often not work out well in practice.

A very excellent guide in evaluating the thought and opinions of people is to base the value granted them upon what they themselves have achieved. If they are mere writers, mere talkers, mere reformers who do little but make a noise, find fault, suggest, criticize, have much to say, their opinions might well be disregarded entirely. When a man who has made a success in handling men, in achieving things, expresses an opinion, it is well worth considering, particularly if it pertain to activity which he has mastered.

The more ignorant, the bigger fool a man is, the more he thinks he has the solution to every problem and that his way of solving it is the only way. Our opinions are being formed by fools. Unfortunately for us, many are highly educated and have an excellent command of the English language. But they have failed to develop their brains, failed to develop practical understanding, failed to read the lessons from the past and apply them to the present. They are not men with great natural gifts specialized by a narrowing educational system to have great command of the language and ability to express themselves, but men with their thinking capacities small to begin with and still remaining so.

We need practical men, doers, to solve our problems. We already have too many talkers, theorists, writers, telling us much about conditions but not able to show the way out or do anything about it. These are the men who so freely criticize Mussolini, who is a doer within the limits of his horizon. They may abuse him, but if they possessed his ability as a doer and his practical understanding, they would talk less, think more.

We get some idea of the caliber of our liberal thinkers in the views many express relative to the civil war in Spain. They see in this civil war the consequence of oppression by the Catholic Church and by capital exerted on the poor classes. There is some justification for this. Where they make their great mistake is in attributing all virtues to the loyalists, seeing no badness in their conduct, and seeing only vicious aspects of fascism in the revolutionists. The mere fact that the Church has oppressed the Spanish people, and that the wealthy classes have joined hands in doing so, has caused the people themselves to be ignorant, illiterate, primitive. Therefore when they get the upper hand they become vicious, unheeding, slaughter those whom they consider their enemies. One can understand their action, can sympathize with their misfortune, but one should also realize that the advance of civilization will not be served by the primitive. On the contrary, improvement in civilization demands the greatest intelligence, the highest development of man, as far removed from his primitive ancestry as he can be advanced. The loyalists are not without merit or without error, and the same can be said about the revolutionists. When our liberals take such a one-sided, prejudiced view of a case, one can but lose confidence in their ability and honesty. There is much right on either side in the Spanish situation, and much wrong.

We can apply the same criticism to the development of theory, practicalness and human feelings as we can to the narrowing influence of specialization upon the individual's development. We have many institutions who appeal to human feelings to such extremes as to become impractical. We have many institutions that go to extremes in the development of theory. Quite commonly this extreme development of theory and sentimental human feelings go together. On the other hand, very often the practical man is too practical. He employs theory and human feeling only to the extent necessary to achieve success in his practical undertakings. We have many institutions that are too lacking in human feeling. As a result, regardless of their constructive worth to society, they are subject to attacks because of their lack of human feeling. This is particularly true of big business and industry generally. They must cultivate more human feeling and those who attack them must cultivate more practical understanding.

Christianity is a religion of theory. Christ was an able man for his day and he endeavored to answer the problems affecting human conduct to the best of his ability. He, however, was not a practical achiever. He was a theorist, and this tendency to theory has been passed down through the church and exists today. This is not only true of Christianity; all religions to a great degree are religions of theorists and theory. The great modern facilities for the spread of opinions in the way of books, magazines, newspapers, radios, are giving still greater value to the promulgation of theory as opposed to practice. We have too many theorists telling us how to do things, what we should do to correct ourselves, but their ideas are impractical of application. Theory is of no value whatever unless it can be practically applied, and the application of sound theory demands that it be applied by practical, able men.

When we associate Christ with theory, we should also associate with Him human feeling, the desire to serve one's fellows. If our wealthy people, our big business men, would appeal to human feelings, there would be little or no feeling against them. As a result we would have internal harmony. The tendency of able practical men is to neglect theory and fail to give sufficient consideration to human feeling. They should carefully consider theory, apply it where practical, and realize that unless they can appeal to man's better nature, obtain the support of other human beings, their practical ability will achieve far less than if associated with more human feeling.

We can apply this lack of human feeling to practically all existing economic institutions. We do unfortunately experience too much sentimental feeling in those institutions that have stressed it to the neglect of practical living. Substantially, we should make our theorists and our sentimental well-intentioned people more practical. We should also make our able, practical men more cognizant of their duty to understand theory and human feeling and obtain sympathetic support from the public.

Closo and Presento are direct enemies of the development of vision in leaders. They are the great restraining influence on present-day leaders in all countries of the world. These men fail to seek the essentials of human existence and those things that would make both their own country and the world fine places for humans to live in. They concentrate their attention on problems of the present that seem of importance to them but which often have little or no relation to the solution of the big problem of improving man himself.

Wise legislation requires a detached viewpoint, objectivity. With this of course should be associated great ability and determination to act wisely. The development of objectivity is a positive essential among the ablest statesmen. We must strive to promote its universal possession, which will not only solve the problems of government, but will also solve many of the problems of the individual.

Our affairs are being conducted by leaders who have no more ability to handle their jobs than the average citizen, the great difference being that the average citizen does perform his tasks in a fairly satisfactory manner, whereas those who are entrusted with our destinies are failing lamentably to acquit themselves in a creditable manner.

For a nation to advance it must have leaders abler and of higher character than the average citizen, able to lead the way forward to better things. When we have leaders who lead by following the mob, finding what it likes, what will appeal to it, promising, flattering, telling about grievances, condemning capital, condemning all who oppose them, all who are successful, we are having the very reverse of sound leadership. Instead of the people being elevated by their leaders, they are being lowered.

Looking to the future from conditions as they now exist is a disheartening task. Our country, the world, is badly off; there seems to be no sign of improvement in the immediate future; the indications are that conditions will get worse. Let us think over this a moment. If this is the situation, it must have causes, and in order to correct it, the causes should be eradicated. We may attribute most of our own troubles in our country and in the world to the utter incompetence of the leaders who are at present conducting the affairs of nations. They promise much, blame others for their failure. If a private business man had a section of his business that was not paying and discovered that the man in charge was unequal to the task, he would remove him and place a competent man in charge. The same sensible action should be exercised in solving our problems of government. If we have men inadequate to the task, remove them. Find men who are competent and put them in charge. If we seek men to do this we will not find them among politicians or among those who make much noise. We will find them among men who have made a success of their lives and who work more than they talk.

Who among the great men and women of the past asked for benefits, pensions, doles, relief for themselves? Not one. They gave not money but wise counsel, work, devotion. It is their example we should follow, not the example of the quitters, those demanding doles or benefits, telling hard-luck stories, seeking personal gain under the guise of helping others.

Those men who wish to go down in history as being great will only be able to do so by doing things that contribute to man's good in accordance with the truth. Nearly all rulers, statesmen, soldiers of the past look pretty small when their real worth and contributions are analyzed. Those that stand out do so for moral character, scientific achievement, or as a result of having been a helpful influence on their time. Those who will live forever will be the great thinkers who have sought truth, those who have advanced science, man's welfare, knowledge, fought disease, ignorance, and so forth. How many of the great of their day are now looked back to with respect, admiration, thankfulness? Few, oh so few! Take heed, you who would be great and live after death.

Thoughts

The United States must lead the world toward sanity. No other country is in a position to do so; our failure to take the lead shows the poor quality of our leaders.

Did great men make their times, or their times make them? Both. They mutually influenced each other.

Great leaders should consider two factors in making their plans: The application of their plans to the world as it now is, and the future world.

It is relatively easy to find men to carry out plans and orders; far less so to find men to plan and give orders.

The success of a ruler depends less upon the basic soundness of his measures than upon his ability to obtain support for them. A sound measure poorly supported may bring disaster.

Neither the average worker nor the average citizen desires strikes or war. It is his incompetent leaders who cause both.

Politicians by their conduct and talk are doing much to undermine the character of the citizens and thus lower the moral standards of the nation.

Our leaders are attempting to lead us by facing the mob, trying to anticipate what it will think and do. They seek to advance in that direction with the mob following them. They have their faces turned toward ignorance, their backs toward knowledge.

If the hundred ablest statesmen were selected by an infallible power, there would be few if any politicians among them, provided, of course, that the need for obtaining votes from the rabble did not enter into the picture.

The world has yet to see, and man to have, a real statesman.

Who believes that the world is better off today than in 1914? We have gone down hill since then. Unless we find able leaders and adopt sane measures we will continue on the downward path.

It is useless to teach or talk good citizenship unless we have leaders who will set an example which the citizens may follow.

It is not capital. Why not place blame where it belongs? Blame self first, then when you can with justice place no blame there, seek elsewhere.

It is claimed by the opponents of the capitalistic system that the capitalists control the country and use their power to oppress the worker. If this be true, how much worse are not the politicians, men through whom they work, men sworn to serve honestly and faithfully and who in their speeches advocate right and justice to all?

We have too many high-sounding words among our politicians. We want deeds, examples, as exemplified in action, and not a lot of fine-sounding words and phrases.

Let the loonies go on unhampered with the government of our country and the world, and when they have discredited themselves and their measures, sane men may have a chance.

A country permitting itself to be controlled by such contemptible men as Farley, Roosevelt, and Lewis, is suffering from a lack of national mental ability and moral character, and will suffer as a consequence.

If our politicians devoted as much effort to seeking wise measures as they do to denouncing opponents and extolling their own merits, they would be great statesmen.

VI

POLITICIANS

WE ARE STATING A POSITIVE TRUTH WHEN WE ATTRIBUTE THE unsatisfactory state of affairs in our own country and throughout the world generally, to incompetent leaders. However, the leaders of all nations are products of their environment, of existing social institutions. To obtain better leaders, we must improve the environment, improve the social institutions. On the other hand, able leaders themselves will exert an uplifting influence upon their times. We are thus to some extent faced with a contradiction. If leaders are produced by their times, by their environment, they will not be able to improve it. However, all environmental influences are not uniform. There is viciousness and virtue, stupidity and intelligence, industry and laziness. Virtuous, intelligent, industrious leaders can improve their people; good citizens can exercise a salutary influence upon their leaders. It is here we should concentrate our efforts.

We should question existing institutions thoroughly, seek the reasons for the poor standards of leadership, character, and ability among our present-day politicians. Then we should endeavor to improve our political institutions. We should improve the environment. We should improve all things that will contribute toward placing able leaders in control of our affairs. We must elevate the standards of citizenship so as to appreciate the merit of able leaders and support them. Our present-day politicians are not leaders in the fullest sense. They are products of vicious political institutions.

They reflect the worst aspects of society. We must modify our political institutions so as to place leaders of character and ability in control of our government who will elevate the standards of citizenship and give us efficient government.

The worst feature of our democratic government today is its effect upon the character of the citizen. Our politicians are corrupt, self-seeking, set a bad example to citizenship. They are men of neither ability nor character. They appeal to much that is base, low, and selfish in obtaining office and remaining in office. We must so reform our political institutions as to have the offices of the government appeal to men of ability, character, fairness, and a desire to serve the public to the fullest extent of their ability.

Our present-day politicians are much like the office seekers who beset Lincoln after his first inauguration. Lincoln commented on their pernicious activity by remarking about being beset for jobs by office seekers in a house on fire with destruction threatened. Our senators and representatives especially are excellent examples of the same conduct. They have much to say in the halls of Congress about abuses, they ask for jobs for their friends, money for their constituents; they fail to look at themselves, to see just what puny, insignificant, contemptible people they are. They have no understanding of the vast problems of the world. They do not see existing threats to civilization. They see only their limited field of government benefits and talk. They resemble the old Aulic Council of Austria; clearly unable to understand practical measures of war, of administration, but much concerned with their own immediate comfort and interest. Our senators and representatives are short-sighted, insignificant men. They are unfit to have a voice in the councils of a great nation. Their unfitness is clearly displayed by their unwillingness to admit faults in themselves and to blame the poor capitalist, the big business men, because attacks on him are popular. Yet these big business and industrial leaders are the men who keep the affairs of the country operating.

Most of our politicians have developed from lawyers. This

is not a good background from which to build statesmen. A man who studies law spends much time in mastering statutes. His mind is developed along a specialized channel. He tends to pay much attention to technicalities. If our legal system were a simple one really serving the citizens, the training of a lawyer would not be incompatible with being a statesman. The legal system we now have is so cumbersome, so far removed from equity and endeavors to do justice, that it exercises a bad influence upon the development of anyone pursuing law as a profession. Our legal system has been developed by lawyers. We have but to see the vast amount of crime in the country and the operation of the civil law in practice to see that it is a very poor system. People who desire justice will avoid going to law to obtain it, but those who wish to use the law for their own advantage are all too willing to make use of its technicalities. Lawyers who are unable to establish a sound beneficial legal code are unequal to the task of conducting the affairs of our nation. Our leaders could better be taken from almost any walk of life other than lawyers.

Politicians should be gentlemen, seek the truth; not abuse opponents by undeserved ridicule and belittlement. But politics has reached such a low estate that no one is able to make a success of it except by such methods. We should accept the politicians of both sides at the evaluation given them by their opponents. We should remove the discourteous fellows from office and permit gentlemen to discuss problems in a gentlemanly way.

One result of our government being in the hands of professional politicians is that they resort to obtaining public offices for their supporters in order to consolidate their political positions. From a highly ethical standpoint, this is abusing their offices. They should, as government officials, endeavor to obtain the most efficient government employees. When, instead of doing this, they secure the appointments of their own friends as a means of assuring themselves of re-election to office, they are serving not the nation but themselves.

Politicians are probably the worst influence in our country today. They claim to be leading in the right direction and serving the welfare of the nation. In reality they are merely throwing out a smoke screen of promises while they seek to advance personal interests. They do much harm by their control of, and influence upon, the public schools, preventing them from showing the younger generation the ills of democracy and the bad features of present-day politics.

Our politicians of today are prihuman. They think in terms of the present, with little regard for the future except in as far as their own immediate future interests are concerned. Enlightened government demands that it be conducted by adhuman leaders who will consider the future; who will look a hundred years, a thousand years, ahead.

The so-called social-reform legislation of our present era was inspired by people with good intentions but little understanding. It is adopted by the politicians because popular and catchy. In its final operation the politicians are about the only class consistently favored. They obtain office for themselves and friends. The poor fellows who vote for them get little other than promises.

One hears much about quarrels, disputes, arguments among politicians. They have forgotten that their duty is to serve the citizens of the country, to give us a good government. They have confused their official duties with their personal lives just as children sometimes do; they have developed a kindergarten outlook which expresses resentment against those who disagree.

Criticism by politicians is generally overdrawn, exaggerated, largely untrue, influenced by the desire to obtain votes. Every speech we hear by them should be divided by two, three, five, ten, or some greater number, to evaluate properly. In a vast number of cases the speech should just be disregarded, being nothing but the outburst of a man who has made nothing but mistakes, trying to blame them on others.

Criticism to be helpful should be constructive; should be made in a calm, searching frame of mind in an effort to obtain an answer to the problems under consideration. Calmness and reason are but little used by politicians. They substitute therefore criticism of others, denunciation, ballyhoo. They are the only ones who have the right answer; everybody else is wrong. "Do what I say, boys, and everything will be all right."

Our government spends six hundred thousand dollars a year for publishing the Congressional Record, a means utilized by senators and representatives to have their speeches printed and circulated among constituents to show just what good fellows they are. Why should our federal government be required to publish such rot to advance the personal interests of politicians?

Our politicians are herd reflectors. They tell the herd what it would like to hear, promise those things that will prove popular with it, tell it that its members are virtuous but are being abused by the capitalists. Politicians reflect the prevailing popular thought on any subject regardless of whether it be right or wrong.

A real test to apply to a statesman is to ask, "Does he flatter us, tell us what we already believe, or does he seek the truth, point out our shortcomings with suggestions for correcting them?" If we apply this test to our present-day politicians we will find none who can bear up under it.

Professional politicians make their living from politics, obtain supporters by dispensing public office and ·benefits. There is a great temptation among politicians to spend other people's money. It takes men of high character to avoid the indulgence of this temptation. Our present-day politicians cannot be considered men of high character. A very high quality of citizens, however, would produce high-grade politicians. They would judge the politicians upon merit, ability, service for the public good. They would not permit their support to be purchased by the spending of government money in the form of benefits for ostensibly good reasons, but actually contributing towards unsound economic conditions although serving to give the politician more power and retain him in office.

Our politicians have adapted themselves to the demands of the situation by becoming divided into two somewhat general classes: First, the political manipulator such as Mr. Farley, who himself lacks the ability to attract votes but is able to manipulate party machinery. Quite frequently these men are of poor moral character; so poor indeed that they make poor candidates. The other class is the elective type, such as Mr. Roosevelt, who have pleasing personalities and have much to say about benefiting the common man. They are able to convince a large part of the electors that they are honest, upright, deserving persons striving for the welfare of the country. These men very often pass the dirty work necessary to obtain election to office to the party manipulators. Thus we see Mr. Roosevelt permitting Mr. Farley to do many unethical things and taking great care not to inquire too greatly into what Mr. Farley does. These political manipulators, particularly in the large cities, do not hesitate to conciliate the criminal vote and the vote of the lowest type of citizens in the community, just as the vote-seeking politician takes good care not to antagonize the political manipulator.

A superficial thinker hearing our politicians rant would think that they were great influences striving to help the common man. As a matter of fact they are making up in volume of noise for lack of sound action. They are a discredit to democracy and are bringing about its inevitable downfall in this country. They have had full reign for a sufficiently long time to show that they are incapable of governing. The first step in instituting sound government is to get rid of our present-day politicians and so modify the institutions that similar creatures will not again be permitted to obtain control of the government.

Our politicians are about average men, products of their time and calling. Having some knowledge of men, ability to obtain votes, skill in obtaining offices for supporters, they make enemies of those whose enmity will be of value from the political standpoint. They take great care to conciliate those whose enmity would be dangerous to their political future, doing this with great skill, crying out their virtues to the public at the same time. They are willing to promise all things to all men and willing to conciliate, just so they obtain votes, offices, and power. It will be interesting to see if in their attempts to conciliate all, they eventually lose the support of the majority.

Politics is so dirty, so vicious, so crooked, that a man of character will not select a political career. He does not care to use his ability for the benefit of selfish interest groups, selfish constituents; has no desire to dicker with vicious politicians. Our government will be incompetent, undeserving of respect, until we reform the institutions so as to both encourage and obtain able men of character to conduct its affairs. The politicians have done us great harm and are continuing to do so. They are the ones who have contributed to poor understanding of economic problems and to class feeling. They do not attempt to educate the people to a proper understanding of economic problems. They do not understand them themselves. The only qualifications they possess is the ability to flatter, please, promise, and obtain votes.

Our politicians are men of poor character. This has been true for many decades. Years back they permitted themselves to be purchased by the money interests, failing to correct the abuses then existent. When feeling was aroused against those abuses, they gradually swung over to the side most popular. They promised reforms, bought votes by giving government benefits, penalizing the deserving, rewarding the undeserving; the while crying their virtues to the world and always fighting the great battle for the downtrodden.

Our politicians have discredited themselves to anyone who will take the trouble to reflect on the subject. Look back over any presidential campaign: the same twaddle about the people, about democracy, about their own merits, about their opponents' vices; truly a disgusting performance, and yet we call ourselves a sensible, virtuous people. If this situation is ever corrected it will not be by politicians. Sound reform measures will be bitterly opposed by them, for their benefits would then cease. They have passed many laws, levied many taxes, talked much, done many things except think soundly and act with judgment. Whereas in the past they permitted themselves to be bought and controlled by wealth, today they cringe before any organized group of voters able to threaten them. Capital in the old days had no recourse except to buy them, much like racketeers today, yet our politicians admit no vice in self or virtue in capital.

In the early stages of our national existence, capital to a considerable extent really abused labor. The politicians of that day not only failed to prevent this but were themselves bought by capital to do as capital desired. This abuse was so apparent to all that labor organized in self-defense and obtained the support of the public in its endeavor to obtain better treatment. Now labor is so strong that it is persecuting capital, disregarding the interests of the public, and again politicians, in keeping with the policies of their predecessors, are failing to solve the problems but are permitting themselves to be controlled by labor, doing whatever it wishes. Clearly, institutions are at fault that put men in control of the government incapable in the first place of controlling capital, and now unable to control labor.

The same politicians who were instrumental in causing the Civil War by their incompetence later gave the country corrupt, incompetent government. They failed to solve the economic problems of their day and we are today suffering from their incompetence and corruption. If they had properly regulated the ruthless capitalists of their period instead of permitting themselves to be bought by them, and had this attempt at wise solution of economic problems been continued, we would not be suffering as we are today. How long will the American public permit itself to be deluded by politicians? They brought about the Civil War. They had a most corrupt government following the Civil War. They have failed to solve adequately the problems of the day, and yet they place the fault of it all on capital. It is by no means beyond the bounds of possibility that their incompetence and promotion of class feeling will result in causing another civil war. About all they do today is denounce capital, flatter the voter, and make promises, pass laws that burden industry and complicate the problems still more. When will the American public learn better? When will they understand that men of ability do not continually denounce others? This extreme denunciation by politicians prevents decent men from entering public life. If our government problems are to be solved we will have to have decent men to do it; not our present-day politicians.

The striking labor unions who appeal to violence, the relief workers who picket city halls, threatening legislatures and politicians and demanding benefits, are not as guilty as those who have brought this situation about. The guilty ones are the politicians who have made rash promises to practically everyone who had little, to obtain their votes. These promises have not been fulfilled. If these people were sensible, they would, instead of venting their anger against innocent parties, transfer it to the politicians who have failed to live up to their promises.

But these very same politicians who brought about this situation will convince the misled people that they themselves are the victims of some other vicious person, namely capital. Capital has been abused, fought, regulated for so long that everyone is willing to blame all existing ills upon it, and the politicians will doubtless succeed at this yet for a time. It seems unreasonable to believe, however, that they will be able to do this .indefinitely. Even the most stupid person should realize that the politicians have promised many things that have not been fulfilled, and that the fault, therefore, must be with the politicians.

To the thoughtful person, the actions of the politicians in blaming their lack of success upon capital, upon opponents, shows conclusively their inability to control the government. To one versed in economics, it is apparent that their measures are unsound, that persecuting capital, raising wages, restricting hours, giving benefits to many people, handicapping industry by regulations, heavy taxes, the burden of social reform, are breaking down the economic structure, tending toward greater distress for all. This cannot be the fault of capital. It is the fault of unwise economic policies which are directly inaugurated by our rulers. They and they only should be blamed. If they were able men this situation would not exist.

Two pictures on the same page of a newspaper I just glanced at express to my mind very forcibly our existing condition. One of the pictures shows fighting with clubs, fists, stones, between men desiring to go to work and other men who would not permit them to do so. The other picture shows a committee of senators and representatives engaged in investigating the evasions of income taxes by the wealthy. Here are these men, our rulers, investigating violations of law, if they exist, that they themselves have caused, by abusing the wealthy and by subjecting them to exorbitant taxation. They spend their time investigating, to see if wrongdoing has been committed, while decent citizens are being subjected to violence in violation of constitutional rights. The unwise measures of these very politicians have brought about the resort to violence, and yet they ignore it. They go on persecuting the wealthy taxpayer, stirring up more feeling against him, seeing no fault in themselves, making no effort to help the law-abiding American citizen who wishes to go to work and maintain himself by his own efforts.

We may well ask, why do not the politicians now in control of our government solve the problems of the day? Why do they not correct the evils they so heartily denounce and bring about that great era of prosperity and righteousness they so fondly extol? The government is in their hands. They have the power. Why do we not obtain results? The answer to this question is incredibly simple. They are incompetent. They are able to talk, bluster, make much noise, denounce, belittle, attack, criticize but they are unequal to the task of thinking, of understanding the issues confronting them and of solving them. Clearly, we have been ruled by noisy people long enough. They are convincing evidence that noise alone is insufficient to solve the problems of today. Let us apply this common-sense thought and seek for men to administer public affairs who will think, who are competent; who will resort to sensible action instead of noise.

When the American people refuse to listen to politicians who denounce big business and monopoly and place the blame for existing conditions where it rightly belongs—on the politicians themselves—they will have advanced from infantilism to maturity. It should be apparent to any reasonable person that the politicians govern the country, pass its laws, enforce them, and should be able to control monopoly and big business. When, instead of doing so, they denounce the latter, they admit their incompetence and blame a scapegoat to conceal their shortcomings.

We have many laws that cause evil, and yet our politicians are unable to correct them; they likewise fail to enforce the laws that are in existence. This points to the utter breakdown of government if permitted to continue. We must have laws that are fair to all, and the laws must be enforced. It is for this purpose that government exists.

The attitude of our politicians in control of our national and state governments during the sit-down strikes represents the heights of cowardice, incompetence, and stupidity. Our government has indeed come to a low point when those controlling it not only refuse to enforce the laws but actually stimulate insurrection within the country, encourage one class of citizens to attack others, disregarding the rights of the public.

The recent remark made by Governor Earle of Pennsylvania in one of his speeches that, "from a moral point of view business should be given fair play but that actually it was not important," sheds great light upon the character of our politicians and the reasons for existing unsound economic conditions. It shows low standards of public life when a prominent man can make such a remark. It shows his incompetence and lack of moral character. If business is not given fair play, why should anyone else receive it? It is because business is afraid of not receiving fair play in the future that it is reluctant to expand and support the people as it would if encouraged. Our democratic institutions have fallen to a low estate indeed when our leaders deny the need for fair play, deny the obligations of moral law. Those who defend our democratic institutions so vociferously should give this matter some little thought. If they do not promote moral character, maintain high standards of civic virtue, they are unworthy. It is less the form of government than the character of the men who control and set the example that is important. A democracy can be as vicious as any other form of government when in the hands of despicable men. This is our condition today.

Politicians are not sound thinkers. They adopt that view which will give votes, will be most popular. They defend this view so eloquently that they finally believe it themselves. Their conclusions are invariably unsound. They do not go deep enough into a subject to find out just what is wrong. They arrive at the conclusion that is most popular and defend it most eloquently. Our politicians talk much, reason little, display much passion, exaggerate, misstate, appeal to prejudice, class feeling, anything to down their opponents. Such a state of mind does not permit of deciding questions upon merit.

Illusions in the mind are conditioned by anticipating occurrences that have occurred before. For instance, you have become accustomed to waiting for an elevator. As it comes down, its motion is reflected through a window or by the light or shadows. You ring for the elevator and, if thinking about it, you can well have several illusions of seeing the shadow or light or reflection, thinking it has arrived, whereas it actually has not; the activity and thought is entirely mental. This is a type of conditioned illusion. Merely thinking, anticipating the arrival of the elevator, activates brain cells having impressions recorded upon them, with the result that the belief is entertained by the mind that certain anticipated things have occurred.

This form of conditioned illusion may be transferred into a mental viewpoint, a conclusion, an obsession. A politician or reformer, for instance, desires to accomplish certain things. He wishes for certain results. His mind dwells upon them so long that he becomes convinced that certain measures will accomplish certain things, and in time he believes they have been accomplished. Likewise his belief, constantly repeated, that capital is causing all the woes of man, stimulated by many others thinking in like ways, results in the creation of a mental illusion. He has been so convinced by thinking about it, by absorbing the same thought from others, by finding reasons to substantiate it, by failing to see anything that would tend to discredit it, that it becomes a mental illusion. The man has developed an unsound mental outlook rendering him incapable of dealing with public questions in a sound manner. We are being governed by these victims of mental delusions.

Our politicians afford an excellent example of Adapto in operation. They have developed great ability to flatter, please, promise; great skill in substantiating popular ideas; and have become unable to reach sound conclusions. They seek for measures that will be popular, that will appeal to the popular mind, instead of seeking for the underlying truths.

The professional politician by continued attempts to conciliate, to appease, to denounce, to obtain votes, finds only good in his plans, only bad in those of opponents, is undermining his character and his sense of perspective.

An obsession is a strong belief or feeling exercising a strong influence on the individual and sometimes entirely dominating his conduct or thought. It may be true or false, harmful or good. An obsession may be acquired in a great many different ways. The most common means is to acquire it as the result of arriving at a conclusion or belief that is pleasing to one's desires. Often very capable thinkers are guilty of this. They conduct research and do much thinking in an endeavor to find the truth or answers to certain problems. Their original intention may have been entirely honest. But as they become involved in the subject, some particular phase of it will attract their attention. This particular thing, which seems to offer a solution, is then utilized as the main objective. All other features are interpreted with a view to confirming the soundness of the obsession, and all things disagreeing are belittled, disregarded, or attacked in all possible ways. With time the obsession grows upon one and prevents, if it goes to extremes, a sound conclusion, provided the obsession be itself unsound.

Probably the greatest victims of obsessions are our politicians. They develop a form of transitory obsession. Their line of thinking does not reach into the deep recesses of intricate problems and locate the causes. In most cases their mentality is not equal to such a task. They therefore utilize their thoughts to arrive at conclusions that will be pleasing to them and further their political fortunes. They build up any number of these transitory obsessions established merely to obtain votes, although the possessor himself may be convinced of their truth and merit. As fashions change, so his thoughts change. He will drop some of the former obsessions and cultivate new ones. Such mental activity is obsessionistic thought. It is of all things the most unsatisfactory phase of man's life in this age, and until realized and rectified by more healthful mental processes, will be a distinct bar both to the solution of present pressing problems and to the development of sensible public men.

Politicians in applying obsessionistic thought show conclusively the functioning of specialization of thought. After a time Adapto is harnessed to develop the individual along those particular channels, rendering him in the course of time a specialized obsessionist. His mental processes are confirmed in ways leading away from real truth. Understanding of social and economic problems requires a fresh mind, a determination to seek the truth, a groping for causes, and a determination not to permit personal feelings or popular desires to influence the accuracy of the conclusion. This is the direct opposite of obsessionism.

Roosevelt, Lewis, communists, socialists, radical labor agitators are all obsessionists. They have formed certain stereotyped lines of belief or thought as the result of their environment. They are looking at the world, interpreting it, in the light of their own convictions, wishes, and desires. Their convictions are not formed by intelligent reasoning but are more in the nature of absorption from their own herd, with a plentiful supply of popular platitudes, phrases and conceptions that agree or seem to agree with their own. They are unable to understand that other viewpoints can be broader, more disinterested than theirs; therefore all who oppose them are stupid, vicious, selfish. This obsessionism is all too common and is one of many factors, and not the least, preventing both sane conclusions and sensible action. The world is being dominated by madmen. They and the interest groups to which they belong make such an outcry that sensible men seeking sound solutions are unnoticed. When this spell of madness has run its course, the thinker will have his chance if he be equal to it. Now is the time to work and be prepared for that day when it arrives.

The dickering for personal gain among our present-day politicians is very similar to the action of European rulers of two hundred years ago. They failed to recognize that they existed primarily for the task of serving the people and confused the people's interest with personal interest. If anything, our politicians are more despicable than the old absolute monarchs. The monarchs continually stressed the duty of the subject to the sovereign and were more frank about seeking aggrandizement. Our present-day politicians cloak the advancement of personal interest under the noble motive of advancing the welfare of the people. Man's history constantly repeats itself. The student will recall that the kings were overthrown. Nature is just as ruthless in man's affairs as in other ways. The unfit ultimately perish as a result of their unfitness.

Gripe

Mr. McNutt is now trying to build up support in order to become president. He is not doing this by wise measures to advance the public welfare, by studying present-day problems, by pointing out present-day evils; he is attempting to obtain support by making friends with politicians, handshaking, smiling, promising. He, like most politicians, is specialized in such activities. Understanding of the vast problems confronting the world, our nation, is beyond his comprehension. Yet he apparently has a fairly good chance to become president. If he does, he will not contribute anything to civilization. He will continue the policies of present-day politicians. These policies are undermining the moral character of our citizens, are discrediting democracy. A civilization that produces men like McNutt as leaders, has serious faults. Unless the faults be corrected, unless we obtain able, honest leaders, either we or our children will witness the overthrow of our much-vaunted democratic institutions.—*February 24, 1938.*

VII

INTEREST GROUPS

THE FUNCTION OF A GOVERNMENT IS TO PROVIDE FOR THE interests of all living within the country, to give justice, afford a means of settling disputes or disagreements among its citizens. When the government is inefficient, inadequate to this task, very commonly interest groups within the nation organize to protect themselves from injury by others. The very natural tendency of these interest groups is to abuse others themselves when they become more powerful. The various groups now existing within our country, especially the labor unions, exemplify this truth too well. We must improve our government, make it efficient, educate all citizens to see the need for supporting it and being members of one interest group—that of the entire nation, protecting all in their rights and working harmoniously for the greater good of all. With such a citizenry the need for labor or other interest groups to organize for protection will be unnecessary.

Permitting selfish interest groups to grow· and develop in the nation results in creating an environment conducive to such development. Thus Herdo is utilized in support of interest groups and against its better employment of being an ascendent force considering all.

I have before me a clipping from an association organized to protect retired army officers. I will read a brief part of this as pertaining to legislation. "Only through cooperation with other groups such as the American Federation of Labor, the American Legion, Veterans of Foreign Wars, Spanish-

American Veterans, Federation of Government Employees, and so forth, and our personal contact with senators and congressmen, as well as with the war and navy departments, can success be achieved." Let us dwell on this brief statement a moment. Here we have an organization of patriotic citizens somewhat above the general average of intelligence, willing to serve their country, give their lives for it in case of need. Yet we see them here endeavoring to obtain the co-operation of other interest groups in obtaining benefits from the government. In their particular case it is less to obtain further benefits than to protect their own interests.

Some lobbies and interest groups are justifiable under our vicious system. In order to protect themselves from unjust treatment they must band together and obtain support from such sources as they can. The viciousness of this interest-group development is apparent. One interest group will trade with another for support, and the eventual result is that we have a great number of interest groups banded together demanding not only defense from unjust treatment but demanding benefits—a system which is fast making our democratic form of government the most vicious of all time.

The origin of these interest groups can be traced in the development of democracy. Government officials are elected by votes and controlled by votes. It is a simple matter for any number of voters to band together, first in support of desirable measures, but with the passage of time demanding benefits such as pensions, a local postoffice, a harbor improvement, some reform to help the poor, the suffering; gradually developing until our entire government is controlled by interest groups banded together to obtain certain ends. This association of interest groups prevents the consideration of each particular problem on its merit, which is the essence of efficient government.

The cure for this is adequate education of the individual citizens, impressing upon them the need for all citizens to work for the benefit of all; to constitute within the nation one interest group to which all citizens belong, giving justice to all, considering each case on its merits. The situation has now continued for so long and is so bad that its correction will call for drastic reorganization of our entire governmental system. No effective reform can be made while politicians of the present type remain in control. They are products of interest-group methods and unable to adapt themselves to a new conception of having only one interest group for the entire nation. Able men who are capable of understanding this evil and correcting it must be put in control of the government. When such men are put in control they must receive the whole-hearted support of all citizens.

When a selfish interest group obtains special benefits, they are obtained at the expense of other citizens or of other interest groups. The existence of one or more selfish interest groups and their success encourages the development of more. In the initial stage, the selfish interest group may obtain benefits for itself. When, however, it arouses opposition on the part of other citizens and encourages the development of many other interest groups, none will profit. The interest of one will be opposed by many others. As the result we have much internal conflict and all suffer. This is substantially the condition of affairs in our country today.

When the American Legion obtains increased benefits for its members, the money must be paid by taxpayers of the nation. When farmers obtain special benefits from the government, the taxpayers foot the bill. If prices are arbitrarily regulated, the consumer pays. When labor unions organize, intimidate employers, the public pays. When politicians and political parties create class hatred, denounce others, seek office and benefits for themselves, the public pays. All these interest groups fighting for themselves are creating much ill feeling and unsound economic conditions, and are themselves suffering as a result of the unwisdom of their acts. How much more sensible it is to abolish all interest groups seeking to further their own ends; to have all citizens willingly co-operate with all other citizens; to consider the interests of each other; to advance the interests of all; not seek for personal gain for oneself or group at the expense of other citizens or groups. The development of these intensely selfish interest groups within our great democracy, exposes the weakness of our institutions. Selfish interest groups cannot develop to such extremes under other forms of government. We must elevate the standards of citizenship and abolish selfish interest groups or abandon democracy.

The conflict between these many selfish interest groups within the nation is very similar to national interest groups in the international field. Nations oppose each other, go to war, have much ill feeling and all lose. If they would compose their differences, co-operate harmoniously in advancing the interest of all, each would benefit.

All descendent interest groups within our nation must be abolished. All citizens of the country should then unite in joining one nation-wide interest group: that of the American citizens, for promoting the welfare of all, treating all with fairness, thus establishing a feeling of co-operation and of willingness to serve our country. When we have accomplished this and solved our internal problems, we may endeavor to secure a like development throughout the world in which all selfish national interest groups will be merged into one vast interest group including all men throughout the world. They can then work together and solve the problems of the world just as we will have previously set an example of solving the problems within our own country.

The growing development of selfish interest groups and their conflicts with each other when their interests clash is very similar to the condition existing after the Revolution and prior to the adoption of the Constitution. The interest groups then were the separate states loosely bound together by the old Articles of Confederation, fighting among themselves, creating friction and discord. As a result all suffered. They resembled a large family fighting and quarreling among themselves instead of harmoniously working together for the best interests of all. It was this situation that brought about the adoption of the federal Constitution. It was apparent to the abler men of that day that a strong federal government capable of controlling the states was necessary.

The development of our present-day interest groups has reached the same stage. The greatest offender is labor, demanding special privileges with no regard for the public, and there are the numerous other interest groups demanding benefits from the government. In order to correct this we will have to take somewhat similar action to that of the nation's founders.

Our government could be strong enough to cope with the situation, but is controlled by incompetents. The general public looks on somewhat helplessly, doing nothing. The solution is for worthy citizens, having the welfare of the entire country at heart, to assert themselves, to remove the incompetent politicians from office, to revamp the government and social institutions, to abolish interest groups that are abusing their rights, to place honest and able men who will seek the interest of all citizens in control of the government, and to give them full support.

It is one of the functions of government to establish rules for the guidance of its citizens, to maintain order among them, and protect all. A government fails in its duty when it permits interest groups to cause the public to suffer as the result of their activities, or permits internal strife to exist. In this respect democracy is now failing. Our government is proving inadequate to the task of maintaining order when large interest groups have conflicts. Anyone with an understanding of human nature will realize that interest groups are unfit to settle controversies. They very naturally stress those things that are of interest to them, fail to see the viewpoint of the opposing interest group or the rights of the public. It is therefore the positive duty of the government to control them and prevent conflicts. When the government proves unequal to this task, it will sometime, when the evils are sufficiently great, be superseded by another government which will be more forceful and may or may not be more competent.

Interest groups working for certain measures for their own interest are one of the most demoralizing influences on our institutions. They work hand in hand with self-seeking politicians who are willing to resort to any means to obtain office. Selfish interest groups and self-seeking politicians are at the bottom of our misfortune. Present-day legislation is passed more to propitiate interest groups, to please the multitude, than it is to accomplish far-reaching reforms. We are permitting our lowest, most selfish elements to control our government at the expense of the higher deserving element.

The development of these vast interest groups has been a gradual progressive development. It has been encouraged by politicians promising benefits to interest groups in order to obtain their votes. Having separate political parties is conducive to the development of interest groups, because the politicians of the party out of office will make promises to interest groups to obtain their votes and get in office. There is but little difference between the policies of the two political parties in our country today. It would be a wise measure that would reduce the evils of interest groups if we were to abolish political parties as such. We should have the citizens vote directly for leaders without the intervention of primaries or politicians.

The present-day tendency is to promote loyalty to one's interest group, using the government as an agent from which to obtain benefits. Sound government may be insured in the future by the extreme development of selfish interest groups, having so many making such great demands upon the government as to render it impossible to accede to any. Then they may finally conclude to form one interest group for the entire nation and endeavor to serve all citizens. This is consoling to think about, but there are many obstacles in the way. It would seem that the denunciation of capital and the successful is the one thing that all selfish interest groups agree upon. Harmony within the nation will not be promoted by denunciation and persecution of any class within it.

The American Legion bulldozes politicians by saying in

effect, "Give us money or we will put you out of office." What a disgusting spectacle our government has become when organized bodies of voters will threaten their government unless it give them benefits! Not only does the American Legion do this but any aggregation of labor agitators or of people on relief do the same thing, intimidating the legislators into giving them what they wish.

It is very unfair for labor unions or any interest group to get all they can merely because they can get it, regardless of whether deserved or not. This is the reverse of "Right makes might," putting brute force ahead of intelligence, demands ahead of duty. Interest groups following such procedure should pause and consider other people, the other side of the question. Someone must pay for the benefits they are demanding. By using the threat of their organized voting power, they may be able to obtain present benefits. But what about the future? Their methods will discredit themselves and they will suffer. Injustice cannot thrive at the expense of justice, nor stupidity at the expense of intelligence.

The men composing the American Legion are a general average of American manhood. There are many fine men belonging to this organization, yet when they attempt to obtain benefits from the government they are showing conduct unworthy of a decent citizen. They are prejudicing the rights of the deserving veteran who is entitled to government benefits. When so much is demanded for all members of the American Legion, the government will eventually be unable to pay benefits to anyone. This attitude on the part of these men is caused by their environment, the habit that has grown up of looking upon the government as a Santa Claus having vast sums of money to give away. They dwell upon the fact that during the war they received small pay while men at home received large pay, and feel that they should have this equalized. They can think of many reasons why they have been unjustly treated and why they should receive benefits.

They are the victims of poor standards of citizenship, of the failure of our educators to teach real character, intelligence, understanding. Men who are willing to give their lives for their country are not entirely unworthy. There is as much worth within the American Legion as in any body of similar citizens in the country. To correct this situation we must teach higher standards of citizenship, teach a knowledge of human nature, Ascendent Psychology, have all strive for Ascendency. No one should strive for benefits for himself or his particular interest group. If we make this universal we will not have such large groups of really fine men devoting their energies toward measures that are harmful to the nation.

One can severely criticize the American Legion for demanding benefits for themselves and using their voting power as citizens to obtain them. They are but reflecting the spirit of the times, the unfortunate development of our democratic institutions into many interest groups and lobbies striving to obtain benefits from the government. We must bring about a more healthful understanding of the duties of a citizen. Let all work for the benefit of all citizens of the country, ask only for benefits that will benefit all, and not one particular interest group. The American Legion is no worse in its demands than any number of other interest groups. If we can induce all citizens to cease making demands upon the government for themselves, we will bring about a more healthful atmosphere. We must cause all to see the viciousness of organized lobbies and interest groups demanding benefits for themselves.

We must establish a government that will work for the benefit of all the people. At present the government is being conducted by coalitions among interest groups who band together trading votes. This is an unfortunate development but it is one that we must approach in a sensible manner if we are to insure the perpetuation of our democratic institutions and the prosperity of our citizens. Whenever one particular group is benefited by some legislation, some other group suffers. When we cease to benefit one particular group to the prejudice of others, but benefit all citizens, we will have established democracy on a sound footing. We will then have a government supported by citizens intelligent enough to understand the harmful effects of interest groups demanding benefits for themselves.

Members of the American Legion, in addition to showing characteristics of poor citizenship, show their utter short-sightedness. They fail to see that by making excessive demands upon the treasury they are encouraging other interest groups to like efforts. This may cause the bankruptcy of the government, possibly inflation, which will result in everybody suffering, including the really deserving injured veterans. The members of the American Legion are not alone in having such a selfish, short-sighted viewpoint. It is the general attitude of the American citizens to live today, heedless of the future, having little knowledge of economics. The cure for this is to have our educators teach both the duties of citizenship and economics, and to have public men deserving of respect, who have the welfare of the nation at heart and will tell the truth regarding current problems. When our public men flatter the citizens and appeal to whatever means they can to obtain votes, they are breaking down the citizen's character and causing unnecessary suffering in the future.

The conduct of the American Legion in using its voting power to obtain benefits from the government is about the same as that of our educators in getting better salaries and bigger school appropriations, or of any locality striving for federal funds. Each one is encouraged by the success of the other, and the vicious system thrives. Democracy conducted by interest groups intent upon getting benefits from the government is not a form of government conducive to either good character development of individual citizens, or toward an efficient performance of its duties. Interest groups within the nation must be reformed or abolished, or they will destroy our democratic government. True democracy requires that all citizens seek the welfare of all. When they seek to advance the selfish measures of their interest group, or personal interest, they are bringing about the downfall of democratic institutions.

Mendicant interest groups such as the American Legion and radical labor unions are harming themselves as a group in seeking present benefits at the expense of the future. Great harm is being done also to the individual members of these organizations, by confirming them in grievances and demanding benefits, instead of building up strong character through working for benefits.

When we permit interest groups to develop within the country to the degree that the American Legion and labor unions have developed, we are bringing about internal conflict, creating opposing interest groups who consider only themselves and are willing to sacrifice all other groups for their own immediate benefit. This is a short-sighted policy by which they themselves will suffer in the long run. We are introducing within our nation the same situation that prevails in the international field, in which each separate nation is a separate interest group, considers only its own interests, will go to war, will maim and slaughter for what it considers its interests. If we are to avoid discord and civil disorders, we must constitute our government so as to prevent large interest groups from developing.

The civilization of ancient Greece perished as the result of the extreme development of Groupo. Their interest was in their own city and in selfish interest groups within it. Yet considering their times, they were more meritorious, everything considered, than we are today. We are threatened by this same extreme development of Groupo, as shown in the intense national rivalry of nations today and the intense feeling between interest groups within our nation. The Greeks failed to understand this evil and permitted it to destroy them. Can we not profit by their failure, the dictates of common sense and enlightened self-interest, and control Groupo, preventing its development in a vicious form from destroying us?

Our federal Constitution was adopted as the result of enlightened self-interest. Following the Revolution the need became apparent to able thinkers for a strong central government in order to insure a greater degree of prosperity to all of the states. With the loose system of government under the Confederation there was friction between the different states, as a result of which all suffered. It was necessary that a strong government be established, capable of reconciling conflicting interests in order that all might benefit. It is this enlightened viewpoint of a national interest group to which we owe our greatness as a nation, and it was lack of this that caused the ancient Greek civilization to perish. When we apply this same principle in reconciling the differences among interest groups within the nation, causing them to act for the benefit of the one national interest group, realizing that in so doing their own interests will be best served, we may hope to solve our present pressing problems.

A like further consideration may be applied to the entire world. When nations, which are but interest groups, realize that their own interests are best served by giving due consideration to other nations and working together harmoniously for the best interests of all men, the problem of international conflicts will have been solved.

It is not true that the problems of today are so complex as to defy solution. Look back upon history, see where man has been caused to suffer much by foolish, short-sighted interest groups, failing to see that their individual welfare was better served by a broad outlook considering the welfare of all. We have any number of examples from past history from which to profit. It requires merely the intelligent application of principles of proven soundness. Because man has failed to do this in the past is no reason why he should fail to do so in the future. It is a mere matter of mental development, advancing from the primitive stage to an enlightened adhuman stage—instead of facing our problems with a primitive outlook, facing them with an advanced outlook, profiting by the mistakes and successes of the past.

All interest groups are not selfish, vicious in their actions. A good test is whether they make demands upon others, cooperate for mutual interest, promote good feeling. The vicious ones demand that the rest of the world serve them or give them benefits. Our labor unions, the American Legion, political parties, and local groups demanding benefits from the federal government are all in the class of vicious interest groups. They use their power as voters to make demands upon the government. The influence of a virtuous interest group such as the family, whose members ask nothing from outsiders, who work together in a spirit of harmony, is a splendid example of man at his best. The vicious ones are an example of man at his worst. We condemn organized bands of racketeers, gangsters, criminals, but they are less harmful than the interest groups organized for the same purpose, to plunder others, but cloaking their designs under motives that ostensibly show they are virtuous and working for the good of others.

If all selfish interest groups could be induced to apply the same effort toward obtaining benefits for all men as they do for those within their own group, the world at large would be the gainer—likewise the interest groups concerned. They would gain far more by such altruistic efforts than they do by their present selfish efforts.

Extreme interest-group activity such as the American Legion and labor lobbies is simple racketeering, keeping within the law so as not to be subject to penalties therefrom. With a high code of moral law they would be considered even worse than racketeers, for the latter's purpose is apparent, while the former's is clothed with fine appeals to the sympathies of the public, with the real motive concealed. Legislation to protect interest groups perpetuates selfish Groupo and prevents the highest development of Co. Those hurt by such legislation seek to protect themselves. Thus both those who are benefited and those who are hurt are stimulated to stress narrow self-interest at the expense of an all-embracing, enlightened Co.

Considering the great opposition to war in this country, one would think that the American Legion would receive little support in their drive for veteran's benefits. The public, however, is inconsistent and does not govern its conduct by reason. One war mother defended the great expenses involved in paying mother's pensions and other war benefits because their great cost would deter us from entering another war.

Interest groups are a direct product of the democratic form of government when it is permitted to develop along interest-group lines. When, in order to obtain benefits, interest groups band together in an effort to·control sufficient votes to compel the politicians to accede to their needs, democracy has permitted itself to become vicious. All interest groups claim they are working for the benefit of all. They arrive at this belief by obsessionistic thought. "What benefits their interest group will benefit everyone," and they interpret all to substantiate this conclusion.

An interest-group obsession is one held by a particular interest group, which its members attempt to justify by belittling and ridiculing all measures that oppose and by interpreting beneficial things to sustain. The American Legion, for instance, advocates benefits for its members. It does this under the guise of a debt due soldiers, patriotic motives, but as a matter of fact they are abusing their privileges as citizens to compel the politicians to give them benefits for votes. Labor unions demand many benefits from the employer: shorter hours, higher wages, control of hiring halls. They claim economic improvement if these measures are adopted and see no objections to them. Silver miners advocate measures to increase the purchase value of silver and find reasons for doing so by pointing out the great economic results that would result. They admit no faults. Interest-group obsessions of this nature are very harmful. This is particularly apparent in our own country where we have many groups demanding benefits from the government, too short-sighted to see that the demands of great numbers of people for benefits will bankrupt any government and cause loss to all. The best interests of all groups are best served by the welfare of all, and the welfare of all is achieved best by considering the interests of all. This truth is evaded by the interest-group obsessionists; all alike claim they are without fault, and their policies unselfish.

If we understand the functioning of human beings, it will be impossible for violent agitators to arouse groups to unwise acts. Let us take a labor group dominated by agitators. They stress Granto and Grievo, encouraging their members to take the benefits for granted and emphasizing grievances. A state of mind is soon reached whereby the members of the unions think they are being badly abused, and are soon stimulated to violence. We must show these men that it is not in violent displays such as this that their best interests are served. Their interests are best served in contributing to sound governmental policies which will not give special benefits to labor but will treat all citizens alike in an effort to do justice to all, that all may be the better served.

With a universal understanding of the functioning of Groupo in human beings, we should not see instances of communities demanding that the government give them special benefits, that it construct public buildings in their locality. Common sense should tell our citizens that when so many people are making demands upon the government, someone else must pay and in the end they will have to pay themselves.

The same principle applies to groups as to the individual. Let each group try to solve its own problems within itself. An interest group that does this, demands no benefits from outsiders, is an ascendent influence. An interest group that is constituted to use its voting power to make demands upon the public or for any reason demands special benefits, is an undesirable interest group.

Regardless of how high its motives may be, the fact that it demands assistance from others is sufficient reason for us to scan it closely. The best citizens we have are not those demanding benefits, but those who are meeting their own problems without assistance. The same is true of interest groups. The best interest groups we have are those that are meeting their problems by their own efforts; the worst are those who demand that others give them benefits.

The government should prevent conflicts between interest groups. Its function is to safeguard the welfare of all citizens, not particular interest groups. To do this it may be necessary to abolish some of the worst interest groups that are so large and create such ill feeling as to prevent the solution of pressing problems.

To understand just how interest groups are produced, you should master Ascendent Psychology thoroughly. Primarily, selfish interest groups are a descendent application of Groupo. The chapter headed Groupo in INDIVIDUAL ASCENDENCY discusses this in some detail. It should be studied carefully in conjunction with this chapter on Interest Groups. Descendent or selfish Groupo is the primary cause of war between nations and of internal conflicts within nations. The development of interest groups may be supported by many psychas in addition to Groupo. When one's feelings or personal interests are aroused, his entire being is stimulated to a response to protect what he believes threatened. Man can protect both worthy and unworthy things. Descendent interest groups are unworthy. None of the members of these descendent interest groups will admit their unworthiness. They themselves do not understand the basic human urges that cause them to believe and act as they do. The mere aggregation of a number of individuals having somewhat common interests tends to stir up a desire for self-glorification.

A gathering of lawyers, for instance, is often productive of much praise for themselves and the law, but of little effort to correct the many ills inherent in the legal system. They are flattering ignorance, promoting sloth, deluding themselves into believing they are serving man, whereas they are an obstruction in the way of sane thought on legal matters and retard man's development.

We see this exemplified throughout our society in many ways. Who has not heard school teachers, members of a political party, doctors, scientists, extolling their own merits and virtues? Many act as though they are carrying the burden of the world upon their shoulders. Such activity on the part of presumably intelligent, highly educated men, shows the existence of Infanta and Groupo. Despite our education, our knowledge, our self-glorification, we retain within ourselves the mental processes of the child, of primitive man. Selfish, unreasoning interest-group activity is a manifestation of this.

Thought

If the American Legion employed the same energy it now uses to obtain benefits for its members in promoting good government, it would be a truly creditable organization.

Gripes

Turn the veteran's bureau over to the American Legion; then they can both write the checks and find the money to pay them.

A convention of teachers has prepared an indictment of American society for the treatment it accords one million public school teachers. They accuse many communities of interfering unduly with the private lives of the teachers; organizations such as the American Legion attempt to dictate policies of which the teachers disapprove. It is not unusual for teachers to be reprimanded and even dismissed for teaching accepted facts which, however, were disapproved of by prominent members of their community. Even textbooks have been modified to overcome this opposition.

The greatest criticism of the teachers is directed towards the undue interference with their private lives. They state that many communities expect the teacher to sell his body and soul into bondage and to relinquish the rights of American citizenship. They complain because hedged about by regulations which determine how they shall dress, regulate their recreations and social contacts. They claim that it is even sometimes specified at what time a teacher must be in at night, the hour at which she must retire, the place where she can obtain room and board; even social activities are often prescribed.

Then they state, if we are to preserve democracy, we dare

not risk an impairment of the freedom of democracy in school. Unquestionably, the teachers are receiving inconsiderate treatment by certain groups, certain individuals, certain communities under particular conditions or with regard to certain things. This, however, is but natural in such a large institution as our public schools.

I fail to note appreciation by the teachers for the support the schools do receive from the public. They criticize harshly many other groups. The recommendation by President Roosevelt for nearly a billion dollars for school aid, however, met with their warm approval. They are worse than those they condemn. They condemn others for being unpatriotic citizens and yet they are only too willing to support measures to plunder the federal treasury to obtain money for themselves.

Like most other reformers, they themselves are without faults; everybody else is at fault; all citizens should fall on their knees and worship teachers, give them all the money they want, place them on a pedestal as being superior beings. This is our educational system, the social institution that has most to do with forming habits of thought. We do not have far to seek for our existing national and international difficulties. It is the fault of our school system ably supported and assisted by our religion and politicians.—*February 25, 1938.*

VIII

OUR GOVERNMENT TODAY

WHY IS IT THAT MAN, WHO IS NORMALLY A SENSIBLE CREATURE, is now supporting measures intended to contribute to his welfare that are but little removed from insanity? All situations have their explanation, and this can be explained also. Any number of small influences contribute toward this, but let us mention a few of the more important ones: Self-glorification of our country and democracy generally with no attempt to point out the ills; the unfairness of some people possessing so much wealth and others suffering want; the abuse of privileges by many wealthy people; unjust treatment of employees; the failure of our schools to teach moral character and intelligence, to point out the errors of democracy, and to profit from the past history and blunders of man generally; the coming into power of labor; the sympathetic support which it receives from the public in recognition of the fact that labor had been abused; the abuse by labor of its increased power; the development of lobbies and interest groups to vicious extremes in attempting to get benefits from the government for their particular groups regardless of the welfare of the nation as a whole; the specialization of politicians in flattering, pleasing, buying votes, seeking measures that are popular, and failing to seek sound ones that would solve national problems; the corruption of politics generally; the general feeling of sportsmanship of the average American who wishes to help the underdog, the underdog being in this case the poor fellow, the worker, or anyone who happens to have a grievance; the development in response to this environment of a great many impractical intellectuals and reformers who have much to say about solving the problems of the day, improving the conditions of man, expressing good wishes, but with no sound conception of measures required to bring about results, merely adding confusion to an already confused situation; a religion which makes virtue unattractive, looks to the past for inspiration, retards mental development, says many things noble in their purpose but harmful in their effects.

We may make fun of the orgies and frenzies of savage tribes, but we ourselves are no better. Considering the advanced knowledge we possess and our vast educational facilities, we should be rated somewhat below a savage tribe not possessing these advantages. We are the victims of a vicious environment, of a development of Herdo, in which sound thought is nonexistent, but in which much nice talk, Wisho, Infanta, exist.

The downfall of nations has been caused more by lack of practical intelligence than by viciousness. They proved unequal to the task of controlling the influences molding their environment. As a result they were overthrown by these forces creating an environment that prevented their survival. There is evidence of that in our institutions now, a great deal of talk and wishing to better conditions but nothing practical done; the influences controlling our environment go on uncontrolled, gradually creating an environment that will overthrow our institutions.

The attitude of pure science is illustrative of this. The pure scientist seeking knowledge can be of assistance in increasing the fund of man's information, but through losing track of practical everyday life he is of little value in solving the problems of living, and to a considerable degree is harmful. Our educational system is practically helpless for the same reason, inability to understand and solve practical problems.

We talk much about reform but do little to help matters;

the insidious influences continue to grow. Yet our politicians say nothing of the actual basic causes threatening our destruction. Their principle effort is to condemn the wealthy, flatter the poor, and make promises.

We have a government attempting to regulate all activities of the nation, but which is unable to protect the citizen who asks nothing but the right to support himself and his family. This same government willingly gives vast sums to those who demand benefits. Common sense should tell us that this is the reverse of sound policy. Give nothing to those who demand free benefits, and give the utmost protection to the man who wants to work. He is the one who has made our nation great.

In analyzing the condition of affairs in our country today, one is amazed at the marvelous contrast between the efficient conduct of the affairs of our large corporations and business generally, as compared with the insane and inefficient conduct of public affairs. This contrast is so unusual as to demand explanation. The explanation is relatively simple. The business and industries of the country are being conducted by practical men who are attending to their business, conducting improvements, looking for more efficient means of management. They are so occupied with their own affairs that they do not attempt to run the affairs of the country or the affairs of other people.

On the other hand, we have a great many idlers, noisy fellows, would-be reformers, politicians, agitators generally, who have no constructive work to do and are not practical minded. These people denounce the viciousness of existing institutions, stir up feeling, promise reforms. These are the people who are trying to run our country and who have brought about existing conditions. Unless we take steps to correct this situation, they will make matters still worse. These same noisy people attack the efficient managers of business and industry and accuse them of viciousness. As a matter of fact, if they were as efficient as the big industrialists are, present conditions would not exist.

Capital is receiving persecution today because such action is popular to the unthinking. The mere fact that some have much and others little seems so unfair that those having much are very open to attack. Those having little or nothing are only too willing to ascribe this difference, not to their own lack of sterling qualities in the slightest degree, but to the vicious actions of those who have more than they. How stupid! They should realize that persecution never reforms the one persecuted and harms the persecutor the most by intensifying his animosity and lessening his ability to see matters in a true light. How simple and sensible to enroll capital to fight with and help the government! But our rulers are not sensible, and simple measures are beyond their comprehension.

The actions of politicians, labor, and reformers generally in attacking big business are a close approach to insanity and are in effect a form of mass insanity. Business supports the government by paying the taxes. It supports the individual citizens by affording them work. It is the government's duty to help all business, for in doing so it helps all the citizens. And yet our government, with the support of a great number of citizens, fights business, attacks it, handicaps it, regulates it to strangulation and subjects it to heavy taxation. Continue this policy and disaster is inevitable.

Our government shows its utter incompetence by attacking capital, thus showing that it is unable to control it for the best interests of the country by insuring its helpful co-operation. Any government that persecutes any class within its jurisdiction thereby admits that it is unable to control. This is a sign of inferiority. An inferior person, unable to control the superior ones commonly belittles and denounces to show that the fault is not his.

Is it not evidence of national insanity that the industry that supports nine-tenths of the people of this country is continually persecuted and belittled by the government, by social reformers, by practically everyone who is dissatisfied with existing conditions? Blaming all this fault on industry is positive insanity. Industry is but a reflection of the existing social order and institutions under which it is living. It is as good or as bad as they. The so-called robber barons have been denounced as being very bad individuals. They were fully as good as their times, and as a matter of fact better. Nothing can exceed the low standard of conduct of public men of the decade immediately after the Civil War. We hear them denounced but little, but the wealthy have been denounced unsparingly.

Denunciation of all wealth is a most vicious thing and shows stupidity and Infanta on the part of those doing it, combined with envy, jealousy, sense of inferiority, and many other manifestations of mental disorder. If you wish to bring about far-reaching social reforms, cease to attack wealth, cease to attack business. Co-operate with them in an effort to solve the nation's problems.

The men who are conducting the industries of the country are doing splendid work. They are able specialists who have risen to their positions of great responsibility by merit, a far different situation from that prevailing in the case of our politicians and social reformers who have risen to their positions by lack of merit, lack of ability to do practical work. But they are capable of writing, of talking well, of belittling others, of making promises and plans for what they choose to call social-reform measures. In effect we should reverse our present social standards, put these denouncers to work and put the men who are working in control of affairs. If our government were as efficiently conducted as the average large corporation, we would have an efficient government.

Our inefficient methods of conducting government business are well illustrated by our failure, our unwillingness, to register aliens, with the result that we have vast amounts of bootleg immigration into the country. Instead of having a nation for Americans, we are permitting a conglomerate mass of undesirable people from foreign lands to come at will, obtain benefits from the government, vote corrupt officials into office, and demoralize our institutions. The limitations we place upon immigration to some degree prevent desirable immigrants from foreign lands from coming here and encourage the undesirables to do so.

A vicious development has grown up in our government by which the administration obtains support for its measures from members of Congress by the use of patronage. That is to say, if the administration gives certain offices to friends of a congressman or senator, he will vote for the desired measures. This has a lowering effect upon the moral character of our national life. Measures should not be decided by patronage. They should be determined upon their merit. This development alone is sufficient to discredit our entire political system. When our leaders, instead of seeking the welfare of the nation, seek offices for their supporters, we have a government undeserving of respect.

Government to receive respect must deserve respect. Demagoguery in high places lowers the tone of national affairs. The effect of our government being dominated by men of such universally poor character is shown in the lessening respect for· authority by the citizens and in their greater attention to the privileges of citizenship than to the duties pertaining thereto.

A democratic government in which politicians of slight ability and character seek office by flattering the multitude, trading government benefits for votes, lowering the moral qualities of a nation, cannot prove successful. No government is fit to exist that degrades its citizenry.

The desire of the politicians to get office and remain in office once elected causes them to conciliate the numerous interest groups by voting benefits to them. This has resulted in constantly increasing government expenditures, which in time the government will be unable to bear. The solution of modern problems of government and economics requires calm consideration by the ablest men we can find. Able, unselfish men will disagree as to the advisability of certain measures. When we introduce the selfishness of interest groups, prejudice, appeals for votes, we are confusing the problems beyond any hope of solution.

Our Constitution never contemplated relief by the national government to individual citizens. That was certainly a local state affair. Yet our national government has embarked upon it because not expressly prohibited. It appealed to the public and politicians because of easy money, jobs, attractiveness to voters, appeal to sentiment and good intentions.

When the government pays benefits of any kind, it stimulates many to try to obtain them. These individuals are often needy and in a condition which attracts pity from other people who are all too willing to assist them in obtaining government benefits.

Existing government policies are neither modern nor progressive. They possess many of the same unsound features that destroyed Rome and Greece, with much flattery, cajolery and promises to the masses incapable of fulfillment and so vicious in their ultimate effects as to make the conditions they bring about worse than the ills they are intended to correct.

If we have a government deserving of respect in the highest degree, the citizens will willingly pay essential taxes. When, however, the government is undeserving of respect, when the money raised by taxation is prostituted to unworthy uses, the citizens will be less willing to pay taxes and are less to be censured for not doing so. Thus in order to insure the willing payment of taxes, we must have a government deserving of respect.

To have a government of this nature we must have a society that encourages good conduct and worthy people. The worthy people should control the government in the interests of all, and if necessary use force to control the unworthy. At present our general trend is to permit the government to be controlled by unworthy people who denounce the worthy. We must reverse this tendency if we are to solve the problems now awaiting solution. We must endeavor to bring out the best in all and encourage future generations to do likewise. If we set a good example today, generations that follow will benefit, and having themselves thus benefited, will be encouraged to do likewise for the generations that follow them. Thus over a period of many generations we may hope to elevate the affairs of man to standards that will be a credit to him.

Our existing government policies are essentially promoting an environment in which mendicancy is rewarded and honest industrious effort is penalized. If these policies are permitted to continue the number of mendicants will tend to increase and the number of honest self-sustaining workers will decrease. Eventually the burden upon the latter will become too great and the entire system of so-called social reform will clash. This is the most damnable result of our present-day reform measures. It is the opposite of what far-reaching reform should promote. The honest self-sustaining worker should be encouraged at all costs. All citizens should belong in this class and there should be no mendicants. When this condition exists, we shall have a healthy social order, a healthy economic condition and high standards of citizenship.

To the thoughtful person the conduct of our politicians and our administration arouses only feelings of disgust. It matters little to the administration how high-minded or able a person may be who disagrees with their policies. They denounce him as being selfish and having ulterior motives. On the other hand, any person who agrees, regardless of how vicious or selfish, is a virtuous, fine citizen. This is the government that is controlling us. How can we expect anything else but chaos?

Our leaders have so confused present-day issues, have done so much to obscure the truth and spread unsound beliefs as to prevent the adoption of sound measures. Hope for better things seems to require that our present leaders be permitted to pursue their unsound measures to such extremes as to discredit both themselves and their measures.

There is more talk about social reform today and more efforts are being made to improve individual welfare than ever before. Unfortunately, these efforts are being directed by men not equal to the task. They are storing up problems for the future by concentrating upon measures that will receive present support. Eventually the burden of all these reform measures will be too great to bear and conditions will be far worse as a result of unwise efforts made to improve them. The American public has yet to learn that a let-alone policy is far better than impractical measures.

Unpleasant as it may be to face the facts, our government is nothing more nor less than racketeering of the most vicious nature. Our politicians resort to all means to obtain votes and they grant benefits to an endless number of voters. These benefits in turn are paid for by heavy levies upon other citizens and by borrowing vast sums of money which are charged to future generations. It is no different in principle from a band of racketeers who levy tribute upon honest business and apply the proceeds to their own use. We condemn the racketeers. On the other hand our government racketeers are conducting their activities under the guise of social reform, of bettering the condition of the common man, in such way as to obtain the support of a great many well-intentioned but foolish people.

The worst feature of our existing governmental policies is the effect upon the youth, upon the character of the future generations. We spend vast sums of money for the maintenance of educational institutions intended to educate our youth and make them better citizens. At the same time we maintain a government that by its policies and general behavior is breaking down the very moral fiber of our youth. Wise government would plan for the future, would avoid placing burdens upon future generations, and would strive to establish an environment that would be conducive to the development of the highest character.

Our policies from an economic standpoint are unsound. We are burdening the future with vast debts and are establishing a government that is a very parasite itself, that takes from the most deserving class of its citizens for the sake of giving to the undeserving. This has created constant demands from many people for further benefits from the government, with the result that instead of the efforts of our citizens being directed toward the solution of their own problems, their effort is directed toward demanding that the government do something for them. When this viewpoint is transmitted to young men, they can never develop into good citizens. No institutions have a right to exist that break down the moral character of young people.

This subject will bear further thought. The more talk we have about doing things for other people and improving the world, the worse we make it by unwise action. The very restriction the government is placing upon the development of industry is preventing young men from getting jobs, leaving them only the alternative of demanding help from the government. When you convert a young man into a person demanding something for nothing, you have taken from him the incentive that will make strong character and a strong individual. There is a vast amount of good in our young men if we but develop it. Unfortunately our unsound policies are preventing the development of the good and encouraging much that is undesirable.

There is a ray of sunshine in the future, however, which we can hope for to improve conditions. When they get so bad as to be generally known, the citizens should be aroused by having the evils causing this brought to their attention. It should then be possible to reform the institutions, correct the evils, and prevent their recurrence. To bring this about we should devote all our efforts to increasing the understanding of the citizens and arousing a greater conception of their duty as such in order that at some time in the future they may be able to act wisely in bringing about sound reform of our political institutions.

Our government today is not much more inefficient than it has been in the past. However, in the early period of our history, the doctrine that the least government is the best government prevailed widely. An increasing social consciousness has been developing of recent years, creating demands for additional action by the government to correct evils. This has resulted in a great extension of government activities. The harmful effects of inefficient government are more apparent when it undertakes to direct so many activities. Evils exist that are apparent to all and the demand for government action meets with wide support. People are more insistent upon action of some kind than that it be wise action. If they were as equally insistent upon wise action it would be forthcoming.

The great development of our country from the adoption of the Constitution until quite recently was not due to assistance received from the government. It was due more to the fact that the government permitted each individual the fullest of liberty and the enjoyment of his individual efforts. Government control was so slight as to be negligible. Now, however, we are endeavoring to control many things through the government. This tends to crush individual initiative and prevents development.

Our country was in a very unsatisfactory condition after the Revolutionary War. This condition became so bad as to result in the adoption of our Constitution and the creation of a national government having sufficient power over the states to insure liberty and freedom of action to the individual citizen. We today possess a national government having sufficient legal power to act. It is in the control of incompetent men, however, as the result of the gradual deterioration of our institutions—largely due to the fact that the politicians promise benefits to any group of voters for the purpose of obtaining their vote.

Thus the problem we are confronted with today is not lack of a national government. It is lack of ability to administer the government, lack of public understanding on the part of citizens, lack of a good citizenship which will support a government instead of demanding to receive benefits from it.

Just as the situation became so bad after the Revolution as to result in the adoption of sensible measures, so may we hope that when the situation becomes so bad as to be generally recognized, sensible measures may be taken to correct existing evils. It is to be hoped that the distress and suffering that will be caused by the present unsound policies will result in rejecting such unsound measures in the future. If this happens we can well afford to let this madness take its course in order that character and intelligence may control.

We can despair of the future of American civilization when we see many parts of the country unfit for decent men to live in because dominated by violence. A self-respecting working-man sometimes cannot go to work without being threatened by attack by strikers. We see our national government and local government supporting striking laborers in their violence, and public opinion says little. This situation seriously cripples industry and causes unemployment and distress throughout the nation. We can blame the politicians, but the American citizen should receive the greatest share of the blame. If he would spend less time tooting his own horn, bragging about the merits of democracy, trying to tell other nations how they should run their business, and behave like a decent citizen with due consideration for others, we would have a nation worthy of respect. When American citizens stand by and permit violent agitators to attack decent workingmen, they are showing a woeful lack of manhood and intelligence.

Our government has shown, by its attitude toward labor violence, its inability to correct economic ills or to enforce the laws. What is the sensible thing to do? Replace the incompetent men now in control by men who are capable of correcting the economic ills and willing and able to assert the power of the government against any group that assails it.

One of the functions of government is to settle disputes among its citizens, giving justice to all. This our government is failing to do in the case of capital and labor, with the result that the latter is using force to attain its ends. If this be permitted to continue, the inevitable result will be civil war at some time in the future, for decent citizens will not always submit to being controlled by irresponsible labor leaders.

Our government is controlled by officials who refuse to enforce the law, who are in sympathy with those who are violating it. If a government conducted by officials sworn to enforce the law fails to do so, there is but one means left for the law-abiding citizen—resort to revolution or civil war. It is impossible to remove these officials by impeachment or by any means less than revolution. This makes it a bad situation because those who undertake to remove them will be blamed for causing a civil war. These same government officials have stirred up this agitation by telling the poor that they were doing much to help them, blaming all the troubles on capital, pursuing unwise policies that increased unemployment. The average citizen does not think very much or understand a great deal and is easily led by plausible talkers. The result will be that when civil war comes in our country it will not be between the good and bad citizens, but many good citizens will be arrayed against each other and the consequences will be very unfortunate. The cause for this will be due entirely to incompetent government officials.

Revolutionists tend to be very cruel when their passions have been aroused by what they believe to be injustice. We can see this by looking back over history and observing the French revolutionists, the Russian revolutionists, and the Spanish civil war today. It is by no means improbable that we will have such a situation in our own country. There has been so much denunciation of so many people that great ill feeling exists and we may yet see the most shocking scenes of bloodshed.

We, in the United States, are living on top of a smoldering volcano. The decent citizens of the nation are permitting the most vicious elements within it to control the government and dictate its policies. (This vicious element could have been curbed very readily. As a matter of fact it has been stirred up by our own government.) The vicious elements feel that they are suffering great injustices; and when the decent citizens revolt against abuse they likewise will feel they are being badly treated. We will then have two elements within the country both of whom feel they are victims of injustices. This feeling, with their passions aroused, may result in the most horrible scenes of violence and slaughter.

It does not take a great deal to cause us to revert to savagery. Real or imagined wrongs will easily put anyone in a state susceptible to brutality. Note how vicious many women have been in Spain, France, Russia, Ethiopia. Anyone who adds to this feeling of resentment on the part of any group of our citizens is assisting in bringing about an unfortunate revolution. This will be caused not by the men who will have to fight, risk their lives, and suffer, but by the well-meaning reformers, agitators, and politicians, who are claiming to do so much to improve conditions in the country, and by the weakly sentimental who are unwilling to restrain violence by meeting it with like violence. Their weakness will result in requiring far greater force to restrain than would have been required initially. We need strong men in control of our institutions; not weak, sentimental people who can do little but promise, flatter, and stir up class feeling.

Sound reform is almost impossible in our country without civil war. So many unsound measures have been passed, so many interest groups have been appeased by special legislation, so many people are deriving benefits from existing conditions, that great opposition will be encountered against sensible measures. It is quite possible, however, that if conditions are permitted to continue as they are now, the system will destroy itself. It will become apparent to even the most stupid that far-reaching reforms must be put into operation.

This is a pleasing hope to look forward to, but by no means a certainty. It is both possible and probable, but we have such incompetent leaders, the people have been deluded for so long, that existing ills may be perpetuated indefinitely. The nation may struggle along as best it can, with the same talk of reform and helping the underdog. If so, there will be a continued breakdown in the moral character which, in time, will make American institutions unworthy.

Probably the most threatening condition tending toward civil war is that our federal government gets the support of vast numbers of voters by benefits, in effect buying votes by the use of government funds. This prevents the normal functioning of democratic government. For democracy to be a success, demands that each citizen vote honestly for officials of his choice. When the government gets into the control of men who use its finances to buy votes, under the guise of benefits, it becomes impossible for the law-abiding citizen honestly to serve his country by means of the ballot. When this situation is recognized and sufficient resentment is aroused, those who are supporting the government will not forever remain content to support vast numbers of other citizens.

We have had organized bands occupy state legislature buildings and demand relief, intimidating the legislature by violence to grant their demands. This is not government; this is intimidation by mobs controlling the government. The relief workers who did this are not without justification. They have been promised much by the politicians and the promises have not been fulfilled. They are generally the most worthless class of people in the nation who have been on relief, getting benefits for a long time, becoming confirmed parasites, and will demand benefits throughout the balance of their lives. This relief situation, combined with unemployment, is a very serious problem for the future. It is entirely uncalled for, and brought about by incompetent government stimulated to unwise measures by interest groups, labor unions, and reformers. The politicians, unwilling to admit their inability to solve the problem, have always found a scapegoat in capital. As a matter of fact, capital has been doing its part very well, and if it were left alone, the present unemployment would not exist. The unwise persecution of capital, labor agitation, and interference by labor with management is bound to discourage capital from developing new enterprises.

Thoughts

The existing condition of affairs in our own country not only affords convincing proof of the incompetence of our leaders but displays the utter inability of the masses to understand or support sound economic measures. We have in the past five years spent twenty billion dollars for the purpose, as stated by the spenders, of improving the condition of the forgotten man. We are now experiencing a business depression as a result of this unwise expenditure and government regulations generally, which the government is unable to ward off or improve. The general understanding is that if the business recession does not improve within a few months by some miraculous means, the process of government spending will again be started. One cannot but have a feeling of hopelessness as to man's future. The optimistic view can hope that the failure of these unwise policies and the distress thereby engendered will finally discredit them and permit the adoption of sensible measures supported by a sadder but wiser body of citizens.—*December 20, 1937.*

The patriotic citizen can only be inspired with disgust with the present American government—too inefficient, too weak to solve internal problems or insure respect for the law, and so weak that foreign nations may sink American warships with impunity. Yet if anyone expresses his lack of confidence in the government, he is immediately denounced. What are we headed for? Only the future can tell. When the utter incompetence of our government has been understood by the citizens, it may be possible to institute sensible measures; but by that time much harm will have been done; perhaps not limited to our own nation but having world-wide ramifications.—*December 20, 1937.*

The existing conditions in our country justify revolution, rebellion, on the part of the decent citizens. They should protect themselves against the racketeers who now control the government by plundering decent citizens to get money to buy votes and keep themselves in office.

IX

THE ENACTMENT OF LEGISLATION

LEGISLATION SHOULD BE ENACTED AFTER CALM DISCUSSION. Here democracy is seriously at fault. The average politician makes appeals to whatever will obtain votes. All too often the merit of legislation is not considered with full regard to its final result, and much harm is done by misstatements.

All legislation begins as a certain proposed bill or measure. This is followed by discussion of the reasons for supporting or opposing it. The intent of those framing the measure may be good; it will be as good as their ability and knowledge warrants. More often than not the measure suggested is unsound. Legislators arrive at conclusions by letting their own feelings, the appeal to the public, and the effect on their own future fortunes govern. When the measure is later put to a vote, the same conditions decide whether it will be opposed or supported. Certain objections or additions may be agreed to by compromise. This does not conduce to sound legislation. The measure should first be prepared by experts knowing what they are about, the advantages stressed and the disadvantages eliminated to as great a degree as possible. Then instead of a compromise, which comes more from conflicting interests than from the merit of the measure, a real attempt would be made to obtain sound legislation.

The tendency of the democratic form of government to correct all ills by laws must be guarded against. This tendency is less that of democracy itself than of the politicians who, in their endeavor to obtain votes, will promise to do things to

benefit the voters. Our legislation has resulted in many unsound measures being put into operation. If the quality of
the laws now in effect within the borders of the United States
were as great as their quantity, we would have wonderful
institutions. Quantity does not of itself produce quality; on
the contrary the increase in quantity decreases the quality.

Sewy is prominently displayed in the discussions on the
floors of Congress, in state legislatures, and in fact all political gatherings. It is least displayed by the directors of our
corporations at their board meetings. Regardless of what the
politicians and agitators may say, business men conduct their
directors' meetings in a far more sensible manner than our
political meetings are conducted; less oratory, less ballyhoo,
more knowledge, more desire to obtain facts and arrive at a
sensible conclusion.

The general tendency of legislators in a democracy is to
talk on the legislative floors to their constituents in order to
please their vanity, to say many things that have no direct
bearing upon the question at issue. The greater the size of
the legislative body, the more unwieldy it becomes, and the
greater the amount of futile talk. Reducing the size, increasing the intelligence and ability, inaugurating a policy of discussing questions in an effort to obtain a positive answer,
would do much to elevate our legislative bodies from their
present mediocrity to respectable assemblages.

Many of our voters use their voting power to obtain benefits from the government; many voters who do not pay taxes
are perfectly willing to vote taxes upon others. The question
arises whether it would not be possible to limit the franchise,
preventing abuses such as this. Unquestionably, if the non-
taxpayers did not vote, and other citizens could not vote for
officials who would give them benefits, the electorate would
be more responsive to sound measures. If we could give the
right to vote to a group of citizens selected by an impartial
board for ability and merit, many of the existing abuses
would be eliminated. On the other hand, it would tend to
arouse resentment on the part of those who were not per-

mitted to vote. The best method seems to be to educate all to a better understanding of the duties of citizens and a higher code of conduct.

A great evil that has developed in our legislative assemblies is that of swapping votes. That is to say, members will vote for the measures of another member if in return they receive his vote for their measures. All measures should be determined on their merit with due regard to their effect upon the entire country—not determined by the swapping of votes of legislators in the interest of themselves, of their political fortunes, or of particular constituents or interest groups whom they may be attempting to favor.

As illustrating how much legislation is passed in our country, I will recite a recollection of my own. In the year 1910 I was a resident of the town of Branford, Connecticut, and a member of the National Guard Battery existing in this town. A move was inaugurated to have an armory built by the state to afford us better accommodations. This attracted the support of the townspeople and of the two members of the legislature furnished by the town. Eventually the appropriation was made by the state legislature. Some time after this we had a big party in celebration and the two legislators who were instrumental in the enactment of the bill made speeches. The remark made by one of them that impressed me very forcibly was, "Whenever any other member of the legislature approached us on any measure of his own, we had but one reply, 'How do you stand on the Branford armory?' " Meaning by this that they were perfectly willing to vote for measures of other members of the legislature if in turn these other members would vote for the Branford armory. This is a very vicious way of enacting legislation. The question of whether or not the Branford armory should have been built should have been determined upon its merit.

When an appropriation is obtained not upon merit but by means of political wire pulling, swapping votes with other legislators, great harm is liable to ensue. Worthy measures will sometimes be enacted, but many unworthy ones as well.

The system tends toward extravagance. This armory incident occurred some twenty-seven years ago. It had been going on for years before that, and we are now beginning to suffer from the consequences. It is nation-wide, and this is one reason why we have such large local, state, and national debts. The cure for this is to arouse a greater understanding of the citizens' duties to the government. We should have it understood that each particular question involving an appropriation will be determined upon its merits alone, not by means of organizing groups to demand appropriations.

We see this abuse throughout the country in demands from cities and towns for federal appropriations for the construction of new post offices. Whenever abandoning an army post is contemplated, the residents nearby at once protest vigorously to the federal government. However worthy their local pride may be, these questions should be determined on their merit. Our government is breaking down largely because of this attitude of American citizens, short-sighted in its final outcome.

Many of the men advocating the building of post offices, or supporting drives for obtaining money from the federal government for their communities, are among the finest men in those communities; big business men who should know better. Yet because everybody else is demanding benefits from the government, they feel that, "As long as everybody else is getting government money, why shouldn't we?" And the vicious system goes on. The more one thinks about the conduct of what we presume to call sensible American citizens, the more one becomes disgusted and hopeless for the future. The only hope is that when these unwise measures run their course, the errors will be pointed out and corrected. It is to this end our thinkers should strive; educate the public to understand and build sound institutions on the wreck we are about to make of existing ones.

The real merit of democracy is the fact that though people are long suffering and will submit to much misgovernment, when it is apparent that certain evils are very bad, public opinion will be aroused to insure their correction. But by this time the evils have done much harm. While we may consider this willingness to correct evils a merit of democracy, we must also consider the serious weakness that corrective steps cannot be taken beforehand and receive sufficient support to render them effective. Thus, instead of waiting until the ills stir up public opinion to correct them, wise action beforehand will prevent the ills from developing. This is what scientific government would accomplish.

It is often difficult to determine whether to take steps to correct or prevent an abuse or to let it run its course and correct itself. Serious abuses are very likely to have many ramifications and may do more harm in an indirect way or upon other things than in their own limited scope. Abuses of this nature should be treated beforehand, prevented, but there are other cases where from a practical standpoint it is better to let the abuse run its course until sentiment is stirred against it rather than to attempt to correct it by action that will not be popularly supported. Wise statesmanship should decide the best action after calm reasoning. This, unfortunately, is not done. Questions are decided too much in ignorance, with regard to their influence upon politics, to self-interest, to hatred, to anger, or to anything but calm consideration.

Our democratic institutions have developed to a condition in which there is so much opposition to worthy measures that by the time they have been amended to overcome objections, they have lost much of their merit. We are fast reaching a hopeless muddle in which no measures can be enacted except those paying benefits great enough to attract votes.

The need for compromise in all measures under the democratic form of government results in emasculating them of strong features and permitting the weak ones to remain. It is questionable whether any sound solution to present problems will be found by a democratic government. The very nature of these problems requires a strong policy, carried out by able men with no half-way measures or compromises.

These problems have been made worse by half-way measures, compromises, or unwise interference. The whole economic and governmental structure is so hopelessly involved as to require drastic reconstitution. Such drastic action would be opposed by so many people as to prevent its being carried out by a democratic government. Thus the ills from which we are suffering are created by our democratic government, and due to the weaknesses of this form of government, cannot be corrected by it. If by some means we could correct the unsound conditions and start our democratic government off again under more fortunate auspices, it might meet the demands provided an energetic effort to elevate the citizens to a full conception of their duties as such was made.

X

POLITICAL PARTIES

POLITICAL PARTIES ARE UNSOUND FROM THE STANDPOINT OF Ascendent Psychology. They tend to develop descendent Groupo, loyalty toward their political party instead of developing an ascendent Groupo including all citizens of the nation. This loyalty to one's own party, by its very nature, will often transcend the interest of the entire nation. The very development of political parties is conducive toward descendent selfish Groupo, the exact opposite of what an elevating government should strive for.

Our political parties have degenerated into machines dominated by professional politicians resorting to all measures that will obtain votes. They are far more concerned with political strategy than with principles of citizenship and manhood. Their general policy is to promise to give everyone whatever he wants, to study the whims and fancy of all, flatter, promise, and try to please them—anything to get their votes. They do not wish to have a definite aim to strive for, for fear they will lose votes or because someone might object to that aim. They do not wish to be either liberal or conservative for fear they will lose votes in either direction. The tendency is to claim to be liberal and at the same time to flatter the conservatives into believing that the politicians have high moral motives. It is no credit to the intelligence of the American citizen to listen to politicians and vote for them, hoping and believing that they are sincere in their virtuous attempts to reform. It does not take deep inquiry to determine that politics is the most vicious, dishonest institution in our country. It is easy to denounce the bankers and industrialists, and the wealthy because this is popular; but their conduct, bad as that of many has been, is on a far higher plane than that of the politicians who are denouncing them and trying to persuade the citizens that they are establishing a better moral atmosphere.

Political parties have developed into effective political machines designed to get their members benefits and offices. They do not exist for the benefit of the country as a whole, but for the benefit of professional politicians. Politicians are skilled in the practical applications of means to influence the mass of voters.

Their parties are built up initially around the ward heeler, a person of no great consequence but having some understanding of human nature, the ability to make friends, to do favors, and to control votes. By virtue of his ability to control votes he obtains from the political machine or boss small government contracts, offices, or benefits. His interest is not in the welfare of the country or in supporting wise measures; his interest is to control votes and employ political power for his own ends. The immediate boss above him works in a somewhat similar way by promising benefits to his various ward heelers; by virtue of this increased mass of votes he obtains benefits from those higher up.

This system continues up to the large city, state, and national machines. Support is given in some localities by criminals and the most vicious elements. The politicians in the public eye have much to say about crime and criminals and the misconduct of their opponents, but they carefully refrain from inquiring too closely into the actions or antecedents of their supporters.

Political parties constitute an interest group designed to serve the politicians, not the nation. Our politicians do many things to get and keep in power that have nothing to do with the public welfare. By abolishing political parties and having government officials elected by direct vote of the people, this abuse should be greatly lessened.

Political parties prevent the citizens from exerting a direct choice as to whom they shall elect—for president, for instance. With two political parties dominated by professional politicians, who nominate what they call the available candidate, the self-respecting citizen may be virtually disfranchised. He may have two candidates to vote for, both of whom are unworthy of his support.

Our division into political parties has another evil in that it may cause the candidate for president to obligate his office, if elected, to serving certain interest groups. Let us suppose the contest for president is quite close and one of the candidates is willing to promise certain measures to an interest group to advance its interests. This action, however, is of such a nature that it cannot be made public. It is a secret arrangement between a candidate for president and a leader seeking benefits for his interest group. By this means the presidential candidate, when he becomes president, is obligated to serve someone of whom the people do not approve and for whom they did not vote.

Party loyalty is vicious to the best interests of the country and to the most efficient government. The development of political parties has resulted in many voters allying their interests to the political party and placing it above the government itself. Political parties must go if we are to have efficient democratic government. They confuse thought and place an interest group in control of the nation. They attack and belittle opposing political parties regardless of the soundness of their measures. They do much to create ill will. No political party is deserving of loyalty to itself before the country, particularly so when the political parties are dominated by professional politicians who have developed great skill in manipulating conventions, obtaining votes, flattering the voters. At the same time their specialized development in this direction has prevented them from mastering the principles of government.

No political party ever admits error. All are errorless, pure, unselfish. It is bad mental exercise to toot your own horn, to be unable to find fault with yourself or the party to which you belong. There may be some human beings or human institutions that are without fault, but if so, they are so rare as not to be generally known. Accepting as a basic principle that man inherently possesses faults, wisdom dictates that he frankly acknowledge them and endeavor to eradicate them entirely or minimize their effects. When we permit our government to be controlled by those individuals or those parties that never see error in themselves and never commit faults, we are being controlled by people who by their very sayings admit their inability to control themselves. Anyone unable to control himself has no right to control others.

One of the bad features about our present political system that keeps the best men from entering politics is that, regardless of how good their record, how well they exert themselves, how efficient their performance of duty, they will be viciously attacked by opponents who employ all means to discredit them.

The division of our politics into two political parties results in the party not in power making rash promises to obtain votes. When it gets into power it attempts to carry them out in part, and the opposite party employs the same tactics. Thus our government is being conducted by individuals who have promised increasing benefits to the masses of the voters. These benefits paid to the masses must be raised by levies upon those who have been more or less successful in their personal affairs, with the result that this policy penalizes the better class of citizen to reward the less desirable ones. In time it is bound to have very harmful effects upon the economic life of the country. The true development of democratic institutions demands that all citizens have a high sense of duty, that they not demand benefits from their government but that they support it. Unfortunately the development of our institutions has taken the opposite direction. The politicians running for office flatter the people, promise to benefit them, but fail to point out the real dangers threatening the future.

Under the two-party system, a small minority may hold the balance of power. For instance, in many northern states there is a considerable negro minority, and both parties strive to obtain this vote. For many years the Republicans received the solid negro vote, but as the result of shrewd measures on the part of Democratic politicians at the last election, the negroes voted for the Democrats. Thus we have introduced into our political affairs the race question. The welfare of the country is not considered. No government can be efficiently conducted under such a condition of affairs. The politicians endeavor to conciliate all minority groups, do as little as possible to antagonize anyone, with the result that the government is becoming more and more inefficient.

It has been claimed that having two political parties tends to keep the one in power on its toes to do the right thing, because the other party would point out its errors and discredit its unwise efforts. There may be some benefit in this, and undoubtedly there is, because the exposure of unsound methods is always desirable. But the opposition parties go much farther than this. They oppose every project of the party in power regardless of its merit, if it will discredit their opponents or strengthen their own political position.

The loyalty of the politicians is to their own interest group, their own political party, rather than to the country. They are perfectly willing to bring about great distress throughout the nation in order to get political advantage. No more vicious institution for the government of man can be established than political parties that will attempt to wreck the government so they may get in power. We condemn vigorously stock manipulators of the past who would wreck corporations in order to attain their ends, but we are ignoring politicians who willingly and intentionally harm national welfare in order to further their own political fortunes.

Thoughts

Politicians and political parties do not look very far ahead. They are entirely concerned with the present and their immediate personal fortunes.

Our politicians are more often working for the benefit of their party or for themselves than for the general good of the nation. This explains why our government is failing.

XI

THOUGHTS ON GOVERNMENT

HOWEVER UNPLEASANT FOR THE PATRIOTIC CITIZEN, HE MUST face facts. Our desire to be proud of our country should not be permitted to blind us to the fact that we are being governed by incompetent, contemptible men.

The proceedings of the House and Senate reflect credit neither upon their members nor upon their country for either character or intelligence.

Our political institutions are developing in a direction that will soon render it possible for only a spineless jellyfish to obtain and hold office. Politicians only get elected now by flattering the masses and buying the votes of interest groups by promising them government benefits.

Democratic government in the United States is fast becoming a farce in which the least desirable elements of the country are in control. Not until the decent elements assert themselves and assume control can the situation be corrected.

Our government is being dominated today by a wish to help the underprivileged, by adopting methods that appeal to the herd, but which are unsound and which in time will do more harm than good.

Our present democratic government levels down. Enlightened government would level up. That is to say, our government tends to reduce to the level of the lowest classes. An efficient government would tend to elevate all to higher standards of citizenship.

Our government is too contemptible to insure respect abroad, too weak and incompetent to receive it at home.

Our existing social and economic system, considering the increase in knowledge, is more vicious than the old regime in Europe in 1789.

The assassination of Huey Long should give pause to all. This act was committed by a high-type man to eliminate an unworthy leader. It is a terrible commentary on our day that such a situation should exist. It may be the forerunner of many similar acts. Permit this to continue and we are bringing about rule by violence and a reversion to savagery.

From a legal, technical view, the government now in control of our country is legal. It has been put in office by the voters misled by the promises of the politicians. It does not, however, live up to either the letter or spirit of the Constitution which it has taken the oath to support.

No program of the government, however worthy in intent, will materially aid in the solution of man's problems that does not use sound measures of improving the moral character of its citizens. Can we truthfully say that our government is doing this today? No, on the contrary.

I have some respect for Mussolini. I have some respect for the British government but I have no respect for our own government.

Landon's man Taft said, "Nothing which concerns this nation can ever be simple again." What an inane remark! Only simple methods will work. Making simplicity difficult is easy to do but profitless.

We must stop making simplicity difficult. Let us reduce all our complexities to simplicity. Make them so simple as to be understood by fresh young minds.

The first nation that attains sanity in the conduct of its affairs will rule the world. Let us be first.

Politicians, labor leaders, nationalists the world over are alike in their primitive mental processes. Their opponents are always vicious, low, and deceitful, while their supporters are virtuous, noble, and truthful.

Our government is just what the people are. Any government will be as good or bad as the people composing the nation, and no better.

Our government is failing because we have too many people who demand much for nothing, and because we permit the foolish to dominate the wise, giving consideration to quantity and little to quality.

A nation cannot long remain great if it fails to protect men in their right to work.

The rogues have been in the past more practical than idealists. Our politicians are rogues, some with a greater sense of duty than others, but nevertheless all rogues differing only in degree. The idealist must become practical in order to put high ideals in control and overthrow the rogue. The mere fact that rogues are more practical than idealists is both a problem and a promise for the future. To whip the rogues we need not become rogues ourselves, but we can employ the methods by which they succeeded, and can discard the faults that have caused idealism to fail in the past.

Give the greatest possible liberty to the individual, to business, industry, and corporations, with a minimum of laws and regulations, government and taxes, and the maximum of character, intelligence, and service.

The best defense against communism, socialism, and vicious democracy, is to establish a country where all are so happy and prosperous as to be above wanting anything that these can offer.

Among the many reasons for the failure to solve the present problems, not the least has been that the government, religion, and science do not work together. Of these three, only science has contributed anything of real lasting value, often against the opposition of the other two. Why not in future profit by the errors of the past and have these three work together, improving education, the environment, and all agencies affecting man's welfare?

Unless we can get a majority of our people to think soundly, support sound measures of government, future generations will have a poor country to live in. At present the best way to accomplish this seems to be to let popular reform be tried, to prove its futility, and thus to give sound measures a chance to be carried out.

A dictatorship has many advantages over a democracy in accomplishing results. A dictatorship that would not suppress great minds, thought, or truth, but instead would crush the inane, the vicious, and the false, is what the entire world needs—dictatorship methods to advance democratic aims. Unfortunately, all dictators claim to do so. If we could only find one who is sincere and able, whom we could trust!

Gripe

The United States is fast becoming a nation of mendicants demanding support and largesse from the government. The decent must either fight to save themselves from perpetual slavery to mendicants or destroy themselves by one hundred per cent birth control—and let the mendicants have a nation of one hundred per cent mendicants and maintain, sustain, and amuse themselves.

XII

EFFICIENT GOVERNMENT

IT IS A DEFINITE, POSITIVE PRINCIPLE OF EFFICIENT GOVERN-
ment that government activities must be limited to an absolute minimum in order to insure efficient performance.
When the government attempts to regulate vast businesses
and engages in extensive activities, it becomes increasingly
difficult properly to co-ordinate all activities. To handle vast
projects of this nature requires the greatest of ability. Such
ability does not exist in the nation, even if we were able to
get the ablest men to accept government positions. We cannot
expect to find it among politicians and their creatures who,
by their very activity, are specialized to promise and please,
not to administer efficiently.

Really efficient government must be conducted by the
highest type of men. There is hope for this being done some
time in the future. We have a high type of service in our own
army and navy, and in some civil departments of the government not influenced by politics. England has evolved a fine
type of civil service, whose members give their best to government service. There is, however, a trend, even in the highest
types of civil-service employees and army or navy officers, to
develop a specialized viewpoint, losing touch with the viewpoint of the man in the street. This is something to be guarded
against. It can be obviated by greater knowledge of human
nature, and a determined effort to develop a broad viewpoint
in oneself.

Many ills of man are so deep and far-reaching as to require

generations for correction. Here is where democratic government is limited. The average citizen desires benefits for himself now, and does not look to the future. It should be the duty of an enlightened government to provide for the solutions of future problems. Our educational efforts in citizenship should endeavor to bring about this understanding on the part of the citizen and make it a matter of pride on his part to work for the interest of future generations as much as, or more than, for himself. This generation should solve the problems of today and anticipate the problems that will confront future generations. If each generation would prepare for the next one, a consistent advance in man's welfare would result.

An efficient government would give much thought to, and plan for, the future. The interests of the future should not oppose those of the present, but where there is apparent conflict, the future should be given priority. Many ills could be prevented entirely by a little wise action ahead of time. For instance, if the negroes had not been brought into the country we would have been saved a civil war and much racial animosity, and a problem that now confronts us would not exist. If we had not let down the bars of immigration and permitted many undesirable foreigners to enter our country we would have less disregard for law and less corrupt government. If the immigration of orientals had been prohibited entirely before they arrived in the country, ill feeling would not have been caused, and we would have no problem as the result of oriental racial animosity.

If we would sensibly apply sound economic principles today, paying off our government debts, we would leave the future generations able to solve other problems and not be burdened by those we are now thrusting upon them. When problems of the present are not solved they tend to become more serious, so that even if they are solved at some time in the future, they leave bad effects behind. This is one of the most serious faults of democratic government. The average man thinks in terms of the present and of those things immediately affecting him. This in itself is not bad, but should not be indulged in to the extreme of preventing thought and planning for the future.

We should leave to our children the best heritage we can, not necessarily material things, but moral and spiritual, and they in turn should do the same thing for their children. If this be done, the children years hence will look back upon us as their benefactors, and have an example to spur them on to similar performance. Could this be impressed upon all citizens so as to insure their whole-hearted effort toward its accomplishment in accordance with their gifts, we would soon have a country and a citizenry of which we could be justly proud.

A government highly efficient, striving to promote the Ascendency of the individual, would have as its principle task the creation of an ascendent environment and the eradication of all descendent influences. We have many influences freely circulating in our country that are pernicious in their effects. They should be controlled, but any attempt to do so will cause great opposition, and we have not the ability in our present government to make such control effective. A highly ascendent environment will not permit anything to exist within it that injures the mind or violates truth.

This would result in a fine body of public-spirited citizens, which is what is required to have a strong nation. The main body of our citizens is sound, wholesome, and self-respecting. It is not the decent citizens who are causing trouble; it is the poor ones, plus the agitation of politicians, agitators, and reformers unequal to the task of solving the problems of the day.

All laws enacted should be considered with a view to their effect upon Ascendency, both of the individual and of the nation. This is one of the reasons why we have so many poor laws in effect. They are not considered with regard to Ascendency. They are enacted as the result of many compromises in efforts to please many conflicting interest groups. This is why we are having such an unfortunate condition today and why it will continue to get worse. Is it not simple to consider all laws with regard to Ascendency? If they advance it, enact them. If they oppose it, do not permit them to become laws. But opinions will differ as to whether the measure will contribute toward Ascendency or not. We must have the ablest men in control of affairs in order that they can really determine whether proposed measures will advance Ascendency. If we teach Ascendency in our schools, cause all people to strive for it, cause it to become generally understood, we can bring about on the part of our lawmakers a greater ability to determine whether suggested measures will promote it or not.

Thoughts

It is essential to efficient, competent government to consider all measures with regard to their effect upon the entire nation, not to conciliate interest groups or compromise the benefit of all to bring about agreement between factions.

One great reason for failure to solve man's problems is that few men can visualize all conditions and influences in their proper perspective and use them for man's good.

XIII

REFORM OF OUR GOVERNMENT

IN THIS CHAPTER I WILL DISCUSS BRIEFLY THE REFORM OF OUR democratic institutions. The following chapter, Scientism, will deal with a form of government somewhat different from democracy. It is possible that our democratic institutions can be improved and furnish efficient government. The merits of democracy are so great that we should consistently endeavor to improve the agencies entrusted with the conduct of public affairs. A weakness of our democratic government today is in part due to the fact that the founders of the nation themselves did not trust democracy. They attempted to prevent unwise action by law. This is unsound. Unwise action can best be prevented by high standards of citizenship and leadership. Any action that we can take to further these two essentials of democracy should be resorted to. If we apply wise measures now, we may yet save our democratic institutions.

We have made great advance in many sciences, but we have made none in advancing the science of government. This lack is what is holding us back today, and it is the one we must overcome if we are to advance the welfare of the nation.

Knowledge generally is greater than it has been in the past, and it should now be possible to solve many problems of human existence that have heretofore defied solution. Before attempting to solve these problems we must perfect the government, establishing one that will be capable of grappling with the questions of the day.

We must perfect our government institutions in order that each citizen may be enabled to get the most out of life and that future generations may be stimulated to an advance toward the highest standards of human perfection.

Scientific development has brought·about advance in the utilization of many natural forces. This has had vast influence upon society. Neither our government nor science is able to control social forces. What is the solution? Drastic change in both our government and our scientific outlook. There is much wrong with today's affairs, and science is as much at fault as any other agency. The Defeato attitude of scientists, claiming that they have harnessed natural forces and that man is unequal to handling them, is an admission on their part that they are hopelessly incompetent. If science is worth anything it should be able to find means to control man himself.

Our democratic government has failed to produce really able men capable of conducting the affairs of the government. This being so, it is unwise to enlarge the government any more than is absolutely essential to the performance of the minimum government duties. By this means the incompetence of the politicians will be prevented from doing much harm. When we enlarge government functions and entrust them to unskilled hands, we are inviting disaster. Our liberal thinkers are making this worse by constantly demanding that the government shoulder increasing burdens to carry out the reform measures they advocate. They, however, fail to recognize that they are entrusting these measures to politicians, to men who are only capable of pleasing the voter, and who are unable to conduct government efficiently. They had better direct their efforts toward reforming the government and producing one competent to carry out reform measures.

Sound reform is impossible without the removal of our present politicians from office. It may require a dictatorship to accomplish this. They have the faculty of stirring up the public mind to such a degree as to make it almost impossible to remove them without the use of force. The national environment has been poisoned by them. It is questionable whether politics can be reformed so as to put respectable men in control. If we could remodel our educational system, correct the environmental influences, declare a moratorium on all vicious attacks, it would be possible to bring up a new generation adequate to the task of honest government. Our present generation is so deeply prejudiced, so confirmed in unsound ideas, so helpless in the hands of politicians, as to make it almost impossible to achieve sound government by constitutional methods.

From a practical standpoint under existing conditions, a most effective measure to reform our government and improve our democratic institutions would be to remove all existing politicians from office. Not only should they be removed but they should be forever disfranchised. All creatures of theirs who have profited likewise should be removed from office and permanently disfranchised. This would provide for a great reform in our institutions. Those who have specifically plundered the public for years would then have been removed and their future influence prevented. Drastic as this measure is, it would be of little avail unless accompanied with a campaign of citizenship education which would insure higher standards of citizenship and higher standards of political life. The removal of the present incompetents is not sufficient of itself. We must reform our institutions in such manner as to prevent like incompetents from again obtaining control.

Instead of having a democracy which is a government of all the people, let us have a government by the workers, disfranchising both the Philistines and Philistiners and letting the workers control. If with this be combined means to reform the Philistiners and eliminate the Philistines, in time all citizens of the country would be workers and we would again have a democracy of all the people.

The system of checks and balances in our federal government is on the whole more harmful than beneficial. The reliance of a democratic government should be upon an intelligent civic-minded citizenry. The government should be constituted to promote the elevation of the citizens to the highest conception of civic duty. A government possessing a system of checks and balances does not elevate its citizens, but it does give great opportunity for the politicians to place the blame for their ill-advised measures upon persons or things other than themselves.

Constitutional restrictions and checks and balances may prevent unwise measures to some extent, but such prevention may often be harmful. When many reformers have ideas they wish to try out and have a considerable following, the best means to discredit them is to give them full power to try out their measures. When their unsoundness has discredited them, sound measures may be forthcoming. This is an expensive method of government, but it would be more effective in bringing about a better government than the system of checks and balances we now have. It would educate the citizens to a higher conception of their duties as citizens and a better understanding of economic problems.

For instance, if the New Deal administration had been unhampered by the courts, by the Constitution, or any other check or balance, it would have long ago discredited itself by the failure of its measures. Strangely enough, the best friends of the New Deal administration have been those who have most bitterly opposed it. They have given the members of the administration a scapegoat on which to blame their failure. They blame the courts and capital for their inability to improve conditions. Blaming others is an admission of incompetence. Able men do not blame others for their own failures. This thought would be driven home to the citizens if the government had full control. It could not then abuse capital so freely. Doing so would show the falseness of its policies and its inability to control those it so freely denounces.

Our government was established on the principle that it was a government of laws, not of men. This principle has been adhered to until recently. The object of the founders of the Constitution was to create a written document that would regulate the conduct of government, a written document containing fixed principles which would protect the citizen in his rights and which the courts were bound to observe.

The difficulty of amending the Constitution and the demands of changing conditions have resulted in the courts modifying their interpretations of the Constitution. The Supreme Court and other courts have been reading interpretations into the Constitution to respond to public opinion and demands for social reform, and to appease organized labor. Considerable pressure is brought upon judges to cause them to give what is called progressive or liberal interpretations of the Constitution. If a judge attempts to interpret the Constitution as written, he is called reactionary, which is unfair.

The Constitution itself should be changed to meet the demands of progress. Failure of the legislators to do this should not cause the intimidation of justices to give decisions more in accord with public opinion. This undermines the principles under which our government was established and tends to render the courts unnecessary and useless.

If judges make interpretations of the Constitution in accord with public opinion, the Constitution itself is useless. It would be far better to do away with it entirely than to distort its provisions to meet the demands of the public. Such action tends to build up a disregard of the law by the judges themselves. If the judges do not respect the Constitution or the law, others will not do so.

The division of our Congress into a Senate and House was made as the result of a compromise in the adoption of the Constitution in order to reconcile the interests of the small states as opposed to the interests of the large states. From the standpoint of wise legislation there is no justification in having two lawmaking bodies. Their use as a check upon one another may prevent unwise legislation from being rushed through at times, but it is equally harmful in preventing desirable legislation. The feature of electing both representatives and senators from the states seemed natural for that age, but it is having a pernicious effect upon our existing political life by making the senators and congressmen not representatives of the nation as a whole but of their own states or districts. As the result, they attempt to obtain benefits for their constituents that are not for the best interests of the nation as a whole. This could be corrected by having a small number, say from twenty to thirty members, constitute the legislative branch. They should be elected by direct nation-wide ballot. The president and vice president should be elected the same way. This would result in having them responsive to the nation as a whole. It would place better men in control of the government and would do much to improve our democratic institutions.

Having large legislative bodies makes them unwieldy, conduces to oratory and appeals to the voters instead of to the soundness of measures, and causes a generally lower standard of ability. A selective senate, say of a dozen or a score men elected by national referendum, would be a body far superior to one of several hundred. When the legislative assembly does consist of several hundred men, it usually results in a score or so of the abler ones becoming the leaders and dominating the others.

A small efficient group of able men, replacing both our present House and Senate, can conduct the affairs of the nation far more efficiently. Their meetings should not be open to the public. They should be more in the nature of quiet conferences, seeking the merits of laws undisturbed by undue oratory, denunciation, or pressure from interest groups or the public. Only the decisions of this conference should be made public. All members should support a definite policy once agreed upon. When there is danger of disagreement, a national referendum should be called for.

These able legislators should encourage the public to understand public questions. They should present both sides. They should not denounce or belittle. A high code of conduct on their part and on the part of the citizens would demand this. Our present legislative bodies employ too much talk and denunciation. There is too much imputation of vicious motives to others. We should have a legislative body that will seek the most satisfactory solution after weighing all advantages and disadvantages. Probably one of the greatest weaknesses of democracy is the tendency to resort to words, to develop noisy leaders capable of making noise but incapable of sound action. Let us eliminate the noise and substitute in its stead character and ability.

The use of national referendums would be a great means of preventing politicians from being browbeaten by the voting power of combined interest groups. When labor, for instance, demands the passage of a law establishing a minimum wage, instead of Congress passing on the matter directly, it could refer it to the people. This would obtain a direct decision from the final source of authority and prevent members of Congress from being unduly influenced by consideration for their political fortunes. When the American Legion demands benefits, instead of Congress passing on the matter, refer it to the people and get a direct vote on it. Many public questions could thus be solved quickly and fully, and their demoralizing effect upon political life would be removed.

National referendum by all desirable citizens would give a fair decision on government questions, separate them from personalities and politics, and make for better citizenship. The use of popular referendum to determine controversial questions would relieve Congress from the need of compromising on many measures and provide a clear-cut vote giving a definite answer to a definite question.

A great handicap to efficiency in government is caused by the conflict of present conditions with those of the past. The basic principle behind the adoption of our Constitution was that it was a confederation of states. The national government was established to correct unsatisfactory conditions of that day. The founders of the Constitution attempted to limit the powers of the general government to the barest minimum and retain the independence of the states to the greatest extent.

Today, our national government is encroaching upon states' rights. It has expanded its activities sometimes wisely, sometimes unwisely. This has been brought about in part by new economic questions, improved communications, and many problems that did not exist when the Constitution was adopted. This has resulted in the duplication of government activities by the states and by the federal government, which often causes friction and unnecessary expense. It is a distinct bar to economic development.

It would be far better if we entrusted the national government with all powers it chose to exercise, making the states themselves in part administrative units of the national government. If we employ a nation-wide referendum on public questions and if all important officials of the national government are elected by direct nation-wide ballot, we would be extending the principles of democracy directly to the citizen. Laws then passed by the national government will require that state officials themselves enforce national laws. We will have to rely upon the entire body of citizens to avoid abusing this power. Democracy is government by the people. Why not let them decide questions of nation-wide interest? The rights of the states would then be protected by the entire citizenship of the nation.

We have many unnecessary governmental subdivisions, much duplication of effort, many unnecessary officers and offices. This has been pointed out by able men desiring to reform the institutions of government, but the opposition of politicians and other interests is so great that the abuse remains uncorrected. We are building up a vast bureaucracy containing great numbers of unnecessary employees who must be supported by the government. These people and their supporters have votes and it is impossible to dislodge them. Any measure, no matter how beneficial, has disadvantages, and when any move is made to simplify government functions, it is viciously attacked not only by those who will suffer the loss of benfits but by many others who find other objections to it.

Unquestionably the cost of government could be greatly reduced by efficient reorganization of government subdivisions, and the taxpayers would reap the benefit. State boundaries could be modified, boundaries of cities, of counties, of townships, in the interest of efficiency. We need more centralization in some cases and more decentralization in others. If we can have small communities capable of conducting their affairs in a creditable manner, we should encourage them to do so, without hindrance by the central government. On the other hand, certain basic policies must be inaugurated by the central government and maintained throughout the nation to insure a reasonable degree of uniformity and control questions of national import. In our efforts to simplify the governmental structure we should therefore attempt to decentralize as much as possible, retaining for the central government those essentials required for its proper functioning.

Many of our states are ill bounded. They include much territory having people whose interests are not in common. What, for instance, have the people of western Maryland in common with those on the eastern shore, the people of east Tennessee with those in the vicinity of Memphis, the people of Cairo with those in Chicago? The existence within a state of localities differing greatly in their nature results in inefficient government. Their interests conflict, and as the result, compromises are entered into which are satisfactory to none.

We could well consider granting separate statehood to the large cities. New York City should not be a part of New York State. It should be a separate state of its own; the same for Chicago, Philadelphia, and other large cities having a greater population than many states. When a large city exists in a state having separate interests, there is a conflict of interest between it and the balance of the state. This friction could be avoided by separating them from each other, forming distinct political entities.

The better communications of today render the consoli-

dation of unnecessary units of local government advisable.
In some cases great consolidations could be made. In others
it would be desirable to permit small communities to exist
and conduct their own affairs when they are doing so efficiently. In modifying local governments we must consider
the people residing therein, and do nothing to break down
a fine spirit of local pride and civic duty. Small communities
have the advantage that they can obtain the support of the
citizens more effectively. They promote voluntary efforts by
their citizens in lessening the cost of government. Our small
frontier communities would co-operate to build or repair
roads and bridges, and to serve the entire community. This
was done by voluntary effort and did not require the expenditure of vast sums of money. When we consolidate such
communities we tend to lessen this desirable spirit of co-
operation, causing the people, instead of relying on their own
efforts, to rely upon the government. There are both advantages and disadvantages in large and small local units. We
should endeavor to minimize the disadvantages and strengthen
the advantages so that the people may obtain the most simple,
efficient government practicable.

All police and employees of local governments should be
considered employees of the federal government as well, and
should have the task of enforcing federal laws as well as local
and state laws. We have too much duplication of effort, which
is both wasteful and inefficient.

We should elect only a few of the most important officers.
The task of selecting other government officials could de-
volve on those elected to perform executive duties. This
would permit them to select able, congenial men, insuring
harmony in the governmental structure, provided we elected
able men to the key positions. Having the voters vote for a
great number of minor officials confuses the issue. They do
not know these men, and their duties are such that the average
elector is not directly concerned. He should vote only for
those few officers whose duties are important enough to
justify his attention. Having fewer men to elect, he can be

expected to exercise greater discrimination and select better men.

We should do away with political parties as such and provide for direct elections. This would enable each citizen to vote for the man he considers best qualified. Direct elections would be somewhat similar to direct primaries. Each citizen could write on the ballot the name of the man he desires elected. In practice it would be found that in many cases a majority would agree upon the same man. In other cases, additional elections would be required to eliminate candidates having but few votes. Practical problems unquestionably will arise in a direct election of this nature. Nevertheless, the benefits in elevating the standards of citizenship and of leadership would be so great as to require its employment. Our citizens today do not often have choice in their selections. They very commonly must vote for or against a candidate selected by politicians through political manipulation. If we do away with political parties, we also do away with present-day politicians. We encourage the development in their stead of statesmen appealing to the best interests of the citizen and advancing efficient government. To insure the success of direct elections we require able, unselfish citizens, the same essential need required for the success of democracy itself.

The development of civil-service reform as a means of correcting the spoils system is an example of new evils arising from a reform measure. Unquestionably, laws to protect civil-service employees from political spoilsmen are better than the spoils system. However, the laws to protect the civil-service employees may become a means of protecting the inefficient and incompetent and prevent the reward of those of real merit. The true correction of the spoils system is to find means to appeal to the best in human nature, to place the government in the hands of men who will select able servants, who will not use government office to further selfish ends. Civil-service laws would then be unnecessary; the able public servant would be rewarded in accordance with his merit and the undeserving one would not be unduly re-

warded. This is the true basis for government reform. Trying to effect reforms by law does not get to the heart of evils.
While it may correct some of the most obvious manifestations
of evil it may in time be the means of developing still greater
ones.

XIV

SCIENTISM

THE DEVELOPMENT OF OUR POLITICAL INSTITUTIONS HAS RE-
sulted in placing our government in the control of men who
make politics a profession. It is necessary that they obtain a
a following of voters. As a result they are specialized in obtaining votes, pleasing the voters, appealing to the public,
rather than masters of the truths essential to efficient government.

There is considerable feeling against politicians as such.
They have discredited themselves in the eyes of many thoughtful people by their conduct and their failure to conduct
efficiently the affairs of government. The attitude of the
average citizen, when he thinks of politicians, is to realize
that politicians as such are not very worthy individuals, but
he does not pay much attention to the matter, looking upon
them more or less as a necessary evil, and hoping that things
will come out all right. When they cease to come out all
right, it is possible that these thoughtful citizens may be
united in support of a policy promoting a general reform of
our government institutions that will prevent politicians,
as we now know them, from being in control of our institutions.

Able public-spirited experts engaged in fighting crime or
insuring honest, efficient performance of public duty, invariably demand that their activities be separated from politics. Our military and naval forces offer an excellent illustration of this. How efficient would they be if they were entirely

controlled by the politicians, made a political football? This demand that government activities be separated from politics in the interest of efficiency is in itself a most serious indictment of our existing political system, of our politicians, and of our democratic institutions. Our politicians are entrusted with affairs of government and should conduct them efficiently. Instead of this we see our most efficient public officials demanding that they be released from political dominance and interference.

This condition is largely caused by the politician's efforts to obtain office or retain it, to associate the interests of his party, his associates, with his own, using public office and public service as a means to advance his personal interests, the interests of his party and his friends. No efficient government can be developed under such system. The true solution is to entrust the government to men who will perform their duties efficiently, serve the public, and consider the future.

We have specialists for most things in modern life. Why not have specialists for the conduct of our government? Our government affects us more than any other one thing. The very best specialists we can obtain will be none too good. Government, to be successful, must be conducted by practical, able men who understand man and are able to direct his affairs to the best advantage. The government of the future must be conducted by master scientists under a form of government which I shall call Master Science or Scientism.

Scientism is the conduct of government in accordance with scientific truth, in which master scientists are in control of the affairs of state for the best interest of all, regardless of social status, class prejudice, or interest groups, with the future welfare given more consideration than present benefits. Master scientists are men of ability and understanding, adequate to the tasks of carrying on the affairs of government and appealing to the higher nature of man rather than to his lower nature. In conjunction with Scientism, there must be associated a determined attempt to elevate the citizens of the world to the highest possible status from the standpoint both of intelligence and character. Master Science demands that all peoples, nations, races, be viewed with an unbiased eye, the best of each adopted for all, the bad discarded. Then we may hope to have a world worth living in and be proud to be a part of it.

Master scientists must possess human appeal, practical ability, knowledge, and character, and must be broad minded. The average scientist today possesses knowledge but is inclined to narrowness of viewpoint. The average politician possesses considerable human appeal but is commonly lacking in the other essential qualities. The able business and industrial leader commonly possesses the practical ability which our scientists today lack. The master scientist will combine in himself the finer qualities possessed by the politician, the scientist, and the business man, be a specialist in the wide field of human affairs and possess great vision capable of seeing the ultimate consequences of far-reaching social and governmental measures before they are put into practice.

We might roughly divide geniuses into two types, those who acquire the ability to handle men and those engaged in pursuits in which this quality is not exercised. The true master scientist should be a genius and he should be of the type qualified to handle men, having a thorough understanding of the principles governing human nature. He must also be able to select essentials from a large mass of scientific knowledge and assemble it into a synthesis for the solution of practical problems advancing the welfare of man.

The reason we have poor leaders is because we do not have them specialize in master science. They specialize in too many other factors tending away from the direction of master science and increasing their inability to grasp the issues awaiting solution. Incompetent leaders have been in charge of the affairs of man throughout his entire history. Our present-day ills are caused by incompetent leaders. Therefore, the true solution is to produce able leaders, put them in charge, and support them. Amateurs have been running the world long enough. Now let master scientists do it.

We possess universal narrowness of outlook because of specialization in the production of narrow specialists. Migro and Adapto function in the case of the typist, the clerk, the bookkeeper, the doctor, the scientist, anyone pursuing a particular form of activity either to make a living or as the result of interest. We are all the victims of a cloistered mind to this extent. The cure for this situation is to master the principles of Ascendent Psychology and seek broadening interests. We have had relatively few men who possess great synthesizing minds. This very lack is caused by our specialization in narrow specialities. If we create a greater interest in all, develop a broader viewpoint, we will be establishing an environment favorable to the development of great synthesizing minds and the production of master scientists. Not only will we have able men capable of solving world problems, but we will have an enlightened citizenry that will give them intelligent support. The development of this universal broad viewpoint is essential to the solution of present-day problems and future advance.

The development of master scientists requires intelligent use of Migro and Adapto. Misuse of these two psychas is a large factor in the existing low standard of leadership. Our writers, for instance, who largely influence public opinion, have devoted much effort to literary activity, reading the works of other writers, absorbing much theory and little of the practical. This establishes their definite viewpoint and they write books of a similar nature. They have beautiful words, express fine sentiments, but they are superficial. Instead of advancing knowledge, they confuse it. Somewhat similar influences are exerted upon our educators, in fact on all those now leading in the establishment of public opinion.

With universal understanding of Ascendent Psychology and the development of master science, we can place within reach of all people the literature that will teach basic truths, that will convey understanding of human nature and of practical problems of government and society. Our leaders then will be able to exercise Migro and Adapto in mastering master science and in time we will have able master scientists adequate to the task of conducting man's affairs. Accompanying this development will be the existence of a universal ascendent environment which of itself will be conducive toward promoting understanding of master science. All our institutions, such as religion and education, will be constituted to further it. We are today foolishly employing Migro and Adapto to prevent the development of master science. When we employ them properly to advance it, amazing progress will be made.

Specialization to the extreme of developing a laboratory outlook or becoming a hothouse scientist is of value in that certain specialized forms of knowledge are thereby rendered available for man's use. If we recognize this truth and apply it properly, all is well. But when we permit the hothouse scientist, the man with the laboratory outlook, to conduct the practical affairs of life, we are inviting disaster. We are permitting a specialist in one field to dictate to us policies in another field of which he is ignorant. The development of the master scientist is the direct opposite of the laboratory outlook. The very nature of his task demands a broad outlook, a great human understanding, a deep searching into the essentials of problems with not too much emphasis on any one phase. It requires a perspective view giving to each its proper part in the whole picture.

All sciences exist only to serve master science. We have as yet made no attempt to master the truths of master science. We have many people talking enthusiastically about doing good, but they know little or nothing about the basic principles of human nature and the truths of master science. We must concentrate on these. When we have mastered them in some degree and applied them to improving our government and solving our problems, we may hope to attain a reasonable measure of success. Our efforts heretofore have not been intelligently directed toward accomplishment. Neither have they been in accord with such knowledge as was in existence. They were too much controlled by the mere desire to help, to do good, with insufficient understanding. All too often measures intended to accomplish good have resulted in harm.

The difference between master science and ordinary science is quite similar to the difference between Ascendent Psychology and ordinary psychology. Present-day psychologists admit that man is a creature of his environment. They accept this as a fact but fail to suggest means to employ it. Ascendent Psychology recognizes that man is largely the creature of his environment and suggests means to improve the environment and thus improve man. Thus Ascendent Psychology seeks to master the principles underlying human nature for man's improvement. Ordinary psychology merely makes an attempt to understand them; it makes no attempt to employ them. Present-day science generally undertakes to master the laws of nature but does not attempt to harness them for man's good. Master science will not be satisfied with understanding nature's laws alone but will have the aim of controlling nature's forces to improve man, to add to his happiness, intelligence, and character.

The absolute need for having master scientists to control our government should be apparent to all. We have but to look back over the past history of man and see where he has failed miserably, without exception, because of incompetent leaders. It is true, the leaders are produced by their environment. We must direct the efforts of our churches, of our schools, all environmental influences, to produce master scientists, to create an environment conducive to their production. We must teach the people the principles of human nature, show them how they are being led by politicians who appeal to their feelings and not to their common sense. We must teach them to control themselves by their conscious minds. If we can start this now, even in a small way, it will grow. As it grows it will become increasingly impossible for politicians such as we now have to control our institutions by denunciation and appeals to prejudice and hatred.

By having all people in the nation strive for Ascendency, the standard of intelligence will be improved, rendering it relatively easy to produce master scientists. The very nature of Ascendency itself is conducive to the development of master scientists. Unquestionably we have very many able men today who have inherited naturally great mental gifts, but due to lack of understanding of how to develop them, they have remained dormant. The teaching of Ascendency would enable them to make use of their dormant talents and develop them to their maximum extent. We could obtain many master scientists from men who are now manual laborers.

Create a demand for master scientists and the supply will be forthcoming. To become a master scientist a man requires great gifts and their development. He should study all problems affecting human welfare, seeking for the profound truths underlying them, and for sound solutions. With men of great gifts and with this effort continued over long periods, Adapto will produce master scientists.

Many people develop a dominant interest in life. I will describe this by stating that a dominant interest is an interest in a particular thing that dominates the thought and conduct of the individual. A fond parent may be so wrapped up in a child as to consider all other factors with relation to this one dominant interest. An intense love affair while at its height constitutes a dominant interest. One of the great secrets of genius or of great achievement is the possession of a dominant interest exercised toward the accomplishment of a definite aim. We can use this to great advantage in the development of master scientists. Let us create the demand for master scientists and endeavor to bring about the supply. The ideal way would be to impress upon the young at as early an age as possible the fact that master scientists are able men who have devoted their lives to the study and mastery of problems having to do with man's welfare. The earlier in life they start thinking about this the sooner their development begins and the greater possibility there is of developing them into scientists. With this understanding and incentive, many of our most gifted young people would establish the desire to become a master scientist as their dominant aim. Many would succeed and the problem of government would then be solved.

Scientism is the only sound means of government suited to modern conditions that will meet the pressing problems of the day. Existing conditions have not produced master scientists capable of conducting scientism. We will first have to produce them before we can make it a form of government. But we do have sufficient able men who could adequately meet the problems of today if they were put in control. If we do so and encourage the development of master scientists, the future will have no lack of ability to conduct governmental affairs.

No such government as scientism has yet existed in man's history. Some nations have been governed by oligarchies or aristocratic bodies, but they were not selected for their ability as master scientists. They inherited their positions or acquired them for other reasons. By establishing a selective senate of master scientists we are obtaining what efficient government requires, that is, government by the ablest men available. If these men are able and conscientious, and if they insure that their successors will also be able men, scientism will be successful. Past history has shown the failure of government as the result of corruption and incompetence succeeding able leaders. The greatest care must be exercised to see that the master scientists are the best from all standpoints and that they take great care to avoid having harmful influences creep into scientism. The essential thing is to insure that they are succeeded by men as good as or better than themselves.

If scientism be established as a form of government, the members of the selective senate themselves should select members to fill vacancies. It would be desirable to prevent the body from becoming too conservative and behind the times. This could be prevented to some degree by establishing fifty-six years as the maximum age for master scientists to be members of the selective senate. We could nevertheless permit members to retain their seat through life, giving the benefit of their age and experience, but subject them to the control of members under fifty-six years of age to determine their suitability to remain in active service within the senate. They would have a vote on all questions except those having to do with the eligibility of men above fifty-six.

Scientism must provide for an exercise of democracy of a superior kind to avoid falling into a rut. Actually, scientific government must be a combination of scientism and democracy. We must associate a certain amount of democracy with scientism in order to prevent the master scientist from losing contact with the public and getting into a rut. This can be accomplished by providing some means of referendum whereby the public can express its views. What scientism aims to do above all things is to eliminate the politicians, the agitators, those who stir up feelings and emotions to the prejudice of facts and understanding. When such a referendum is held only the intelligent citizen should vote, and each should do his own thinking. No vicious attacks, demagogic tactics, or action to obscure issues should be permitted. The object of scientism is to abolish the worst features of democratic institutions and retain the good.

A group of twenty or so master scientists, selected for their ability as such, could govern this entire nation efficiently, doing away with political controversies, appeals to interest groups, class hatreds, and ill feeling. The fact that we had in control of our government twenty of the best men capable of conducting it would insure its respect by the citizens. This government itself would resort to all reasonable measures to elevate the standards of citizenship.

Conclusion

From the standpoint of human nature and science generally, scientism offers the best solution to the successful conduct of man's affairs. Politicians, the creatures of democracy, devote their efforts to pleasing the prejudices and feelings of voters and compromising issues, and are thereby developed in that direction. Master scientists, seeking for the truth, the real causes, the most satisfactory means of accomplishment, will be developed in that direction. Their efforts will not be to please and retain office, but to solve the problems. The very efforts made will harness nature's forces in achieving it. Truly this is science in its highest form, harnessing the forces of nature to man's use instead of, as in the past, just blundering along, blindly, in accordance with the whim of a fickle multitude.

Scientism will permit of hearing and heeding the people's voice. It will not permit the existence of politicians creating discord in their efforts to advance self-interest and obtain office. Master scientists will seek public support for measures designed to advance the welfare of all. Master scientists will not do as politicians commonly do, seek to obtain public support to advance their own self-interest. The vast body of people as a whole are sound. Master scientists will endeavor to retain this soundness and be guided by it. Our present-day politicians do not appeal to the more elevating and constructive influences of the people. They appeal to passion, prejudice, the primitive, whatever feelings they can arouse to obtain office and advance themselves. Master scientists will consistently and unremittingly appeal to man's better nature.

XV

LAW, ETHICS

MULTIPLICITY OF LAWS, RIGIDITY OF LAWS, AND REPRESSIVE laws alike distract the attention of the individual from creating an inner urge within himself to further good conduct. The existence of laws of these natures attracts his attention to forces outside himself. Good conduct must come from within, must be imbedded upon one's subconscious mind, upon his very being. We should therefore modify our laws and legal procedure to encourage the individual to look within himself and establish a high code of conduct by his own efforts.

A wise government will not seek to cure all ills by legal enactments, nor to create character among its citizens by statute. Instead it will seek to raise its citizens to such high standards that repressive laws will be unnecessary. Who can make the bad good by law? It cannot be done. But you can have the deserving citizens control the nation and control the bad so as to minimize their harmful influence. If the problem were intelligently approached, the vicious could be eliminated entirely.

Our legal system must be entirely recast, simplified, and reduced to essentials. We should regulate as little as possible by law and encourage voluntary good conduct on the part of the individual by improving the environment, intelligence and moral character of the individual citizens.

Our laws should both reward and promote good conduct. They do not do this today. In many cases they actually encourage dishonesty and unethical conduct. Our divorce laws

168

are an example of this. In some states the laws regarding divorces are very rigid. The result is that couples resort to unethical practices to meet the legal requirements for obtaining a divorce. This conduct is reprehensible but less so than the laws that require it. No one should be condemned to live forever with someone he dislikes. Sensible laws would provide an honorable means of relief.

One of the most serious crimes a citizen can commit and one which we not only do not punish today but which we tolerate and encourage, is the betrayal of citizenship by using its powers to obtain benefits from the government. Such conduct breaks down the very moral fiber of the nation.

It is not necessary for a person to commit a serious offense to be an undesirable citizen. The commission of many trivial offenses is an indication of undesirability. Anyone who disregards the rights of others, who lacks consideration for them, is not a desirable citizen.

All descendent conduct such as lying, misleading, misstatements, is conducive toward crime. We should not try to prevent such conduct by legal enactment but should rather attempt to do so by education and the creation of an ascendent environment that will not permit of such conduct. We must teach each person to realize that any such action on his part or on the part of any other person tends to lower the environmental standard of conduct.

We should consider the character of the individual, the effect of his acts upon the public, rather than arbitrarily set forth certain requirements by law for him to live up to. When such requirements exist, undesirable people will attempt to get around them; but when their character throughout their entire life is the question at issue and their contribution toward being a good influence is made the determining factor, they will endeavor to improve their character and be a good influence in the community.

The most successful moral and legal code will be one in which each person is encouraged to do right of his own volition because that is the proper and fitting thing to do. The

use of fear and punishment as deterrents will still be necessary to restrain the vicious but the need for its employment
should be reduced to a minimum.

Teach all to do right, and all except a small portion will do
so. We must strive for a universal moral enlightenment which
will modify our economic and social systems to conform to
what is right and encourage all to do right. Those who refuse
to do what is right should be segregated or removed from
contact with the better class of citizens. Unfortunately our
legal system at present tends to curb all, because the few
abuse their privileges.

All human experiences demonstrated the futility of attempting to make people good and happy by legal enactment.
The true, sure method is the development of an environment
which is conducive to the development of character, the promotion of knowledge and the increase of understanding. An
enlightened educational system and religion will help advance
this aim.

Trying to regulate human conduct by a great many laws
will be both unsuccessful and harmful. Assuming that the
people are trying to follow the laws implicitly, they are misus-
ing their effort in finding out what they may do rather than
developing their ability to do what is right.

Attempts to read human rights into statutes cannot help but
be harmful in their effects. When you define what is right
by legal enactment, you encourage people to do only what is
required by the statute, discourage them from raising
themselves to extreme nobleness. You further encourage
individuals to interpret the statutes in an effort to get whatever benefits they can thereby. Many people are willing to
take whatever they can, feeling that the mere fact they can do
so justifies their action. An enlightened legal system should
not permit this. No suits should be permitted that are not
equitable and just. It should not be possible for the undeserving to obtain benefits in ways that deserving high-minded
people would not employ. No matter how enlightened a legal

code may be, it must be flexible and must be administered by enlightened judges in order to insure justice.

The commandment "Thou shalt not steal" is not adhered to for the reason that the churches attempt to prohibit too much and fail to apply proper methods. Fear seems to have been religion's main way of insuring good conduct. We must appeal to the good within each person to accomplish this. Teach each one to be good. In overcoming the acquisitive instinct, which all have, and stopping pilfering, for instance, we should appeal to the individual, show what a small cheap thing this is and how one is more than repaid for not doing it by the increased feeling of self-respect acquired by such wholesome restraint. If we can start this, we begin a good moral development and promote good habits. This would advance self-interest because all would benefit from the goodness of their neighbors.

If man's conduct is only influenced by hope of gain or fear of loss, he may well perish. There is a higher conception of doing duty to self and to others. History has many such examples. We must make these truths so universally recognized that all can understand and comply with them. Lack of knowledge and understanding are more to blame for our present ills than viciousness or desire for gain.

We will not be able to call ourselves a moral nation until it is possible to leave jewelry, money, or valuables in public places unguarded without danger of pilfering. Let everyone make a resolution now, and adhere to it, not to pilfer anything of however slight a value. Could this acquisitive habit be overcome we would be on a fair way to developing such universal good character as to insure a future world free from evil.

In developing universal good character we should stress and impress upon each individual the fact that by committing offenses against others he is the sufferer in the end because his privileges are limited through measures taken to restrict bad conduct. If there were no crime or misconduct in the world, every person would benefit. This is a far-sighted viewpoint to which we must educate our people.

Give everyone as much liberty as possible, in all ways, at all times, in all things. Repress only when this privilege is abused and then only the offenders, not others. Let the deciding factor in all legal measures be the ultimate human good. Let us make our legal system such a one that the virtuous will prosper; that will assist in eliminating the helpless, weak, and unvirtuous.

Equity and the effect upon man's future interests should govern in all cases. Its effect upon moral character, upon the environment, should be weighed. Nothing opposed to Ascendency should be tolerated. It is possible to conceive of a society so fine and high that courts, lawsuits, and litigation will not exist within it.

The line between honesty and dishonesty should be made clear and unmistakable, and the laws reformed so that the subtle cannot work around intricacies of law and that the moral are free from annoyance by them. The law today promotes discord and has much to do with the economic difficulties and poor moral standards of our people. Altruism on the part of all results in each having more.

We should classify all acts that tend to oppose Ascendency as being illegal. Our present-day lawyers are all too often only concerned with the legality of acts, and not with their righteousness. If we wish to have an ascendent legal system we must have regard for what is right. This need not oppose the statutes. They should be revised and made to be in accord with what is right. Our legal system should not condone any conduct which is unmoral, i. e., opposed to the best that is in or that can be developed in human beings.

It should not be possible for a moral act to be illegal, nor for an immoral act to be legal. When politicians in control of our government give jobs and vote benefits to friends and others for their own selfish aggrandizement, they are committing a serious wrong. This is tolerated by our present code. It is such conduct as this that cannot readily be regulated by a legal code. We must therefore concentrate on raising the standards of ethics, using the law to support the highest possible standards.

An enlightened legal code would demand a higher standard of conduct and example from the wealthy and powerful. These are the ones who set the example and influence others. The poor and ignorant will do as those in power do. If we insure good conduct on the part of the powerful, a great contribution will be made in improving the conduct of those less powerful.

Our legal code unfortunately does not differentiate between moral and legal. We should in effect abolish the legal aspects and make of our legal code a moral code, a code of conduct, one that will not only deter bad conduct but that will promote good conduct; that will help those who are trying to live the better life and restrain those who are a bad influence. An enlightened legal code must work in conjunction with sound government measures endeavoring to eliminate undesirable people from the environment in order that they may not harm others by their example.

XVI

LAWS

OUR ENTIRE LEGAL SYSTEM IS TOO COMPLEX, TOO INVOLVED, TOO cumbersome. The vast mass of statutes, precedents to be consulted, diverts the attention of the lawyers from the merit of the case into mastering the printed word. Attempting to reduce human conduct and acts to statutes results in greater attention being paid to the statutes than to the conduct. A great simplification of law could be brought about that would result in having laws that would be less than one per cent of those in existence at present. They could then be readily understood and be a real contribution toward improving the character of the citizens.

Much of our present unsound economic condition is due to an unsound legal system. We worship the statutes and forget that they were originally intended to serve man. We can, by adopting a sensible code of laws, do much to bring about sound economic conditions. The law should endeavor to prevent undesirable people from having any influence upon business or industry which, if controlled by decent people, will not require regulation and government interference.

Law that prohibits action should not be employed if it can be avoided. The fact that certain people are doing things which are against the interests of others shows the existence of forces or circumstances causing them to do so. The sensible means is to control these forces, and guide them into constructive channels. When we attempt to prohibit their manifestation, we drive them into harmful hidden channels.

Our present legal system is based too much on repression instead of expression. Instead of tracing evils to basic causes and either eliminating these causes or leading them into constructive channels, we try to prohibit them entirely, which is utterly impossible and causes disrespect for the law and further violations of a similar kind.

From an economic standpoint, a complex legal code employing many courts, many lawyers, is very injurious, not only because of the cost of this vast institution, but also because of the bad effect it has upon the development of honest industries which are hampered by its provisions. Too many honest people and honest corporations are being threatened by people who employ our legal system to obtain benefits for themselves. No sensible system would permit this. Before a person enters a suit in a court, he should be required to be of good character. This provision would eliminate about nine-tenths of the legal cases we now have. Why should the public maintain a system that is designed to serve vicious people who employ it as a means of annoying decent people?

A sensible legal code would provide means to determine the constitutionality of laws when they are passed, not years later. We have many examples of the constitutionality of laws being determined many years after their passage, rendering a fair decision impossible because of the great harm resulting to innocent persons. This affords a good example of statutitus, of narrow customs in which our courts are not permitted to decide constitutionality of laws until some person directly interested institutes suit. Common sense would indicate that some means should be established to show that when a law is passed and put into effect it is constitutional and will not be declared unconstitutional after the public has accommodated itself to its requirements.

Unintelligent laws may defeat their object. The double liability of stockholders in the national bank system, for instance, is a bar to the increase of the amount of capital outstanding, with the result that the banks, instead of being strengthened by this law, which is the intent, are rendered less strong by their attempts to evade the additional liability. We have any amount of unwise legislation of this nature throughout the country; foolish attempts to better conditions that in their final ramifications result in greater harm.

We have laws supported by vast numbers of people for the most trivial reasons, and likewise we have measures opposed for the most trivial reasons. Laws should not be enacted unless they serve a great good, and they should not be opposed unless they would prove harmful to Ascendency. We must look more to the future, see what the effect of suggested legislation will be upon it, have greater knowledge of human nature, of master science, and be controlled by truth, knowledge, and understanding.

We have too many laws prohibiting such basic human acts as sex, which are impossible of enforcement, and discredit the law itself. They tend to drive evils into concealment where they are worse than if they were permitted in the open. Our failure to recognize that sex promiscuity exists results in giving us a very high ratio of venereal disease. Frank acknowledgment of this evil could result in having all venereal diseases eradicated.

Our laws are heartless and cruel in their operation under unusual circumstances. There was a case not very long ago where a girl about twelve years old was raped and became pregnant. Because of the wording of the law, no one undertook to order or permit an abortion. As a result this poor little girl was required to bring into the world a baby produced by a criminal act. This is cruel, unjust, brutal. Such a legal system has no right to exist; yet we stand by and permit it to operate.

We should strive to attain the ideal of a minimum of lawsuits and litigation by practical means. This can be gradually achieved. Any lawsuit requires two parties. If both are highly moral it may merely be a matter of misunderstanding, but too often under present conditions, a righteous person is being subjected to annoyance by a unrighteous one. If we eliminate the undesirable element from our population, deserving citizens will not be subjected to annoyance by them. It will then be possible to arbitrate disagreements in a fair-minded manner and there will be no occasion for lawsuits. This is an idealistic view which our lawyers will laugh at, but we have no reason to repose confidence in them. They have only been successful in discrediting the law and are unable to conceive of any measures which will improve it. There is a certain amount of selfishness in their outlook in that they obtain their living from a complicated mass of legalism. If law were simplified, many would have to obtain their living elsewhere.

Our legal system as now constituted of itself creates litigation and increases the number of courts. A sensible system would reduce litigation to a minimum and by this reduction require fewer courts and officials, would lessen government costs, and would cut down ill-feeling generally.

Our legal system is condemned by many of the ablest lawyers themselves, but they do not seem able to reform it. Like government, it has so many people being benefited by its present form that any change will meet with great opposition. Our attempt to reduce everything to writing makes it so cumbersome as to prevent justice. Our legal code is a reflection upon our nation, and a reflection upon the quality of the lawyers who permit it to exist as it is at present.

Does capitalism teach that the strong and cunning can overreach the weak and helpless and take their money so long as they adhere to prescribed ways? No. But our legal system does and our lawyers support it and the politicians maintain it.

The ineffectiveness of our legal system is shown by the wide prevalence throughout the nation of gangs of racketeers intimidating legitimate business and extracting tribute while the law remains practically helpless. Attempts on the part of these sufferers to invoke the law are more likely to cause more suffering and they therefore willingly pay tribute—truly a terrible reflection upon our enlightened civilization.

We should try to have our legal system so constituted, so

administered, as to prevent unjust gains from being obtained under it. We today have many abuses in breach-of-promise suits, alimony, damages for accidents, nuisance suits, and other means by which people utilize the law to obtain money from others. A sensible legal system would prevent this abuse. It would be designed to administer justice, to reduce law suits to a minimum. It should never be possible to make a wrong right by making it legal; on the contrary, it should always be possible for a wronged person to obtain justice. This is more than our present code provides.

Our legal system is at fault in permitting itself to be abused for the collection of damages by unjustified legal actions. One person resorts to sharp practices of this nature and wins; another follows his example, and it spreads. Each feels that if others do so, why should not he? By this means we are promoting bad conduct, penalizing the deserving who refuses to abuse the law for his own interest in favor of the undeserving who is all too willing to use the law to further his own ends. This is a false conception of what law is for, and under no circumstance should it be permitted. The law should prevent the vicious from using it to persecute the virtuous. Not only is such action highly unjust, but it tends to break down the integrity and character of the individual. When the example is spread of the law tolerating its abuse, it continues to grow. Thus our legal system is creating the abuses it is supposed to prevent.

Many people instituting damage suits are of very poor character and have no just claim. We should not permit the law to be abused by such people. They should rather be segregated and removed from the environment. Our court calendars are cluttered up as the result of action by undesirable citizens who thus prevent desirable ones from obtaining justice and having their cases promptly disposed of. For example a drunken man was killed in an automobile accident entirely as the result of his own conduct; yet his family, supported by a lawyer, did not hesitate to sue the railroad company in an effort to obtain damages even though without justification. Sympathetic friends testified that the man did not drink, although he was a confirmed drunkard; that he was not drunk at the time when actually he was. Here we see law being used for selfish ends supported by supposedly respectable citizens. We must bring about a higher conception of public duty in our country, greater respect for the law, a realization on the part of all citizens that when they tolerate evil conduct on the part of others they are being unjust to themselves and to the entire community.

When it is necessary to reduce certain principles of law to specific statutes, in the interpretation of these statutes, the intent behind the act should always be considered. Regardless of the reading of the statutes themselves, they should never be utilized for improper purposes, such as permitting shyster lawyers to persecute honest people, or to make use of an injury in an accident in which the injured person was at fault. It should not be possible for shysters to exist under a sensible legal code, yet the shyster trumps up a claim and often obtains damages. This discredits our code, penalizes honest people, rewards the dishonest. We should, instead, reward the honest and penalize the dishonest.

Unjust suits could be greatly reduced. The law should provide for taking suitable measures against those who prefer unjust suits. A certain element of danger would then exist in such action and offenders would be deterred. We should not permit advantage to be taken of legal technicalities to collect damages or benefits when no moral right to them exists. Neither should we permit of profit by catering to harmful human weaknesses.

Suit for damages should be limited to a reasonable amount of damage actually sustained. We commonly hear of suits for fabulous sums such as a million dollars for relatively trivial damages. It might be well to levy a tax upon each suit for damage, graduated in accordance with the amount sued for. Complete records of all suits made and received should be entered upon the life dossier of all concerned. This would afford a means of determining whether they are fit to institute a suit for damages.

We are attempting to cure many ills, reform many abuses, and improve morals by statutes. All this succeeds in making the statutes bulky, clutters up courts, lessens justice, discredits law, and fails to correct the ills for which the measures are intended. Such action increases the cost of government, decreases government efficiency, and confuses issues to such an extent as to prevent a sound wholesome outlook or perspective. The very existence of vast quantities of government enactment shows the utter incompetence of our government. Simple methods are the essentials of truth, of understanding. No one can understand a complex jumble of statutes contradicting each other and causing conflicting opinions between the ablest lawyers in the land. If the ablest lawyers cannot agree on interpretations, how can we expect the average citizen to understand?

One of the worst faults of the American is in attempting to cure all ills and improve morals by legal enactment. This fails, discredits the law; only the lawyers benefit. We would do better with one-tenth of our present laws and more freedom for the individual. The land of the free is fast becoming the land of the freedomless. Laws of this kind are a harm in many ways. They perpetuate evils which they are designed to help. The causes which should be treated lie deeper than mere legal enactment can reach. Do for each person what will encourage him to do his best for both self and others. This principle carried into practice would do much to further the solution of present-day difficulties.

Quantity of written law does not improve human conduct. On the contrary: when we have vast quantities of statutes it does not mean by any means that we have a virtuous citizenry. We have more crime, more lawsuits, and more laws than any country in the world that claims to be civilized. With fewer laws, more sensible and greatly simplified, and with concentration on character development and intelligence, we could reduce our crime and legal controversies. Few simple laws favor good conduct; voluminous complex ones oppose it.

When will our people realize that passing vast numbers of laws will not correct either morals or poverty? How can we have liberty if we have a multiplicity of laws and a vast bureaucracy to enforce them?

All our present-day ills are caused or contributed to by our laws, passed to accomplish certain reforms, but whose far-reaching effects operate to our prejudice. These laws were enacted by amateurs who could not foresee their ultimate effects.

Vast numbers of laws attempting to correct all the ills of man will not accomplish much. The more laws, the more difficult they are to enforce, the greater the annoyance to honorable citizens, and the easier they are for the unscrupulous to circumvent. Fewer laws will accomplish more. They can be more readily enforced. They harass less. Instead of asking for statutes to help them, people will meet their own problems and be strengthened in so doing.

Having unnecessary laws in effect that cannot be enforced tends toward disrespect for law. It promotes the habit of ignoring or violating laws. A true principle is securing respect for the law is to reduce all laws to a minimum and to those that are enforceable. Having done this, see that they are enforced—more by building up character than by repressive measures; but when the latter is necessary, use with vigor.

Thoughts

There are many injustices possible under existing laws. It is too rigid and carries out erroneous ideas.

Multiplicity of laws is positive evidence of inefficient government.

We have too many laws as the result of trying to become moral by statutes, and prosperous by legal enactment. They have not succeeded for we are neither moral nor prosperous. Let us clear the deck and start anew, giving each person the utmost liberty and freedom. Help them be moral and prosperous by their own efforts.

When will the American people cease to try to correct everything by laws? When will they realize that the conditions they hope to correct are only aggravated by the passage of many laws which prevent sane action?

XVII

JUDGES, LAWYERS

REGARDLESS OF HOW GOOD A LEGAL SYSTEM MAY BE, ITS EF-
ficiency depends upon the judges, the men entrusted with the
task of administering the law. We should endeavor to obtain
the finest men in the country as judges, encourage them to
decide questions on merit, and reduce the legal code to such a
simple form that their initiative will not be hampered in
administering justice. That is to say, consider each particular
case upon its merit and give a decision based upon justice.

Many civil cases could be referred to boards of arbitration
who would have the same standing as courts and whose decision would be final. They would consider the merits of the
question submitted to them and insure that justice was done
to all concerned.

Courts should consist of about nine able men familiar with
the matter at hand and understanding human nature. There
should be no lawyers permitted before this court, no arguments. It should be the mission of the members of the court to
ascertain the facts and rule on them. There should be no
appeal from their decision, no cluttering up of records or unnecessary delays.

It is a serious reflection upon our present-day courts to see
the way in which they permit decent citizens to be abused
when used as witnesses. This should not be permitted. A
self-respecting citizen should be treated courteously as such.
Our courts often treat the honest witness far worse than the

criminal who is on trial. The accused has protection; the witness, none. The more the opposing lawyer can discredit and belittle him, the more he attempts to do so.

Lawyers as a class are cynical of human virtues. This may be attributed to the fact that a lawyer's clients are seeking to get the most and give the least, and he is paid to assist them in doing so. This is bound to affect his viewpoint, and he develops contempt for humans, believing that they are all seeking their own ends; he and his legal system encourage this conduct. The law is sought by those desiring to cheat, overreach, get something for nothing, use legal machinery and litigation as a means of gain; it is shunned by the man seeking justice. When our courts invite the latter and repel the former we may improve them, not before. Our legal system distrusts man so much that it does not give judges freedom to act. The code is so inflexible that it cannot assist those seeking justice.

One of the great faults of lawyers is that they spend entirely too much time in mastering statutes and rules of procedure, but all too little on equity, justice, and human nature. Delving into statutes, dealing with words, spending much time on procedure, tends to kill real thought and originality. The law is one of our institutions that is farthest behind in this day of scientific advance. This has been caused by the specialization of the lawyers in a very narrow field to such a degree that they are unable to reform their outworn institutions. Our present legal system is unscientific and was devised without thought of future effects. It worships the past to the exclusion of the future.

Nine-tenths of our legal cases are caused by the law itself. The lawyers prosper on litigation. They are interested in having as much litigation as possible and are opposed to measures that would lessen it. Reform of the law cannot come from the lawyers. It must come from some outside source, someone who is not a member of the legal fraternity. Our lawyers have grown up in an atmosphere of legal phraseology, statutes, and technicalities, and are unable to approach the task of reforming the legal code with an open mind.

Our present legal system permits of too many delays and is unnecessarily costly. Both these conditions are aggravated by the lawyers. They resort to all means to win their cases. They do not hesitate to obtain delay for the most trivial reasons when they think it will benefit their cases; neither do they care as to the increased cost thrust upon the public. We have had cases drag through the courts for years. With the passage of time it becomes more difficult to decide a case upon its merits. Witnesses will disappear, die. In any case it is far easier to remember what took place yesterday than what took place several years ago.

The tremendous costs shouldered by the public in some criminal cases are ridiculous. I note a brief notice today in which a witness retained by the state for a period of twenty-three months has incurred hotel bills and bills for personal expenses for about eight thousand dollars. During this period he has been guarded by detectives drawing a salary from the public of three thousand dollars per year each. This is entirely unnecessary. When a man is tried for an offense, the trial should proceed without delay. It should be possible to complete the trial within a period of a few days. The innocent man would then be free or the guilty man punished. The moral effect of such trials would be an excellent deterrent. We would have far less crime news in our papers. The rights of the public would be protected and the taxpayer would have less cause for complaint.

Our present-day judges and lawyers are victims of bad environmental influences. They have grown into a deep rut to the same degree that our churchmen have. Both judges and lawyers are products of our present-day legal environment. There are some basic truths contained in our present law. It has developed through the ages to what it is at present. It records much of man's experience. We should retain what is worthy. We must, however, revise the law with regard to our greater knowledge of human nature. To perfect the law, it will be necessary to improve the environment surrounding the judges and lawyers. If we can give them a more wholesome outlook, a broader viewpoint, we can employ their knowledge in developing a system of laws and a legal system that will be adequate to modern needs.

XVIII

CRIME AND CRIMINALS

THE GREAT AMOUNT OF CRIME EXISTING IN AMERICA IS A reflection upon our institutions. The existence of a large amount of crime is an indication of inefficient government and of low standards of conduct among the citizens. Crime is further contributed to by unsatisfactory economic conditions and undue sentimental regard for criminals. Disregard of the rights of the public by organized interest groups is very similar to crime. When any group resorts to action to obtain benefits for itself at the expense of others, it is guilty of the same offense of which the criminal is guilty. The criminal places self-interest before the rights of others and selfish interest groups do the same thing. In some cases these interest groups resort to organized violence to obtain their ends. In other cases they resort to the use of their voting power as citizens. In both cases the result is the same. They, in effect, are criminals. When we see the existence of so many selfish interest groups, we can expect many criminals. The action of organized interest groups, indeed, is sometimes more cowardly than that of criminals. They rely upon protection by virtue of their numbers. When we abolish selfish interest groups, we may also hope to greatly reduce crime and criminals. Crime is a product of a descendent environment. The more ascendent the environment is, the less crime will exist. Efforts to control and reduce crime must include efforts to establish an ascendent environment.

The largest single cause of crime in this country is the

prevailing poor standard of conduct. So many are seeking their own ends without regard for others and will do wrong if they feel it will be to their interest. A great amount of hypocrisy and deceit exists which contributes to this. How can we censure criminals from following the example set by others? When politicians seek votes by trading benefits, when we have so many citizens demanding largesse from the government legally, why should not criminals hold up and rob? Many other people do it in ways the law does not classify as a crime, but which are as serious an offense; sometimes more so. To lessen crime, we must prevent the elevation of corrupt people to the control of our institutions. With a good example of conduct set by our rulers, criminals will have less justification for following a life of crime. Before you punish the followers, punish the leaders. Then you will not need to punish the followers.

I remember a boy in a C.M.T.C. camp who stole a hat. His excuse was that someone stole his. This boy was basically good and would respond to good influences. If the good did not beckon, he would respond to the bad, but somewhat less readily than to the good. Here lies a means for good but little utilized. If we make the good predominate in our environment, the bad will decrease rapidly. The example of others influences greatly, especially among the young and children. When we have presidents, cabinet members, senators, big men the country over, resorting to duplicity, treachery, lies, bribing, abuse, threats, stealing, for their own ends, how can we blame a criminal for doing the same? He is less at fault than they. Our politicians and lawyers do worse, but under cover of the law.

Our law, if it is ever to be any good, must not permit wrongs to be done under its protection. We must have a truer conception of right and wrong, give no legal protection to wrong however skillfully disguised. It should be considered, and in reality is, a crime for anyone to set a bad example which causes another to commit a crime. The man who causes is worse than he who does, regardless of legal technicalities. If we had no one setting bad examples and all set good ones instead, who would then dare be bad? No one. Can we achieve this? We can. How? By keeping this aim in mind and working toward it, using all weapons to attain it, the weapons being those that elevate, not degrade.

The idle rich, by their ostentation and lack of consideration, help produce bad feeling that tends toward crime. It seems, and is, very unfair to a poor man that he has little or nothing and someone else less deserving has much. Education along with sensible reform would eliminate economic evils, give all a good living, tend to distribute wealth, and prevent its accumulation in the hands of the undeserving.

In some recent labor disputes policemen, attacked by men endeavoring to enter a plant they were guarding, used their firearms, with the result that several men were killed. Their action has been criticized by a great many well-intentioned people who abhor the use of force. They have been criticized for being unnecessarily brutal. This criticism is unfair, and made by people who do not sufficiently understand the difficulties under which the police operate.

Considering the vast amount of disturbance in the country, particularly by labor, I think that our police forces have displayed admirable control. Relief workers have spat upon them, have called them names. They have had rocks thrown by strikers, they have received personal abuse and insults. They are the custodians of law and order and they are entitled to respect. When our law permits them to be insulted with impunity by organized groups, we are bringing about conditions conducive to civil war and to such incidents as that in which several men were killed.

When policemen have been subjected to insults and annoyance for a considerable period of time, and suddenly such violence is employed against them as to require retaliation on their part, past offenses are brought to their mind and they are more likely than not to retaliate vigorously. They cannot be blamed for this. It is a trait of human nature. Rather than denounce policemen for being overvigorous in asserting the law, we should denounce those who violate it and particularly those who stir up agitation, who foment disorders, and above all, those officials at the head of our government who neglect to use their influence to prevent such manifestations of lawlessness.

Whatever may have been due these particular policemen in the way of censure, there is far less due them than our high government officials should receive. There has been a committee of congressmen investigating this riot—brought on by their own promises, failure to redeem them, and agitation generally. When we have a civilization that permits guilty men to investigate the conduct of more worthy men, we are bringing about a bad situation.

Incompetence is often a worse crime than criminal acts. Our criminals do not do as great harm as the incompetent statesmen the world over who are making war inevitable and will cause the killing and maiming of millions.

If we intend to cure crime, we must start at the top and remove our existing politicians from the control of our institutions. They are a direct cause of crime by setting a bad example themselves and contributing to the lowering of the moral standards of the entire nation. They are unquestionably a large factor in giving us the distinction of the largest criminal record of any nation claiming to be civilized. They cater to criminal elements for votes, they fail to prosecute when this will be to their advantage, and at the same time they talk in the highest tone of virtue and good. They preach a code of conduct entirely different from that they live. Criminals are not fools by any means; they are but accepting the example of the politicians in following a life of crime.

We condemn harshly criminals who rob, steal, and plunder others for their own benefit, but we applaud such action on the part of politicians. Our politicians have not the interest of the nation at heart. They are serving themselves. They are far worse than criminals because in their endeavor to serve themselves they place around all their acts an aura of virtue, of duty, of service to the country. By reason of this their vicious acts are not detected by the average citizen, which permits them to do vastly more harm than the most vicious criminals in our midst, who, because unable to clothe themselves in a mask of virtue, are condemned by the public. Our politicians are deserving of greater condemnation than the criminals. As a matter of fact many of them owe their election to conciliating the votes of criminal elements. They take good care in large cities not to prosecute criminals too vigorously, not to inquire too closely into the antecedents of their ward heelers and supporters. By obtaining the support of criminals and near-criminals, they are elected to office and assume to control the government in the interest of honest citizens.

A large element in crime is pure selfishness. The individual will do whatever he wishes for his own interest with little regard for others except when deterred by fear of consequences. The real criminals are those who take more than they give. If all gave as much or more than they received, there would be no crime. This is a question for each person to ask himself and his duty to accomplish.

Much crime is promoted by the indulgence extended criminals through many well-meaning people who feel that society is more at fault than the criminal. By reforming social ills, having a good environment, those who resort to criminal acts will have forfeited their right to special consideration.

An intelligent person has a more natural tendency toward good character than the less intelligent. It has been observed among children that lying, cheating, and stealing is more common by the less intelligent under the same environmental conditions. This, of course, is a tendency only, because we have many stupid people of fine character and many intelligent ones of poor character. But the more intelligent a person is, the more readily he can be taught to see the need for considering the rights of others and for contributing toward an ascendent environment. This is particularly true if the bad conduct is certain to result to the disadvantage of the offenders.

Our newspapers have a bad influence on the stimulation of

crime by giving much publicity to sensational crime news. We should realize that many of our citizens are morons and near-morons, and that the effect of having sensational crime items constantly placed before them will encourage some in similar endeavors. Many weak-minded people commit crimes just for the sake of the publicity they will receive. They want to see their names in the paper, be much talked about, have people exclaim over their cruelty and viciousness. They glory in this sort of thing and are stimulated to commit crime by receiving this great amount of publicity. This should not be permitted. We should not permit newspapers to stimulate the feebleminded to criminal acts harming decent people.

Violent acts may be induced by thought. Constant thought on rape or murder may gradually result in the development of an uncontrollable desire to commit either, with the result that when an opportunity is afforded, the act is committed. Thus we must teach all to have healthful thoughts, not think about committing violent acts. When crime is induced by thought it more commonly occurs in people of poor mentality, primitive, willing to give way to the feelings of the moment.

We often see crimes committed by degenerates, usually with a sex connection, in waves. The reason for this is simple. When a crime of this nature is committed it receives great publicity. This publicity causes other abnormal people with similar tendencies to think about committing such offenses. This concentration of thought on the desire makes the urge greater, with the result that they commit the offense.

An example of thought leading to crime is afforded by the Leopold case, in which a young man of good family, obsessed by thinking of committing a perfect crime, murdered a young boy in cold blood. Other factors contributed such as Bruto, lack of Primo, Co, and sensitivity, but thought of evil was a contributing factor and decisive in this case to the commission of the deed.

Movies may be an agency for implanting in a child's mind, by the power of suggestion in an attractive form, evil ideas leading to crime and vicious acts. Producers should consider the effect upon the public and present pictures in a truthful light. They should carefully avoid putting a halo around evil that would lead childish minds in that direction. Wholesome home influences and education stressing beauty, truth, and right living will assist in preventing healthy-minded children from being influenced by vicious suggestions.

In general there are two classes of criminals: those born with criminal tendencies, and those born without the inherent tendencies but who are the victims of a vicious environment. The two classes merge into each other. The creation of criminals as a result of bad environmental influences is within easy power of correction by sensible action. Many who inherit criminal tendencies may, if brought up in an environment not conducive to crime, be developed into desirable citizens.

Visualize a prisoner in a guard house, passing bread crumbs out from between the bars to a bird, speaking soothingly, kindly, to the bird, encouraging it to seek and eat the bread crumbs. Just another victim of a poor environment. Unquestionably there is good in him. Society has failed to teach him how to use his mind to control his conduct and to develop himself into a good citizen.

The individual can be developed toward either crime or virtue. Development toward crime is less easy than that toward virtue, for man is basically good and is only turned toward evil by misapplication of effort, by poor environment, and by lack of understanding of what constitutes good conduct. There is a direct relationship between Co and savagery. Co is a development raising man from savagery to a higher being. The criminal who lacks Co is a reversion to the primitive.

Crime is due in great measure to arrested development from Bruto to human, or undue prominence given Bruto traits, strengthening them and preventing the development of the more human traits. Bruto indicates the survival in the human being of instincts or desires more appropriate to the jungle than to civilization; a person whose ethics are those of the jungle, a reversion to prehistoric ancestors; a person whose development has not outgrown his jungle ancestry.

The degree of advance of a human being is shown by his ability to control his own actions by means of his conscious mind. A person dominated or controlled by Bruto instincts is an animal having the physical conformation of a human being but lacking other human attributes. Lack of a sense of responsibility in the individual shows the retention of Bruto or Infanta in the make-up.

The criminal lacks Extro, sense of moral values, and cannot put himself in the place of his victim and feel the pain and injustice of his acts; he lacks the quality of pity. Extreme sensitivity is a development of the higher type human being. Callousness, or lack of sensitivity, shows defective functioning of the glands, a lack of development, and points toward the primitive. Many criminals are so because utterly heartless, unable to visualize the sufferings of others and caring less.

Physical disease may tend to stimulate crime by exciting acts of viciousness. Physical deterioration, malfunctioning of glands, and so forth, may withhold from the brain the essential fuel required for the advanced human being. This results in his reversion to the primitive, seeking to satisfy his wants by petty acts of theft or similar offenses, without regard for others.

Crime and abnormal behavior of any kind bear a distinct relation to the primitive and infantile. The more one observes such conduct, the more striking the relation becomes. It is not at all unusual for the physical development of the criminal's body to be retarded in certain respects; certain organs have failed to mature fully. In many criminals and those guilty of abnormal behavior there is a similar retarding of development of their mental processes. The brain has not developed as it should. The feeling of sensitivity is not what it should be. The victim was originally not very well endowed mentally and was not subjected to proper educational and environmental influences to overcome this deficiency. Very often he is thrown in with bad associates and subjected to bad influences. A temptation is indulged which, giving pleasure, is repeated and eventually built into his behavior pattern. One can detect in some cases the direct opposite influences of those producing genius. The development of genius requires inherent gifts and consistent activity to develop them. He is led to this by natural liking and by fortunate circumstances. The criminal and abnormal person is led in the opposite direction by inclination and circumstances.

Bruto is a remnant of savage animal traits. We have advanced from savagery through evolution. There is a trend toward further advancement and there is also an atavistic tendency, a failure to become civilized, a regression to the primitive tendencies of the past. Bruto exhibits itself in individuals in opposition to Co, to Ascendency, and to intelligent thought. It represents a general inclination to a mere brutal existence, satisfying the self and immediate desires and failing to develop the highest moral character.

Bruto tendencies may be accentuated by brutal treatment. In the Middle Ages in the most backward countries in Europe, the brutal treatment which some peasants received retarded their fuller development into human beings and caused the retention of the more brutal animal traits, accentuating these to the exclusion of more desirable characteristics.

The more cruel and primitive the environment, the more the tendency to Bruto exists. Contrarywise, an ascendent environment tends directly to lessen the development of Bruto. The environment either tends to develop the individual away from the savage instincts of the past or toward regression. It may encourage the retention of the more brutal feelings in man at the expense of finer ones or it may advance the latter.

Crime, stealing, and cheating in an adult may be considered as being the result of the persistence of Infanto and Bruto, evidenced by a craving to satisfy his desire without thought of others. This is because he reverts more to animal instincts, has atavistic tendencies, and is little touched by the tender sympathetic feelings of advanced human beings. Such conduct is confirmed by Adapto, with the result that we have a criminal produced by natural causes to start with, further confirmed by an environment conducive to their development.

XIX

PROTECTION OF THE PUBLIC

THE ILLS OF MANKIND ARE SO DEEP, SO LONG STANDING AND strongly entrenched as to prevent correction without the use of brute force. One must be careful in applying force not to lose the support of the worthy element who wish good to prevail but are too sentimental to permit using force to down evil, believing that good can and will prevail without force and that force will harm good. There is a germ of truth in this, but one must be practical and face conditions as they exist. Force is a double edged weapon that cuts either way. Christ's enemies, who caused him to be crucified, made him immortal. Had they merely ignored Him, He might have lapsed into oblivion.

If we employ force as ruthlessly in advancing man's welfare as it has been employed in the past for religion, nationality, rulers, and retarding advance, real good could be accomplished. Force is not the best method, but it is one of the strongest and most effective, and will succeed where other methods will fail. It gives immediate results. Care must be used in its exercise, for it may bring about or encourage evils greater than those it is used to cure. The mildest methods that will be effective should be employed; the more forceful ones used only when required. Force should be used in somewhat the same way as surgery on the human being; let nature effect its own cure, but when surgery is necessary, use it to assist nature.

The use of force in the past has discredited it. It has been used in repressing intelligence, freedom, and inquiring minds, and it has caused great harm. Education to improve moral character is advocated instead of force. The problem is too great for education alone; force should be associated with it but intelligently controlled, with full understanding of the bad results of its harmful use. The ills of man are too numerous, too universal, too vicious, too deep-seated in our social order, to permit of cure without the use of force. In effecting these cures, force should be used as little as possible, for its use has serious drawbacks. When used, it should be assembled in such overpowering manner as to make resistance useless, and thus render its actual employment unnecessary. Make it a moral force that will not be opposed by any except the vicious who must be controlled in any case. Savages, the primitive, the brutal, can be more readily controlled by force than any other means. In many cases force is the only method that will control them. They are incapable of fine moral distinction. The man who cut off the head of Archimedes annihilated a splendid intellect which was helpless against brute force.

Force is the means by which man conquered beasts. It, combined with intelligence, is what produced civilization. It is what restrains the vicious today. It is what preserves our national freedom. Force can be misapplied and used for bad ends. It has been so used in the past by dictators, governments, rulers, having their own opinions, their own standards of morals and conduct and determined to impress them upon their citizens. They used force, repression, to accomplish this. This is an unintelligent use of force. It is abusing it. Because it has been thus abused is no reason why it should not be employed in advancing man's Ascendency. We must recognize the fact that we have many individuals whose intelligence and conduct is more that of the jungle than civilized life and that many of these people can only be controlled by force. They are beyond appeals to reason and character.

A puny pup displays the bravery of cowardice when he growls at a St. Bernard dog because he knows the latter will not hurt him. We often see this same bravery of cowardice exhibited in human beings. A weak person, knowing that his feebleness will prevent retaliation, abuses the generous tolerance of the more powerful. We see this feeling exhibited by pickets during strikes, jeering the police because the latter are unwilling to hurt them. We see it exhibited in a somewhat different form by some prominent speakers in our own country who denounce our preparation for war, our army, and our navy, yet do not hesitate to denounce foreign rulers abroad. They do not give much thought to this contradiction. They are protected from harm by those they are attacking, by the very army and navy which they consider useless. We see this exhibited by any number of agitators who take advantage of our laws granting free speech to everyone, and attack others most viciously, knowing that they themselves will not be punished for such abuse. This bravery of cowardice evaporates very rapidly when prompt and effective methods of retaliation are employed. Tolerance of abuse can be carried too far when it makes cowardice appear to be bravery.

Fear and force are powerful agents in controlling men, but not the best. They are more in the nature of driving, whereas the best method is to inspire a desire to advance of one's own volition in the right direction. But for those who will not voluntarily advance toward what is right, fear is an efficient means of control. The mere fact that sufficient force exists is enough to intimidate them without its actual application. Aside from the physical force there is moral force, which is very strong. No person is willing to lose the good opinion of others. Fear of losing the respect of those you like is a real incentive to good conduct.

Intolerance and force can be used as potent weapons in advancing man's welfare. Their use in the past has mainly been in ways opposed to human welfare and against the real truth. Now let us harness them in the direction of truth and in ways to advance human welfare.

Intolerance can well be a great good if it be properly used. Tolerance of evil conduct encourages it; tolerance of vicious, selfish minorities encourages them in their vicious work. We should not tolerate having theorists and other impractical people oppose measures which would accomplish real good to such an extent as to defeat the desired measures. Intolerance in the past has been mainly employed by the privileged, ignorant, and prejudiced to restrain the intelligent. Let us now reverse this process. Let the intelligent use it to repress the ignorant, the vicious, and those causing misery in the world.

Crime is a great burden upon the community from the standpoint of economics. We maintain hundreds of thousands of criminals in jails and penitentiaries, our police forces are large, and many measures are taken to restrain criminals that restrict the freedom of honest citizens.

Criminals should be removed from contact with decent citizens so as not to contaminate others. When we attempt to repress them and permit them to circulate, their feelings are hurt and they are a bad influence on those with whom they come in contact. They endeavor to justify their conduct and induce others to follow their example.

It is unfair to the public to waste money in attempting to reform criminals. Justice to the public requires that the criminal be given a reasonable amount of assistance to seek the right path by his own efforts, and that this be done without undue cost or burden to decent citizens. We must not permit our feelings to penalize the deserving for the benefit of the undeserving. The effort and expense of reforming criminals could be better used in removing them entirely from the younger generation, preventing them from producing another crop of criminals by example and association. In those cases where the tendencies toward crime are the result of the perpetuation of primitive atavistic traits or tendencies in the individual, reform is impossible.

We should give less consideration to the criminal and more to the decent self-respecting citizen who does his work, minds his own business, brings up his family, and maintains the nation. He and his family should receive full protection from all evil-doers, whether they be the victims of circumstances or not. We can sympathize with those who were brought up under bad environmental conditions, but we should sympathize still more with those who are deserving citizens.

The rights of the deserving law-abiding citizen should take precedence over those of criminals. Our present law protects the guilty and fails to protect the law-abiding. Under this inefficient criminal code we have the highest crime rate of any civilized nation. It is very expensive, it lowers the environmental standards, and promotes crime by its very efforts to protect the innocent. What was originally intended to protect the innocent has been utilized by the guilty in protecting themselves, rendering it almost impossible to secure a conviction.

Our present code places the burden of proof upon the government. This is unfair to the public. The accused should be required to show his innocence, protect himself, show why he is a desirable character. This would not penalize the deserving honest upright citizen who has lived a good life, but it would render it possible to judge an undesirable person using his entire life as a means of reaching a decision. He should really be the first witness examined in his own case and required to answer fully all questions asked of him, thus giving full opportunity to confirm his truthfulness or discover falseness.

An innocent man should be only too willing to testify fully as to the facts in his case. The guilty man, by remaining silent, requires the state to produce all evidence to convict him of the crime. In many cases under our present code it is utterly impossible to produce the evidence required even though such a man has a vile record.

Our present day legal code has developed from the past, and, we must remember, a rather ignorant past. We should utilize the principles underlying human nature and build a new code upon them that will actually promote good behavior.

In abolishing crime we must use the mildest measures in order to insure the support of the tender-hearted who dislike hurting or seeing others hurt. If anyone must be hurt, let it be those who most deserve it, not those who least deserve it.

Drivers who fail to consider others and cause accidents by reckless driving of automobiles are but little removed from criminals. They lack Primo, Co, and Extro. They are not desirable citizens and should be effectively curbed. The extreme toleration we grant those who cause automobile accidents results in extreme carelessness on the part of many.

Every driver at fault in an accident should be forever barred from driving. Adequate records should be kept of every traffic offense; many offenses will show that the individual is clearly unfit to drive, either physically or mentally. It is unfair to endanger others by permitting irresponsible or unfit drivers to do so.

We should prohibit driving by those whose reactions are inadequate to the task of safe driving. In an ascendent environment this would not be considered a disgrace or a humiliation to which one should take exception. It would merely be a recognition of the fact that we are all gifted in different ways. We should not attempt to do what our gifts do not enable us to do well when it may injure others.

Lynching is harshly condemned by practically everyone. It is a bad thing. Nevertheless it has some justification. It is produced by ineffective legal machinery. During the settlement of the California gold fields, the law broke down, and the citizens had to organize vigilance committees and administer summary justice to the vast number of criminals who were terrorizing the community. We have considerable lynching in southern states today, largely of negroes who have attacked white women. This lynching is contributed to greatly by the ineffectiveness and delays of the law in summarily disposing of guilty offenders. If the law were efficient, if it functioned quickly, properly, and terminated the affair in a few days, there would be far less lynching. Thus the greatest single thing we can do to reduce or eliminate lynching is to establish a most effective legal system that will deprive the lynchers of any justification for taking the law into their own hands.

Based upon a scientific analysis of the laws governing human nature, our present methods of preventing crime violate these principles in many ways and directly contribute toward poor conduct. This is mainly because we endeavor to define what may not be done by statutes, with the result that the selfish individual often devotes much effort toward discovering means of getting around the statute when his own interests will be served thereby. A scientifically correct legal code, instead of doing this, would encourage the individual to look within himself for evidences of bad conduct and then to endeavor to correct them by his own efforts. When our criminal code encourages this and tends to penalize deviations from it, it will be employing the scientific truths governing human nature.

We put a premium on lying by requiring the state to prove the guilt of the accused. We should not have a criminal code that encourages lying, but should develop all possible means to discourage it. Lying itself should be considered a most serious offense, even though it be indulged in to save oneself. Civilized communities demand trust in others; trust demands that we believe what others tell us, and lying is a direct opponent of this. It is descendent action, and all descendent action should be discouraged in an adhuman society.

We permit many crimes that are far more serious than others which are prohibited. The transmission of venereal disease; selling inferior articles or harmful foods or medicines for profit; the action of politicians and agitators in fomenting class hatred and making misstatements, thus contributing to lower moral standards—all are serious offenses yet not punishable by law. If we permit these serious offenses to go unpunished, we have a legal system that is unworthy. We must develop a legal code that will punish moral crime, elevate public opinion and the standards of the citizens, so they will not tolerate misconduct of a harmful nature on the part of anyone.

Our criminal law has been developed as the result of many abuses of the past in order to protect the rights of the innocent. It has gone so far in this direction as to afford the guilty too many opportunities to escape punishment. It does not adequately protect the community. Our criminal code is so extensive, so involved, as to require specialists to interpret it. It has gone to extremes in defining crime in its rules of procedure and of evidence, making it more important to comply with all legal requirements than to give justice or protect the community.

In defining criminal offenses our present-day law is too arbitrary, too rigid, too narrow. The same crime may be committed at different times and be far more severe in one case than the other, yet our law does not recognize the differences, the conditions under which the offense was committed, or the past record of the individual. A man of fine character may be led to do things that are punishable under our present-day system and have ample justification for doing so. The law fails to recognize this. We are punishing people for violating statutes, instead of encouraging good conduct.

For illustration, the crime of murder and its close associate, manslaughter, has many legal classifications. A sensible legal code would consider the character, previous record of the offender, the victim, and the conditions under which the offense was committed. It should be a far less serious crime for a high type person to kill an undesirable one than it would be for an undesirable citizen to kill a desirable one. Yet our legal code punishes one offender as severely as the other, regardless of his individual worth. This is bound to result when we attempt to classify human conduct and punish by statute. Each individual offense should receive due consideration in an effort to do justice to those concerned and to the public. Murder is a terrible crime and should be discouraged. He who resorts to violence as a means of revenge is harming his own character, even though he has much justification. A good legal code would render it unnecessary for an individual to resort to violence in order to obtain justice.

The general object of our present-day criminal law is to deter crime by fear of punishment. This is not a very high conception of law. It is an inheritance from the past and has been developed by man in an endeavor to insure good behavior by those means he considered most effective. A higher conception of criminal law would be to prevent crime entirely and to promote good behavior.

No such system of crime prevention has been adopted by any nation. The existing criminal law has been much criticized but no practical methods of improvement have been suggested that would modify the principle of preventing crime by fear of punishment.

Each person who commits a harmful act sets a bad example and is contributing to crime, even though he may have committed no legal offense. Here is where our present legal code is at fault. We have developed the attitude that all things that are not prohibited by law are permissible, and as a result more harm is done by harmful legal acts than by illegal ones. We must modify our legal code to recognize this fact; try to prevent all acts that harm others. Instead of classifying crimes as we now do we should seek to evaluate the final effects of the offense upon the individual himself and upon others. If such acts are harmful they should be discouraged even though not expressly prohibited by statutes. The best method to insure this is to keep an active record of each individual throughout his life. Let him know that he is constantly on trial to determine whether he is an asset to society. When he ceases to be an asset to society, he should be removed from it. This will permit all acts of whatever nature to be effectively judged for or against the individual.

Human nature being what it is, fear will ever be an important factor in controlling the conduct of man. The more vicious, infantile, or brutal a human being may be, the more he is influenced by fear and the greater the need for insuring his good conduct by fear of punishment. This is a truth which we must not permit sentimental considerations to blind us to. For those who are lacking in understanding, inflamed with passion, or controlled by primitive instincts, fear is the most effective means of control. The mere fact that ample physical force exists and will be unhesitatingly applied to repress misconduct will deter the most vicious. This is not the best way to control people, but we must remember that we have many individuals having the appearance of human beings but the desires of the jungle, and in controlling them jungle methods will be most effective.

The use of punishment as a deterrent for crime is effective but it is not the best method. It is repressive. To obtain good character we should encourage positive means of expression, encourage the individual to be good voluntarily. When force, or threat of force, or punishment is used to require individuals to be good, they are likely to seek means to get around the statutes or laws that define just how far they may go; whereas if we encourage them to express themselves in constructive ways, they have no incentive to do so. They should seek within themselves, find means for developing the best in them in order that they themselves may profit by it.

Severe punishments do not deter crime. Rather they promote it by rendering it less possible to obtain a conviction. Tender-hearted citizens dislike voting a death penalty upon another person. As the result, it is imposed so infrequently as to cease being a deterrent to crime.

Life imprisonment, if carried out, is a most brutal form of punishment. Euthanasia is far more merciful. When you imprison a man for life you destroy the mind, the high moral qualities of a man, make him a beast, whereas painless death quietly returns him to the place from whence he came.

The use of death as a deterrent for crime, especially when revenge is sought, hardens and coarsens people and will be opposed by the tender-hearted to such an extent as to defeat the object desired. Great understanding would consider death without cruelty or suffering the greater mercy, but until public understanding is brought to see this, the present feeling must be considered. Death as a penalty should be administered in a painless manner. Hanging, electrocuting, and brutal methods should be abolished. Criminals who desire painless euthanasia should be accorded that privilege.

The criminal is generally a person showing infantile or

Bruto traits. He has failed to develop consideration for others. This may be assisted by poor environment or generally retarded mentality. It does not necessarily have anything to do with physical disease, although disease may contribute to it. There is a great relation between mental disorder and poor health. Anything that tends to break down the physical structure of the individual tends to break down the mind also. In abolishing crime and mental disorder, we should attack disease and ill health as well.

In eliminating crime and evil-doers from our midst, we cannot be guided by such an unsound statement as, "Judge not lest ye be judged." It is true that we all have undesirable tendencies in our make-up. It is also true that by effort we can overcome them or turn them into desirable channels. This being so, those who control their own undesirable tendencies should take steps to control those who do not. This requires that the latter be judged. This judging should take in not one offense alone, but their entire life.

If we employ the principles of Ascendent Psychology, we can very readily classify criminals as distinct from decent citizens. We will find that they uniformly lack Co and Primo and are deficient in understanding the rights of others. Having thus classified these undesirables, it is relatively simple to provide for their segregation and elimination. Full development of Co is an advance in man's evolution. Those individuals not possessing it are regressive and possess undesirable traits in their make-up that justify their segregation from desirable citizens and the taking of steps that prevent the reproduction of these characteristics in offspring.

Placing all the Philistines in large colonies would make it possible for the physically able to care for the disabled. Those possessing mental capacity could assist those lacking it. These large Philistine colonies would be aggregations of individuals unable to perform adequately their duties to society. Being placed together in colonies, their various abilities could assist one another. These colonies could become great laboratories for advancing knowledge of human behavior. They would be conducive to bringing out the best in criminals by having them assist others. They offer the soundest solution to many social problems at a minimum of cost.

Thoughts

To reduce crime to a minimum, it is necessary that we have laws that not only will prevent criminal acts, but will actually promote good behavior. To do this will require a form of government superior to any the world has yet seen, and a much higher standard of ethics among its citizens.

More wrong is done in this country today in ways not expressly prohibited by written law than in ways that are so prohibited.

We should remove repression from our law and endeavor to give the individual expression in a form beneficial to himself and others.

In our efforts to control the vicious we restrict the virtuous. We should give the virtuous the utmost freedom and eliminate the vicious entirely.

Those guilty of descendent conduct should be removed from possibility of contaminating others. If this be done, it will be unnecessary to regulate the good by statutes hampering their ability to enjoy life as they wish.

A rotten potato will infect a whole basket in time if left alone under favorable conditions. Why should we let a rotten human infect wholesome ones, even in a small degree?

If we segregate, eliminate, and prevent propagation of those individuals dominated by Bruto instincts, we will be using nature's laws in eliminating Bruto from man.

Be merciful, but remember that civilization itself is based upon force, and force alone can restrain the vicious. Mercy can go so far as to become a weakness that harms more than it benefits, for the vicious will take advantage of it.

A tender-hearted person suffers more in administering punishment than do those who receive it. Therefore all should be careful to avoid incurring the need for punishment.

The doctrine of pacifism or passive resistance is a denial of the very force used by man to insure survival, subdue savagery, and achieve a measure of civilization. Wise use of force is essential to further perfect this civilization.

Would you stand idly by and permit a brute to violate innocent children? No. You would kill him, even though realizing that he was a victim of a vicious environment. Those who are good must be protected against the bad at any cost. Reform the bad if you can, but above all do not permit them to harm the good, regardless of the force required.

Moral force is a power among the moral, physical force among the vicious. In a conflict between the two, moral force will be worsted unless it be supported by physical force.

Physical force is not the best to use, unless used in such way, with such overpowering strength behind it, that resistance is useless and it becomes a moral force.

Fight for the right, give life, all that you possess, that right may rule in the affairs of man. Let not a high ideal of refusing to hurt others prevent the virtuous from fighting for virtue. The unvirtuous have no such scruples and will overcome the virtuous if not opposed by the same weapons with which they attack. Virtuous people are in general of two classes, those of passive virtue who, while virtuous themselves, do not wish to harm the unvirtuous but would prefer to reform them; and the positive, those who will fight the unrighteous. Positive action is required. Nothing less than force will control the unvirtuous.

XX

OFFICIAL DOSSIERS

AN INDIVIDUAL RECORD OF EACH PERSON SHOULD BE KEPT BY
the government from the time of birth, extending throughout life as a means of improving the citizenship of the nation
and reducing crime. Such records would also be available for
use in the study of eugenics and euthenics. The record should
be started at the time the child is born, the attending physician making necessary entries on a prescribed form regarding
parentage and any other information that would be of value
in the future.

Thereafter all persons having anything to do with the life
of the individual would submit suitable reports to the office
of individual records. The family doctor, for instance, would
make reports of childhood sicknesses, ailments of any kind
that would be worth entering. The school teachers would have
regular forms to submit periodically to file with the records,
giving essential data. When the child attained maturity and
went to work, the employer could be called upon to submit
essential information periodically.

Any conduct of an unethical nature would be entered
against the individual record, as also any conduct considered
worthy of special mention. We would thus have during the
life of each individual a complete record of him. Men who
were expert in consulting these records could readily determine the individual's worth to society. Means should be afforded for having experts consult individual records and
submit reports to those entitled to the information. Reports

could be submitted by several different experts to increase accuracy. This should be regulated to prevent abuse which can readily be done.

An office for maintaining individual records should be established in each of our smaller units of local government with specially trained personnel in charge. Standard forms could be established for all entries in order to insure easy filing. Those who make entries upon the life records should be extremely conscientious. All should realize the importance of this as contributing not only to the welfare of the present but also the distant future.

By using individual records for each individual from the time of birth, it should be possible to determine whether he is a desirable person. If undesirable, he should be segregated with other undesirables away from the desirable people. This would result in time in our entire citizenship consisting entirely of desirables, would result in the abolition of much mental disorder, crime and poverty and would release the desirable citizens from the burden of caring for the undesirable. It is toward this we should aim. Our present reform measures are penalizing and handicapping the desirable citizens.

Once individual records for each person were established and all misconduct entered therein, they would become a great force for good behavior. No person would willingly wish to have a bad record, and would take care to conduct himself well. In addition to this, it would bring the matter forcibly to his attention, impress upon him his duty to set a good example to others and to avoid being thoughtless.

When a divorce is granted the divorce courts granting it should determine the causes. If one of the couple shows evidences of bad character, a complete report of the circumstances should be entered upon his official dossier. This would assist in preventing the abuse of marriage and divorce.

These records would be of great benefit to insure honesty in business enterprises. People would be less willing to permit debts to remain unpaid or to misconduct themselves in any way, because of the reflection on their records.

With the adoption of life records, we should adopt an entirely new criminal code in which, instead of trying a person for one offense, he should in effect be on trial throughout his entire life. His previous record should count in determining whether or not he should be segregated. Thus, instead of having to obtain evidence for one single crime as we now do, giving the criminal the benefit of all doubts, we would have a complete record of his entire life, and it would be very easy for any board of skilled men to determine whether or not he was a desirable citizen. When a person is brought before this board, he should have the right to call witnesses and obtain statements from them which would be checked by agents of the board. These witnesses would be careful not to violate the truth, because in so doing they themselves would become subject to adverse entries upon their own records. If these life records are established and well administered they offer a great means for eliminating crime and raising the standard of behavior to a higher level than has yet prevailed in any community.

We should endeavor to find some means of marking children upon birth so they can be forever identified. If this is not practical, each person should be required to have on his person at all times a suitable means of identification in order that he could be readily identified. Each person should be considered a member of the nation's police force and have the right to demand the name and address of any other person for good reasons. Much misconduct is condoned and many individuals misbehave because they can get away with it. If, instead of relying on our inadequate police force to prevent this, each good citizen considered himself to be charged with the preservation of law and order and the improvement of the environment, and made it his business to report misconduct in this way, the misconduct itself would cease. Securing the co-operation of all desirable citizens, in an earnest endeavor to prevent misconduct and insure good conduct, would make it impossible for anyone to misbehave and escape detection.

It is very difficult today to secure convictions for crime for the reason that the evidence is not forthcoming. By the use of life records, it should be readily possible to obtain vast quantities of evidence to determine whether a person is undesirable.

Most criminals obtain favorable evidence from their friends, who themselves are criminals or depend upon crime for a living. These witnesses often discredit reliable witnesses under our present system. All witnesses brought before a board to determine desirability of a citizen would themselves be subject to examination of their individual records and it could be readily determined whether their testimony should be considered. In the eradication of crime, racketeering, and gangsters generally, we are failing to make use of one of the greatest agencies available, the very environment and friends of the criminal. If he lives in a low environment surrounded by criminals and they attempt to protect him, the life records would show this and all could be segregated as being undesirable. By this means the vast criminal localities could be abolished entirely, removing their bad environmental influence upon the young and diminishing crime greatly.

The use of life records sensibly administered, with a wise means of crime prevention, will accomplish marvelous results. No such enlightened measure has ever been attempted by any nation. It should be incumbent upon us to put it into operation and demonstrate to the world that not only can crime be controlled, but that a system can be established that will of itself promote good behavior.

If for any reason one has a grievance against another person for poor professional services, abuse, cruelty, or anything of the kind, he should have the right to make a complete report on the proper form to be entered on the life record of the offender. This would prevent many people from abusing others because they know it would show up on their life record.

Any person who observes another misconduct himself should submit a report to the office of individual records giving the circumstances therein. He should make this report in duplicate, one copy to be filed with his own record, and one with the record of the person guilty of the offense. When an adverse record is charged against any individual, it will then be possible to consult the record of the individual making this adverse report to determine whether his own character justifies belief.

Giving the right to each citizen to make reports of others would not result in harming those against whom the report was made, because it would be possible to check back upon the record of the person making this report. If it developed that he made many unjust reports or was an irresponsible person, he himself could be classified as being undesirable.

To give each citizen the task of reporting his neighbor's misconduct is unusual, but with the development of a high-type citizenry it could be taken as a matter of course. In actual practice it would rarely be employed. People will not behave badly when to do so would harm themselves more.

Most citizens today dislike making complaints against others, for the reason that they dislike causing trouble. They are sometimes subjected to so much annoyance through our antiquated legal system that they prefer to suffer in silence. We should educate our citizens to a realization of the need for conscientious effort on the part of all to curb bad conduct. We have many people who resort to unethical practices and remain unpunished because no one takes the trouble to prosecute them. If each person having knowledge of unethical practices makes a report of them, so many reports would be entered upon the offender's record as to condemn him and warrant his segregation. This fact alone will prevent bad conduct on the part of those so tempted. In carrying out this system, we must reward those who are conscientious enough to make reports of bad conduct by seeing that they are caused no annoyance because of their efforts.

Official dossiers would be evidence of scientific intelligent co-operation. The essence of successful human institutions is co-operation. This co-operation must be by the intelligent deserving citizen. Scientific co-operation is profitable not only from the standpoint of one's own character but in a material way as well. When we ourselves co-operate, we promote a good example. When all members of a society co-operate in essentials toward improving their society, they solve social problems. When we are assured that our neighbors will behave with consideration and with virtue we have more respect for them. If the virtuous are not penalized by the conduct of the unvirtuous or the need for supporting them, their own problems are much easier solved. Let us have a society constituted entirely of virtuous citizens co-operating with each other in the highest sense. Let us not permit ourselves to be penalized by the unvirtuous either to the extent of supporting them or having our own freedom restricted because they abuse theirs.

In addition to the official dossiers maintained in the citizen's immediate place of residence, a central office of record should be maintained for the entire country. This could include all foreigners while they were in the country. Its primary object would be to afford a ready means of identification of criminals. Having complete fingerprints and other life records of criminals in the central office for the entire country would facilitate their identification and conviction.

The keeping of official dossiers of each person will be a cause of some expense to the government. It is possible that each person might be called upon to keep his own official dossier. This would be good instruction in citizenship, would attract his attention to himself and the need for behaving well. It might be necessary to impose penalties for failure to keep complete personal records. The existence of high standards of citizenship would make it a personal obligation.

It is possible that they might be kept by the employment of the honor system alone. We are so accustomed to existing low standards of citizenship and conduct that it is difficult to visualize just what standards the most enlightened human institutions would contain. We do know that the most wholesome civic institutions will rest upon citizens of a high sense of duty and conduct. It is by no means impossible that, instead of requiring the government to keep an official dossier for each citizen, each one would do it for himself, not only as a duty but also with real pride in doing so.

The fact that we had instituted a system of individual dossiers for each individual would be evidence of a scientific approach to the solution of human problems. These life records would be so closely associated with all conduct of the individual as to stimulate greater thought and effort to understand him. They would have a great influence upon economic conditions, upon crime, upon sex, marriage, and all social activities, whether individual or collective. They would be positive evidence of the existence of master science itself.

We should not attempt to accomplish too much by the use of life records at first or employ master science so extensively as to discredit it. We must develop master science to a point where it will be able to solve human problems. This will be a constant never-ending perfection of knowledge. The life records themselves would give great information contributing toward this perfection.

When we have good records of each individual and his relatives extending over many generations, we have definite information of great value. The development of the life records themselves will require time. What we today may regard as of great importance may, with greater advance in knowledge, become relatively unimportant. We should, however, endeavor to make them complete in essentials but not to the degree of becoming overburdened with detail.

XXI

CONTROL OF CRIME

BY FAR THE GREATER PART OF PRESENT-DAY CRIME IS OF AN economic nature. Many authorities on crime stress unsatisfactory economic conditions as being the greatest factor in producing crime and criminals. This is true to some extent. However, the greatest single factor in the production of crime today is the fact that we stress economic reform and neglect moral reform. There are many people living in slums, in poor conditions, suffering deprivation. They have constantly before them examples of the wealthy, of the injustices of modern life and they hear much denunciation of capital, of wealthy people, and of conditions generally. They, however, do not hear much about their duty of living a good life and setting a good example. They are not told that if each individual person in the country considered others and performed his duties well, economic injustice would cease. Thus our efforts to bring about economic reform are attracting undue attention to economic evils and neglecting the true point of reform, the individual himself. The development of high standards of moral character will greatly lessen economic injustices.

In eradicating crime, we should harness the laws of nature in promoting the survival of the fitter by establishing an environment that rewards virtue and is not conducive to the survival of the vicious.

In the crime-ridden districts of our large cities we have young children reared to a life of crime. The environment is sometimes so evil that they have little choice except a life of crime. A sensible government, a sensible society, would not permit such conditions to exist.

To abolish crime, remove the bad environmental influences that produce it. Trace it to its source, eradicate it, and at the same time elevate the environment.

A high standard of public opinion that condemns criminal acts will be the greatest deterrent to crime. It is our tolerance of wrongdoing, our lack of strong public opinion that encourages crime to prevail so widely. We must teach our citizens to realize that by tolerating misconduct they are harming both the criminal and themselves. They encourage the criminal to continue his life of crime, they encourage others to follow his example, and generally lower the standard of conduct, permitting it to fall more to the level of a criminal than to raise all to the standards of the best people in the land.

Police have great difficulty in obtaining evidence. Most people dislike causing trouble for others. They dislike the embarrassment of being faced by those whom they accuse of crime. If they do testify in court, they are frequently abused and not treated with proper consideration. We should bring about on the part of the citizens a better conception of their duties as citizens and encourage them to report all misbehavior that comes to their attention. We should further see that they are rewarded and not penalized for this effort. If all good citizens will co-operate with an efficient police force and system of crime prevention, crime can be almost entirely eradicated.

The most effective means to prevent crime and insure good behavior is to concentrate on a drive for Ascendency, causing all individuals to strive for it. We must teach them to realize that every time they commit a bad act or do wrong, that they themselves are being punished because such action is impressed upon their behavior patterns, making them more vicious. Who will admit being a vicious person? No one. The most vicious criminals try to justify their acts. If we can cause them to be honest with themselves, cease to explain away their misconduct but face and correct it, we will be attacking evil at its source.

Gangsters frequently accept death rather than talk. This is largely because in their eyes being an informer is the lowest thing one can do. If we could cause them to look upon acts against society in the same light, this desire for the approbation of others would be used for beneficial instead of harmful purposes; would tend to eliminate crime rather than to produce and perpetuate it.

Under a perfect system, criminals would find crime would not pay and would thus become decent citizens. Certainty of detection and segregation would be a great deterrent. No person with reasonable intelligence would attempt to follow a life of crime if it was unprofitable. Here is the true solution to the problem of crime: not severe sentences or an elaborate legal code, but simply the application of scientific truths to insure good behavior.

Crime may be both inherited and acquired. If inherited, examination of the unfortunate by able, practical men well versed in the principles of human nature would indicate such to be the case; if acquired, the environment should be corrected.

Adapto can assist in adapting the individual to a life of crime as well as to a life of virtue. It therefore becomes the duty of society to see that an environment conducive to crime is not permitted; on the contrary, that the environment be conducive to virtue.

We have crime committed by many people who would have been normal citizens had they not been subjected to the influence of a bad environment. Therefore one of the best ways to combat crime is to strive for an ascendent environment that will not tolerate influences within it contributing toward crime. At the same time we must recognize the fact that many individuals have regressive tendencies, are practically born to be criminals and lack the ability to develop Co and Primo. To improve the environment and maintain it at a high level, we must segregate these undesirable individuals from their contaminating influence upon others. If we try to create the best environment possible and strive to eliminate the most undesirable citizens, crime can be reduced to the barest minimum, almost cease to exist.

In tolerating misconduct on the part of many, we permit them to set a bad example for others and lower the standard of conduct generally. We must so educate everyone that they will feel the responsibility of being a good influence and of setting a good example. Have this feeling so well established that any departure from it will result in the offender being condemned by public opinion. Such a view will be far more effective in the prevention of crime than laws, courts, and punishment. Have each individual possess a strong desire to live well and have them receive appreciation from others for doing so or condemnation for failing to do so.

Our police are far more efficient in the performance of their duties than are the laws or the courts. During an epidemic of sex crimes upon young girls the police, in a relatively brief period, rounded up a couple of hundred men known to be more or less moronic and given to sex crimes. In many cases the men had been previously convicted of sex offenses and later released. It is unfair to society, to children, to permit such persons to be at large. A sensible criminal code would provide suitable means of restraint.

Rapers, nymphomaniacs, sadists, homosexuals, and other victims of sex perversion should be encouraged to seek assistance from a suitable public agency set up for that purpose. This agency should arrange some means for their abnormal desires to obtain satisfaction in ways not harmful to others, taking care to avoid the influence of bad example. This would avoid attacks on innocent persons.

We should establish in each city, and other suitable subdivisions, an official corresponding to our present chief of police or sheriff, whose task it would be to insure good conduct within the district entrusted to his care. He should be an expert in this and have an efficient force of police to assist him. Life records of all inhabitants would be available to him. The task of this official should be to prevent crime and insure good behavior. He should endeavor to classify all individuals within his jurisdiction as to whether or not they were desirable. Those whom he considered undesirable and not fit to be at large, should be presented before a court with a view to segregation. With the development of this system, in time it would be a reflection upon these officials for a crime to be committed in their jurisdiction.

The spirit of competition and comparison could be utilized in reducing crime in different localities. When the crime percentage of a certain locality was above that of others, it should require investigation. A reason exists for this, and it could readily be found. This reason would unquestionably be the existence within the community of a great number of undesirable citizens. They could be promptly segregated and as a result, the crime ratio would be reduced.

If we can greatly reduce the prevalence of crime, we will also be contributing toward world peace by lessening the possibility of war between nations. If we have such a high standard of conduct as to almost entirely abolish crime, other nations will be impelled to adopt our methods. This will result in somewhat of a world-wide striving for Ascendency. When we combine this with high standards of living and economic security, the influence throughout the world will be overwhelming.

This comparison of crime and individual conduct with war is not inappropriate. Just as the existence of crime in a nation indicates poor standards of conduct, so does war indicate poor standards of conduct by nations. The poor conduct of the individuals is the direct result of the prevalence of primitive characteristics and lack of Co, Primo, Extro, and the finer adhuman qualities. The existence of war is a reversion to primitive savagery and failure on the part of nations to possess Co, Primo and Extro, and a high degree of adhuman development.

A criminal trial should not be to determine the guilt or

innocence of the accused. It should be to determine whether or not he is a desirable person and whether he should be permitted freely to circulate among desirable citizens. His whole life record should be examined to determine this,·and if it be found that he is unfit to be at large, he should be segregated. By this means we will make certainty of punishment a relatively simple task.

Our police at present have records of many criminals whom they know are living lives of crime, and yet they are unable to obtain evidence against them. If we use a man's whole life in determining whether he should be left at large or not, we could very easily break up bands of racketeers, criminals, and gangsters. They could all be segregated. Their environmental influence would then cease to exist, thus preventing the perpetuation of the conditions producing them.

The court constituted to classify individuals as desirable or undesirable should be composed of experts trained in this particular line of work. All people would be considered desirable until, as the result of misconduct, the question arose as to whether they were to be considered undesirable and so classified. In effect each person would be on trial to prove to society his right to remain at large and retain the privileges of citizenship. When he proved undeserving of them, they would be withdrawn.

When the court has determined that a certain person is undesirable and should be segregated, he should be turned over to a criminal bureau. This would be composed of experts who would study each individual case, see if reform measures were in order and determine the methods of control to be employed.

Criminal courts should be composed of nine judges who would be specialists in human nature and all things that have to do with misbehavior and good conduct. They should inquire thoroughly into all matters brought before them, and determine whether or not the individual should be permitted to be at large. If these men are wisely selected and are specialists in this work, we can well do away with appeal from their decisions, particularly if unanimous. Various degrees of review may be established in case of votes of six to three, seven to two, or eight to one.

These courts should not permit lawyers to appear before them. Our present-day lawyers make use of technicalities, use many words, discredit the law, and prevent justice. Able judges can obtain the facts without the intervention of lawyers, without arguments, without emotional appeal, their task being simply to determine whether or not the individual is fit to remain at large. They have his whole life record to consult, and under such conditions it should not be difficult for them to arrive at a fair decision.

We could obtain excellent material for judges on these courts by using retired officers of the army and navy. War is a young man's game. The older officers could render many years of excellent service on these courts. Their very experience in handling men gives them a good practical understanding of human nature. With further training in this specialized direction they would make excellent material for judges.

The control of crime would be facilitated by having two separate and distinct types of courts or classification boards. One would consider primarily the rights of society. The other would be directed toward consideration of the criminal himself. The court primarily considering the protection of society would determine whether or not a certain individual was fit to be at large. When it reached the decision that he was undeserving of this privilege, the offender would be turned over to the criminal bureau. He would then be examined by a court or classification board considering the interest of the criminal himself. This board would decide whether or not efforts should be made to reform him. If it seems possible to reform him, he could be placed in a suitable institution developed with this object in view. If he proves undeserving of reform, this court could classify him as being undesirable and have him permanently segregated in a criminal colony.

The existence of these two types of courts would greatly

facilitate the protection of the public and the reform or segregation of the criminal. At present the criminal receives
much consideration and society little. It is commonly accepted that society should attempt to reform the criminal.
This is erroneous. The criminal should be given an opportunity to reform himself. If he fails to do so he should be
permanently segregated. When a citizen is first brought before a court for classification as to fitness to be at large, this
court is to consider only his effect upon society. If he is not
an asset, not a deserving citizen, he should not be permitted
to lower environmental standards. This court would not
have the task of punishing the criminal; it would have the
task of removing undesirable influences from the environment. It accomplishes this by turning offenders over to a
board of experts whose task it is to control his future welfare.

Scientific measures to control crime must be entrusted to
the hands of experts. This applies to both police officials and
public officials generally having to do with improving the
conduct of the citizens and to the courts which sit in judgment upon criminal cases. We should no longer permit juries composed of nonexperts to decide questions for which
they are clearly unfit.

The right to trial by jury was an endeavor to protect the
rights of the individual and to insure him a fair trial by his
fellow men. Like many good intentions, it does not work
well in practice. Our juries are composed of average citizens
selected not for particular ability in this duty, but simply
because they are on the jury rolls. While the members of the
jury receive pay, most people strenuously object to serving
because of its interference with their work and have a general dislike of such duty. Thus we find the average jury composed of men of about average intelligence; some may even
be below average; some are levelheaded men capable of giving a fair decision in the case presented to them. But on the
whole, trials by jury are a poor means of insuring justice.

By having our courts composed of experts in human nature, we can do away with the present abuse of pleas of in-

sanity. It is not at all unusual for criminals to plead insanity under our present code, be adjudged insane, then later claim recovery and be released. Vicious action against wholesome citizens whether done by an insane person or a sane one must be prevented. The true method is the removal of such offenders from society.

To control crime we must base our acts upon understanding of human nature. Criminals are human beings. Their acts are dictated by urges governed by basic laws. The conduct of criminals is guided just as much by these laws as the conduct of the most intelligent persons. We must base our control of criminals and the reduction of crime upon sound principles. In the discussion of crime and criminals in these few chapters, I have avoided the repetition of much matter published in the volume INDIVIDUAL ASCENDENCY. This volume discusses human conduct and very naturally has much to say about criminal and abnormal acts. To understand the causes of crime and the reason for the existence of criminals, you should possess a thorough understanding of Ascendent Psychology. The volume INDIVIDUAL ASCENDENCY gives a good basis for such study.

The perfection of Ascendent Psychology will require the efforts of many able thinkers striving to do so. As we perfect Ascendent Psychology, we can perfect our means of controlling crime and improving conduct. Criminal acts and good conduct are intimately related. When the standard of conduct improves, criminal activities decrease. Thus to control crime, we should elevate the standards of conduct of all citizens. As this standard improves, crime will be lessened.

Thoughts

Much crime is caused by the desire for gain. If we make it unprofitable to commit crime, crime will decrease.

Treat evil at its source, not its effects. Do not drive it into hiding but bring it out into the open.

We punish criminals after they commit crime, instead of correcting the conditions that produce both them and crime.

Racketeering and gangsterism are examples of Apro and Ampro exerted in a descendent way. The members of criminal gangs are encouraged in their viciousness by receiving the applause and approval of their follows. Raise the moral tone of society so all condemn wrong and crimes, and criminals will cease to exist.

It is not practicable to reform confirmed criminals. Their behavior patterns are so confirmed toward a life of crime as to make the task of correcting them so difficult as to be unfair to impose upon society.

If the efforts spent in trying to reform people with marked Bruto instincts were spent on those capable of responding to the stimulating influences of Co, we would soon solve our crime problem. In a nutshell, eliminate or segregate those not amenable to reform, and concentrate the effort now wasted on them on worthwhile individuals.

Tolerance of evildoers and attempts to help or to reform them encourages near-evildoers to emulate them, whereas a policy that makes evildoing unprofitable would deter them.

We have many adults with childish minds. They should be treated as children, not too indulgently but fairly and with some degree of strictness.

Crime and vicious conduct are very similar to a contagious disease. They contaminate all those with whom they come in contact. When we recognize this fact, we may by intelligent efforts control viciousness.

I have less sympathy for the criminal than for those he injures by his acts or influences by his example.

Tolerance of evil encourages its continuance.

XXII

THE CAPITALISTIC SYSTEM

THE PRIMARY VIRTUE OF THE FREE CAPITALISTIC SYSTEM IS that it readily adapts itself to changing conditions. From a scientific standpoint it is sound. It is an exemplification in social institutions of the principle of force-adaptation, of the herdé principle and of evolution. These natural forces are unrestricted by government regulation. They adapt themselves to changing conditions. If our government restricts its activities to a minimum, all social institutions, including the capitalistic system itself, will readily adapt themselves to continued changes. The government also must adapt itself to changing conditions.

The primary duty of the government is to insure a maximum of happiness, moral character, and intelligence among its citizens and provide for the improvement of future generations. The best means for the government to bring this about is to encourage high ethical standards which of themselves will prevent serious abuses. One great fault of our government today is in bitterly attacking big business, blaming many of the country's ills upon wealthy individuals. This creates friction.

The government should educate the public to an understanding of existing problems and promote harmony. This is the true method of solving all economic problems; not by denouncing the capitalistic system and attacking business but by insuring the harmonious co-operation of all citizens in furthering the common welfare.

Our ills are not all produced by capitalism, neither is all good destroyed by it nor will our ills be eradicated and good prevail when capitalism is overthrown. The ills from which we are suffering are less the product of capitalism than of incompetent government and the selfishness and lack of understanding of the individual citizen. Despite this, the general standard of living in our country is higher than that of any other country in the world. If we adhere to the present system and assist capital in fulfilling its obligation to the country by wise measures, we can further raise the standard of living and make capital a real servant of the people.

We should not condemn capital as a failure without giving it a chance, and it has not as yet had a chance. We have too many impractical people with insufficient understanding of economic problems, who condemn capital for all existing ills. The crying need of the world and of our country is more intelligence and greater moral character. To judge from some of our liberal thinkers, capital is the only one lacking in these essentials and the stupid, ignorant people are the ones who possess all the virtues and ability.

A successful capitalistic system demands a minimum of government regulation, activities, expenditures, ownership, and interference. An extension of government regulation and interference tends to hamper industry. An increase in government activities, government reform measures, government expenditures, and payment of government benefits places an increasing burden upon constructive business. The payment of government pensions, for instance, and relief money, encourages parasitism. That is to say, a large number of people receive pensions or benefits who do nothing of a constructive nature in return therefore.

The prosperity of the entire nation is best assured by having all citizens engaged in constructive work producing wealth of permanent value. When the government undertakes to maintain or support some citizens, their constructive effort ceases. This not only causes a large decrease in the production of wealth, but they become a burden upon the remaining workers who are producing constructive wealth. The money paid nonproducers must be raised by taxes paid by those who are working.

The capitalistic system is sound from the standpoint of human nature. Its development can be traced through the psychas, beginning with the basic one of survival. Socialism, communism, fascism are unsound, not in accord with human nature, for they are not conducive to man's highest development. We have but to create an ascendent environment to make of capitalism an ascendent force. Capitalism will adapt itself to the environment and have moral standards as high as the environment itself.

Capitalism has not the power to raise or lower the environment, of itself, but can be made to contribute to either, depending upon the wisdom with which it is controlled. This control must be exercised by the government and is best obtained by striving for an ascendent environment. We should develop managers of industry of such high character that they will conduct its affairs upon a high moral plane.

The capitalistic system stimulates mental development more than any other economic system. This is largely by the encouragement the individual receives from the realization that he will profit from his own efforts. He is thus stimulated to great achievements and to great exertions. Communism, socialism, and fascism stifle mental development for the very good reason that the individual's activities are limited and he is not so certain of reward if engaged in independent activity. He therefore usually enters the government service to obtain success in life with the result that his individuality, originality, and personality are crushed, stifled and prevented from developing freely because he must always consider the desires of those above him and must conform to their orders whether right or wrong. He is less willing to question the soundness of policies because the average government official, unless he is of an exceptional type, will not encourage subordinates to find flaws in his policies.

Liberty and democracy thrive best under the capitalistic

system. The utmost freedom and liberty in making a living also includes the utmost liberty and freedom in other ways. The less the government interferes with the individual, the simpler the form of government and the less the amount of government activities, the more liberty and freedom all citizens have. Attempts on the part of a government to help the individual citizen not only penalize the more efficient to reward the least efficient but also hamper liberty and freedom.

All history shows that mental development requires, not repression but the fullest expression, and that this is best assured by letting each person live his own life with a minimum of restraint. If we have an ascendent government that endeavors to develop an ascendent environment, the capitalistic system will be more successful than in the past.

We should permit the freest development of those business concerns that are able to survive by giving better service to the public. Department stores are not the most efficient business concerns because of their delivery charges, charge accounts, and special services rendered. However, if people are willing to pay the additional cost of maintaining these services, there is no reason for the government to interfere. If more efficiently conducted businesses, having no charge accounts, delivery charges, or rendering other services, can undersell the department stores or give a better product for the same price, the department stores must meet this competition. We will find many people, however, who would rather receive service and pay more, than be bothered with seeking the lower prices.

The free development of business permits concerns to develop suited to the demands. Here is where the great benefit of the capitalistic system is seen as opposed to socialism. Institutions under the capitalistic system will adapt themselves very readily to the public demand, giving what the public desires. Enlightened government would not interfere with this adaptation but would direct its efforts toward educating the public in the direction of Ascendency. With the public demanding Ascendency, business would be bound to conform.

. Capital is being denounced on all sides, and yet there is a high degree of trust on the one hand and integrity on the other when you can drop a deposit in a night opening for the convenience of late bank customers and rest assured that it will be properly credited. We may say the same for transactions on the floor of the New York Stock Exchange, where millions of dollars worth of securities are exchanged in fractions of a second by the simplest methods; no iron-bound contracts, nothing but the integrity of those with whom you are dealing. Those who attack capital so viciously could well emulate some of its integrity in their own lives.

It is much the fashion to attack Wall Street, the stock exchanges, speculation, and denounce them for all existing ills. Like all the rest of the country, they are far from perfect, but they do render excellent service and are often unjustly attacked. On the whole their moral character is higher than that of those who attack them vigorously, and the service they render is better performed.

Much of the feeling against capitalists would subside if we would institute means to require the bad ones to behave and permit the good ones to carry on their good efforts unhampered. All are not self-seeking. The great error of our social legislation is that we are hampering and giving a bad name to the good capitalists in our efforts to control the bad ones.

Many fortunes were made possible by inventors, soldiers, discoverers, geniuses and brave adventurers who themselves received little reward. This contradicts the statement that capitalism is vicious and that men crave money alone. Any number of men value many things more than money. It is toward the cultivation of this quality and of men of this type that our efforts should be directed.

Capital should reform itself as much as possible and afford less justifiable grounds for attack. The demand for profit is sometimes carried to extremes. The salesman in the Orient selling razor blades who advocated the marriage of native women and white men because their children would have heavy beards and thus give a market for his product, illustrates the extremes to which capital will sometimes go for profits. At no time should capital resort to the promotion of aims whose social effects are harmful, for profit. Capital itself should withdraw from a field, however profitable, if it has a bad effect upon social institutions. We cannot expect capital alone to reform itself. It should be assisted by the public who should strive to understand the problems with which it is faced. Blaming all our ills upon capital is unfair and unwarranted. If the effort now devoted to attacking, belittling, and ridiculing the capitalistic system were exerted toward improving it and eradicating its evils, progress would be made to as great a degree as intelligence was displayed.

It is not the capitalistic system that is at fault; it is incompetent government allied with ignorance, class feeling, and stupidity. We should encourage capital to perform its duty to the nation.

Despite all its abuse, waste, lost motion and duplication, the capitalistic system is far more efficient than socialism would be. The mismanagement of a socialistic government would be worse than that of our present government.

Socialism tends to reward the undeserving and unfit at the expense of the deserving. Capitalism tends to reward the deserving to a greater extent than it does the undeserving, thus being more in the interest of man than socialism. Capital should demand a reasonable profit, have pride of service and give good value for value received. Many business concerns do this now, and they should be encouraged.

The vast quantity of social reforms and regulation which our government is employing to control capital prevents it from functioning as it should. We should give it a real chance to perform its function, release it from the restraint to which it is being subjected and encourage it to the utmost.

Socialism stresses economic injustices unduly. It does not recognize that the government, either socialistic or capitalistic, must be one of character to be really capable of doing justice to all. If we have character on the part of all, social-ism will not be needed. We do not have socialism in our country, but most of our attempted reforms follow the general aims of socialism, that is, to improve the economic well-being of the citizens. The economic well-being of the citizens cannot be greatly improved unless we improve their intelligence and character. If the effort now being directed toward economic reform was directed toward developing intelligence and moral character among the citizens, we would unquestionably have more success in the solution of our economic problems.

The advantages of socialism are outweighed by its disadvantages. Both socialism and capitalism must be controlled by character if they are to advance man's welfare. There is greater possibility of injury to character under a socialistic government than there is under a capitalistic government. Socialism limits individual freedom of action. It is a system benefiting the failures and appealing to the impractical well-meaning; it deadens progress and tends toward mediocrity.

Many fine people favor socialism as a cure for our ills. Practically, it offers as great evils as we now have. Poor moral character and lack of mental ability are the real faults. Let us improve these; good government and institutions will follow; evil will diminish and tend to disappear.

Socialism aims to solve most ills by having equal incomes for all, thus abolishing the ills of the profit motive. There are many more people undeserving of an equal share than there now are getting a greater share. The excess of the latter is in the long run spent in some way. The aim of socialism is better than its methods.

Inherently, despite its defects, capitalism can do more in building character than socialism. Socialism tends toward bureaucracy, rewards the many at the expense of the few, the below-average at the expense of the above-average and superior, and penalizes thrift, industry, and ability to reward waste, indolence, and mediocrity.

Socialism and communism are opposed to democracy. We

have an example of that in Russia today. The vast mass of people in Russia have as little to say about the conduct of their government today as they previously had under the czar. Yet when the czar was overthrown, the Bolsheviks claimed to be serving the interests of the people and democracy. Communistic Russia still claims to be advancing the interests of the people. To insure a definite policy, they have found it necessary to impose a most ruthless dictatorship. All citizens are required to carry out the behest of government officials.

To obtain advancement under a socialistic government, one must constantly seek the favor of those under whom he is serving. Unlike the capitalistic system in a democracy, he cannot change employers at will. There is but one employer, the government. He must get along with this government, even though he may be under the direction of an abusive minor official.

Let us make the best of our present system, raise the standard of business ethics, encourage each individual to develop himself, to be a good citizen and protect him against those who do not live up to this obligation. Let us encourage the greatest freedom of effort, enterprise, and thought, and stimulate the individual citizen to the highest achievement. We can make a real success of capitalism if we make the effort.

XXIII

UNSOUND ECONOMIC POLICIES

A DEMOCRACY IS NOT WELL FITTED TO CONDUCT ECONOMIC reforms. We should recognize this fact and reduce government interference and regulation of economic matters to the absolute minimum. When the government starts a policy of economic reform, the various interest groups throughout the nation endeavor to obtain legislation benefiting themselves. The reforms attempted will rarely be sound. They will generally be designed to appeal to selfish interest groups and to obtain the support of uninformed voters.

Sentimental considerations are also a great contribution to government extravagance and unsound economic policies. Our national, state and local governments alike spend vast sums on monuments, cemeteries and useless memorials. An excellent example of this is afforded by the expensive memorials constructed by our national government in France. If our participation in the battles of the World War excelled other nations as greatly as our cemeteries and monuments do, we would have a most creditable military record.

Indulgence in sentiment of this nature, is employing display to make up for lack of merit. It is very similar to employing talk instead of work. The record of our soldiers should speak for itself. It will not be improved by vast memorials or expensive cemeteries. On the contrary it shows a weakness on the part of American citizens to glorify themselves. We would do far better to direct this effort into constructive performance of practical value.

The economic measures of a democratic government are not determined by soundness but by popularity. We cannot hope to attain sound economic measures when appeals are made to the voter who tends to see present benefits and not future harm. We must do two things: Raise the standard of intelligence of the voter so he will understand economic problems better and endeavor to establish a government able to function efficiently.

One of the great causes for the existing unfortunate condition of affairs in our country, is due to the action of the politicians in denouncing capital and the wealthy, for the simple reason that such action is popular with many voters. Whenever such attacks are made, we should study the past life of the attacker and those whom he is attacking. We will often find that the man who viciously attacks is unworthy and that the man who is being unjustly attacked possesses merit.

We can well ask who built the railroads, our large utility concerns, our large automobile-manufacturing establishments, our large steel- and iron-manufacturing plants. Our politicians have not done this. These various industries have been built up by men of ability. We should defend them against unjust attacks.

When a politician attacks our business and industrial leaders, we should be careful to see whether such attacks are justified. In general, attacks by the politicians are not justified. They are more in the nature of meddlesome, incompetent people who have failed in life, who are unable to accomplish constructive achievements but who possess the ability to talk, flatter, and obtain votes.

By virtue of their power as rulers of the country, the politicians undertake to point out to our business and industrial leaders their errors, tax them heavily, and try to regulate their affairs—affairs which the politicians themselves could not efficiently conduct. If we were to dismiss our big industrial leaders today from their positions and let our miscellaneous assortment of politicians take over their executive positions, in a relatively brief period our industrial efficiency would be seriously impaired. Yet these men, who are unable to conduct large industries, are regulating and telling others how to conduct them. In effect, they are directing the operation of industry without responsibility.

On the other hand, our industrial and business men have the responsibility but are unable to exercise it properly due to regulation emanating from incompetent politicians. Our politicians have had nothing to do with establishing and building up these industries. When, however, the industry is successful, they are all too willing to attack, to impute false motives to the successful managers of it, to tax it heavily and to subject it to stifling regulation.

How vicious is our political life when, in order to get office, politicians attack business, the very institution that supports all the people! It is entitled to both protection and assistance. Prosperity cannot exist until this fact is recognized.

It is unfair for us and for the politicians to blame industry for all ills and expect it to find the cure and solve national problems. Such effort should rather be exerted on the average citizen himself, improving his character, developing his intelligence and insuring his co-operation with industry for the solutions of common problems. Industry is not at fault; it is man himself.

We are attempting to control business and industry through politicians and bureaucrats. The men most competent to control industry are those who have proven successful in its development. If we reduce government interference and regulation to a minimum this will automatically be effected. The able business and industrial leaders will be directly in charge of affairs which they are well qualified to handle.

It has been so often repeated that Wall Street and capital are vicious that many believe this to be the case. It is unfair to persecute any class; Wall Street and capital are better than those who criticize and denounce them so unthinkingly.

This denunciation is so general because it is politically popular and is a ready means for the inferior and jealous to explain away their failure.

Our industrial men somehow keep the country going in spite of attacks from all sides, interference and regulation by the government, and payment of heavy taxes. The general average of the active business men is above the general average of any other class in the country from the standpoint of character or conduct; they are, on the whole, able men, courteous and reliable, giving as good or better service than they receive.

The attacks directed against them have been based more upon feeling and prejudice than knowledge. The fact that they have been so universally condemned by the stupid, the prejudiced, the worthless, only proves their merit. When worthwhile men attack others, we should heed. When worthless men attack worthy men, we should not heed.

Our business men, industrial magnates, bankers, and others concerned with the control of the industries of our country, deserve great credit for their ability to carry on the affairs of the nation, supporting the citizens therein, under all the attacks they have been receiving for many years. If these attacks continue, industry will be unable to function efficiently and as a result, the citizens of the country will suffer. Industry is supporting the nation in spite of itself.

Labor alone cannot achieve great things. It must be well directed. We owe a debt of gratitude to the so-called robber barons. They were as moral as their times and far more practical and able than our reformers of today with all their education, access to modern knowledge, and desire to help man. If we had to choose between the old robber barons and our present-day reformers, give me the robber barons.

I observed in the newspaper today (January 7, 1938) an account of Mr. Henry Ford's efforts to build automobiles from soy beans and his general attempt to develop and use farm by-products in the manufacture of automobiles. He has developed a new-type tractor and is endeavoring to reduce the cost of tools for the farmer. Contrast this constructive achievement and attempt by Mr. Ford with the vicious attack made upon him a short time ago by Mr. Ickes. It is an outrage that such a splendid man, contributing his best to the industrial welfare of the country, is subjected to attacks by our own government, a government which fails to protect him from labor racketeers, a government which encourages them to attack him, a government which interferes with him when he attempts to discharge inefficient workmen. One could desire the harshest fate for our governing officials if it were not for the fact that innocent people will suffer with them. We must place decent men in charge of the government who will conduct its affairs as efficiently as Mr. Ford does his automobile plant, who will promote the welfare of the farmer as much as Mr. Ford is trying to do, who will be as great a contribution to constructive achievement in government as Mr. Ford has been in industrial development.

We are today witnessing a strange anomaly in American life. A great industrialist, Mr. Henry Ford, is waging single-handed a struggle for the preservation of American institutions against our own national government which is supporting labor racketeers endeavoring to intimidate Mr. Ford. What right has the C. I. O. to demand that Ford workers organize and join their unions? If the Ford workers choose to organize, why should they not do so themselves without the employment of coercion by labor agitators?

What right has the National Labor Relations Board to dictate to Mr. Ford whom he shall employ? The problem of maintaining discipline in a large corporation employing a hundred thousand men is a difficult task. It can best be met by promptly discharging those who show poor quality, who are discontented and create ill-feeling among fellow employees. One agitator can do much harm in upsetting the good feeling that should exist between employers and employees.

When the employer is prevented from discharging agitators, when he is required to take them back into his employ as the National Labor Relations Board has directed Mr. Ford to do, they return to their job with increased prestige. They can very easily encourage others to follow their example, and in a short time the fine discipline prevailing in the Ford Corporation will no longer exist.

We see evidence of this break-down of labor discipline in our merchant marine as a result of unwise government interference. When our government succeeds in producing similar conditions throughout our industries generally, the public will suffer and the deserving laborers as well.

The most discouraging feature of the whole situation, however, is the fact that our government is lending its support to an organized group of racketeers and that this action arouses little comment from the public. Public opinion acquiesces in whatever our government attempts, as long as it is associated with an expressed desire to help the underdog regardless of law, or the rights of others.

The mayors of several important American cities today (January 17, 1938) made additional demands upon the federal government for assistance in carrying the relief burden of their cities. They claim that the cities themselves are unable to do so and that the federal government must help in some form. These demands and the existence of such conditions afford much room for thought. It shows, for instance, that the much-vaunted New Deal policies have not solved the nation's problems after five years of attempts to do so. It shows the development on the part of local governments of a willingness to pass the buck to the federal government for relief. It shows that economic conditions themselves are basically unsound.

Is this not conclusive proof that our reform measures have been unsound in all respects? Have they not been of such a nature as to administer mere palliatives to a diseased condition? Continued demands for more government payments for relief or for public works is an example of administering additional palliatives. Why do not our leaders face facts, tell the public the truth, and evolve a sound solution? They are incompetent, unable to do this. They can denounce others, blame capital, anyone but themselves.

These continual demands of local politicians for additional payments from the federal government are bound to lead to inflation. No government can continually pay out vast sums of money for relief, and for public works, and assist local governments in carrying their burdens. Yet when this inflation arrives, these same politicians will admit no fault in themselves in bringing it about. They will still find someone else to blame. If they were as good in performing their duties as they are in denouncing others and finding scapegoats, they would be efficient administrators indeed. No far-reaching reform measures of any kind can be effected as long as we have such miserable creatures as our present-day politicians entrusted with their execution.

The great reform that all true reformers should seek should be a means of placing able, honest, sensible men in charge of the administration of the affairs of government. Our reformers lose track of this basic essential. They demand reforms of all kinds by the government. Of necessity these reforms are entrusted to the hands of politicians, a class far more in need of reform than any other class in the community. But these very same politicians denounce the big bankers, the big business men, the industrial leaders. From the standpoint of character and ability, our industrial and business leaders are far superior to our politicians. Of the two they should be the ones to regulate the politicians rather than have the politicians regulate them.

France affords us a good example of a government by incompetent politicians and unsound economic measures. The government has failed to balance the budget because of the opposition of many interest groups to economical measures; the labor element has been active in demanding increased benefits. As a result of these and many other contributing factors, the franc declines in value. The decline of the purchasing medium is the equivalent of a cut in wages and is a direct levy upon many types of capital.

This is not understood by the people generally. Instead of facing the facts frankly and endeavoring to meet the problem, there is much denunciation of some evildoers, and no sound thought toward a solution of the economic problem. As the result, the laboring classes will not be bettered; there will continue to be just as much hardship and suffering as ever. The people will struggle along somehow. The government will appeal to the influences of the moment rather than seek sound measures.

It is, of course, possible that at some future time the error of all this incompetence may be revealed and sound, corrective measures taken. In a relatively small country such as France, however, it will be difficult to put her house in order by herself. This is true of all European nations. The solution of all economic problems of the day in all countries of the world requires greater international understanding, and mutual co-operation among the nations and among groups within the nations.

Unsound government policies are not restricted to the internal affairs of our nation alone. They display themselves in international affairs and in foreign trade. The incompetence of our government in domestic affairs is on a par with its incompetence in international affairs. Under existing international conditions, a sound internal currency or money policy must take into consideration international affairs. A wise international policy would contribute towards a sound home currency and sound internal conditions. Conditions abroad are bad. Conditions in our own country are likewise bad. The reason they are not worse is because of our vast size, wealth, and efficient industrial system. Incompetent government will deprive us of this advantage if it be continued.

The large gold hoard in the United States may deteriorate in value and prove valueless in time. As other nations lose their gold a commodity or other standard may be adopted by them and they will no longer need gold or want it. It is a useless article anyway, with a false value conferred upon it by being the medium of exchange. Our government's gold policy is very unwise and may prove costly.

The unsettled condition of international affairs and the great amount of currency juggling is very likely to result in a form of currency not based upon gold or silver. Things have been done with money that have never been thought of before. The experience thus obtained may make it possible to do away with the gold standard and adopt one not based upon metallic security.

There are many laws governing the value of currency, not the least of which is that of quantity. Modern economic life demands a ready means of exchange, and people are required to accept whatever the government dictates in order to conduct their business affairs. It is possible that a government could print paper, and by carefully regulating its quantity, could maintain it as a standard of value by manipulation. This manipulation would include varying the quantity of money both by increasing or decreasing the amount in circulation, by buying or selling vast quantities of commodities and materials of all kinds.

While the gold standard has serious limitations, it is far more disturbing to have a standard that offers no certainty for the future, and this development will have disadvantages. Depending on how it is controlled and finally developed, it may be more harmful than, or superior to, the gold standard.

One reason for this vast gold hoard being in the United States is the lack of confidence in European nations. They are constantly threatened by war. Their financial problems have proven too great for the capacity of their leaders. Money will seek security. It will leave those countries where it is being harshly treated and seek those where it receives fair treatment. Money is prevented from doing this to a great degree at present by the restriction on international trade imposed by many nations seeking to advance their own interests.

Much of the difficulties of international trade is caused by the unwise interference of incompetent people. International trade is best served by a policy of freedom. Economic laws control both international and internal trade development. When they are interfered with unwisely, progress is handicapped. All governments should seek to promote the free functioning of economic laws. They should not attempt to modify these laws to further national interests. Attempts to do so will have harmful repercussions in other ways.

The United States, under a minimum of government, reached a high industrial stage and attained a higher standard of living than Europe. The European advance is now held back by tariff walls and heavy internal taxes. This prevents development. Automobiles, for instance, are so heavily taxed as to prevent development of a real industry such as we have in the United States. If our present policies of heavy taxation and limitation on activities of individuals are continued, we will revert toward the lower standard prevailing in Europe, and further progress will be prevented.

Government supervision, heavy taxes, and restraint are preventing business from grappling with and solving its problems. The problems of business are in reality the problems of the nation, because business supports the nation. Business can stand government spending better than government regulation. The spending is only a matter of transferring money from one hand to others, but prohibitive regulation actually prevents business from functioning.

The best government is still the least government, the simplest, most efficient, the one that spends the least, attending only to the essentials and giving to each citizen the utmost liberty. A government with simple activities can find it very easy to keep its finances well regulated. It spends but little and it has only to levy slight taxes to receive all moneys needed for its requirements. When the opposite situation exists, when the government expands its activities and starts spending vast sums for relief and for a vast number of employees, this wise process is reversed.

Consider the vast number of people living in our country. See what vast sums are poured into the government treasury if relatively small taxes or small amounts are paid by so many millions of people. Now reverse this process. Imagine the government paying out benefits to this large mass of people. The tremendous number, even though receiving but small amounts, runs the total up to staggering proportions. This results in floating loans and heavy taxation. At the same time the people who are getting benefits, become confirmed in the habit and continue to demand more and more.

Thus we have the least deserving people of the country demanding that the government support them and pay them benefits. The worthwhile element who are able and willing to make their way are being taxed and required to pay into the government large sums for the maintenance of the worthless. Anyone having knowledge of human nature will see that the receipt of government benefits results in creating a demand for them. Because one obtains them, another thinks he should have them too. This results in many applications for unjustified reasons. Many vicious, unscrupulous people will try to find means to get some of the government money that is being so freely expended.

Another effect from this free expenditure of government moneys is the fact that much unconstructive effort is exerted by many to obtain benefits, whereas if the government were not paying out benefits they would have to apply their efforts in the direction of sustaining themselves. No one with the slightest knowledge of human nature would adopt such a policy. From the standpoint of material welfare in the future and of the moral development of the citizens it is suicidal.

There is but one answer—we are being governed by incompetents, by politicians who have been willing to promise anything and everything to obtain votes to place themselves and their friends in office. This is the most vicious development of democracy ever seen. The most unsatisfactory phase of all, on the part of the thinking observer, is that there is no denunciation of the politicians, no denunciation of the reformers or of those demanding benefits, or of anyone except the poor capitalist who has to pay. It causes one to be pessimistic and think that the human race after all is not worth surviving and may just as well perish.

The vast amount of unemployment in our country today in conjunction with the high labor cost and industrial activity is convincing proof of the unsound policies of our rulers and of the great ability of American industry to adapt itself to unsound conditions. Our government by its unwise policies has contributed to the present unemployment and has hampered industry in innumerable ways. Despite it all industry supports the nation.

The best interests of the entire nation are served when all the people within the nation are working. Unemployment is positive evidence that something is wrong. Instead of fighting industry our government should encourage, support, and assist it in all ways possible in order that work may be found for everyone. A sensible government will inaugurate sound economic policies so that industry will be encouraged to embark upon new enterprises, with the certainty of being rewarded for its efforts.

Unwise government policies, with suggestions of further interference at a moment's notice, render it impossible for industry to plan for the future with any degree of certainty. When to this uncertainty we add the labor policy of the government which permits any group of agitators to abuse their employers, we can readily see that the blame for this unemployment is not upon industry but is squarely upon our rulers. Instead of frankly facing this issue and co-operating with industry in an effort to reduce unemployment, our politicians consistently attack industry and blame all existing ills upon it. The industrial leaders are less able to fight back. They are more interested in conducting their affairs.

We, the public, must defend industry from the attacks of our own government and place honest men in control capable of administering the affairs of government and doing justice to all citizens. The fact that a man is successful is no reason why he should be persecuted. His very success should entitle him to protection. We today are adopting the policy of attacking the successful and attempting to glorify the unsuccessful, those who lack the ability to care for themselves, who continually demand more benefits and higher wages and at the same time do as little as possible to honestly earn what they get.

A weak government that permits itself to be dominated by such a low type of citizenship is unworthy to remain in control of affairs. It contributes to existing class feeling, complicates present problems, and is storing up trouble for the future. Not the least among its acts is the creation of vast amounts of indebtedness; creating a burden upon future taxpayers that is as unnecessary as it is unjust.

Payment of government subsidies, such as those being paid to silver producers, cotton growers, and farmers, to increase production or to decrease it, may be productive of good if in the direction of sound economic development. They are more often productive of harm, particularly under a democratic form of government, when the industries concerned are depressed as a result of natural conditions and demand assistance from the government. By virtue of their political influence they are enabled to obtain this assistance, based less upon merit and future economic development than upon the amount of political pressure they bring to bear. The payment of government subsidies tends to increase the demand for them both by those receiving them and by others envious of their success.

Such payments moreover tend to prevent the natural adjustment of industries to changing economic conditions and requires sound industries to support the unsound. This may become such a burden as to undermine their soundness. It is better to let all survive by their own efforts and merit. Let the weak solve their own problems and be strengthened by the effort, not make the strong weak by the very burden of carrying the weak.

The increasing number of men engaged in nonconstructive work further increases the burden on the workers. Nonconstructive work is that which accomplishes nothing of value in serving man, such as extra clerks caused by a complicated system of administration which could be better done by a smaller number if the methods were simplified and efficient. Our legal system, for instance, costs much, hampers much, and helps little. Extension of government activities increases employees, causes more taxes, more employees to collect them, and becomes more inefficient with the increase in size. In time this will result in making the citizens of the country exist merely to support their government. Here is where our democratic government will soon crash. It will some day reach the point where there will be insufficient citizens supporting it, and too many being supported by it.

Our natural wealth is declining, or remaining at a standstill, which is the same thing, when we allow for the increase in population, however small it may be. This is being concealed by the devaluation of the dollar, and various other factors which prevent one from getting a clear view of the picture. Large numbers of unemployed over a long period of time indicate that industry is not using available labor because new industries are not being developed, buildings are not being constructed, old equipment is deteriorating and not being replaced.

To increase the wealth of the country and of the individual, we should put as many people to work as possible, accomplish the greatest amount of work practicable, and make as much of this work as possible of a permanent, constructive value. This work should be done by private citizens, and the wealth created owned by them, not by the government. These are sound means to increase the general wealth and prosperity. They are being violated by our policies of today. Work is discouraged. The government is encouraged to take over increasing activities, and no effort is made to increase the percentage of work of enduring value as compared to that of little permanence.

If we endeavored to establish a more unsound economic policy than the one we are now working under, we could not do so. Our government borrows vast sums of money, creating vast debts. It pays vast sums of money to many people in the form of pensions and benefits. It creates vast numbers of office holders in an effort to carry out many reforms. It interferes greatly with business, handicapping it so it is unable to function properly. It attempts to establish maximum hours and minimum wages, creating unemployment, and having done this it spends federal funds to take care of the unemployed, resulting in increasing the national debt, necessitating further taxation and further burdens upon industry. The extension of government activities is resulting in many businesses owned and operated by the government competing with private business, which further increases government cost by the incompetence of government operation, and discourages the increase of private enterprise. All these attempts to improve our economic condition are only making it worse. We have incompetent people doing it, and the policies they adopt are unsound, being based upon appeal to the voters and the present. They fail to look to the future and seek sound measures regardless of popularity. The present unsound policies eventually will result in harm to all; not the least is the great harm done moral character.

A government policy that takes from those who have and gives to those who have not will only succeed in increasing the latter and decreasing the former until finally there will be too few of the deserving to support the undeserving. The burden will be too crushing. It would be interesting to let this policy continue and see just what the net result will be. We are enslaving a large portion of our population to maintain others, and yet we claim to have abolished slavery years ago. This actual enslavement is being done by people who fondly believe they are improving the welfare of man.

Even the most stupid will some day begin to question the value of these unsound economic measures when, despite all the glowing promises, they realize that they are no better off today than they were many years before. When this time arrives, however, there will be plenty of people to explain why

the reforms have failed and to advocate many others perpetuating the existing evils.

The sensible men in the country must get together and
make an effort to educate the public to a proper understanding of economic problems. The people will respond. They
will do right if they but know. So far as I can see, no one is
attempting to teach them sound economic truths, to even
give them the slightest idea of the direction in which economic security lies. We can well blame our politicians, agitators, Wisho liberals for this condition, but the able business
men are guilty also. They do have some understanding of
the fundamentals of business, and they should make it their
problem to find means to educate the public to an understanding of their problems.

Appeals of business men to science to solve the problems
will not do. Our present-day scientists are as theoretical, impractical, and unfit to deal with human affairs as our impractical writers. We must develop master scientists who
have minds trained to seek for the true answers to human
problems; not to seek popularity in the interest of any one
class, but to seek the interest of man himself.

XXIV

DEBTS

LARGE GOVERNMENT DEBTS ARE A VERY UNWHOLESOME INFLU-
ence. This is particularly true when they are tax-exempt.
Because they are tax-exempt the governments, national, state,
and local, can borrow vast sums at low rates of interest. This
constitutes a constant invitation to borrow more and more.
When we combine tax-exempt bonds with heavy taxation on
business and discouragement of productive enterprise, we
convert what would normally be constructive capital into
unconstructive. Men who would normally promote new enterprises invest their money in tax-exempt government bonds
instead of doing so.

Increase in government debt in our country is stimulated
by heavy income taxes. A wealthy man can get a better return for his money by purchasing tax-exempt securities than
he can obtain from industry. As the result, capital is being
forced into government securities instead of seeking new
industries, which would give greater employment, stimulating business generally. The ease with which government
debts can be floated results in too much money being borrowed, placing a heavy burden on the future, and making
the economic structure unsound.

The government debts in this country, local, state, and
federal, amount to something over fifty billion dollars and
are constantly increasing, rendering economic conditions
more unsound. Wise government would take steps to reduce
this debt and pay it off entirely. If this were done the large

amounts now invested in government bonds would seek investment in private industry, causing a great stimulation of business.

Government debts generally are bad because they must be paid for by the taxpayers. The fact that the government can borrow money and spend it results in unnecessary extravagance and the spending of money for purposes that could well be dispensed with. The government should set the example of living within its means. Large government debts increase the burdens of taxes for interest payment. If greatly overdone, they threaten inflation, which is disturbing to confidence and has an unsettling effect upon business.

There is a simple truth which forms the basis for sound fiscal policies. Have more people paying money to, than receiving from, the government. Have larger sums paid in than are paid out. In a vast population, if each person contributes payments to the government, a vast sum is soon accumulated even if the amount contributed is as small as a penny or nickel. By contrast, when the government undertakes to pay out to many, the treasury will soon be exhausted.

Large government debts penalize the workers by creating a privileged class within the nation, namely the holders of the government bonds who thus receive benefits from the government in the form of interest. A vast government debt has much the same effect of creating dependents upon the government as unwise relief measures, payments of pensions, and similar expenditures.

The existence of vast government debts results in parasites receiving benefits at the expense of industry and workers generally. That is to say, the bondholders, from whom the government borrowed the money, receive interest on their bonds and this must be raised by the government through taxation upon other people who must work to create wealth in order to pay taxes which in turn are utilized to pay interest to parasites.

The term parasite is used here to emphasize this statement. Most bondholders are worthy citizens. However, their money could be used to better advantage if invested in industrial undertakings that promote industry or business and afford employment. Payments to bondholders by the government are payments to unproductive capital through taxes upon productive capital. If no government debt exists there will be less unproductive capital by virtue thereof. Then much unproductive capital, having no avenue for employment in government indebtedness, will be required to become productive capital.

The diversion of capital into government debts not only has the bad effect of depleting the capital market and causing higher interest rates but imposes further burdens upon industry by virtue of the increased need for taxes with which to pay the interest on the government obligations. This tax burden serves to discourage business expansion causing unemployment and expressing itself in other harmful forms depending upon the skill with which the government is administered. The expansion of government debts inaugurates a vicious circle pressing increasing burdens upon the people in an infinite number of forms but in such an obscure way as not to be readily discerned.

Large government debts tend to raise the rate of interest, even though the interest paid on government obligations be low. This for the reason that the government obligations absorb such vast quantities of capital as to lessen the supply of available capital for loans to other borrowers. Suppose, for instance, that we could by some means liquidate our some fifty billions of national, state, and local obligations. This fifty billions of dollars of capital would have to seek employment elsewhere. If conditions were such as to offer security for the future, the interest rate on even long-term loans would decline to a very low point. When well-intentioned people advocate an increase in government debt to furnish employment and accomplish other social reform, they are actually contributing toward a condition that tends to neutralize their good intentions. They are creating a far worse situation then the condition they are endeavoring to help.

The existence of vast government debts depresses real estate and all property values. This is caused by the fact that such a large amount of capital tied up in government securities lessens the amount of capital available with which to purchase and own property; also because the additional charges to pay the interest on government obligations tend to lessen property values because of increased taxation.

All government debts in our country, whether national, state or local, should be liquidated. Their existence is unjustified and unnecessarily complicates our economic system. These vast debts exist because of the weakness of our politicians. They appropriate money to conciliate voters. They are unwilling to levy taxes; instead, they borrow money. If no government debts existed, taxes would be less, capital would be unable to obtain investment in government bonds, and would be required to invest in industry. Also the number of government employees required to administer this vast debt and collect the taxes would be lessened. All sensible thought points to the elimination of government debts; instead we are increasing them, the opposite of sound principles.

All debts, whether public or private, are in the direction of unsound economic conditions. It is better for individuals not to owe money and it is better for all governments not to owe money. Being in debt can easily become a confirmed habit. We have many people who go through life without ever being in debt to any degree, and whose credit is always good. We have other people who are continually in debt and hopelessly extravagant. It is the thrifty class we should emulate in the conduct of our government affairs and we should model our institutions so as to encourage and promote thrift. We have too many borrowers in our country unable to handle their own affairs. They borrow money from the more capable and then blame a vicious economic system for their own incompetence.

Loans by the government direct to business or to any individual are harmful, for several reasons. They cause the
business or individuals to rely more upon the government
for support than upon themselves or upon other private
concerns. The government is thus establishing a policy of encouraging indebtedness, which is the opposite of the policy
it should encourage, that of decreasing debts. The lending
of money by the government is more likely to be undertaken
with regard to political implications than assisting sound
business developments. If it were not done, business would
find means of meeting the situation. It is toward this that
the government's efforts should be directed.

It would be well to discourage borrowing and the habit of
indebtedness by prohibiting advertising of money to loan by
lenders. It might be desirable to limit charge accounts and
charge sales of all business concerns where such action would
not unduly interfere with the orderly conduct of business or
prejudice rights. It would be unfair to restrict present purchases of farmers, for instance, who often must wait a year
before their crop is harvested and the money obtained. Naturally some means must be provided for them to pay expenses until they receive payment for their crops. Provident
farmers, however, could well be a year ahead and avoid the
need of borrowing money.

Mortgages, loans, and leases should be discouraged and
positive ownership encouraged. We should have less renting
and more home owners. The development in our cities of
apartment houses, in which citizens cannot acquire homes
but must pay rent throughout their lives, is not a desirable
condition. It would be far simpler and better if each person
owned his own home. They are then rewarded for good care
and have no cause for complaint regarding rent and service.
This problem may be met in large cities by the development
of co-operative housing projects by congenial people.

Bond issues, mortgages, loans, and all forms of indebtedness are bad. They exaggerate booms and depressions. When
money is to be easily had in boom times, people borrow very

willingly, becoming hopelessly involved in debt when business starts to decline. As the depression becomes more marked it results in bankruptcies and foreclosures. It would be far better if, instead of having people lending vast sums, they owned the enterprises. The bad effect of indebtedness would then be minimized in depressions, because fear of foreclosure would not exist. Owners cannot overextend themselves so readily if they are limited to their own funds. Sound economic conditions are promoted by reducing debt to a minimum; not to the extent of preventing development of enterprises, but to prevent it from becoming too great a burden for industry to carry.

Loans tend to increase property values and penalize those borrowing the money. Suppose, for instance, that we were to prohibit all mortgages on farms, that all farm property must be unencumbered and owned free of indebtedness of any nature. If this policy was adopted suddenly, there would be a great drop in farm values. This would render it possible for many to purchase farms outright.

This same inflation of values is also apparent in stock-market loans. When the stock values become very high, conservative investors are unwilling to purchase the stock. They, however, will loan to others for the purpose of purchasing the stock. This tends to force stocks beyond their actual worth. If we were to prohibit purchases of stocks except for cash, prices would not rise so far above actual worth.

The sudden adoption of a drastic policy to prohibit loans, borrowings, and indebtedness, would be unwise. No such change should be made in economic policies without giving the economic system full opportunity to adapt itself to the new changes. We should not prohibit stock market loans, farm mortgages, or borrowing suddenly and entirely. We should, however, inaugurate the policy of discouraging overextension of credit by wise measures that will tend toward the establishment of a sounder economic system, lessen creditors, lessen debtors, and encourage those who have money to buy property outright.

If we discourage loans, those people possessing money will, of necessity, have to make direct investments. That is to say, they will buy land, farms, or stock, and become direct owners rather than unconstructive capitalists of a parasitical nature, lending money to others who take the risk while they themselves shirk the risks.

Installment purchases are not conducive to the soundest economic conditions. They tend to stimulate purchases but the resulting indebtedness during a business decline tends to exaggerate the resultant depression. The best method is to have all people pay as they go, have as few debts as possible. Installment purchases may be desirable for the purchase of articles of a constructive nature.

On the whole, installment buying should be discouraged. Levying of a light tax on installment purchases would assist in discouraging them and encouraging cash purchases. They should not be discouraged to the extent of imposing hardships on those who really needed installment purchases.

The general policy should be to reduce debts not to the extent of restricting business activity, but to insuring as sound an economic structure as possible at all times. The fewer debts, the sounder it is. It is possible to conceive of a society in which each person has ample money and no one owes to others. Under such conditions the ill effects of depressions and booms would be greatly minimized.

The general government policy should be to discourage installment purchases, particularly those for luxuries. It might be well to prohibit advertising, soliciting or encouraging people to borrow or make installment purchases. An educational campaign could be conducted in an endeavor to have the public pay cash for all purchases, doing away with credit abuses. It might be wise to prohibit installment purchases of inexpensive articles of little value. Why should one purchase something for ten or fifteen dollars, or even twenty or thirty, on installments? It might be advisable at times; but generally one can get along without inexpensive articles until he is able to pay for them in full. Making a minimum limit for installment purchases is repressive legislation and not desirable; but this disadvantage may be outweighed by the advantages. All installment sales are a burden on business and the consumer must pay the additional cost involved. If they are reduced or abolished entirely, he would benefit ultimately.

In competent, skillful hands, the levying of taxes in varying amounts and as required upon debts or loans would be a valuable mechanism in preventing credit inflation and in controlling prices, foreign exchange, gold imports, and financial activities related thereto.

Suppose, for instance, there was a business boom in our own country and the government wished to prevent its expansion to undue proportions. At the same time it wished to avoid the influx of gold from abroad. Instead of raising the discount rate, which would tend to attract foreign money, we discourage further loans by placing an internal tax upon them. Thus we are able to check expansion in our own country and check the influx of gold from foreign countries at the same time.

Taxes on loans must be levied with due consideration to their ultimate effect. We may divide loans into two general classes, consumer and capital. Consumer loans are those in which money is borrowed by the consumer to make purchases. Installment sales are in this classification. Capital loans, however, are of an entirely different nature. They are loans made to capital to establish new industries, enlarge the plant, increase the capital investment. They therefore directly contribute toward an increase in employment and general prosperity. They are less harmful than consumer loans but may be very harmful if overdone. For instance, if great amounts of capital loans are incurred at the height of a period of prosperity and immediately thereafter a depres-sion ensues, the borrowing concern may be forced into bankruptcy.

Consumer loans have a good effect in creating a demand for more products. But they are basically unsound because the product when delivered is not paid for in full. They exaggerate booms by creating a far greater demand for goods than is justified, and, the demand having been previously overfulfilled, there is much less demand during the following depression.

Knowledge of the difference between capital and consumer loans is essential toward proper understanding of loans and the effect of taxes made upon them. Both can be either beneficial or harmful. Capital loans may be a positive necessity at times. Consumer loans are of a more questionable nature.

Both consumer and capital loans are harmful at the heights of a boom but would be extremely beneficial at the low point of a depression. If we could apply these sensible principles, we could to some extent avoid their abuse. But who knows at the time whether the boom is at its peak or a depression at its lowest? We can to some extent regulate this sensibly by keeping statistics regarding the quantity of loans in existence. When they exceed a conservative level, taxes on them should be levied in increasing percentages. When they are below this conservative level taxes may be reduced, and when very low, abolished entirely. Taxes in this way on loans would lessen their volume in periods of prosperity and encourage their increase in periods of depression. These would both be constructive influences on the economic structure.

Thought

Government debts are a direct debt and charge against each citizen. Why cannot they understand this? So simple!

XXV

TAXATION

OUR METHODS OF TAXATION TODAY ILLUSTRATE ANOTHER weakness of democratic government. Taxes are levied not to improve economic conditions but to effect social reforms and please the masses. We must educate our citizens to realize that regardless of how the taxes are levied, the average citizen pays for them indirectly if not directly.

There is a limit to the taxes which industry can pay without serious injury. When the burden of taxes becomes too great, the natural tendency is for industry to retrench in all ways possible. This results in unemployment, lessens the demand for products and decreases the ability of people to purchase. As a final result, less money is raised from the taxes. The lower the taxes, the more evenly distributed, the more readily they can be collected with less harm to industry.

Taxes should be levied not only to raise revenue but to avoid cramping enterprise and business development. They should be considered with a view to their ultimate effect upon business and be designed to stimulate and increase business profits, and as a result increase the ability of business to pay taxes.

Regardless of all efforts to levy taxes upon the wealthy, the average citizen in the final analysis pays his share. Taxing the rich is politically popular and makes it possible for heavy taxes to be levied because the rich have relatively little voting power. These taxes must come from industry in some form, and are passed on to the consumer in whatever ways are open. Much of our present-day economic difficulties are due to unwise taxation and the increasing costs of government. To attain a sound economic foundation, the reduction of government expenses to the barest minimum, thus permitting the reduction of taxes, will be of the greatest benefit.

The conflict of jurisdiction between our states and federal government is resulting in burdensome taxes being levied. When both the federal government and the states apply taxes to the same things, confusion is bound to ensue, and unfairness results. Some of our taxes by this means are confiscatory. A sound policy must be established whereby the national government will control, to some extent, the state governments in the matter of taxation.

When we pass many laws establishing very high taxes, it causes people to resort to all possible means to avoid paying such confiscatory taxes. This is only natural. We are losing revenue by such high taxes, and are creating a bad spirit in encouraging taxpayers to seek all possible legal loopholes to avoid payment of them. All taxes should be levied in a fair manner without too many laws and regulations. The spirit of co-operation should be encouraged among taxpayers so they will willingly pay their share without seeking means of evasion.

Our income taxes are entirely too high. Fifteen or twenty per cent is about the maximum that should be levied. When taxes are raised beyond a certain definite limit, instead of increasing tax receipts, they decrease them. Wealthy people are driven to invest in tax-exempt securities and seek all means of evasion. If the taxes are reasonable, we encourage good citizenship, co-operation, and willingness to contribute to the support of the government.

People would willingly pay high taxes to a good government for good uses. They cannot be blamed for being reluctant to pay high taxes to a corrupt government dominated by politicians who spend government money to conciliate interest groups and obtain their votes.

An appeal to the wealthy to will their property to a government working for the nation's good might result in more income being obtained by voluntary contributions than by the present confiscatory taxes. When you treat people unfairly you build up resistance and cause them to seek means to evade the unjust treatment. Our tax system is unjust. We abuse those who pay the taxes instead of encouraging them to co-operate willingly. You should treat high-minded people generously and obtain their support; not fight them, treat them harshly, and alienate them from you. This is the real solution to our economic problems. A high-minded, capable government supported by all citizens would soon make our country a real heaven.

An efficient government worthy of respect would provide for taking over estates or foundations having unsound objectives. Many eccentric individuals of wealth will their money to purposes affording no constructive values to society. A wise government would provide for suitable means to convert this money into constructive use. There is danger in the abuse of this power. Unless we can have efficient government by able men, it had better not be attempted.

All churches and trusts of all kinds should pay taxes. We have much real estate that pays no return, making the burden upon the taxpaying public heavier. If these welfare institutions cannot carry on their welfare and fulfill their obligations to the government, they should not exist. This is a somewhat ruthless viewpoint, and there should be exceptions in certain special cases. Our neglect at present is in letting good intentions alone determine whether they should be taxed, and not real merit.

Vast sums of money are spent in building churches that look well and that are of little use. This money could be better spent in the construction of simpler buildings. If our religious institutions can become a real asset to the intellectual and moral life of the nation, it may be desirable to extend certain tax exemptions to them in furthering this development. When they are a real service, we may well grant them freedom from taxation; when they are of no service, they should be taxed. When they are, as so many are today, a distinct detriment, heavy taxation would be in the interest of the country, both for the revenue derived and in order to discourage the development of useless, harmful institutions.

Government debts are intimately related to taxation. Politicians are reluctant to levy taxes on the voter because of their unpopularity. They therefore resort to loans to meet the vast expenditures required to fulfill their political promises. Our government debt is now reaching a dangerous condition. It is still increasing. This increase will either result in further taxation or inflation. Both of these conditions are bad and a bar to the development of new industries.

The devaluation of the dollar by forty per cent by the Roosevelt administration was, in effect, an inflationary step. If this has been done once, it may be done again and yet again. Devaluing the dollar is a means of levying taxes in a concealed form. It has been a common expedient of governments of all times to meet pressing financial problems.

The bad feature about dollar devaluation and inflation is that it is a direct tax upon, or confiscation of, the property of the most deserving citizens. Not necessarily those who are wealthy, but the conscientious citizens who desire to provide for their families by taking out insurance and accumulating a nest-egg for future eventualities.

Sound taxation policies are essential to efficient government. The government should spend less than it receives. It should be frank and honest about matters of taxation and set an example of good conduct to its citizens. If the government resorts to discreditable financial measures, it encourages its citizens to do likewise.

Taxes should be levied upon capital in such a way as to encourage work and enterprise. They should not be levied in such a way as to confiscate profits and discourage work and enterprise. Probably the best way to accomplish this result is to reduce taxes to a minimum. When we compel the successful to pay vast sums of taxes, we are penalizing ability and industry.

Large government debts, large government expenditures, heavy taxation, and inflation alike penalize the industrious and enterprising. On the other hand, a minimum of government debts, expenditures, taxation, and absence of inflation rewards industry and enterprise. We should endeavor to bring about this wholesome condition. The requirements, however, are contradictory. To pay off our vast government indebtedness will require heavy taxation. This could be done in time by an efficient government if expenditures were reduced to a minimum, and taxes levied in ways to bring a good return without unduly penalizing enterprise.

The use of a capital levy in a small way might be helpful toward accomplishing this. A capital levy would tax capital itself. It would not tax profits from capital. In this respect it is wholesome. There are practical difficulties in carrying out a capital levy. It requires high standards of ability in the government and high standards of citizenship. We lack both these requirements.

The development of sound measures of taxation demands that we educate our citizens to an understanding of the harmful effects of unsound government policies. This is a task that our schools should take upon themselves. They do not do this today. They do not teach sound economics to their students. They do not point out the evils of taxation.

In bringing about sound taxation methods, we must reform our political institutions and our schools; require them to contribute toward an understanding of fiscal policies. This is not difficult. We must teach the citizens to look upon the government as a business concern that must be financially solvent, a concern that will not burden the people by taxation but which will make the burden as light as possible. The more efficient the government, the less need there is for taxation. We must change the common attitude of our present-day citizens. They demand benefits from the government. Instead they should be willing to pay to the government in order to make it solvent.

The ratio of taxation in the United States is constantly increasing as compared to national wealth and national income. It is estimated that one-fifth of the national income today is taken by the government in the form of taxes. Taxes are levied in so many indirect ways that the average citizen is often unaware of their existence. When one-fifth of the national income is paid to the government as taxes, it is bound to have a harmful effect upon business and industry. It is bound to cause unemployment. When such vast sums of money are levied by the government in taxes, uncertainty is caused as to future tax policies. This uncertainty further contributes toward the reluctance of industry to enter into new enterprises.

A wholesome system of taxation should have a very broad base. That is to say, all citizens in the country should pay taxes. When we levy taxes upon the wealthy alone, we encourage discrimination against them and promote unsound economic conditions. The poor people do not realize that, regardless of how taxes are levied, they pay them in the end. They foolishly applaud taxation of the wealthy, not realizing that they must pay them anyway in some form; either in high prices for goods purchased by them or in unemployment.

If, instead of taxing the wealthy alone, we tax all citizens, they would appreciate the evils of government spending to a greater degree. Suppose our workingmen were taxed as heavily as some of the wealthy people are today. Suppose when they receive ten dollars for a day's pay they were required to pay five dollars to the government in taxes. They would protest most vigorously.

Sensible methods of taxation under a democratic form of government call for high standards of unselfish citizenship. When the poor applaud efforts to tax the wealthy, they are not being good citizens. Politicians who resort to such methods are violating their trust. We should educate our citizens to full understanding of economic problems and the harmful effects of taxation. Taxation is intimately associated with government expenditures. The less money the government spends, the less it need raise by taxation. Therefore, the interests of all citizens are directly concerned in efficient, economical government.

XXVI

CORPORATIONS

THERE IS MUCH WASTE IN ALL ECONOMIC SYSTEMS. IT SHOULD be the endeavor of the government and of all citizens to reduce this waste to a minimum. Any waste, no matter how caused, results in the consumer paying for it, either by higher prices, poorer service, or inferior goods. Similarly, the elimination of waste tends to reward the consumer by better prices, better quality and better service.

Large corporations should be encouraged when they tend to reduce waste, duplication, and price conflicts. It is far better for the nation's welfare to have one firm make a reasonable profit with good service to the consumer than to have several losing money by too much competition. Small businesses should be encouraged and protected when rendering good service. Consolidations when in the public interest should also be encouraged.

Large corporations, managed by able, public-spirited men, are a distinct contribution to modern economic life. Modern conditions demand large corporations. This development can, of course, go to extremes. They may become so enlarged as to become unwieldy and inefficient. We should not penalize all large corporations. We should, if possible, make our economic system encourage large corporations serving the public and discourage the development of those not rendering service commensurate with their size.

Large concerns can very often render better service to the public than small concerns. They can often give better prices, handle a better product, and furnish better service to the consumer.

A large business can abuse its power by putting small concerns out of business. We should not permit such unfair practices. We should, however, permit a large corporation to develop naturally. When it can give better service to the consumer than many smaller concerns, it should be permitted to develop unhampered. When we pass laws limiting the activities of corporations, designed to protect small business, we are, to some extent, penalizing efficiency, rewarding inefficiency, and penalizing the public. We should encourage the most efficient methods and at the same time the highest ethical standards. These two are imperative to the development of sound economic institutions.

Large corporations or worthwhile business concerns possess many virtues. They have vast amounts of capital invested in their enterprises, and have much to lose from poor products, poor ethics or conduct of a nature that will prejudice the public against the purchase of their product. A large concern cannot abuse the public without having it become generally known. By virtue of its size it is required to establish a reasonably high code of ethics, whereas the small, insignificant business concern can resort to sharp practices with less danger. Many small concerns thrive on bad practices, and when discovered change their names, their locations, and repeat the same things over again. A large corporation cannot do this; neither can a large corporation exist unless it fulfills a need, answers demands of human wants.

Big corporations are unjustly attacked because of bigness and the popularity of attacks on them. The annual report of one, recently published, shows the payment of about ten dollars in dividends and about six dollars in taxation. The stockholders of a corporation, who shoulder all the risk and responsibility, are getting but little more than the government, who has no responsibility. If we had adequate statistics relative to the amount paid to labor, we could more truly evaluate the worth of corporations. Large corporations are highly helpful institutions. They pay large taxes to the government, they render service to the public, and yet they are attacked, persecuted and regulated by incompetent people.

Corporations are a development of modern industrial life and are essential to the conduct of vast enterprises. Evils can creep into corporation management just as readily as evils can creep into the government or any other activity of man. Effort should be directed toward raising the ethical standard of the citizens, the government and the corporations, so as to lessen the abuses resulting from the aggregation of vast amounts of capital in private hands.

There has been in the past much stock manipulation in corporations, the payment of high salaries to the management, favoritism in the promotion of employees and the making of contracts with the friends of the management. Corporations have sometimes been wrecked for the purpose of stock manipulation or other reasons. This is not an inherent evil of corporations or big business itself. It is an evil resulting from the misconduct of men. If our corporations are controlled by men with a high sense of honor and duty, such abuses will not exist. It is toward this standard we should strive.

The holding by one corporation of stock of another should be regulated so as to prevent corporations from developing which exist almost only on paper. A small corporation should not be permitted to own stock in a large one. The general development of corporate structures should strive to provide for the elimination of stock ownership of one corporation by others. The general object of building up corporations by stock ownership is to develop their own field of activity and not to invest in other corporations.

In limiting ownership by corporations of stock in other corporations we should not go to extremes and prevent the development of more efficient corporations by combinations through ownership. When combinations are in the interest of the public or in efficiency they should be encouraged.

The general policy of the government should be to simplify capital structure and to avoid unnecessary duplication of stockholdings. When a small corporation holds stock in a larger one, it but serves to complicate the capital structure. The government should require reports showing all stock held in order to have statistics of value regarding stock ownership. The object of this report would be to furnish information regarding the capital structure of corporations in an endeavor to simplify them.

In building up sound corporate structures, increase in the quantity of common stock should be encouraged, lessening preferred stock, bonds, and generally reduce debts to a minimum. A corporation is in a far sounder financial condition if all these obligations are converted into common stock.

Wise regulation would endeavor to raise common stock to the highest possible standard, insuring uniform income, and lessening the amount of bonds and senior issues. This could be facilitated by permitting savings banks, trustees, and similar units to invest their funds in common stock. If we take steps to make common stocks a good investment, they should prove just as sound as bonds. Our efforts to insure greater safety to savings banks and to people having savings accounts is a short-sighted view which prevents the development of the soundest economic structure, in which the interests of the individual would be even better served. Our present policies tend to encourage bond issues and preferred stock at the expense of common stock, whereas we should encourage common stock and lessen the bonds, indebtedness, and complicated issues.

The development of corporations affords a means for the workers and citizens generally to own the corporation by the purchase of their stock. We should build corporations into institutions serving the public and owned by the public, affording the thrifty an excellent means of investing their savings and securing a reasonable return. We should let

corporations grow to full size, and encourage stock ownership so the workers will own them, if possible.

A large floating supply of stock is a good thing. It provides
a wide market reducing fluctuations, there being such a
vast quantity of stock on hand for purchase or sale that the
market is less unsettled by either heavy buying or selling.
We should therefore promote sound ethical methods on
the part of brokers, encouraging them to furnish the best of
services.

Taxes should be levied on small stock holdings to discourage many holdings of such small size as to constitute a
nuisance in correspondence, payment of dividends, and legal
technicalities concerned therewith. A minimum holding
having a certain market value should be established, and
amounts less than this should be considered a nuisance and
required to be liquidated. The same principle applies to
transactions in odd lots of stock which are so small as to
result in annoyance and wasted effort.

There should be but one agency in the country capable
of granting the right to incorporate. By this means all corporations would be licensed by one agency, and a standardi-
zation of annual reports, accounts, and so forth could be
brought about.

Supporting corporations on the verge of bankruptcy may
be desirable or it may be harmful. In many cases it would
be better to have them liquidate their affairs and start anew,
unburdened by debt. On the other hand, it is possible that
a small loan may enable them to survive, and with improvement in business conditions, place them upon a sound footing.

Discriminatory regulations and taxation against chain
stores and large aggregations of capital penalize the efficient and reward the inefficient. Our efforts should not be
directed toward the encouragement of inefficiency and incompetence, as by this means the consumer pays more for
inferior products and poorer service. Our efforts should
rather be in stimulating efficiency, honesty, and a higher

code of business ethics. If a large business concern can be run efficiently, with due regard for service, it should be permitted to do so without restrictions.

Hampering industry because of size is not the answer to economic problems. The answer is efficiency, service, and better products. Natural economic laws should be permitted to function in bringing this about. Size in itself is evidence of efficiency, showing that the corporation or business is well handled and deserving of protection. It is only when large concerns abuse their power by unethical practices that they should be regulated and restricted. If our efforts were directed more toward establishing and maintaining a high code of ethics, less toward hampering efficiency, all would be better served.

Each corporation official and employee should also be considered as being a government official and servant of the public. The welfare of all cannot help but contribute to that of each. The loyalty of each employee should be not only to his corporation, to his employer, but to the entire country. He should give the best service he can to the public. The public should respond by assisting the corporations and the individual employees of the corporation in performing their service to the public.

XXVII

THE FARM PROBLEM

THE DEPRESSION IN THE FARMING INDUSTRY SINCE THE WORLD War has been effected by international conditions in addition to internal ones. The disturbance of the war, and high prices of farm products the world over, resulted in much more farm land being brought into cultivation in the United States. The amount of capital invested in farms was greatly increased. Many farmers overextended themselves in hoping for the continuation of prosperous times. With the termination of the war the American farmers had to meet the competition of foreign nations, and were unable to do so. High tariffs, depreciated currency, and lower labor costs in foreign countries prevented the American farmer from meeting their prices.

The overexpansion of our farms as the result of the war caused overproduction of farm products, resulting in declining prices. Heavy war debts, taxation, breakdown of international credit abroad, rendered foreign countries unable to purchase American products extensively. The general development of international conditions since the war has tended to deprive us of our foreign markets and to require the consumption of the products of the American farms within our own country, except for such items as cannot be grown abroad in sufficient quantities to meet the demand.

Farmers borrowed vast sums when the value of their farms was great. With a decline in farm values and a general depression of the farming industry, these mortgages were in some cases greater than the actual value of the property.

The people who loaned this money to the farmers did so in good faith. Foreclosing a mortgage works a hardship on the farmer, who loses his farm. On the other hand, failing to live up to the terms of the contract penalizes the man who loaned the money. It is indeed a difficult problem, the result of unsound economic conditions and unwise borrowing.

The real solution to the farm problem is efficient government, reduction of taxation, and the establishment of a sound economic system. Efficient, economical government will reduce taxes, thus enhancing farm values. Our present policies have the opposite effects. The farmer is obtaining certain benefits from the government which in turn must be raised by loans and taxation which are a charge against him in an indirect way. When he pays higher prices for everything he purchases as a result of government taxation and government policies, he is not being benefited. We are paying him benefits, making him pay higher taxes, and increasing his expenses. The sensible policy would be to cease paying him benefits, lessen his taxes and reduce his expenses.

The farmers should be encouraged to solve their own problems. When our government attempts to help them, we encourage the farmers to demand more government assistance. We should require the farmers, as well as all other citizens, to stand on their own feet and solve their own problems. Farmers can very easily organize co-operative agencies for distributing their farm products. There is a great deal of waste in the distribution of farm products to the consumer. At present the farmer is the greatest sufferer by this. The middlemen have fixed expenses as well as the farmer. If the farmer can eliminate them and deliver his products direct to the consumer, this waste will be reduced. The farmer will then receive the large profit he contributes today to the large dairies and distributing agencies.

The departments of health in many cities penalize the farmer-dairyman by imposing limitations on the sale of milk within the city and by requiring inspections and pasteurization, raising the cost of distribution. The health of the people should, of course, receive first consideration, but we should endeavor to find means of preserving their health without penalizing the farmer. Here is where science can contribute greatly toward the solution of the problem by finding means of insuring the delivery of fresh milk from the farm to the consumer without danger of disease, and in a simple inexpensive form.

Any means we can employ to facilitate the delivery of dairy products from the producer direct to the consumer will improve the farmers' condition. It is possible that suitable light containers could be filled at the farm, sealed with proper agents, and kept fresh indefinitely. A great difficulty in the farm and dairy problem is in the cost of distribution, causing the farmer to be penalized because unable to protect himself. Our efforts should be devoted toward correcting this situation, not by attempting to repress existing evils, but by working out true methods that will eliminate the evils entirely or lessen their bad effects.

Attempts to maintain farm prices require great ability on the part of those administering the attempt and great knowledge of underlying conditions, so they may be co-operated with and not opposed. The attempt made by the Hoover administration to maintain high prices through the purchase by the government of farm products resulted in driving them to new lows. The vast accumulation of purchases by the government placed such a mass hanging over the market as to render it impossible for high prices to be maintained. It is far better to all concerned to permit prices to seek their own level. When they go down below a reasonable amount, the less productive fields will not be cultivated. In a short time the great superabundance of products will automatically be cared for by the voluntary curtailment of production on the part of the farmers.

Paying bonuses to farmers to restrict production in an effort to raise prices is unsound. The benefits thus paid farmers must be obtained from some other source. This is taking from one person to pay another, and makes no attempt to reach the underlying causes for the farm depression. Such action tends to perpetuate existing evils, whatever they may be. Payment of bonuses to our farmers to restrict production has in some cases resulted in increasing amounts of foreign goods being imported to make up for the scarcity thus caused. The effect is then to reward foreign importers at the expense of the American taxpayer.

International conditions are having a great effect upon the farming industry. The markets of the world are being largely closed to us by tariff barriers. As a result our foreign markets are being lost. This, of necessity, will require a curtailment in farming operations, restricting their production to meet the lessened demand. Our government has attempted to meet this by actually paying farmers not to raise farm products. The normal and sound measure is to maintain a hands-off policy and let the farmers voluntarily curtail their production through the free functioning of the law of supply and demand.

When the government attempts to maintain prices, it interferes with the functioning of the law of supply and demand. The farmer will, if left alone, adapt himself to price fluctuations. When prices of his products are high, he will raise more and thus reduce them. When they are low, he will lessen his production causing them ultimately to rise. When the government sets a fixed price, the farmers do not adapt themselves to high or low prices. They raise as much as they can to obtain the maximum benefits from the price fixed by the government. The government attempts to meet this difficulty by paying them bonuses to restrict production. We are creating a farm problem where none should exist. We are penalizing the entire country by our fumbling attempts to help the farmer.

These attempts to help the farmer are unsound and will prove harmful to him in the long run. A far worse harm is the injury done to the moral character of the farmers themselves. The inefficient farmer demands benefits from the government and receives them. The administration in power receives great political support from farmers by paying benefits to them in various forms. This abuse will continue to grow until it destroys itself. We will then be back where we were before the present policy was adopted. In addition we will have a vast government debt on our hands partly as the result of unwise farm policies. We will have prevented the normal development of the farming industry to meet changing conditions. We will have created much ill-feeling among the farmers themselves. Everyone will suffer. Why can we not be sensible and refuse to employ unwise measures?

The farmers are passing through a period of evolution, of industrialization, somewhat similar to industry. The farmer is purchasing and using an increasing number of labor-saving devices. The horse is being displaced by tractors and trucks. This increases the plant investment and is more efficient. The industrialized farmer, however, like the industrialized business, is less able to bear up in a depression than the unindustrialized farmer having smaller overhead and plant investment. Unwise interference by the government prevents the modernization of farming. We should permit the most efficient to survive and the most efficient methods to be carried out. This will be effected by natural development if not prevented by unwise government interference.

We should encourage the development of means of converting farm products into industrial products. There is a great field here for development. Many farm products now raised can be readily converted into manufactured products and by further research many new products suitable for cultivation on the farm can be developed to be made into manufactured articles.

XXVIII

ETHICS AND BUSINESS

AN ASCENDENT ENVIRONMENT INCLUDES THE DEVELOPMENT OF an economic environment in which the individuals will be rewarded in accordance with their merit, and where descendent conduct in an effort to obtain economic advantages will be impossible. The capitalistic system, in giving the utmost freedom to all, offers the best means of obtaining a sound economic environment. Despite inequalities and injustices, there is a distinct tendency for the most able and energetic to obtain the greatest economic reward. There is also a tendency for the lazy, the worthless, the incompetent, to receive less reward.

The great error present-day government and social reformers make is attempting to do away with the evils in the existing economic system by penalizing the deserving citizen to reward the undeserving. The true method is to eliminate the undeserving, have all citizens deserving, and continually to strive for improvement so that all will be rewarded in accordance with their merit.

Unwise attempts to help those having little will result in additional burdens being placed upon those capable of succeeding by their own efforts. The assistance that is given should be restricted to measures that will assist the individual concerned in developing the ability to solve his own problems. Under no consideration should so-called reforms be attempted that will place additional burdens upon the deserving or render any person less able to solve his own problems and more willing to be a parasite or the recipient of benefits.

In attempting to reform our economic system we must not be impatient and demand the abolition of all evils at once. We must recognize the fact that we have a higher standard of living than has heretofore prevailed in any nation of any time. Modern industrial development has resulted in many new problems and in different ways of living. In solving these problems we must proceed cautiously, making sure that no action taken will prove harmful to character. In considering means of improving economic conditions we should weigh them first by determining what their ultimate effect will be upon moral character. Only when the effect will be good should the suggested measures be put into practice.

In bringing about a sound economic system we should utilize the basic truths of human nature. Men will not willingly lose the approbation of other men. In an ascendent environment, employers, managers, and others in power will not resort to descendent action. They themselves will be a part of the ascendent environment, and will act in such way as meets with the approbation of the people composing it. They cannot do otherwise, for they are especially vulnerable if they do so. Thus effort directed toward the attainment of an ascendent environment directly solves the conflict at present existing between capital and labor, and conduces toward a sound economic system in many other ways.

The great error our government is making is in stressing economic improvement and passing many acts to improve the condition of people who are in poor circumstances. If this effort were directed to improving the intelligence and moral standards of the individual citizens, there would be greater possibility of bringing about a sound economic system. The measures being employed are impractical. They appeal to the masses by flattery and include efforts to take from the Haves and give to the Have-nots. Rather than do this we should educate the Have-nots to a realization that they are at fault to some extent. We should endeavor to bring about such a sound economic system that they will have full opportunity to emerge from their condition of want. Then failure to do so will mark them as improvident, inefficient, and victims of their own incompetence.

We should strive to develop our economic institutions for the future so as to stress character and service, placing moral qualities ahead of profit. Business should be given a reasonable profit and efficient management should be rewarded. The development of character on the part of all individuals will result in the able executives taking just pride in rendering service and in being a real good to the community, in addition to making profits. Heavy taxes on industry by the government tend to restrict it to the profit motive and lessen the good feeling which would develop of its own accord toward rendering better service and improving the general moral tone of business. Business will reflect the moral character of the nation. It is today far superior to the moral atmosphere of our political life. Yet we are permitting politicians to regulate it.

We should not continue to penalize present-day business for the misdeeds of business magnates of many years ago. Neither should we penalize all busines men for the misconduct of a few at present. We should rather encourage the good conduct of the well-behaved business man and correct the misconduct of the guilty one.

We have permitted the solution of our problems to be obscured by too many irrelevant considerations. Common sense should tell us that if each person behaved well and solved his own problems no need would exist for legislation to solve them. This is the vital point. Let us strive for it by making the individual meet this requirement.

Let us give business a chance. Let us apply the Golden Rule for a while and remove all these restrictions that are preventing it from fulfilling its mission. It has been much chastened by past bad behavior and overregulation, and would readily respond to the application of the Golden Rule and a chance to redeem itself.

Business should follow an enlightened code of ethics. Instead of prohibiting certain practices we should encourage individuals to contribute toward improving the code of business ethics by their example.

Forcing capital or anyone to do things against their will tends to build up their resistance and causes them to seek means of evading the requirements. The effort of government should not be directed to forcing people to do things. It should educate them to a responsibility for their duties, resulting in their doing willingly whatever is best for all.

A sensible economic system would make it difficult or impossible for vice to enrich and virtue to impoverish. To bring about sound economic conditions we must combine with them a high moral code, both to be controlled by intelligence. Passion, class hatred, and denunciation will never accomplish results. Cease to belittle the other fellow or attribute false motives to him. If he is really a bad influence, eliminate him from the environment; if not, encourage him to contribute of his best.

We might well start establishing a high code of business ethics by requiring that products be not misrepresented; that the manufacturers and the dealers, state exactly what they are and what benefits or virtues they possess. The dealer should treat his customer as he would himself be treated. Business exists to make a profit but it also has the higher duty of rendering service and being a real contribution to the community. Profits are only justified when these requirements are met.

A government test bureau should be established to test all products that are advertised and furnished to the public. Harmful ones should be prohibited from circulating, those with merit should be encouraged. Those with little merit should be neither prohibited nor encouraged. The government bureau should state the facts to the public that they may know just what they are getting. Honest dealers should be protected, and the buyer also. The rights of honest dealers are prejudiced by dishonest ones. Buyers should not be subjected to exploitation. No concern should handle a product unless it is of a social value, useful, beneficial, and meritorious.

One of the most vicious demonstrations we see of harmful advertising is that shown by the many advertisements guaranteeing the restoration of hearing to old people. These elderly people have suffered physical deterioration in the organs of hearing and it is very difficult, almost impossible, to give them material help. Some contrivances may be of assistance, but most of them are merely means of obtaining money by claims to unpossessed merits. They impose upon the elderly who possess this physical ailment. No business has the right to exist that capitalizes the disabilities or misfortunes of others. If true service can be rendered to alleviate the misfortune or lessen the disability, well and good. When no benefit can be derived and advertising is resorted to only as a means of obtaining money, it is no better than outright robbery and should be condemned with equal severity.

It would be helpful to honest and better business if all articles for retail sale were price-marked at the time of manufacture, giving the date, dealer's name, wholesale price, and retail price. This would protect honest dealers, manufacturers, and the consumer and would tend to bring about better service, better products, and reasonable prices. The consumer's best protection is in dealing with reputable merchants. Any measure that will promote a higher code of ethics on the part of dealers will benefit the consumer.

We see much fraud in financial transactions, such as buying and selling of worthless stocks and bonds. Much of this is done in compliance with the letter of the law. We must establish a code of ethics that goes far beyond the mere letter of laws and regulations. We must establish a public opinion that will condemn anyone who exploits others, who obtains money under false pretenses or without adequate return for value received. We have too many clever men making a living by their wits, lowering the code of business ethics, and harming honest dealers. We must establish a code that prevents the survival of unwise business practices and will reward only those who are the possessors of good moral character, a strong sense of duty to the public, and a desire to serve in addition to making a reasonable profit.

We should endeavor to elevate our economic life to the highest ethical standards. The consumer, for instance, should consider the dealer and endeavor to save him unnecessary cost. The dealer, in appreciation of this thoughtfulness, can then give better products or better service, or reduce prices. Universal thoughtfulness on the part of all will result in a better understanding and a better atmosphere.

The unfortunate part of existing conditions is that the better people are penalized for the misbehavior of the less desirable ones. For instance, the department stores are put to much expense and loss as the result of unnecessary exchanges of goods and unsettled accounts. This loss must be made up by having the good customer carry the bad and pay for his misbehavior. Efficient organization of business would reduce this evil to a minimum, reduce charge accounts, and require that all bills be paid promptly.

All people should endeavor to obtain better service by giving good service, the consumer as well as the distributor. The quiet, well-behaved, long-suffering American citizen, who pays his way, is not the one who causes discord or dissatisfaction. He does not constantly attack existing conditions and demand reforms. It is the agitator types, the less desirable citizens, who are always being mistreated and who demand action to benefit them. It is this noisy class who are dominating our economic legislation, prejudicing the rights of decent citizens. As a result, the ethical standards of business and life throughout the nation are not very high. We are permitting them to be established by the poorer element. This situation must be corrected by the better element taking control and imposing good conduct upon the undesirable element.

The life records should contain a complete business record, showing the commercial integrity of the individual. It would then be possible for anyone doing business with another person to ascertain his reliability with little effort. He would then avoid doing business with undesirable parties and seek desirable ones. This in itself would promote the development of commercial integrity. The activities of modern life cannot be carried on effectively unless you can trust those with whom you are doing business. Any means that tends to eliminate undesirable persons from business will assist in bringing about sounder economic conditions.

Business concerns endeavoring to serve their customers honestly and faithfully are often abused by them. Among the worst offenders are women in prosperous circumstances living an idle life. They employ many ways to abuse the service which the store is trying to give them. This tends to cause higher prices in order that the loss occasioned thereby may be made up; the good customer paying for the bad conduct of others. Such offenders lack Primo and Co. They fail to see fault in what they are doing and they fail to give consideration to others. The same traits are exhibited when people damage property, carry it off, or destroy what does not belong to them. Such conduct is not without its own punishment because the offenders make themselves less desirable people.

Pay cash for all your purchases. Consider those with whom you are dealing. If you can in any way make things nicer or pleasanter for them, do so. You will then be setting an example in conduct that encourages its universal spread and will result in benefits to all. We are all the recipients of many services from many different people. If we co-operate with them we render their problems less difficult and encourage them to give better service.

All people should endeavor to prevent vandalism to property of others, whether it be property of a corporation, the government, or private individuals. This will benefit the individual by developing his consideration for others, thus

improving his character. Too many people are heedless of
what property damage they inflict, thinking that it is the
other fellow's problem. Such an attitude shows thoughtless-
ness, poor character, and lack of consideration for others,
and it marks the individual as being a not very desirable
person. Guests in hotels who abuse privileges by dirtying
up towels unnecessarily, messing up the room, and demanding much service, cause the hotel increased expense which
must be made up by higher charges.

Socialists, communists, and radical labor unions fight
property owners because they believe they are self-seeking
and oppressive. Our property owners are opposing labor for
the same reason. If we make the property owners and labor
unions deserving, neither should have a grievance against
the other. The solution of the problem of capital and labor
is therefore the simple task of making each worthy.

In its final outcome, social-welfare work and labor legislation designed to raise wages and shorten hours benefits the
undeserving at the expense of the deserving and in addition
contributes toward the breakdown of the moral character of
the individual citizens. We should reduce our government
activities and interference to a minimum and concentrate
our efforts on raising the moral character of both the employers and employees. If the employers are high-minded
men they will not abuse their employees, and the need for
government interference will not exist.

When you start interference by the government by attempting to regulate hours, wages, and disputes between
workers and employers, any number of small controversies
are initiated unnecessarily and ill feeling is created between
the two, which should not exist. If both are of high moral
character, problems will be considered fairly and ill feeling
will not exist. The government could well assist in promoting harmony between the two and in protecting the public
whose best interests are served by both capital and labor
working in harmony.

Labor, management, consumer, and owner must all be

considered and must work together, taking losses when needful. If we can bring about this co-operative spirit throughout our nation, all will prosper. This can be done with very little government regulation, by promoting understanding, education, intelligence, and the realization that if all work together, all will profit. Whenever violence, agitation, or ill feeling, is aroused, the public pays; when these are eliminated, the public benefits.

Selfishness, repression, denunciation of others, violence, an attempt to get one's own desires at whatever cost, will not benefit those employing them. Let us cease to cause unnecessary discord and suffering within our nation. Let us place virtue and intelligence in control, make them the sole test of conduct, and use forceful measures to restrain anyone acting in any way opposed to them.

The profit motive is not the real basis of man's ills. The true fault is the failure to develop Co and Ascendo so as to make them universal. The profit motive, the desire to provide for the future, can be used as a great help in advancing both Co and Ascendo. In denouncing the profit motive and blaming our ills upon wealth and those who have succeeded, we are using primitive mental processes. The true method is to develop intelligence, use the highest attributes of the human mind, and convert the profit motive into a force assisting the onward advance of man.

We must solve our economic problems in accordance with human nature. No one likes to be belittled, abused, or mistreated; neither do the really deserving like to receive false praise. But all alike, whether rich or poor, like to possess the well-deserved approbation of others, and they also like to feel convinced that they are fine persons. Let us utilize these basic principles of human nature in solving our economic problems. Let us appeal to the best that is within each, whether rich or poor; not denounce or persecute them. Point out to each what is the proper conduct. Establish a public opinion so universal, so strong, that no one will dare oppose it, and your economic problems are solved without the intervention of government. By this means you have established an economic system based upon the good traits in human nature. Today we are attempting to improve our economic system by a policy of repression designed to arouse resentment and prevent the good traits inherent in normal humans from asserting themselves.

We must so improve our ethical standards that men will not seek profit in ways opposed to man's welfare. They should take more pride in the fact that they are serving human needs, are advancing man's interests, are doing good work, and are contributing their share to making this a better and happier world. We should endeavor to modify our economic system in such way that profits are increased in accordance with the good done. They will then be a real agent for advancing the welfare of the nation. Pecuniary benefit is as naught to the profit of mind, body, intellect, and disposition, in the full knowledge of work well done, a just pride of achievement and of contributing to Ascendency.

Thoughts

The profit motive does not produce our low moral standing. It is the latter that abuses the former. Correct the cause and you correct the effect.

———————

The real conflict is not between the rich and poor but between good and evil, knowledge and ignorance, work and idleness.

———————

The economic welfare of the entire nation is best served by any methods which tend to improve the intelligence and moral character of the individual citizen.

———————

In our effort to control vicious wealth we are oppressing the productive, enterprising wealth that supports and serves our people. Why not leave the virtuous alone and concentrate on the vicious, whether wealthy or not?

Unlimited advertising enables the unscrupulous to cheat the none-too-bright. Unlimited speech and propaganda enables the unscrupulous politician to control the unintelligent mob for his own ends. We will have to protect the none-too-bright against the rogue. It would be better, of course, if we could eliminate the rogue, leaving no one to impose on the mentally dull, or eliminate the latter and the rogues could have no one to impose on. Better still, eliminate both and it will be unnecessary to regulate advertising or restrict free speech.

XXIX

THE DISTRIBUTION OF WEALTH

IT SEEMS A GREAT INJUSTICE THAT SOME PEOPLE SHOULD HAVE so much and others so little. The best interests of all would be served by having a more even distribution of wealth. This, however, is far less important than the quantity of wealth existing. There is a limit to what the billionaire can spend on himself; regardless of how he spends his money, it is distributed in some form to workers; they thus obtain a certain amount of benefit from the expenditures of the very wealthy.

The more wealth that exists in a country, regardless of by whom owned, the better off each individual in that particular country is. This great wealth, even though in the hands of relatively few, increases the wealth per capita, and all are benefited thereby. This is a truth which should be stressed by our economists because it is somewhat difficult for those who have little or nothing to understand.

If the accumulation of great wealth is conducted in such way as to prevent the power thus conferred from being used to abuse, no harm will result. The more wealth the better. No vast accumulations of wealth can be made by any one individual under modern conditions without conferring great benefits upon many others.

Wealth must be kept busy in order to earn a return. As a result new industries are stimulated, new enterprises started, old structures rebuilt and remodeled, all of which gives employment, stimulates activity, and results in raising the standard of living throughout the entire country. The true way to prosperity is not to attack capital but protect it, stimulate it, and encourage it to develop new industries. This increased demand for labor and materials will raise wages and assure work to all.

We may divide wealth into two general classes: that which is well employed and serves to advance the interests of man, and wealth of a parasitical type which aims to serve only the individual possessing it. It should be the government's policy to encourage the first type and to discourage and eliminate the second type. This is a distinction that our legislators do not draw. They pass laws regulating all wealth. In their effort to control the parasitical type they put unnecessary burdens and restrictions upon the constructive.

We must not permit wealth to be gathered and perpetuated in the hands of a few at the expense of and against the best interests of the many, neither must we destroy industry by burdening it with high taxes, overregulation, confiscatory wages and hours, and other extreme benefits to employees. All efforts heretofore made to regulate capital in the interests of the working man are tending to overburden it, making it less able to perform its mission of furnishing work for the working man.

The great error being made in attempts to correct economic ills is to pass a great many laws restricting the well-to-do, taxing them heavily, endeavoring to give benefits to the less well-to-do, and failing generally to recognize that the problem is more of a moral one than an economic one. Analysis of the psychas shows that man is influenced by many other feelings than to acquire wealth. This acquisitive desire is an excellent one if it is not abused.

We should endeavor to establish an ascendent environment that will encourage the individual to consider the future, provide for himself and family, and at the same time consider the effect of his acts upon himself and upon others. There are any number of psychas that can be brought to bear to prevent the abuse of wealth. Those who are successful in business and acquire wealth and power should not be penalized or persecuted for their ability. They should be encouraged to utilize their ability for the benefit of all, and others should be encouraged to do likewise.

The abuse of power or wealth should be considered a very serious offense against the public, and should receive universal condemnation. Once this feeling existed, it is very unlikely that wealthy people would go counter to public opinion in performing harmful acts. They would be so encouraged to develop Ascendency within themselves and contribute toward an ascendent environment, that the thought of descendent acts would be distasteful.

A society founded on such an ascendent viewpoint has not yet existed. This has been because sufficient knowledge of human nature has not been available. Man has failed to model his institutions so as to bring out the best within each individual. Once we attempt to remodel our society with this aim in view, the need for interference in economic problems will become less and less. The individuals themselves will voluntarily refrain from any acts that will be prejudicial to the community.

When we strive toward an ascendent environment of this kind we are voluntarily enrolling the assistance of the wealthy toward this laudable aim, the very opposite of coercion. It is a principle of human nature that voluntary action toward the attainment of definite aims will be more productive of sound results than coercive action. Coercion or force should be employed only against the prihuman, the ignorant, the vicious, who refuse to respond by voluntary co-operation.

When we attempt to coerce people into behaving well, we are by such actions substantially saying that they are undesirable citizens and cannot be ruled by appeals to intelligence and character. This is what we are doing today. Unquestionably we have many undesirable people, but they are far from being a majority. Let us rather endeavor to segregate or eliminate the undesirables and give the fine, de-

sirable, ascendent people full opportunity to co-operate voluntarily in contributing of their best to the welfare of the
community.

Persecution of those having wealth and who have succeeded causes them to protect themselves. Instead of being
persecuted they should be enrolled in the cause of advancing prosperity to all. This can readily be done if the effort
be made. These people are sensible enough to realize that
their own prosperity is dependent upon the prosperity of
the nation as a whole, and efforts to attain their co-operation will meet with a hearty response. Efforts to persecute
them will arouse resentment and make a bad economic situation worse.

It is very unfair to the wealthy to require them to spend
much effort evading income taxes in efforts to conserve
their wealth. This prevents them from using their ability
in constructive efforts to improve economic conditions. The
very imposition of high taxes, so high as to be confiscatory
and unjust, has a bad effect on character. When people feel
they are being unjustly treated, they will retaliate in kind.
We cannot blame the wealthy for using all means to avoid
the payment of unjust taxes.

This is not a good mental state to be in, but it is produced by the action of our government. Not only do our rulers levy these high taxes, but they denounce the rich, persecute them in other ways, and do about all they can to prevent
them from co-operating with the government in the development of the nation's industries. Taxes on the wealthy
should be reduced to a reasonable amount so they will not
feel unjustly dealt with and are encouraged to use their
wealth in developing the industries of the nation.

The feeling against the well-to-do on the part of those
who have little or nothing is in large measure due to a
psychological condition, a feeling of inferiority and envy.
The failure is only too willing to blame people or things
other than himself, where the trouble usually lies. An honest
person would first seek fault in himself before blaming

others. Unfortunately, not all humans are honest with themselves.

Another factor contributing toward this feeling against the wealthy is that the politicians use it continually to obtain votes, as it is always a popular means of getting the multitude on their side. There is some ground for this feeling, too, because wealth has in many cases abused its power. There are, however, many fine people among the wealthy just as there are many fine ones among the poor.

The real conflict in man's affairs is not between wealthy and poor. It is between the intelligent, industrious, considerate and deserving against the ignorant, indolent, selfish, incompetent, and undeserving; a conflict of the workers against the Philistines and Philistiners. You can find good people among poor and rich but you cannot find worthwhile people among the worthless, or worthless among the worthwhile. Here is the basic truth in which lies the solution of all of our present-day troubles. When the worthwhile people assert themselves, govern the country and cease to permit the worthless to control it, sensible action will be forthcoming.

Many wealthy people by their poor example furnish just ground for censure. They should live simple lives and set an example of good conduct. They should use their money in ways that will increase the actual wealth of the country permanently, rather than on display, vanity, pleasure, futile sports, or useless, harmful ways. When they become ostentatious or behave in a discreditable manner, they give justification for harsh criticism. This often takes the form of legislation intended to prevent the abuse of wealth but which hampers the enterprising, successful individuals in stimulating industry and adding to economic prosperity.

The parasitic wealthy must be reformed or eliminated. They discredit the deserving people of means; they concentrate vast quantities of property in their hands, thus preventing its acquirement by the workers. Their idle, useless, existence sets a bad example in causing many to pursue the frivolous, trivial, and futile.

The property of those wealthy people who abuse the privileges and power wealth gives them, and fail adequately to live up to the obligations imposed thereby, should be ruthlessly confiscated by the government and used for the public benefit. Inauguration of the policy of confiscation, however, requires that the government be conducted by the most able upright officials in order that public-spirited citizens be not unjustly deprived of wealth which they have proven their capacity to administer.

The mere fact that abuse of wealth would result in confiscation would be a most effective deterrent to such abuse. It would indeed be so effective as to make its actual exercise unnecessary. This affords an excellent example of what sound measures based upon understanding of human nature may have when entrusted to able, honest administrators for execution. Likewise, it illustrates the harm that could result in abuse by incapable or dishonest officials.

Drastic as such action would seem at first thought, it would be far less harmful than the present popular methods of so regulating and taxing wealth and capital as to hamper its efficient functioning. We are today penalizing all people of wealth, all capital, be it deserving or undeserving. By the outright confiscation of the wealth of those who abuse its power, they alone would be penalized and there would be no excuse to hamper constructive capital.

Inheritance of wealth should be limited to those requiring it, such as children and the elderly. Youth and strength should never be constituted a favored class headed for emasculation. The most a parent can give a child is health, character, education, pleasant and helpful recollections. Let not the good in children be submerged by showering them with wealth and gifts, weakening their characters. Sensible public opinion should not tolerate the injustice to heirs of giving them wealth unearned.

We should find means to break up the very large fortunes

amounting to many millions or hundreds of millions of dollars passed on through inheritance. Those who inherit these fortunes are not deserving of them, if they have not actually contributed toward their creation. Arbitrary confiscation would be too drastic, unwise and disturbing. A better understanding of economic problems and of the individual's duty to society could in time bring about a realization that a successful man was acting against the best interests of society when he left vast fortunes to members of his family.

Care must be taken to avoid discouraging the striving for achievement which not only results in great pecuniary success for the individual but enables him to confer vast benefits on society. An able man who accumulates a vast fortune by his own efforts, furnishing employment to many, developing and producing products of value to society, is as great a contribution to it as the scientist, the educator or any others.

We should encourage successful achievement in economic endeavor as well as in the more strictly social field. The successful industrialist can be a great social contribution. We should encourage successful men to realize their social obligations on the one hand and on the other encourage among the citizens a more healthful viewpoint that will not denounce the successful but will encourage them to give of their best to society.

There is a vast difference between inherited wealth and acquired wealth. Inherited wealth tends to soften those who receive its benefits without effort on their part, and is distinctly harmful to them and to society. Acquired wealth is the life of the nation itself. It is the reward for endeavor. It may be abused, and has been so abused in the past by many, but this could be easily prevented by an ascendent environment supported by a sensible economic system. We should encourage acquired wealth to serve the community and should endeavor to lessen the harm done by inherited wealth.

Our inheritance laws should be corrected so that upon death all property reverts to the government unless the owner leaves it by will to certain persons. This would obviate lawsuits in which distant heirs attempt to get money to which they have no real claim. The government could far better use this than the people who fight in law courts for money they have done nothing to earn.

The right of a man to leave property by will to his children, his family, and for good works, should be guaranteed. With the development of higher standards of Ascendency it is possible that many wealthy men could be induced to will their wealth to the government, thus breaking up their fortunes upon their deaths and leaving a reasonable amount in the form of annuities payable by the government to those near and dear to them.

Inheritance taxes could be levied in an endeavor to obtain a reasonable share of the estate for the government in case large sums were left for other purposes. If used, they should not be so excessive as to cause efforts to evade them. The wealthy will bear their share, are doing it now, of government expenses. We should encourage them to do so willingly, from a sense of duty: obtain their co-operation, rather than employ methods of compulsion.

We should in general work toward a more even distribution of wealth, but gradually, in order to avoid harm. Attempts to prevent large accumulations of wealth by penalizing the efficient and rewarding the inefficient are productive of more harm than good. No measures should be enacted that will prevent individuals from employing their gifts to the best advantage in their own interests and the interests of others.

We should not prevent able men from accumulating wealth. If they have the ability to make vast sums of money, at the same time giving good service, manufacturing good products, and affording work, and if they are a contribution to their times, by all means encourage them. Their prosperity and success are shared by the nation. It is mere envy and bad motives that cause able men, who have succeeded in accumulating large sums of money by real service, to be attacked. Those who attack are displaying by their very attacks their own incapacity and stupidity. Yet these are the people that today dominate our institutions.

Wealth can be abused, has been abused, will always be abused, possibly, but it has also been a great benefactor. The great development of our country, regardless of what may be said, has been due in a very large degree to able men working hard, developing industry, building railroads, furnishing the directing brains for vast enterprises that are essential to such undertakings. Those who condemn them are often unequal to other achievements. Sour grapes, mostly.

We should encourage the wealthy to will their money for the advancement of man and not attempt to hold large fortunes intact upon their death. The object should be to prevent the perpetuation of large fortunes and to facilitate the distribution of wealth. But in doing this we should not violate economic laws and cause more harm than good. It is not the quantity of wealth in the possession of any one individual that does the harm; it is the manner in which it is administered. Our interests had better be directed toward securing good administration of wealth than in repressing it to the extent that it is unable to perform its function.

It might be desirable to grant a special license or classification to the very wealthy people, permitting them to accumulate wealth in the development of business enterprises; upon their death, their wealth should revert to the government, with provision that certain amounts could be left to deserving beneficiaries in the form of life annuities or in whatever desirable form the benefactor wished. The object in doing this would be to contribute toward a more even distribution of wealth, and at the same time avoid discouraging enterprise on the part of able men.

People who obtain real pleasure in life from building up vast industries should be encouraged to do so. Their efforts are a benefit to the country and they should not be restricted. At the same time they should be encouraged to leave the wealth to the government or in a form that will benefit the nation and prevent the perpetuation of vast fortunes.

If we could bring about in our wealthy such a sense of duty, we would have the advantage of encouraging them to exert themselves to the fullest. When estates are left to the government, they should be promptly liquidated in order that other citizens may acquire the property.

Trusts that have been created for purposes that cannot be fulfilled or that are opposed to the best interests of the nation should be taken over by the government and administered for the best interests of the country.

Dead bank accounts, unsettled estates, and all property that does not possess a sound legal status should be taken over by the government. These should be liquidated as soon as possible. The government should avoid holding any more real estate or property than is essential to the conduct of its affairs.

We should find means to regulate perpetual endowments by wise action to prevent them from becoming so great as to prevent wholesome distribution of wealth. For instance, if each person in the country upon his death willed his property to a certain endowment, and this was continued indefinitely, after a considerable time all property in the country would be owned by endowed institutions. This would result in there being but little property left to pay taxes, and this property would be overburdened by taxation. This situation arose to some degree in Europe when a vast amount of the landed property of the nations belonged to the church.

The problem of perpetual endowment has not yet reached serious proportions but is well worth considering. Arrangements can be made for all endowed institutions to make suitable returns to the government, to pay taxes in an effort to prevent endowments from becoming too extensive. Our general object should be to facilitate the distribution of wealth and render it possible for any hard-working citizen to acquire a reasonable amount of property. The good which these endowed institutions do should be carefully inquired into. If they are not an asset to the social institutions, their property should be forfeited to the government and used in beneficial ways.

Income throughout the nation should be equalized as much as practicable by elevating the standards of citizenship. Economic conditions will be improved by the reduction of crime and institutionalism, and the improvement of conduct. Anything that makes the body of citizens more intelligent and of better character directly improves economic standards.

Not the least of wise government measures would be the elimination of parasitism, reducing to a minimum the number of those people in the country who demand or require assistance from others. If all parasites were eliminated, if we had no one who was a burden upon others, we would have a sound economic system without the enactment of legislation to bring it about.

The government's present attempts to improve economic conditions have the opposite effect in that they increase the number of parasites and those demanding assistance from others, at the same time decreasing those who are an asset to the community—the direct opposite of a sound economic policy. The undeserving and incompetent have no place in a sound economic system, and they should be eliminated. They are the ones who get the greatest share of government relief; they benefit from social legislation to the prejudice of the worthwhile citizen.

The undesirables contribute to both booms and depressions. They exaggerate booms by being then able to get jobs and spend their money freely; depressions by being unable to get jobs because of their incompetence and having to be maintained by others.

If we reduce the number of people unfit or unable to care for themselves, we directly increase the prosperity of those who are able to do so. Contrarywise, by taxing the efficient ones to support the inefficient, we are penalizing them. Drastic measures to effect this should not be undertaken. We should rather employ education and wholesome environmental influences. If we could eliminate all the undesirables from our country, unquestionably the economic condition of the desirable people would be greatly improved. Poverty as such would cease to exist and there would be employment and opportunity for all.

A great contribution toward the even distribution of wealth and increase in per capita wealth would be made by the elimination of the Philistines and the reform of the Philistiners. Their elimination would improve the welfare of the workers and increase their proportionate share of wealth.

The distribution of wealth is more unfair than the distribution of poverty. If we take the tenth of our population lowest from the standpoint of material goods and compare them with the lowest tenth based upon individual worth, the two groups would coincide to a great degree. This would not be true if we took two like groups with regard to wealth and worth. It would be found that the worthy group are composed mainly of those possessing less wealth than the wealthy group. The true solution to this problem is on the one hand to prevent the perpetuation of wealth by inheritance and on the other to provide for the elimination of the poor and unworthy by education, birth control, and segregation. We should gradually develop our social institutions so as to further this aim. In time it may be accomplished, poverty abolished, and the injustices of the present unfair distribution of wealth largely rectified.

The even distribution of wealth is facilitated by having no government debts. Government debts are a direct charge against each citizen who must maintain the interest payments, which are obtained by the government from him in the form of taxes. Thus, the greater the government debt, the greater is the burden upon each citizen and the greater the charge upon him. This is not generally recognized, but it is a profound truth.

When we see a government spending vast sums of money for the benefit of the poor, we see a government that is placing an additional burden upon the poor; yet to the unthinking who are receiving government benefits, government debts mean nothing. The man who has nothing pays no taxes and has little to lose regardless of what the government debt may be, according to common logic. But these vast debts are a charge against each citizen and he must pay for them either by taxes on the food he consumes or by suffering the ills of unemployment and unsound economic conditions created by unwise government policies and large debts.

Conclusion

The best interests of all will be served by having as uniform a distribution of wealth as is practicable. The utmost freedom should be preserved to individuals in order that they may be rewarded for their efforts. We should bring about, however, on the part of those more successful, a willingness to share their successes with others. Correct economic conditions so that those who are efficient and capable may work up from their poverty. Those who are unwilling or unable to do so, should be segregated or eliminated. By this means, over a long period the distribution of wealth would tend to be more even, without having any restriction upon incentive.

Attempts to bring about a better distribution of wealth should be made to follow the course of natural economic laws, stimulating effort and industry and taking great care to avoid hampering initiative or restricting the able and energetic. Stimulate them to their utmost by hope of reward, and encourage them to share their reward with the nation voluntarily.

XXX

GOVERNMENT REGULATION

THE GREATER THE AMOUNT OF GOVERNMENT REGULATION, THE greater is the handicap to business. When we add unwisdom on the part of the regulators, the handicap becomes too great. The effect of a great amount of unwise government regulation is bound to result in furthering unemployment, because discouraging capital and enterprising entrepreneurs. Thus the very efforts made by our government to improve economic conditions are making them worse. A small amount of wise regulation could be very helpful, particularly when associated with a determination to solve all problems by encouraging intelligent moral action on the part of all concerned.

Encouraging intelligent action and consideration for others makes the need for government regulation become less and less. The reason we have so much government regulation today is that the regulation is unwise, it tends to increase because it brings forth new problems of its own, and causes many to evade its provisions. Additional measures are enacted to deal with problems produced by previous measures, with the same effect, resulting in further confusion. If our present policies continue they cannot help but result in continually increasing unemployment and distress.

American industry has thrived because of its superior management and its constant search for better methods. It has added greatly to the body of scientific knowledge by its efforts to develop new products. Unnecessarily attacking industry and preventing it from properly developing prevents it from serving the public as it should. It should be encouraged to make profits and invest them in further development and improvements. If it were encouraged to do this, it would soon find means to absorb the unemployed and solve economic problems. It cannot do so when subject to harsh treatment, unwise regulation, and overburdening taxes.

We are blaming industry for all modern ills; industry is struggling along under this abuse, supporting the nation. The ones who should be blamed are those who are entrusted with the government of our country, in failing to control industry properly, stimulate it wisely, and prevent abuses. Our regulation does not prevent abuse by undesirable business men, but it greatly restricts those business men who really desire to serve the public.

The more the government attempts to regulate economic matters, the more uncertain the future becomes. If the government establishes the policy of permitting prices to seek natural levels; if it permits economic laws to function unhampered; able business and industrial leaders can anticipate future occurrences. They will then be able to plan for the future and be rewarded for their forethought if their conclusions are correct.

When the government undertakes to regulate economic matters, this is prevented. Instead of business men judging future occurrences by present conditions, they must become mind readers, trying to anticipate what the president or politicians will do.

It is impossible to forecast what a democratic government will do in the future. It strives too much to appeal to the public, to adhere to popular measures. Its attempts to regulate prices or to help in any particular industry result in increasing demands by many groups for government assistance, in turn causing increasing burdens upon other industrial and business activities. Thus the greater the government interference in economic affairs, the more uncertain the future is. The less the government interferes, the greater the degree of confidence and certainty with which industry may plan for the future.

To provide employment under the existing economic system demands the investment of large amounts of capital. If industry is uncertain as to the future, it cannot be blamed for not investing large sums of money in the development of new enterprises. The present great interference of the government in economic matters, intended to help the forgotten man, is actually doing him harm. The uncertainty as to the future prevents industry from investing vast sums in extending plant facilities and in promoting new enterprises. As a result, a vast amount of unemployment exists and will continue to exist until uncertainty as to the future is removed. It will exist as long as our present governmental policies continue. When industry is given reasonable assurance as to the future, when it is encouraged to perform its duties to society, when it is not attacked and persecuted by the government, it will invest vast sums of capital and reduce unemployment. It is not industry that is causing unemployment; it is the unwise policies of our government that cause it.

Regulation of any kind should be reduced to a minimum in order to avoid harmful effects in its operation. The less regulation, the less law, the better for all concerned. It is less costly to the citizen. It assists in making the government more efficient by lessening its duties, permitting concentration on essentials. Regulations encourage literal compliance at the expense of the spirit. Let us encourage the spirit at the expense of the literal by reducing the regulations to the absolute minimum.

Any large concern, be it a government or corporation, requires the use of many regulations to insure uniformity and accuracy in the conduct of affairs. These regulations should be kept down to a minimum. They tend to become very voluminous and try to provide for all possible contingencies, with the result that those who have policies to carry out have their efforts diverted to looking up the regulations to see what is permissable. If the regulations are few and simple, they can devote their time to facing the issue. On the whole regulations are in the interest of sensible action, but no regulations can apply to all circumstances. Slavish adherence to them is crushing to individual development.

Governments should avoid interfering with and restricting mental development. The development of able minds requires freedom of discussion, of ability to develop in the direction best fitted for the individual in question. We see in Russia today a government that is destroying the minds of its people. All are required to accept the prevalent teaching. They are not permitted to question, to develop originality. As a result, Russia has no science, no great minds. Her effort is being devoted toward the development of material things. A certain degree of success may be attained in this, but she will never attain spiritual or mental Ascendency; possession of these two is necessary to the finer development of the material.

As opposed to the free development of the mind, there is a tendency to extreme triviality or superficiality, which creeps up when no restrictions are placed upon individual development. This cannot well be controlled by the government. It is best controlled by teaching mental development and paying attention to the essentials of life.

Russian communists and Japanese militarists alike are throttling real intellectual values. No government can be a far-reaching influence for good that does so. Intellectual development must be encouraged, allied with the development of moral character, and both together led into channels that will advance man.

An increase in government functions of necessity results in an increase in repression. The increase in government functions requires a great increase in the force of government employees directing their activities not into constructive channels but into channels of a repressive nature in regulating the affairs of others. The business man, the workers generally, who carry on the constructive activities of the nation, are increasingly harassed and burdened by the increase in government functions. Instead of devoting constructive efforts to the solution of immediate problems, they must devote efforts to meeting government requirements. These efforts are not of a constructive nature in the fuller sense. They could be dispensed with if the government did not interfere.

A continuation of the existing government policies will constantly undermine American business and industry and lower the standard of living. We must be practical about these matters. American people are too willing to follow good intentions. They are not sufficiently hard-headed to demand practical results.

Government regulation discourages the expansion of business and the creation of new enterprises. For instance, a man may be considering establishing a branch concern in a distant locality, employing several hundred men and benefiting many. There is a question as to the advisability of the project from the standpoint of personal interest. If, in addition, we add heavy government taxation, government interference and regulation, and intimidation by labor agitators, the most high-minded employer would refrain from extending his activities and from establishing this branch concern. This is actually the condition we are confronting today.

Man thrives best when given the fullest expression, when his interest is aroused, when he is free. The personal element should be considered. Many people can survive repressive measures. Others dislike control and interference so intensely as to go to extremes to avoid it.

The government may cause annoyance in many ways that are not essential to the efficient functioning of government but annoy honest citizens unnecessarily. For instance, the average citizen is perfectly willing to pay income taxes but many seriously dislike filling out the income-tax form itself, giving all the necessary information called for. If we were less governed by theorists, an income tax return could be devised that would be simple, give essential information, and yet not unduly harass the taxpayer.

Such a simple income tax return would be to the interest of the government itself. When you have many returns coming in containing vast amounts of information, the task of assembling this information is so burdensome as to be impractical of execution, with the result that little essential information of value is obtained. If the return is simple and restricts itself to essentials, fewer clerks are required, the taxpayer is less annoyed, and the information on the return is available in a simple form.

One great objection to the extension of government functions is the fact that a government is less able to adapt itself to changing conditions than private industry. Suppose, for instance, that the policies our government are carrying out today had been in effect a hundred years ago. The vast industrial development of our nation would have been impossible. The next hundred years may be as fruitful in changing institutions. If government activities are limited to a minimum, society will adjust itself to changes naturally. This is especially true under a government dominated by democratic institutions.

Changing conditions may result in distress being experienced by certain industries or classes of people. If left alone, they would adjust themselves to these changes. On the other hand, when the government interferes, the interference is more likely to prevent the development of the change to its natural solution.

The government may pay bonuses to distressed individuals, thus perpetuating outworn institutions and placing a burden upon other social institutions which are also trying to adapt themselves to changing conditions. We do not know what conditions will be fifty or a hundred years hence. Not knowing, we certainly cannot plan intelligently beforehand.

We should meet the practical problems of the day. We should encourage the development of intelligence and character and provide in whatever way possible for future generations. This action, however, should be of a helpful, constructive, positive nature, encouraging natural forces that may be in operation. It should not be of a repressive nature preventing progressive advance.

Government regulation is reminiscent to me of the operation of our army motor pools. At Fort Bragg many years ago the officers in charge felt that there was too much waste of army transportation, too many motor vehicles being used, with undue consumption of gas and unnecessary cost to the government. They drew up a set of regulations requiring that all vehicles be put in one pool and that a certain procedure be gone through before a vehicle could be dispatched upon any mission. The use of motor vehicles decreased very materially at once, and they flattered themselves upon the success of their policy. This success, however, was achieved by passing the burden over to others. Officers, instead of attempting to receive government transportation through this intricate procedure, would use their private cars. Noncommissioned officers and enlisted men would do likewise. Some of the organizations who possessed funds purchased cars which they could operate without restriction.

An excellent example of over-regulation is afforded by a major in command of a battalion of field artillery, whom I knew well. He was a hard-working officer and devoted much effort to the most minute details of administration and to appearances. He gave many orders and published many memorandums. The result was that his battery commanders and other officers generally had only to carry out his orders. Instead of being capable officers, able to think for themselves in emergencies, they were more in the nature of messenger boys doing as told. This particular officer had a very excellent peacetime battalion. That is to say, it looked well and functioned well under peacetime conditions. He bore a high reputation for efficiency among his superior officers. However, the initiative of his subordinates was killed. If his battalion had ever gone into action, it would not have functioned well.

Modern war requires great common sense and judgment on the part of junior officers and even among the lowest ranking private at times. Proper training will encourage this individual initiative, try to cause each individual to think, to solve his own problems. Then, in an emergency when out on his own, he will be able to meet it adequately. Unforeseen conditions are always arising in war.

No one man can supervise all the activities in a battalion of field artillery. The policy established by this particular battalion commander was effective under peacetime conditions but its very exercise would have prevented effective service in war. Such effective service that would be rendered under war conditions would be due more to the inherent quality of personnel able to make up for the deficiencies of their leader. History contains many instances of this kind; superior troops have won in spite of the incompetence of their leaders.

A somewhat similar instance is afforded by another officer whom I can think of. He was a battery commander during the war. He trained his battery to a high degree of efficiency both for war and for peace. His men liked him. He was solicitious about their welfare and adopted a sensible policy of training designed to produce an efficient battery of field artillery for service at the front. While he encouraged the initiative of his subordinates he did so much work himself that they were unable to exercise their responsibility as they should. This particular battery commander was killed in action during the war and immediately thereafter his organization became relatively inefficient as compared to the other batteries in the regiment. Prior to his death it had been the outstanding unit in the regiment; now it was the poorest.

Proper training of troops will consider the possibility of loss of officers. Therefore a battery commander or any other officer should so train his unit that if he is killed in action or for any reason becomes a casualty or separated from it, it will function just as well or nearly as well without him. That is to say, he has trained his subordinates to carry on without being present himself. This particular battery commander, while an excellent officer, failed to provide against the contingency of his death.

I have observed many instances in the army of officers, active, energetic, stirring up much activity about them. Unless their activities are sensible, well-planned, in accord with human nature and of practical application, intense activity may be productive of more harm than good. It places the men under an additional strain, for instance, because not knowing just what to expect the next instant. Men very easily get disgusted under such conditions and while outwardly results may appear satisfactory, the spirit of confidence and mutual co-operation is lacking. More often than not more sensible, if less active officers, obtain better results.

Some of the most efficient organizations I have seen in the Army were commanded by men whom one can almost accuse of indolence. The reason for their success was that they obtained the whole-hearted co-operation of their officers and men. They did not harass or annoy them or indulge in useless activity. They permitted each man to perform his duties with the result that each one could do so. Each one could consistently plan ahead knowing just what would be expected of him.

One can of course permit a let-alone policy go to extremes. There must be leadership and effective training; but of the two I believe that useless activity is far more harmful to the efficiency of a fighting unit than a let-alone policy. The latter does at least encourage each individual to solve his own problems and to meet them. The former inhibits and prevents this.

After all is said and done, an efficient organization contains a great number of individuals. They live together, sleep together, fight and work together. A certain feeling of pride and loyalty is built up within their own organization. Quite often the men will find means to solve problems when left alone in a better way than if their commanding officer attempted to solve them himself. General Sherman once commented on a somewhat similar condition. He stated that the young officers in his army solved certain problems of supply better when he left them alone than he could possible have accomplished by a vast number of regulations and orders.

Many years of service in the army have shown me the great harm done by the existence of vast numbers of regulations in crushing originality of thought and initiative. Regulations are essential to insure the orderly conduct of a large concern, but they should be limited to essentials and to a minimum. The tendency is for regulations to grow. Some new incident will occur that has an unsatisfactory effect which those in authority will attempt to prevent in the future by new orders and regulations. These in turn will require changes in other existing orders in time with the result that the mass of regulations continues to grow. The practical man who has work to do and must comply with these regulations is then at a serious disadvantage. Instead of meeting the problem confronting him in a sensible manner, he must go through volumes of regulations to see what is permitted and must comply with them.

We have in the Army many officers who will stick to the regulations literally. They are, on the whole, not able officers and are clearly unfit for service in war when the exercise of initiative and responsibility is required. We have other abler officers who will willingly shoulder the responsibility and disregard regulations when necessary. These officers are not products of army institutions; they are able in spite of them. The vast number of officers lie between these two extremes, tending to give a sensible interpretation to regulations as required but naturally complying with them as far as possible.

There is, however, some justification for the existence of this vast mass of Army regulations. If all officers would never commit an error in judgment, never do anything foolish, the regulations would not be needed and would probably not exist in such large volume. However, officers, like other human beings, will act foolishly or hastily at times. The regulations are designed to prevent action of this nature and also to be somewhat of a guide to insure sensible action. The regulations may help those prone to make errors or blunders, but they will handicap men of ability capable of meeting whatever problems confront them.

The true solution would be to have all officers of great ability. This, of course, is impossible. The next solution would be to recognize the possibilities of error but to adopt regulations that would encourage the able man, would not handicap him and which at the same time would be sufficient to insure the orderly conduct of affairs. When you increase the regulations, you decrease the development of constructive ability and sound thinking. When you decrease them, make them more practical and sensible, it has the opposite effect.

Associated with the vast mass of army regulations is the great development of labor-saving clerical equipment such as typewriters, mimeograph machines, and so forth. The readiness with which reports can now be submitted has resulted in calling for an unnecessary number. The army paper work is voluminous; much is entirely unnecessary. I sometimes wonder how Napoleon managed to fight his wars without typewriters and mimeograph machines and how our own great Civil War was conducted without them. Actually, instead of being a help to efficiency, they are a distinct hindrance in many ways.

One can compare the staff of General Sherman with the present staff of an officer commanding a similar body of men. There are so many staff officers about that they get in the way and prevent action. General Sherman had so few that action was instantly forthcoming when necessary. The greater the amount of regulation and administrative detail, the greater is the effort that is diverted not only into unconstructive channels but into what often are to some degree obstructive channels.

Government regulations generally, the existence of numerous laws, regulations, and red-tape, are the result of pernicious activity. Their original justification was to serve the public. In the endeavor to bring about this service, they have grown to such mammoth proportions as to reverse the process. The public must serve them. This not only prevents the public from efficiently conducting its affairs, but it must support this mammoth structure. The more support it receives, the more it prospers, the larger it becomes. Thus measures, originally intended to assist the public, grow and grow into an increasing burden upon the public itself. This is just about the logic of our reform measures and our existing system of government administration today.

Thoughts

I want my life controlled as little as possible by the government, such control to be limited to the absolute minimum required for the protection of the interests of others. When such regulation is administered, I demand that it be under the direction of worthy men.

I have sought diligently for evidence, among our senators, representatives, and other leaders, of attempts to assist business and industry, to stimulate them to renewed activity. Private industry supports the people of the country. A sensible way to insure the common welfare is to stimulate industry to expand and furnish employment to all. I have been unable to detect any evidence of such action on the part of our leaders. On the contrary I hear of much money being appropriated for constituents, hear much denunciation of big business, and hear of new laws to control business. We have not far to seek for the unsatisfactory economic conditions afflicting us. They are being caused by repressive measures. What we require are measures that will encourage expression; measures that will encourage constructive action. Instead of this we have measures that prevent expression; that prevent constructive action.—*March 2, 1938.*

XXXI

ECONOMIC POLICIES

TWO SIMPLE PRINCIPLES SHOULD BE FOLLOWED BY THE GOVERN-
ment in trying to improve economic conditions. It should
interfere as little as possible, and this interference should be
skilled. Today we are interfering very much and the interference is unskillful, thus violating these two principles.

All economic problems should be approached in a sane,
quiet way to decide on action that will insure the greatest
good to all men, present and future. Unfortunately our government does not consider economic questions in this manner. There is too much agitation by lobbies and interest
groups who demand benefits from the government or special
measures that will redound to their benefit. Inefficient government is the cause of our poor economic system.

If our economic problems were sensibly approached, they
could be solved with little difficulty and all deserving people
given reasonable assurance of a fairly comfortable living.
Industry could accomplish more in solving economic problems if it were less hindered by the government. James J.
Hill once said, "If all the legislatures of the various states and
the national congress would disband for ten years, such prosperity would follow that no one would be in dire want." Let
us not harass, abuse, and hamstring industry, but let us stimulate it, encourage it to the fullest extent in order that man,
whom it supports, may be well supported.

One of the great reasons for the rapid development of our
country and the attainment of a higher standard of living

than any other country was due to the freedom granted the individual in his selection of an occupation and location. Curtailing this will decrease national prosperity by lessening individual initiative and discouraging the enterprising from exerting their utmost efforts.

The true solution of our economic problems requires that the individual be permitted the fullest liberty in all respects, and that we create an environment so elevating that power will not be abused. Let us try the honor system for corporations and business. Instead of hampering them by regulation, give them a chance to regain their character and serve their fellows. Industry supports all people in one way or another, therefore it should be encouraged in this task, that it may perform it well.

Our institutions must be so organized that each person is engaged in constructive work adding to the wealth and well-being of man. When men are not working, they are being supported by someone else, which increases their burden. The more people at work, the more they do and the more constructive its nature, the better off all will be. This is a basic truth not generally recognized, the violation of which is probably more at the base of our economic ills than any other single thing, unless it be moral and mental ills. This is an added argument against socialism, which would further discourage the increase of wealth by giving the indolent worker as great a reward as the energetic.

In a crude form of society relying mainly upon hand work for its existence, labor must be worth but little in order for extensive works to be undertaken, because otherwise the cost would be too great. In a highly civilized, mechanized society, labor gets higher pay and greater projects can be undertaken because the fewer men, by the use of machines, can do a great deal more work. More wealth is thus created and in its creation more work is projected, which requires more men. Thus a highly mechanized society will give work to all if properly controlled. The living standard also will be higher. We see this exhibited in our own country today even

under the inefficient administration of the existing government. What would not superior control by a really efficient
government accomplish?

When you limit the hours of work and reduce the number
of people working, you are making all poorer. The more
work that is done and the greater the number of persons
working, the greater the wealth and the per capita share of
wealth. Hence all are richer as a result.

Increasing the number of people getting government benefits, lessens the number of those engaged in producing wealth.
It increases prices by raising taxes, lessens production by discouraging industry, and decreases exports by raising internal
prices higher than those in foreign countries. It prevents the
production of wealth, making the nation poorer. Decreasing
the number of those drawing government benefits increases
the number of workers engaged in productive enterprise,
lessens the cost of the government and the cost of industry,
increases the national wealth, and makes the nation richer.
It also increases foreign trade, because prices being less, our
commodities are more readily salable abroad.

To develop a sound economic structure, we should reduce
idleness and parasitism to a minimum. Idleness produces
nothing, and parasitism imposes a burden upon constructive
workers. The more people we have engaged in constructive
work, the higher the standard of living will be and the
greater the per capita wealth. Anyone who produces something that is an asset to society, is a constructive worker. It
may be in a very humble.capacity, a street cleaner or a scrubwoman. Useless activity should be reduced to a minimum.
Politicians and undertakers are useless from this standpoint.
Harmful forms of activity should be reduced to a minimum.
Many of our writers and reformers, who try to tell other
people how to conduct affairs or how they should be conducted, are performing a harmful form of activity because
they prevent sane people from being heard and sensible
measures from being adopted.

All parasites are supported by someone, in some cases by

an immediate member of the family, in other cases more indirectly by workers. The latter case is true when we have wealthy people who inherit wealth, derive a vast income from it, and contribute nothing whatever to society. Even though they do spend much of their income for purchases and the employment of personal services, the vast sums paid to wealthy parasites are extracted from the common workman.

Parasitism is unquestionably one of the greatest evils of our economic structure. In endeavoring to eliminate it, however, we must be careful to avoid the employment of unwise measures productive of greater harm in other ways or perhaps bringing about other problems requiring corrective action.

Action by the government in extending credit to help business encourages poor business concerns to rely upon the government for assistance and discourages business generally from carrying its own burdens. This is somewhat similar to the creation of parasitism among individuals. Government benefits to any industry tend to build them into parasites of a kind, rendering them less able to adapt themselves to existing conditions without assistance from the government. Such assistance must be paid for by taxes levied upon other industries. The true method is to correct the conditions that handicap industry and strengthen it.

A government supported by taxes on business should not in any way compete with business, regardless of how well-intentioned the effort may be. Low-cost housing projects are an unsound economic move when made by the government. They prevent private industry from meeting the problem; once the activity is started it tends to grow because of the political influence of those benefited by the government activity. The net result is to lessen the amount of taxpaying property and increase that owned by the government, whose losses must be made up by taxes on the constantly decreasing amount of private property. As the government activities increase, private activities decrease. This is accentuated by the fact that private business cannot compete with the government, which is enabled to make up losses by taxing them. We should endeavor to obtain real figures on national income and in furtherance of this aim should have each citizen pay taxes and submit an annual report so we may have a clear picture of the standing of the citizens of the country. The payment of taxes by all citizens will be a benefit in many ways. They will understand the duties of citizenship better and will soon realize that efficient government lessens the burden upon them in the way of taxes. They would then be less willing to support large government expenditures because they would have to pay higher taxes. It is easy for anyone to be in favor of spending large sums of government money when they do not pay for it.

A small contribution by each of a hundred million people makes a large sum of money. When the government receives money from vast numbers of people it is soon in sound financial condition. When the government reverses this process and pays out money to millions of people, it will inevitably go bankrupt. The bankruptcy of the government is not the worst of these evils. Still worse is the lowering of moral character which demands that the government support them.

One cause for the real wealth per capita failing to increase as rapidly as we should expect in this era of labor-saving machines is the fact that so much effort is being put into things that are of little value and in the constant growing demand of the public for more service; the individual is doing less and less for himself and demanding more service from the government or from other people.

To increase wealth, efforts should be concentrated on essentials. They may be educational, spiritual or material such as better homes, furniture, roads, forests, farms and so forth. If we discourage the useless and devote that effort to permanent structures of value, we can greatly increase the national wealth.

The more we discontinue unessentials which, by the way, include vast numbers of government employees immersed in red tape and complicating civilization, the more effort we can employ in improving the beauty of the country, having better homes, and in adding to things of a positive nature that will be of use to future generations. The effort spent on funerals and care of graveyards is waste effort. Not only is it wasted, but it is also harmful from a psychological standpoint. We can find any number of ways in which great effort is being spent to no end, and in many cases to harmful ends.

Much effort is wasted in the production of useless articles. Much is wasted in futile forms of activity that produce nothing of value. Much is wasted in the production of articles that are required by harmful conditions. The vast amounts spent on war and armaments, for instance, do not help man in a positive way. They are to some extent a form of insurance by one nation against attack by others. But from the standpoint of man as a whole, they are a distinct harm. Much activity is diverted into armaments and preparedness for war that could more properly be spent to increase the value of man's possessions permanently and improve living conditions.

Futile social activity that accomplishes nothing is a great waste of energy. Man should have pleasure and amusement, but some of our society people go to the extreme of living for pleasure, for amusement, for futile activity, and produce nothing constructive throughout their lives. Each person should contribute to society by indulging in some form of activity that produces something of value.

To establish a sound economic structure, the elimination of useless and harmful articles will be helpful. We produce a vast quantity of products that are distinctly harmful. We also produce many that are useless and many others of little value. We should bring about demands on the part of the public for useful articles and encourage manufacturers to produce them. This will tend toward an increase in the wealth of each individual person and a higher standard of living as well.

The vast sums of money wasted in the consumption of liquor, tobacco, and useless luxuries would be sufficient to make all persons in the country prosperous if this effort were directed into constructive channels. Instead of purchasing liquor and other useless articles, the effort should be directed toward building a home, or something of a constructive, enduring value.

There is no justification for anyone to suffer want in a properly governed, civilized United States. The money spent on nonessentials, beauty preparations, poor literature, and amusement, is more than enough to give all a good healthful living.

Not only should we endeavor to raise the lowest living standard, but also to lower the wasteful luxurious high standards. Extreme luxury is such a bad social and economic influence that some of its worst features could well be prohibited by law. The bad influence of extreme luxury is exhibited in business booms. During a period of great prosperity, the less well-to-do and even the poor, having much more money to spend than they are accustomed to, indulge in luxuries. The result is those firms dealing in luxuries do a great amount of business and overexpand. When a slight business setback appears, the luxury firms are the first ones to suffer. The economic structure has adapted itself to their enlarged capacity and as a result, when they suffer from the effects of a depression, they transmit additional impetus toward setting back other firms not dealing in luxuries.

Thus luxurious living tends toward unsound economic conditions exaggerating the periods of prosperity and depression. When we endeavor to raise the living standards of the poor and lower the living standards of the extravagant, we are approaching a mean of wholesome living standards for all, which is beneficial from both a social and economic standpoint.

We should simplify methods of distribution in an effort to reduce the cost to the consumer. This can better be done by reducing the restrictions under which industry operates and encouraging it to solve this problem itself. Unwise government interference prevents this by interfering with the normal functioning of economic laws.

Wholesale houses should not allow discounts or special prices to any person. Make the price uniform for all. The present practice of obtaining purchase orders to make purchases from wholesale firms is a matter of considerable expense to the firms concerned. This finally results in the prices to the average consumer being greater, to pay for service rendered favored ones as opposed to the general public.

Laws restricting branch banking, chain stores, and consolidations prevent more efficient distribution. Distribution and selling are the big problems for industry to solve. It is being prevented from doing so by government interference. With assistance from the government, much waste could be removed from our economic system and the benefits passed on to the consumer.

The desirability of co-operative enterprises, such as apartment houses owned by the tenants, seems apparent; but the average person would rather pay rent to avoid the annoyance of ownership and the difficulty of reconciling the ideas and opinions of many individuals. While desirable, co-operation seems to be impractical, except under the most favorable conditions. However, the government should encourage it, where practicable.

An efficient government must provide means for keeping in touch with the action of corporations in order to prevent abuses. The boards entrusted with this duty should not be too formal and rely entirely upon hearings. A far better way is to have specially trained investigators go out and actually see themselves what is going on; get first-hand information. An expert investigator by this means can obtain more knowledge of what conditions are than any number of boards conducting hearings and questioning witnesses, following a regular form of procedure. Investigators could also be members of administrative boards and later meet and decide questions based upon merit and first-hand knowledge. They could then, if necessary, summon additional witnesses to complete their information.

A great deal of prosperity could be brought about in a brief period under the direction of wise government. Present restraints retarding business are imposed either by the government or by labor unions. If natural laws were permitted to function, the country would soon be in a most prosperous condition. We should have economy and efficiency in government with a minimum of government interference in business and no competition by the government with private industry. We should have a definite policy established for the future which would remove the existing uncertainty of industry regarding the future. If we abolish labor unions and permit wages to find their natural level, all people would soon be employed producing wealth. The restraints imposed by labor and the government have, unintentionally on their part, created a firm foundation for an era of prosperity. The removal of government and labor restraints and the existence of a definite policy for the future would be sufficient to bring about a period of great business activity.

An enlightened government having the interests of its citizens at heart would endeavor to minimize the effects of ruinous competition. The interference of the government in regulating competition should be reduced to a minimum and only employed when absolutely necessary. It is far better to encourage among business men themselves a greater spirit of co-operation and a recognition that ruinous competition harms all and should be avoided. But under some conditions the government should act. For instance, our railroads are being subjected to unfair competition from buses and trucks using public highways. They thus have lighter fixed charges than the railroads and are often able to take away profitable business from the railroad. Buses should not directly compete with railroads over long hauls particularly, and the same applies to trucks.

Government ownership should be reduced to a minimum. It competes with private industry, does not pay taxes, increases the cost of government, complicates its problems, increases inefficiency, and results in increased burdens of taxation upon the citizens. It also prevents the distribution of wealth in the same way as trusts, endowments, and large estates do.

Government ownership of all enterprises, or socialism, results in giving the individual less freedom. Such a task is too large for any government to handle effectively. The government will be more efficient if reduced to a minimum. The smaller any undertaking is, the better it can be understood and handled. Such control would level people down, not up. Government ownership rewards incompetence and improvidence, penalizes thrift, and crushes ambition and thought.

Ownership of all by the government would lessen the amount now received by the wealthy, but would also lessen the amount received by the able, thrifty, and hard-working. In addition it would lessen the total wealth of the nation by discouraging private enterprise and giving an even greater share to the undeserving than they now receive.

These same disadvantages of extreme government ownership apply to increasing governmental functions, as we are now doing. The greater the burden of government, the greater its interference, the greater harm to the citizenship; the less government, the more efficient it is, and the greater the chance of each individual to reap the reward of his own efforts.

The more government activities we can pass over to private corporations, the better, for many reasons. The government will have less work, fewer conflicting duties, will be less cumbersome and more efficient. The fewer tasks it undertakes to perform, the more efficiently it can perform them. When the government extends its operations into commercial fields, it competes with private business. This discourages the development of private business, thus lessening the amount of property available for taxation. At the same time government costs are increased because of the inefficient government operation as compared to efficient private operation.

The less property the government owns, the less operations it undertakes, the greater will be the field for private ownership, and the more property there will be for taxes.

Services rendered by the community, such as garbage collection, water, heat, power, and gas can well be handled by high-minded civil concerns who can charge a reasonable amount for the service rendered and obtain a reasonable profit. All municipal activities possible should be turned over to private enterprise. Our postoffice department should be turned over to private enterprise. Many other activities now conducted by the government could likewise be disposed of.

Vast stimulation of activity in Alaska could be brought about if the government would sell all public lands there to private corporations, encouraging their development. Great natural resources exist in Alaska and should be tapped. A policy of setting aside vast reserves and interfering with development, is preventing Alaska from becoming a real asset.

The same considerations apply to the public domain in the United States. Practically all could be sold to private corporations, possessing a public spirit which would insure development not only from the standpoint of present profit but for future benefits, also.

Much of the national park service and other activities could likewise be relinquished to companies organized to develop and maintain them. The present policy of the government in buying back land that it previously gave away or sold prevents development by private individuals and lessens the amount of property available for taxation.

We should provide for suitable grouping of oil companies in order to avoid injurious competition and protect the interest of the public as well as advance the welfare of the companies themselves.

We should provide for the organization of public-utilities corporations into logical units that would simplify capital structure, lessen operating expense, and contribute toward better service.

We should take steps to rescue our railroads from their present unsatisfactory condition. We should provide for federal incorporation, consolidation into strong systems, and the abandonment of duplicated or unprofitable facilities.

We must educate our citizens to have greater understanding of economic problems. Our schools do not do this today. This is not entirely the fault of our educators. It is more a reflection of existing influences. We have had so much publicity about the abuses of wealth and capital that our environment and our educational institutions themselves are dominated by it.

High standards of conduct and intelligence on the part of all citizens result in far-reaching material gains to the community. If we have such high standards of citizenship, we create an ascendent environment that prevents abuse. Our present-day labor agitators and politicians could not exist if our citizens were highly intelligent and unselfish. We would have able men conducting the affairs of government; incompetent men could not do so because intelligent citizens would see the weakness of their methods. Intelligent citizens would not tolerate leaders who would denounce the successful and exaggerate the grievances of the unsuccessful. Able citizens would support able leaders employing sensible measures to correct existing ills.

We must teach our citizens to realize that the more wealth there is in the country, the more all benefit from its existence. We must not confuse the existence of wealth with the distribution of wealth. Let us all work together to create the greatest possible amount of wealth. This is best accomplished by having all people doing work of a constructive nature. Then after this wealth is produced and while it is being produced, we should give thought to equalizing this distribution. We must, however, insure that the distribution of wealth encourages its creation. We must carefully avoid any action that prevents its creation.

Large profits made by industry or business are not necessarily an evil. If they are made without abusing labor or the rights of the public and are wisely invested in promoting other enterprises or in good works, profits are a positive good to the country. Instead of being discouraged, they should be encouraged.

Any business or industry to be successful must make profits. In a period of intense business activity, the profits will be large. Quite commonly during periods of depression they will be nonexistent; losses may result instead. It is far more economical for a business to expand than to contract. That is, when it is adjusted to a large volume of business and for any reason the volume decreases, it is difficult to make the necessary readjustment to prevent loss. The period of prosperity has resulted in enlargement of the plant and overhead to give better service, superior products, larger sales, and so forth.

Our politicians, reformers, and labor leaders in general stress large profits and condemn them harshly. This is both foolish and unwise. Unless large profits can be made, capital will be discouraged from embarking in new enterprises, thus causing unemployment. Many firms will be forced into bankruptcy during a period of depression because of insufficient reserve on hand to tide them over.

From a practical standpoint, the government and labor leaders should be as anxious to have business make profits as business itself. When profits are being made they increase tax receipts and lessen demands for relief. The short-sighted view of the labor leaders permits them to see only the immediate profits made by business and not the future benefit of large profits guaranteed to labor. The attempts being made to limit profits prevent the capitalistic system from functioning properly. The true policy is to promote profits, encourage business and industry—and in the long run labor, government, and the public will all profit.

The profits received by all capital over a long period are comparatively low, probably not in excess of four per cent. Yet the opinion prevails that capital makes enormous profits. Business does make large profits during periods of great business prosperity but also often operates at a loss. There are innumerable expenses which capital must meet. In order to have an incentive to do so, it must be assured of reasonable profits. When we attempt arbitrarily to limit profit and guarantee benefits to the employees, regardless of business conditions, we discourage capital. There must be a very safe margin of profit in order to provide for eventualities and enable the business concern to survive a period of poor business conditions.

It is very common today to hear large profits made by big business and wealthy people denounced as evil. Just where do these profits go? Try to visualize a wealthy man making vast profits from his business. What will he do with them? Mr. Henry Ford plows them back into business, enlarges his plant, improves his product, and, be it remembered, has always maintained a high wage scale for his employees.

There is a limit to the amount of money a person can spend upon himself. Even the parasitical wealthy who draw income from inherited wealth without effort on their part spend their profits on social activities, clothing, automobiles, expensive residences, travel, and similar ways. This is not the fault of profits; it is a human failing, a human weakness responding to poor environmental influences. We have instances where wealthy ne'er-do-wells spend vast sums in multiple marriages and divorces, breach-of-promise suits, sex entanglements, and so forth. This again is not the fault of profits primarily. It shows weakness of character. By virtue of the possession of vast wealth, this weakness can be indulged and attracts widespread attention. The same weakness exists among many of the very poor but because of their relatively obscure position and inability to indulge their propensities for lack of money, they attract far less attention.

The true solution to large profits is an improvement of our social institutions and of human nature. Have those who do make vast profits in business, apply these profits to constructive use either in a better product, better service, enlarging plant structure, promoting new industries—thus increasing employment, or in any means that will enrich society. Many wealth men, even among our much denounced robber barons, have given donations to charity, philanthropy, and educational institutions. Many have willed vast sums for noble works. We see throughout the world many libraries, hospitals, and similar institutions established or assisted by wealthy public-spirited citizens.

If all profits from business are utilized for constructive service to society, they are beneficial and should be encouraged. It is not profits we should prohibit; it is the abuse of profits that should be prevented. This prevention should not be exercised through repressive measures any more than necessary. Abuse of profits can be prevented by better social institutions, higher standards of conduct, and a greater sense of duty and responsibility on the part of successful people. They could be brought to this wholesome viewpoint by encouraging action of a positive nature. When they are denounced, regulated, and repressed, this wholesome development is handicapped.

The short-sighted policy encouraged by our labor unions —to prevent capital from obtaining profits and securing all profits for the labor unions themselves in the form of increased salaries, shorter hours, and other benefits—is harmful to labor interests. When you prevent profits, you prevent the development of business and industry and cause unemployment. When you encourage profits, you encourage the development of new enterprises which create more work.

Let us encourage profits and at the same time encourage their use in constructive social service. Profits in themselves are not harmful. If they are produced by a business that gives good value for value received, they are wholesome. If such profits, when made, are applied to constructive uses, they are still more wholesome.

Thrift is still a desirable virtue. The responsible citizens seeking to attain economic security, to provide for their families and their old age, and to have nice homes, are the backbone of the nation. We should make the practice of thrift universal and have all citizens capitalists in their own right. Thrift has a very great economic value. It tends toward a more even distribution of wealth. The great fortunes are accumulated by the spending of much money by large numbers of people. When this money is spent on luxuries and unnecessary things, it tends to impoverish the man who has but little and enrich those who have much. For all money spent one should get a reasonable return, either in a material way or in the form of pleasure of a worthwhile type.

Thrift is an excellent guarantee against business booms and depressions. The thrifty person will spend consistently. When he is making large sums of money, he will not spend large sums contributing toward an unwholesome business boom. Likewise, when a depression occurs he will have sufficient savings on hand to avoid the need for seriously curtailing normal expenditures. Thus thrift on the part of all citizens contributes to more uniform purchasing power. A person who is thrifty, is not inclined to become indebted. If no debts exist, unhealthy booms and depressions would not occur.

Extravagant spenders are the ones who contribute to both booms and depressions. If all money, all wealth, all property were evenly distributed, the spenders would rapidly spend or lose their share and the more thrifty would retain what they had and obtain that belonging to the spendthrifts. It is these spendthrifts who demand assistance in times of depression; who demand relief from the thrifty. Let us make every one thrifty.

Thrifty people are the backbone of the nation in that they think more of the future than of the present and try to plan for their own future and that of their family by intelligently foregoing trivial pleasures of the moment for future security and benefit. This quality of thinking of the future and planning for it is one which all men should cultivate. If it were universal, we would have far fewer distressing economic problems to solve. It is not the thrifty people who are complaining about economic inequality and injustice; it is the spendthrifts who spend whatever they have, and in time of stress, having nothing, demand that others support them and cry out about the injustices to which they are being subjected. Such people are prihuman. They lack Futuro and possess much Infanta. On the contrary the thrifty are adhuman, possess Futuro and far less Infanta. Let us encourage and increase the adhuman; eliminate the prihuman.

Thought

Economic difficulties are not solved by strikes, the payment of doles, or the levying of heavy taxes, but in having everyone at work, producing wealth, in improving the character, ability, and civic virtue of the citizenry and in reducing government interference to a minimum, giving opportunity and encouragement to all.

XXXII

A SOUND ECONOMIC STRUCTURE

JUST WHAT IS A SOUND ECONOMIC STRUCTURE? A LIST OF ES-
sentials composing such a structure is given below, followed
by a brief discussion of each. These essentials have already
been discussed; the brief discussion given in this chapter is
to summarize the essentials that should exist in a sound economic structure.

It will be noted that the most important essentials are
those having to do with intelligence and moral character.
The great error being made today is to attempt to correct
existing economic ills by law. If we devote the same amount
of effort to improving the standards of intelligence and character, such a great lessening of existing economic ills will
result, as to require far less government regulation and legislation. A reduction in government activity itself makes the
economic structure sounder by making the government more
efficient, encouraging individual initiative and other essentials.

Able, Honest Leaders
Minimum or No Government
  Debt
Minimum of Government Reg-
  ulation
Minimum Repression; Maxi-
  mum Expression
No Government Competition
Sensible Taxation

Promote Equal Distribution of
  Wealth
Promote Efficiency and Initia-
  tive
Reward for Worth
Constructive Legal Code
Discourage Idleness and Para-
  sitism
Practical Men and Measures

333

Internal Harmony
High Standards of Citizenship
Minimum of Government Activities
Minimum of Indebtedness
Consistent Policies
Economic Education of Citizens
High Business Ethics
International Harmony
Thrift

Wholesome Environment
Promote Increase of Wealth
Sound Currency
Improve Conduct, Lessen Crime
Constructive Products
Constructive Activity
Individual Initiative and Responsibility
Wholesome Social Institutions

ABLE, HONEST LEADERS: A sound economic structure demands efficient government under the direction of able, honest leaders. All the sufferings and ills of mankind throughout his entire history have been largely due to incompetent or dishonest leaders. Very often able men have confused selfish personal interests with their duties to the public. A truly conscientious leader will place the interest of the public far ahead of his own wishes, desires, or personal interests. It is utterly impossible to establish a sound economic structure unless the government be conducted by able, honest men.

HIGH STANDARDS OF CITIZENSHIP: A sound economic structure, especially in a country possessing democratic institutions in this modern age, must have high standards of citizenship; a willingness on the part of all citizens to cooperate for the benefit of each other; a willingness to serve the government, to advance the interests of society; a willingness to sacrifice personal interest when there is an apparent conflict with the interests of society. It is also essential that citizens of a superior type exist in order that they may possess the ability to recognize able, honest leaders. Then, having recognized such ability, place it in control of affairs and give it the most loyal, unselfish support.

MINIMUM OR NO GOVERNMENT DEBT: If neither the state, local, nor national government had debts, there would be less burden upon the public in the form of taxes with which to pay the interest; tax-exempt securities would not exist to afford refuge for unconstructive wealth; property values would be higher because of the absence of government debts and because those now owning bonds would invest in physical property.

MINIMUM OF GOVERNMENT ACTIVITIES: Have all government activities reduced to the barest minimum. This lessens the number of government employees, lessens taxation to support them, and increases efficiency.

MINIMUM OF GOVERNMENT REGULATION: This does away with repressive restraint on industry and permits the citizens to devote their activity toward constructive efforts. They do not then have to employ much effort in complying with government regulations.

CONSISTENT POLICIES: A consistent economic policy so business, industry, and all concerned may plan definitely for the future.

NO GOVERNMENT COMPETITION: Under no consideration should the government compete with private enterprise in any way. When the government does so compete, it penalizes private enterprise and causes a duplication of facilities.

ECONOMIC EDUCATION OF THE CITIZENS: The government should educate all citizens to an understanding of economic problems. This would ensure the wholesome support by the people of sound policies.

SENSIBLE TAXATION: Taxation should not be levied to appeal to the popular voice. It should be levied on as broad a base as possible so as to insure that all citizens directly pay taxes. Their interest would then be aroused in the economical administration of the government. The levying of indirect taxes should be reduced to a minimum. All taxation, in fact, should be reduced to a minimum by a simplification of government functions and in all practicable ways.

HIGH BUSINESS ETHICS: The government should endeavor to establish high standards of business ethics among all citizens. The citizens should be encouraged to set a good example of conduct and consideration for their fellows. All social institutions should consider it to be their primary duty to promote good ethics.

MINIMUM OF INDEBTEDNESS: The government should endeavor to maintain private indebtedness of all kinds at an absolute minimum. Not to the extent of handicapping private enterprise, but to establish sound economic conditions.

INTERNAL HARMONY: The government should by all possible efforts maintain harmony between capital and labor. It should not attack, handicap, or restrict big business and seek the support of labor for the purpose of obtaining votes.

INTERNATIONAL HARMONY: Our government should endeavor to promote international harmony, solve the problem of world peace, and encourage the removal of obstacles to international trade. If we can solve our own problems at home, we can obtain increasing respect abroad. Unquestionably, our internal economic problems will be greatly assisted by sound international conditions. If we establish sound economic institutions within our nation, we can assist toward sound international conditions which, in turn, will react upon internal conditions.

THRIFT: The government should encourage thrift on the part of all citizens. If all people are thrifty, they will become owners of stocks, of property, and more directly interested in the maintenance of sound economic conditions.

PROMOTE INCREASE IN NATIONAL WEALTH: The government should encourage the increase of national wealth, encourage all to produce more. This would increase the per capita wealth and the standard of living.

PROMOTE EQUAL DISTRIBUTION OF WEALTH: The government should endeavor to promote the more even distribution of wealth; but not by unwise measures that would handicap industry. It should employ measures that will encourage voluntary action on the part of individuals toward promoting the reduction of large fortunes and increasing the ownership of property by those having little or nothing.

SOUND CURRENCY: A sound currency should be maintained

that will prevent the existence of threats to future inflation or deflation.

PROMOTE EFFICIENCY AND INITIATIVE: The government should encourage the fullest initiative on the part of all citizens. It should encourage the development of economic institutions that will reward efficiency and penalize inefficiency. This is best accomplished by a minimum of government interference. The very laws of nature itself function in economic matters. The inefficient concern, be it large or small, will pass out of existence because it will be unable to meet the competition of the efficient organization.

IMPROVE CONDUCT; LESSEN CRIME: The government should endeavor by all possible means to improve the standard of conduct on the part of all citizens. As conduct improves, crime and misconduct are reduced. A great burden is placed upon the economic structure by the wide prevalence of crime and bad conduct generally. Much crime exists that is recognized as such by our present criminal code. Much bad conduct exists that is not so recognized. With high standards of citizenship and high standards of ethics, crime will be reduced. Aside from the increased spiritual and moral gain, there will be a vast gain in material values. The government today spends vast sums to repress crime. Honest business is penalized by dishonest business. Let us have all business honest and crime reduced to the barest minimum.

REWARD FOR WORTH: The government should endeavor to establish institutions that will reward in accordance with individual merit. The ablest, most deserving citizens should obtain the greatest reward.

CONSTRUCTIVE LEGAL CODE: We should establish a constructive legal code that will simplify and expedite the liquidation of bankruptcies, insolvencies, bank failures, and so forth, and will facilitate the closing out of the weak, unsound institutions; promote the survival of the strong and solvent.

CONSTRUCTIVE PRODUCTS: The government should encourage production of articles of constructive value and lessen the production of the futile, useless, and harmful. Instead of having the services of many directed toward producing and distributing articles that are not essentially constructive, direct this effort into the production of constructive articles such as better homes and home comforts. The permanent wealth of the country will be increased; likewise the per capita wealth, the standards of living, comfort, and knowledge.

MINIMUM REPRESSION—MAXIMUM EXPRESSION: The government should adopt policies employing a minimum of repressive measures, and contrarywise, encouraging the fullest, freest expression of all individual citizens. The greater the amount of repression employed by the government, the greater is the effort required to enforce such measures. Repressive government activity is unconstructive; measures encouraging expression are constructive. The need for repressive action by the government to prevent abuse will be lessened by the voluntary wholesome expression of the citizens.

CONSTRUCTIVE ACTIVITY: A sound economic structure will encourage constructive activity on the part of all citizens. If all are engaged in constructive activity, the per capita wealth is increased, the standard of living raised, and all benefit.

DISCOURAGE IDLENESS AND PARASITISM: The less idleness and parasitism existing, the sounder the economic structure. The government should endeavor to lessen these evils by education and by wise social measures tending to eliminate the idlers and parasites in time. Their elimination requires great thought for the future. Idlenesss and parasitism are the opposite of constructive activity. Those engaged in constructive activity must support the idle, the parasite. If we abolish idleness and eliminate parasitism, those engaged in constructive activities are less handicapped.

INDIVIDUAL INITIATIVE AND RESPONSIBILITY: The government, schools, and all social institutions should encourage each individual to solve his own problems. It should be forcibly impressed upon all citizens that if each one makes his way in the world without the need of help or assistance from others, that all benefit.

PRACTICAL MEN AND MEASURES: Successful businesses are invariably conducted by practical men carrying out practical measures. We must carry out the same policy in the conduct of affairs of government. Place practical men in control and have them carry out practical measures. One of the great contributing causes for our present inability to solve economic problems is the fact that the government is conducted by impractical men carrying out impractical measures. Our very environment is formed by impractical men advocating impractical measures. Public opinion is guided entirely too much by literary theorists, well-meaning reformers and good talkers. Practical men act. Impractical, theoretical men talk and make much noise. A sensible economic structure will never be established by noise. A sensible public opinion dominated by practical men advocating practical measures will contribute greatly to a sound economic structure.

WHOLESOME ENVIRONMENT: We should endeavor to develop a wholesome environment. A wholesome environment will recognize the need for a sound economic structure. Instead of having individuals or interest groups claiming to possess all merit themselves and attribute viciousness to others, we should have a wholesome environment that will recognize that there are two sides to any question, that economic problems must be solved in accordance with economic laws and in accordance with truth. An individual or interest group advocating specific measures cannot alter truth or economic laws. A wholesome environment will seek for the truth. It will seek to master economic laws and guide economic affairs in accord therewith.

WHOLESOME SOCIAL INSTITUTIONS: Wholesome social institutions will promote wholesome economic measures. The churches and the schools are two very vital social institutions. They can contribute greatly to the understanding of economic problems. Primitive men created religion largely to advance the solution of economic problems. They would offer sacrifices to their gods in an endeavor to obtain good crops and would resort to any number of measures to influence the gods to improve their economic well-being. We will do well if we make this practical application of religion today—not in the superstitious manner primitive man employed, but to advance understanding of economic problems.

True religion will not only minister to man's spiritual being but will also seek to advance his material well-being. The injustices and sufferings of an unsound economic structure prejudice the development of the spiritual side of man's nature. When the churches contribute toward sound understanding of economic problems in an endeavor to lessen injustice and suffering, they are serving man's spiritual needs as well as his physical needs.

The churches could do a vast amount of good in lessening class hatred, selfish Groupo and promoting good will. A practical religion will find means to promote the brotherhood of man by showing the positive need for it. The churches should cease to denounce the present and glorify the past. They should teach the people of the present day how to profit from the past; show them how such efforts make them better themselves and will establish a firm foundation upon which future generations can continue to build.

The religion of the future will demand a high degree of intelligence on the part of its people. The schools can contribute greatly to the improvement of this intelligence. All social institutions should contribute in whatever way they can towards being a wholesome influence on the economic structure.

Conclusion

These economic essentials afford an excellent means for analyzing economic measures or policies. If sound they should be in accord with these essentials or contribute toward bringing them about. If they fail to do this they are unsound and should be rejected.

Suppose such a sound economic structure as this had existed in 1929. The boom of that year could never have reached such unsound proportions, the panic could not have occurred and the resulting depression would not have developed.

The essentials listed in this chapter as composing a sound economic structure, have been selected with due regard to the future. I have attempted to profit from the past and have applied the principles of human nature in developing an economic structure that will bring out the best in man's nature. If we stress mental and moral attributes in building up a sound economic structure, we will be building it upon a firm foundation; one that will endure.

Man has made great progress since he was a mere savage. He can, by intelligently controlling the forces affecting his development, make just as great an advance in the future from his present state. Man's physical needs must be adequately provided for in order to insure mental and moral development. Physical welfare is easily insured by the application of intelligence and consideration for others. These, in fact, are the qualities that have led man from savagery. They are the qualities that will advance him to a still higher state of being. Let us place spiritual, intellectual, and moral welfare first in creating a sound economic structure. Material prosperity will then follow as a matter of course.

XXXIII

CAPITAL AND LABOR

THERE ARE ALWAYS TWO SIDES TO A DISAGREEMENT BETWEEN
two persons. Each very naturally sees the good points of
his own side, and the bad points in his opponent's. As a result they are unable to agree. Sometimes the most bitter
enmities are established and exist throughout life. The
same condition exists with regard to conflicts between labor
and capital. There will generally be some right and some
wrong on each side. It requires an impartial outside agency
to settle the dispute. This should be the task of the government but it is one which the democratic form of government is ill-qualified to deal with. Generally when a democracy interferes in a dispute between the poor and the
wealthy, it will take the side of the poor, because that is
popular, and decide against the wealthy. This is substantially
what is occurring in our country today.

Unquestionably there have been disputes between capital
and labor in which right was almost entirely on one side
and the other side were the aggressors. Decades ago employers often treated their employees unjustly, did not consider their welfare, and thought only of profit. The attitude
of the anthracite coal mine operators in 1902 was certainly
unfair to their employees, but the pendulum has now swung
the other way. We still have many employers today who have
a somewhat similar view but they are relatively few. Capital
has been on the defensive for years. Public opinion is so
strongly aroused against it as to prevent serious abuse.

Capital, the big business and industrial leaders, are now the defenders of democracy, the defenders of the public, and their opponents are the labor agitators and our own politicians. Capital is outnumbered, but numbers do not necessarily win, as history well demonstrates. Justice, truth, and ability are a strong combination. They may yet defeat the politicians, our national government, and the labor agitators. The average American citizen desires a square deal and is willing to accord it to others. There has been so much denunciation and misrepresentation that he is confused. Present the facts, the truth, and he will support those who are fair.

To the fair-minded observer, it is apparent that the radical labor unions are being unfair to their employers. On the other hand, we should expect from such men of ability as the big industrialists a greater understanding of conditions. The short-sighted capitalists of the past are in large degree responsible for the present unfortunate condition by failing to perform their duties to the public and abusing their power in their day.

The present attitude of the wealthy does much to arouse resentment against them; they do but little to bring about better understanding. Wealthy parasites who attend social functions, have their names in the Sunday supplements, travel from resort to resort, and get involved in disgusting love and divorce affairs, arouse resentment against the wealthy, and justly so.

We cannot condemn the wealthy as a class any more than we can condemn any other one class of our citizens. There are fine individuals among them and there are worthless parasites. Nevertheless, with all due fairness to them, they should have a better understanding of the problems of the day and be able to lead labor, not have it drive them.

Capitalists should take the public into their confidence. They should show their problems of production and of costs; show where the money goes. There are an infinite number of ways in which they could bring about a better feeling. The politicians attack them because it is popular to do so. They have failed to reply to these attacks in a satisfactory way. This is discreditable to the many able managers conducting our business enterprises.

This, however, is understandable. They have not spent time in developing their knowledge of public questions. They have specialized in the conduct of their businesses, and do not see the outside problems which threaten its downfall. Here is where the need for wise government comes in.

The failure of the government to take such action as to show readily where the corporation's money went, how much for wages, how much for the management, how much for taxes, how much to the bond holders and stockholders, does not discharge the capitalists and corporations from this responsibility. It is their task as citizens to educate the public to a proper understanding of the usages of capital.

The fact that they have failed to clearly show the relationship between wages, profits, and taxes, shows a lamentable lack of foresight on their part, neglect of the duties of good citizenship, or a pure desire to conceal. If they are concealing, they do much to justify the feeling against them. If they are not concealing, it is pure stupidity and a reflection upon their ability.

With all the ability our capitalists have at their command, they should be able to present to the public a true picture of corporate management in all aspects. They have unquestionably done much to bring about the existing labor agitation through failure to demonstrate that they are an agency working for the benefit of the country.

In times of great prosperity and activity, capital can make great profit on its investments, but in times of depression, the profit is rapidly turned into a loss. This is not appreciated by labor leaders, and rarely, if ever, mentioned by them. Anyone at all familiar with business will see that a plant built to accommodate a great rush of business and to operate most efficiently upon that basis will, with the decrease in business, have a correspondingly high overhead, which will become increasingly greater as business declines. Here is where the most violent labor agitators do much harm. They do not understand the problems of capital. By encouraging their union members to demand more and more, they render it increasingly difficult for capital to develop properly.

Many people support collective bargaining, feeling that the worker should have some means of protecting himself against the employer. Unquestionably if an employer abuses his power, the workers should have some means of protection. The bad feature about collective bargaining that is not stressed by those advocating it is that whenever labor unions are organized, there is a class within them which constantly agitates for more and more. It is this class which generally controls them.

Thus labor unions and collective bargaining tend to promote friction between the employer and employee when the employer really intends to do his best for his employees. There was a time in the past when labor was justified in obtaining protection from unjust employers. At present it is persecuting the just employers.

Few employers abuse their privileges as employers, and it should not be necessary to penalize all. Efforts should be directed toward correcting the few rather than punishing the many. The fact that a man has been sufficiently successful in life to employ others seems, under prevailing beliefs, to make him a vicious person to be attacked at will.

In discussing the problem of capital and labor we should consider the following factors, which exist in all good-sized corporations:

1. Dividends to stockholders and interest to bondowners
2. Payments to the management in salary
3. Payments to workers in wages, shorter hours, and other benefits
4. Lower prices, better products, or better service to consumers
5. Plant enlargement, improvement, and research

Look over these five classifications for a moment. They must all be considered in order that the best interests of all may be served. It is interesting to note that the labor unions, which always strive for wages and so forth, neglect all four others. If carried to extremes, this causes the other four interests to suffer and eventually will cause labor itself to suffer. If labor is getting such high wages that dividends are not paid, that efficient management is discouraged, that prices must be put so high as to discourage consumers from buying the product, and that plant enlargement and research is prevented, labor suffers from unemployment.

Karl Marx is having as much effect on prevailing thought as Benjamin Franklin had on the thought of the last century. Franklin himself set an example of a poor boy rising to prominence by his own efforts, and his writings were a great incentive to many others to follow in his footsteps. Many of our successful men owe the initial impulse to strive for success to his example and writings. He was a good influence in stimulating individual effort, and a great contribution to the advance of our country.

Karl Marx is having a bad effect. He stressed the conflict between capital and labor, but failed to add anything to its solution. He attracted attention to the evils of capital to the exclusion of its merits, and extolled the merits of labor, ignoring its faults. Many liberal thinkers have followed his path, which has been in general to attack capital and compel it to treat labor fairly. This has resulted in creating friction where harmony should exist.

It has attracted attention to the economic problems of man, and neglected the spiritual ones. If all people in the world, whether poor or wealthy, were intelligent, considered others, and realized that economic problems were difficult of solution and that their solution required the whole-hearted effort of all, they could be solved.

Any effort that creates friction between capital and labor is effort misdirected and results in harm. No problem can be properly solved if it is approached with bitterness, violence, and in a spirit in which one party is suffering all the grievances and the other all the benefits. We must ignore the agitators who are continually stirring up ill feeling and find men who will seek to solve problems by promoting harmony.

We, as citizens, should face the facts and see that capital is in good hands and functions well. We should prevent our government from stifling capital. We should endeavor to elevate capital to a status commensurate with its responsibility. What we are doing today through our government is to attack, regulate, cripple, and create resentment on the part of able administrators desiring to do their duty to the public. Let us put a stop to this ill feeling between capital and labor by putting a government in control of our nation capable of controlling both and seeing that both receive justice.

Labor should have a direct interest in efficient government in order that taxes on business may be less and their harmful effect in contributing to unemployment and discouragement of industry prevented. This is a farsighted view which labor leaders do not consider. They do not realize that their policies are contributing toward increasing government costs. This causes higher taxes and uncertainty for the future, which reacts upon labor by causing unemployment or reduced wages.

Capital thrives when labor prospers, and labor thrives when capital prospers. The theory that eternal conflict exists between them because their interests oppose each other is an erroneous conclusion that does much to create that very situation. Some capitalists have been brutal to their employees, but on the other hand, there are many employees who do not earn their pay. We should strive to make all employers interested in the welfare of their workers and have all workers interested in the welfare of their employers. Their mutual interests are best served by a spirit of harmony and co-operation.

Capital should do all in its power to improve laboring conditions and remove causes for strife, hard feelings, and suffering. Contented, happy, well-treated workers are more efficient and cost less than others whose pay may be less. If we desire capital to improve the conditions of the laboring man, we must encourage capital, not attack it.

Continued attacks on capital and on the successful are giving the entire world a persecution complex similar to the one fostered by Jewish institutions on the Jews. In both cases there is a real foundation but it has been magnified beyond the bounds of reason, and many other influences are not considered. Labor's interests are being prejudiced by the employment of more or less violence in forcing capital to accede to their demands.

The action of the labor unions in demanding benefits from the employer uses much energy which is thus diverted from efforts which should be used to make the worker more worthy of the benefits he desires. It also builds up resistance on the part of the employer to the demands of the labor unions and an unwillingness to give more than he is forced to, because he is defending himself against injustice. If the labor unions cease to make unfair demands, the efforts of the employer will not need to be used in fighting them and protecting his interests; he would then be more willing and more able to devote his efforts toward advancing the interests of his employees.

The fact that capital may give up the struggle with labor, and move to other countries where its rights are more respected, is one that labor should consider. If a general exodus of this kind takes place, more unemployment will result. This is only being prevented today by unsettled conditions in other nations.

This conflict between capital and labor is now very one-sided. Capital is attacked on all sides, by the government, by liberal thinkers, reformers, and labor unions. It cannot defend itself because the public will not heed. It should be defended by the government and citizens, but both alike fail to come to its defense. When we permit a government to exist by persecuting one class of its citizens for the benefit of others, we have ceased to have a government based upon justice. Injustice has a way of exacting revenge. Past history shows that whenever governments have abused their rights, they have suffered as a consequence.

The breakdown of our democratic institutions is being caused by the conflict between labor and capital promoted by the unwise action of the politicians and liberals. The voting power of the country very naturally is in the hands of the majority, who for the most part do not have great material wealth. The wealthy and well-to-do are a relatively small percentage. The politicians, in their endeavor to obtain office, have utilized this condition by denouncing wealth and capital and arousing the poorer classes against the more prosperous. This is an unfortunate state of affairs. All prosperous people are not vicious, and all poor are not virtuous. If we could array the good against the bad we would be on a sounder footing.

War between nations is the result of each nation selfishly pursuing a short-sighted policy of promoting its own interests regardless of the harm it inflicts upon others. Enlightened statesmanship would see that very often the harm they do other nations results in harm to themselves. The World War and the international situation today show how suffering can be caused by a system founded on selfishness and lack of consideration for others. When nations become moral and decide questions with due regard to the welfare of all, war will cease, and all will be the gainers. So also with regard to the conflict between capital and labor. When they cease to fight and work together harmoniously, both will benefit. The benefits will not only be material but moral. They will have more respect for themselves and pride in duty well performed.

When we have such relations between capital and labor we will be making progress toward international peace and good will. Strikes and conflicts show that we are unequal to maintaining peace and order; that we lack merit, intelligence, and moral character. If we are unable to prevent strife in our own country, where everything is controlled by our government, how much less likely is it that strife can be prevented between nations, having no government over them! The problem of international peace is intimately related to the problem of establishing harmony between capital and labor. When we have solved this problem, we may then undertake to solve the problem of international peace.

Problems of capital and labor may yet involve this country in the worst civil war of all time. Abuse, ill feeling, and violence will result in nothing less if continued. If the problem were merely one of dishonest capital against honest labor, it would be less difficult, but it is more than this. It affects the entire social structure. Labor is today more vicious than capital because so many agitators are inflaming the feelings of the workers by exaggerating the ills under which they live, to the exclusion of the benefits. We must correct this by intelligent action while there is yet time. If this action is not soon forthcoming, brute force will be used.

The action of the radical labor unions is nothing less than civil war, caused by agitators and the ignorant who are all too willing to see a solution only in the one that meets with their short-sighted viewpoint. Our own Civil War was caused by the same element. Grievances magnified beyond reason brought on a bloody war which no one wanted and in which the innocent suffered. Today the innocent suffer and will continue to suffer as long as we permit violent labor agitators to dictate our labor policies, as long as no attempt is made to face facts in a spirit of calm judgment and to solve economic problems with due regard to the rights and welfare of all.

Capital is not at fault in this internal civil war. It is not attacking labor or resorting to violence. Public opinion has been so aroused against capital by bad behavior in the past and by attacks made upon it by reformers, politicians, and agitators, that it cannot resort to violence. If democracy is to demonstrate its fairness, it must be fair to capital and prevent labor from abusing it. This is not only fair but it is enlightened self-interest. The attacks of labor upon capital will cause more and more harm to labor as long as they are continued.

XXXIV

LABOR UNIONS

LABOR UNIONS ARE BAD FOR ECONOMIC AND MORAL REASONS. They tend to bring out the poorer human qualities. Continually demanding benefits and denouncing those who have different views is not conducive to character development. On the contrary, when a man is able to see faults in himself, to see merit in opposing views and to work for what he earns, he is a contribution to the community. When he can see no wrong in himself or his fellows, no merit in opposing views, when his interest is concentrated more upon what he gets than what he does, he is a bad influence in his community.

Labor unions have a bad effect on citizenship and the younger generation. Labor unionists have children who are brought up in an atmosphere causing them to believe that they are being oppressed and unjustly treated. We are permitting labor agitation to break down the very character of American citizens when we permit it to influence young children, unable to understand but believing that their parents can do no wrong. How can a child be expected to do otherwise when his parents feed, clothe, and are kind to him? Naturally he will believe what he absorbs in the home.

If we subject labor unions to critical analysis, employing the principles of Ascendent Psychology, we will see that they are a bad influence unless the members are fine citizens and the leaders of the highest type. Labor unions exist primarily for their particular interest. This results in the development

of selfish Groupo and the stressing of Grievo and other undesirable psychas to the exclusion of desirable ones.

Labor unions are interest groups within the nation placing
their own welfare before that of the nation, too short-sighted
to see that in the long run they can prosper only if the rest
of the nation prospers. A one-sided viewpoint that determines
policies prejudicial to the interests of others should by no
means be tolerated. Policies must be controlled by the public.

Labor unions encourage their members to believe they are
being ill-used and have serious grievances. No such interest
group has a right to exist. If the grievances are justified, a
competent government should correct them. The fact that
these grievances exist shows that our government is not competent and is unequal to the task of dealing with them.
This belief on the part of labor unions that they are always the
sufferers, that they are always being imposed upon, and that
unsound economic conditions are not their fault but the
fault of capital alone, is too childish to consider. When unsound economic conditions exist, they have a reason for
existing. The reasons are more often the fault of labor agitators and incompetent government than of capital.

Labor unions keep their own wages up at the expense of the
nonunion workers. If wages were permitted to seek their own
level, workers would leave those industries which paid poorly
and seek those which paid well. This would tend toward
keeping wages down where they are high and raising them
where they are low. This is a neglected aspect of unionism.
When unions interfere with the natural functioning of economic laws, it may result in wages being higher in certain
strong unionized industries capable of paying high wages, but
they cause them to be lower in the ununionized, weak industries, unable to support higher wages.

When strong labor unions bear but a relatively small proportion to the population of the country, say five or ten per
cent, they can compel their employers to give them shorter
hours and higher wages. The remaining ninety or ninety-five
per cent of the public shoulders this cost. When, however,

the labor unions increase in size to the extent that they compose fifty or seventy-five per cent of the population, it will be impossible to force higher wages from their employers.

The employers and workers create wealth in the form of new products by constructive work. Labor unions do not create wealth or products. Collective bargaining produces nothing of positive value. This is an aspect of labor unions that the public does not consider or understand.

All social institutions that produce something of a positive nature, of value to society, should be encouraged. Those that do not produce anything worthwhile should be discouraged. Applying this line of reasoning to capital and labor unions, we can see that we should discourage or prohibit labor unions entirely and should encourage capital, the employers, and workers to produce.

When labor unions demand collective bargaining and special privileges, they are interfering with the orderly development of industry. The same result is accomplished by the unwise interference of the government or reformers. It is not repressive or negative action that improves the standard of living. It is positive constructive action. Let us encourage the latter and eliminate the former.

The efficient conduct of any industry requires a loyal force of employees working for the best interests of the employer. When we permit unions to step in, we bring about a divided loyalty, resulting in the union members being more loyal to their union than to their employer. Many are more willing to agitate for the union than to work for the employer.

The justification for the existence of labor unions is to protect employees against unscrupulous employers. Let us eliminate unscrupulous, unfair, employers and avoid justifying the existence of labor unions. Labor itself will benefit greatly by this. Incompetent labor leaders have confused unfair, unjust employers with fair and considerate ones and are persecuting the latter unjustly. They justify their action by dwelling upon the abuses which labor has received from unfair employers. Labor's policies today discourage the development of considerate, fair employers. We must reverse this policy. We must encourage their development and eliminate the unfair, unjust employers.

The employers are being attacked so consistently by labor unions that in self-defense they must fall back upon any methods open to them to defend themselves. How much better to have both the employers and employees work together instead of wasting effort fighting each other!

. Labor unions are contributing to unemployment by discouraging new industries from being started. Many people would be glad to enter into business if the prospects for the future were reasonably assured. When they are threatened by labor troubles they will not embark upon new enterprises. Every little while we hear of some small concern being closed up, or factory being abandoned, as the result of labor troubles.

Many small businesses are likewise being given up. A conscientious citizen was operating a small printing business necessitating the delivery of his products by truck. A truck drivers' union demanded that his products be handled through them, regardless of the increased cost. Rather than oppose or get into conflict with them, he closed out his business. Many like incidents are occurring all over the country.

Labor has no responsibility, and is causing greater and greater unemployment by its unwise actions. If we had a strong government that would protect capital from the abuse of labor unions, we would soon have the greatest era of prosperity we have every known. Capital would embark boldly upon new enterprises and there would soon be work for everyone. This plain, simple truth should be apparent to all with a little thought; but few people think.

The labor agitators demand more, our reformers and politicians support them. The employer who pays their wages, supports the nation, and keeps industry going is persecuted, is prevented from running his own business, is required to confer with the lowest type of labor leaders, has his property taken from him by sit-down strikers, and is subjected to abuse on all sides.

What self-respecting man would undertake willingly to receive such treatment? None, if he had his choice. Suppose capital were to go on strike as labor does and refuse to employ anyone. They could cause great suffering, and would be denounced for employing the same tactics that the labor unions employ. If capital is not permitted to do this, neither should labor.

Labor unions lack Primo and Co, the qualities that the insane and criminals lack. By tolerating interest groups lacking Primo and Co, we are contributing toward the development of a population of criminals. There is but little difference in the attitude of a criminal and a labor agitator. Both seek personal gain regardless of the rights of others.

Labor unions show the utmost disregard for the rights of the public in any controversy. One can but glance at the papers and see electric currents cut off, elevators stopped, victims in hospitals left without attention, any number of vicious acts in which these labor unions utterly disregard the rights of the public.

There is but one way to respond to such thought—crush it entirely, prohibit such labor unions, do not permit them to exist. We want decent citizens in this country who will contribute toward the welfare of all citizens and have due consideration for their fellows.

Our violent labor unions are but magnified childish gangs. The same spirit of gang loyalty exists in both; those fellows belonging to the other gang are always in the wrong, and the members of our gang always right.

The fierce antagonism of our labor unions to all who oppose them and their unwillingness to admit any harm in their own acts is a manifestation of primitive mental processes and prevents development. We see this exercised in Russia, where certain beliefs have been established and are taught throughout the nation; nothing in opposition is permitted.

As a result Russia has nothing to offer the world in the way of mental advancement.

Our labor unions likewise have nothing to offer us in the solution of our problems. They demand that their answers be accepted and that those who oppose their solutions be forced to comply with their wishes. There is no difference in principle between the violence of our labor leaders and the government in Russia.

Both alike are obstacles to future development. They appeal to the most primitive mental processes. Only those things that benefit the individual immediately, that are close to him, that he understands, are permitted to exist. The finer, higher considerations for the future, for others, are not permitted to develop because obscured by the very violence which demands that their own present interests be served.

Such an outlook is childish. There is no such simple solution to man's problems. It represents the reversion to violence, the primitive way of settling quarrels. Quite commonly violence is resorted to by those who are unable to command respect in any other way, who lack the ability to think soundly, who lack the moral character to consider others, and who have failed to develop Primo to the extent of seeing faults in themselves and those close to them.

The very nature of labor unions makes them prihuman and regressive, and causes the revival of some of the most unworthy qualities of man at the expense of the most worthy. They stress Grievo, dwell upon grievances and magnify them to such an extent that a wholesome outlook is impossible. A thought inspired by a grievance approaches more the unreasoning animal capable only of satisfying physical needs rather than approaching the adhuman capable of responding to appeals to his intelligence and moral qualities.

The frenzy we so commonly see in members of labor unions displaying their grievances is of a similar nature to the religious fanaticism of ignorant, backward peoples. The labor unions are just as intolerant as the religious fanatics, but far more selfish. Whereas the religious person may, and often does, have unselfish motives, the labor frenzy is intended only to obtain immediate benefits for a selfish group.

Labor unions never find fault with themselves, never admit doing anything wrong or unjust. The problem of capital and labor is not so simple as this. All fault is not on the part of capital. Capital is not persecuting labor today. It is the one that is being persecuted: persecuted not by its best employees but by the most undesirable element.

Buy yourself a labor newspaper sometime and read it. See if there is anything there that appeals to your judgment as a disinterested observer. You will see denunciations of capital, of employers, talk of the virtues of the worker and of the injustices he is receiving. There will be no word of appreciation of any wages, however high, or of any employer, however good.

Communism is somewhat unpopular in this country and, as a result, even the most radical labor unions generally deny sympathy with communistic aims. Actually, our labor unions are more pernicious than communism—far less worthy. Communism demands that the government own and control all property, for the benefit of the citizens. Our labor unions are unwilling to assume the responsibility of owning and operating industry. They demand that the employers pay them tribute; give them whatever they wish. Communism is willing to undertake the responsibility; our labor unions demand the benefits without the responsibility.

Present-day labor unions do not base their demands upon what is right and fair. They strive to obtain as much as they can, regardless of whether deserved, regardless of the rights of the public, the interests of the employer or the future. They do not hesitate to use violence, intimidation, force, any means at hand to obtain their end. No government, no civilization that tolerates the existence of such institutions is intelligently considering the future welfare of its people.

Labor unions holding key positions in an industry will often go on strike because their very power enables them to get benefits from their employers. A small group of a hundred men may tie up the operations of a plant employing thousands. These men go on strike using this vast power to intimidate their employers. They have no regard for other employees or the public.

Labor unions are becoming increasingly vicious with the passage of time. They use force instead of brains, intimidate by numbers—not by righteousness. Their conduct is bad for the individual member in that he seeks solution of his problems by intimidating others and not by his own worthy efforts. The unions reward the vicious, the agitators, and the incompetent at the expense of the decent workers.

The tendency in labor unions is to be dominated by the most violent agitators, who are also the poorest workers. The more level-headed ones are yelled down and not given a chance. No wonder the employers do not want these agitators! No wonder they wish to discharge them! Who would like to employ someone who was continually causing trouble among his employees?

Wholesome labor unions should be encouraged, but only in the smallest units so as to deal only with questions directly affecting the welfare of those concerned. This would do away with many present abuses. It would put a check on ambitious labor leaders endeavoring to use labor unions for their own aggrandizement regardless of the interest of the members. It would prevent labor leaders from terrorizing the community by calling sympathetic strikes.

We have had many cases in which labor unions have had conflicts among themselves. Controversy would arise between two branches of workers—such as, let us say, teamsters and pressmen—over union rights, which would result in blows and an attempt to prevent the employer from operating his business. In this particular case the complaint is not against the employer but against other unions, or union members, and the employer must suffer.

We have seen cases of several groups of union members claiming sole jurisdiction over a particular line of work and preventing any activity whatever from being conducted.

These conditions show that many members of labor unions have the mentality and disposition of spoiled children. We are permitting these spoiled children to dominate our government, intimidate employers and abuse the public.

Could there be any harmony in a large family in which the parents and the older children permitted themselves to be dominated, intimidated, and controlled by spoiled younger ones too immature and too incompetent to know how to conduct the affairs of the family? This is the way we are permitting the affairs of our nation to be handled. The most childish, selfish elements within it dictate the policies, control legislation in their favor, abuse all who do not agree with them, and prevent other men from exercising their constitutional right to liberty and to work.

In some cases two or three rival labor unions will be fighting for recognition, go on strike, and tie up all activities until their rights are recognized. How can anyone deal with groups of rival labor unions unable to agree among themselves? One of the large elements in the high cost of building construction and loss to contractors has been disagreements between separate unions engaged in construction. An electrician is not permitted to saw boards; a carpenter must do it. Conflicts sometimes arise as to jurisdiction between groups, resulting in strikes and tying up constructive activities. Why should the public submit to any such state of affairs?

Labor unions are not democratic. We have but to look over the labor situation in our own country and see where some labor leaders are practically czars, absolute monarchs of the particular unions they head. They dicker with others, make promises and agreements; all ostensibly to aid their unions; but there has been a great amount of dishonesty, seeking for power, self-glorification, and paying off of grudges.

Labor unions are the enemies of many things Americans hold most dear—liberty, the right to act as each individual thinks best as long as he has reasonable consideration for others. Labor unions and radical labor leaders demand that others accept their teachings. Their tendency is to throttle inquiring minds seeking the truth. They and they alone have the right answers, the only solution. They are truth; anyone who questions their infallibility is an enemy of the nation. Their attitude is reminiscent of the religious intolerance of old. The religious zealots demanded that all people believe as they believed. Those who did not so believe forfeited rights, sometimes life itself.

Our labor unions have not as yet required nonbelievers to sacrifice their lives to any great degree, but they have already caused many to forfeit certain inherent human rights: the right to work for whom one wishes without interference, the right to think, to seek the truth, to do what is right. Any institution that attempts to curtail these activities is an enemy to all men, far worse in this day of enlightenment than religious bigots of old.

Our labor unions are direct violators of the rights of individual liberty. Each person has an inherent right to work for whom he wishes, how and when he desires, on whatever terms he cares to make. Organized labor in attempting to curtail this right is causing the breakdown of democracy, of which it claims to be the greatest supporter. The view of democracy held by the labor unions is a democracy in which they have the right to do as they please and no one else has the right to do anything that opposes their wishes or interests.

Labor unions thrive on violence and promote it. Law-abiding American citizens who desire to work and support their families have threats made not only against themselves but against their children and wives unless they do as labor agitators dictate. Is this a free country? Does any government, that permits such a situation as this to exist, itself have the right to exist? Should we permit law-abiding citizens to suffer threats against their families?

Our reformers, who object to the use of force, say nothing about the violent methods used by labor. These labor agitators attack other men through innocent children. Their tactics are but little removed from that of the kidnaper who kidnaps a child, holding it for ransom. We denounce kidnapers. Why then should we not denounce any other people who employ the same means, whether glorified by the name of labor or otherwise? When policemen intent upon preserving law and order attempt to stop this sort of thing, they are booed and often attacked by the vicious element in labor unions.

American civilization cannot thrive, cannot exist, if it tolerates such violence. Is there no manhood in this country of ours that will assert itself to protect children, to protect the honest citizen who desires to work and make a living in an honest way?

The Revolution was fought because George III wished to tax the American colonies. He never went so far as to prohibit law-abiding citizens from working. We tolerate that today. We are permitting ourselves to be controlled by an element far more vicious than George III ever attempted to be. Our forefathers rebelled against his measures, but their descendents submit to rule by worse people than George III.

Has American manhood deteriorated to such a point as to be unwilling to assert itself in defense of what is right? Will we not protect our families, our children, from abuse on the part of anyone? Must we submit to the actions of any agitator who can talk a few morons into following his leadership? Must police officers be subject to attack when they do their duty?

Thoughts

Labor unions have long passed from the stage of seeking justice and are now causing employers to seek justice.

Who are these labor unions? Just interest groups demanding special consideration and getting it by intimidation at the expense of the public. They say they want only justice, but is that not the duty of the government to give? If the government perform its duty, their excuse for existence will cease.

Labor unions are entitled to about as much respect as their leaders deserve. At present they deserve little.

The fact that the government has made no attempt to supervise labor unions in any way, and the mere fact that belonging to a labor union gives immunity, has resulted in racketeers getting in and using labor as a cloak to further their own ends.

XXXV

LABOR LEADERS

OUR PRESENT-DAY LABOR LEADERS ARE PRODUCTS OF THEIR environment, their activity, their thoughts. Granto and Grievo, the misuse of Responso and Wisho, the functioning of Herdo and selfish Groupo, have all been confirmed by Adapto. The result is that they are unfit to direct the policies of labor. Their viewpoint is so distorted as to be unable to see the harmful consequences of their acts. For instance, they continually demand higher wages, shorter hours, pensions, unemployment insurance, and any number of benefits. They say little or nothing about increasing the efficiency of the workers, loyalty to their employers, or loyalty to the government. They are substantially racketeers intimidating the employers into granting whatever demands they choose to impose. They are not farsighted enough to see that as a result capital will not expand, will not promote new industries, that great unemployment will ensue and that the members of the labor unions whom they claim to be benefiting will suffer.

The solution of economic problems will not be facilitated by agitators continually attacking capital and demanding further benefits for labor. They lack understanding of fundamental issues, and are unable to act with regard to the future and the welfare of the nation as a whole.

We must learn that the solution of economic problems cannot be solved by giving way to violence and prihuman feelings. The prihuman labor leader all too often appeals to

363

the prihuman impulses of his followers rather than adhuman feelings.

The average labor leader displays an intense prejudice as a result of Herdo and Groupo influences, as great as the most primitive superstitions. There was often a wholesome attempt at altruism in primitive superstition. In present-day labor violence we see intense selfishness for one's own group with only the claim of righteousness and altruism.

Labor leaders can see but one side of the question. An able man would see the other side. Able labor leaders would see that all the virtue is not possessed by labor, and that capital has problems of its own to meet. They would see that they could better serve the interests of labor by working with capital and rewarding merit. The unfortunate part about labor leadership is that the more conservative level-headed leaders are not listened to, and the more violent, radical element gets in control, inflaming the feelings of their hearers by stressing their grievances.

Read the statements made by the leading labor agitators. Consider if you, as an employer, would be willing to take those men into your employ. Would you want to have a man work for you who continually denounced all your efforts and called you names? And yet these are the men we require our employers to submit to.

Sometime ago, while the maritime strike was in progress in San Francisco, I happened to hear Harry Bridges, a strike leader, over the radio. Knowing but little of the strike's merits, I was interested in hearing what he had to say. He said nothing about specific grievances, the main point stressed being that there were some few stockholders opposing many thousand longshoremen. He made statements denouncing certain people who opposed the strike, made some general observations, but shed no actual light on the merits of the strike itself. My own reaction to this speech was that, if the cause was as weak as the strike leader himself made it, the longshoremen had no justification for striking, and that the stockholders and shipowners were in the right.

The violent labor agitator is a small edition of the jingo, rabid nationalist. Both foment violence to further their own ends. Many labor agitators are victims of unsound minds. They have brooded over their troubles, dwelt on their problems, have convinced themselves that they are right, all others wrong, and that any methods they employ are justified. Many labor agitators are suffering from Inferio. This is why they denounce and belittle their opponents so vigorously. They denounce the successful, whom they envy and can only excel by denunciation.

Collective bargaining as a panacea for labor troubles has obtained much publicity and much support. The labor leaders have supported it strongly. This can be readily understood when we realize that collective bargaining substantially means the organization of labor into unions controlled by them. When collective bargaining is established and labor leaders are entrusted with negotiations with the employers, their power is greatly enhanced.

It is a short-sighted viewpoint that supports collective bargaining alone as a solution of labor problems. Substantially this means that labor unions by numbers alone can intimidate the employer into granting whatever they may demand. Collective bargaining offers no assurance that capital or employers will start new enterprises or remain in business for the purpose of granting the labor unions the benefits they demand. Actually, collective bargaining under the control of labor leaders seeking power and possessing no great ability, will be harmful to all concerned—the labor union, the employer, and the public—unless it be controlled by able, considerate men having due regard for the employers' interests and the interests of the public. No such labor leaders have yet appeared in labor unions. Invariably, labor leaders are for their unions alone and bitterly attack all who do not agree with whatever they advocate.

Men keenly resent an unjust, inconsiderate management, and are only too willing to unite in mutual support against it. They will readily attempt to correct by violence real or fancied wrongs, especially when agitators are at hand to stimulate such action. The discharge of fellow workers for union activities attacks one of the finest of human traits, that of loyalty to one's fellows.

Management must be able and must have the interest of its employees at heart, and labor must co-operate. Violent agitators cannot and should not be tolerated. A few vicious leaders can give a bad atmosphere to the entire body of employees and render harmony impossible as long as they are present. Regardless of how fair one may wish to be toward labor, we cannot ignore the fact that many of their leaders are agitators, stirring up trouble where trouble should not exist, hampering the conscientious employer who desires to do what is right.

Many labor union leaders are more interested in making the employers eat from their hands than they are in the welfare of the members of their union. Unable to make a satisfactory living in any other way, they become agitators of the worst type, stirring up trouble and glorying in their ability to humble the employer. The average employer or manager of today is a far higher type individual than the average labor leader.

Who ever heard a labor leader admit that he made a mistake, that labor was ever in the wrong? Never. It is always their opponents, the employers, who are abusing them. Such an attitude condemns them on the part of the thinking person. When you have reached the conclusion that you are without fault, you admit that you are a fool.

I have sought in vain for evidence of thoughtfulness or understanding of labor problems on the part of labor leaders. Their statements denounce capital, exalt labor, and always seek more pay, shorter hours, hiring halls, and union control without responsibility. They fail to realize that these methods cause more unemployment, and if carried to the extremes they advocate will result in greater misery to the laboring man.

As a class, labor leaders are probably the most undesirable

element in the country. On the contrary, industrial leaders do have an understanding of these problems, as is shown by their words and deeds. The workingman would be infinitely better off if he supported his employers and disregarded the labor agitators.

The tendency of all labor agitators is to think more of their rights and privileges than of their duty and the interest of the employer. From the standpoint of psychology this is a most vicious mental outlook, harmful to the individual and the community. We must have a citizenry who will think of their duties and the interests of others, giving them priority.

Demagogic politicians and the most violent labor agitators do much harm by contributing to the lowering of character by perpetuating class hatreds, prejudices and ill-feeling. They and they alone are right, all others wrong. Truly a ridiculous conclusion which should discredit those holding it. The most violent of our labor agitators display the prevalence of Infanta in their make-up, resorting to the methods of the spoiled child to demand benefits by appealing to the pity of others.

Being a labor leader does not attract the highest type of men. Becoming an agitator and stimulating others to violence will never appeal to a man of high type. The ablest, most industrious men are promoted by their employers to direct the affairs of their companies as a reward for their efforts. The men who become labor leaders are all too often men lacking in the ability to achieve success or attract attention in any other way.

Politicians and labor leaders alike are more concerned with their personal fortunes and power than the welfare of those they claim to serve, although because of their primitive mental processes they believe the two are identical.

The labor leaders bear the same relationship to the rank and file of labor as the politicians do to the citizens of the country as a whole. Our politicians are not the ablest men in the country. They are average citizens able to obtain votes by skillful appeals to the voters. The labor leaders are not the ablest workingmen. They are men able to play upon the feelings of others and obtain leadership by promising benefits.

The same influences work in both cases. If we could raise the standard of our politicians, insuring government by the best men in the country, and likewise raise the standard of our labor leaders so that they are the best workingmen in the country, those who do the best jobs, we could readily solve the problems of government and of labor.

To accomplish this, the influences producing incapable leaders should be corrected. If we can correct these influences to bring about statesmen to control the government and able labor leaders to control labor, there would be less talk, less hard feeling, and more constructive effort.

Does a labor leader exist who has a sound knowledge of economics? No. They all claim that if you pay labor more and shorten the hours and give them benefits, a great era of prosperity will come. We have had more labor agitation in this country in the past few years than the world has ever seen, and the situation is getting continually worse. Is labor at fault? Oh, no! It is the vicious capitalists. Stop and think a minute about this. Does capital benefit from strikes, from disorders, from hard times? It benefits when everyone is prosperous and making money. Any other viewpoint would be short-sighted and foolish.

Labor leaders by their policies have and are causing more unemployment than ever before. The greater their power, the more they abuse it and the greater harm they will do. Are they at fault? Never! It is the naughty capitalist who is persecuting the poor workingman. The labor leaders are virtuous knights fighting for the right; they are clean, inno-cent, darling little fellows who never have an improper thought.

Economic difficulties are caused by many far-reaching causes beyond the power of mere capitalists to create. The labor leaders have contributed their quota to this by their short-sighted and one-sided policies. They are without thought of the distant future, concerned only with the present and with getting all they can. This is virtue for them, but vice if capital takes the same viewpoint.

Labor leaders are created by unsatisfactory economic conditions. If we improve conditions, the labor leaders will be improved. They hope to better conditions. The measures they employ do not take into consideration deep underlying economic conditions. They adopt the popular measures, increasing wages and shortening hours; they fail to see the harm caused thereby. We must educate them to see the error of their ways, to look at the problem from the broad viewpoint of the interests of all people in the country.

Becoming belligerent, appealing to violence for solution, will not succeed. It will stir up resentment and discredit them. Wise action on the part of labor the country over is essential to the solution of economic problems. All must be brought to work harmoniously, that the best interests of labor, the public, and capital, may be served. Labor leaders failing to consider the public, failing to consider capital, failing to take the long viewpoint, are harming themselves. If we can suggest a means whereby the best interests of all can be served, the support of the better element in labor will be obtained and violence will disappear.

XXXVI

LABOR AND CHARACTER

MANY PEOPLE, HAVING THE WELFARE OF LABOR AT HEART, are in favor of labor unions and collective bargaining. They sympathize with the efforts of labor unions to expand and make collective bargaining universal throughout the country and have every laboring man a member of a labor union.

Aside from the other drawbacks to labor unions, there is a serious one which I think merits the greatest attention. We are now witnessing throughout the country a great drive by labor to unionize all industries and all laboring men. What interests me most is the arguments put forward by labor leaders.

This is the point that I dislike most and that I think is the most harmful. They belittle all who oppose them. They find no merit in capital. All the merit is on their side. They contribute to class hatred, they show a lack of understanding of economic problems, they bring about more ill-will. They intimidate, they use violence, and they defend it.

If we are to solve the problems of man, we must appeal to the good within him. There is in each one of us both good and bad. Our mission as individuals should be to eliminate the bad or divert it into constructive channels, and make ourselves as good as possible. Collectively we should endeavor to accomplish the same result; endeavor to make man as good as he can be made. To do this, we must appeal to the good motives within him and encourage bad traits to seek expression in constructive channels.

The actions of labor in attempting to unionize the country has the opposite effect. They appeal to many of the undesirable traits and to but few of the better ones. When they do appeal to good traits, they direct them into harmful channels. There is great good in gratitude and loyalty to one's fellows, but it should be to all men. Labor leaders stress the loyalty of labor to labor unions, disregarding the public. Aside from the short-sightedness of this policy and the bad atmosphere they are creating, their worst effect is upon the moral character of the individual.

Thus I utterly oppose the activities of the present labor unions. I feel that they are doing more harm than good by their attacks on others and in stressing the undesirable qualities inherent in human beings. The future development of man demands that the good be stressed and that the bad be controlled. If it becomes necessary to resort to ruthless force to control the bad, it should be employed. In my opinion the action of labor unions today demands the most ruthless force, that they may be utterly crushed.

But if we decide to crush these labor unions we must likewise crush the politicians, the foolish liberal thinkers, the stupid, the vicious, the selfish wealthy, and many others who contribute directly to the unsatisfactory conditions which cause labor agitation.

What we must have, to bring about this reform, is united action by all decent citizens against those unwilling to appeal to the better qualities in human beings. Very few human beings will admit they are vicious or that they are bad. We need a policy that will be so sound as to enroll all in its support. Then the need for force to repress those opposing it will not exist because they will be in a small minority.

Just how a movement like this can be brought about is worth serious thought on the part of all who have the future of man at heart. It will be difficult, it is true, but our labor agitation is not adding anything to make the problem easier of solution. I would gladly support labor leaders and labor unions if they showed a willingness to consider the welfare of the public, if they were sensible leaders who would appeal to the good motives in men, if they denounced less and resorted less to violence.

Under present conditions, while sympathizing with them, I am forced to conclude that they are doing nothing to solve the problem but are only making it more difficult of solution, that the economic evils from which we are suffering today are caused more by labor than by those the labor agitators blame. It is the repetition of the old story; the more violent the denunciation, the more guilty is he who denounces so severely.

Labor agitation, strikes, and attacks upon wealth have a very bad effect on the character development of American boys. They cannot help but absorb much ill feeling from their elders as a result of this. We might well contrast this condition with that which would exist in a country governed for the best interest of all, where each would blame himself first before adopting the attitude of blaming everyone except himself.

One of the first essentials of character development is to seek your own faults, admit them, and seek to correct, and here is where labor does its greatest harm. It admits no fault with itself and blames all upon others—an unwise and untrue conclusion having bad effects upon the character of anyone believing it.

The greatest harm done by labor unions is their bad influence in opposing Ascendency. Labor unions constitute descendent interest groups intensifying selfish Groupo and contributing toward a descendent environment. Individual members of labor unions have their attention distracted from building up an inner urge to achieve Ascendency, to conduct that opposes it.

Instead of seeking within themselves for means to develop and improve, their attention is distracted to conditions without themselves and to placing the fault there for shortcomings or failure. That fine human quality of loyalty is often converted to unworthy uses when the labor leaders pursue short-sighted policies which do not sufficiently consider others.

There is much jealousy, envy, and feeling of inferiority at the bottom of labor agitation. Combined with this is a wholesome realization of the unfairness and injustice of many existing conditions. The unfairness which is apparent to all affords a ready cloak for the display of undesirable traits.

In the original inception of the labor unions there was often justification for strikes. Conditions in many industries were bad and required correction. Strikes today are often not justified. Many strikes are more a display of Infanta than any other human trait. They resemble a spoiled boy who quits the game because others will not play as he wants them to, saying substantially, "If you won't do this, I won't play." A very simple means to meet this childish display is quietly to tell them that you do not want to play with them. Sever contact, thus avoiding friction. This would be a nice, quiet, dignified way of settling disputes, but one which our benevolent leaders now prevent.

It is impossible to meet all the demands made by all the strikers. We do not protect the employer against any demands, however unjust, from labor unions. An argument often heard by strikers is that fifty or a hundred thousand workers are opposed to thirty or forty stockholders, bringing forth the weak argument that mere numbers are right. This is not so. History will show many cases of individuals crying for right and justice and opposed by the masses. The mere fact that such an argument is brought forth shows the weakness of the grounds upon which the strike is based.

To the average laborer, the unfairness of being born in want as compared to others being born in wealth, appeals. He cannot be expected to understand all the causes for this. Many of our ablest men have differing opinions. But why should we permit this ignorant laborer to decide how this problem should be solved? He attempts to solve it by gang-ing up, making unjustified demands, and causing suffering to many innocent people having no direct concern in the controversy.

What can aggrieved strikers know of economic conditions? In what way are they qualified to determine the righteousness of their action and demand that the public support them? They are not qualified to do so. They lack knowledge and understanding. They are governed too much by self-interest, emotion, and prejudice. Understanding of the economic problems involved requires great ability of a specialized nature. We can seek in vain for this ability among our ablest economists. How much less justification is there for believing that infuriated strikers possess this ability and should be unquestioningly supported!

If we are to permit labor unions and strikes, we should require by law a supervised ballot before any strike is undertaken. All too often we have strikes initiated by a small minority of employees and the use of much intimidation and violence to require members of a union to vote for a strike. If a secret ballot were conducted by a disinterested government agency, violence and intimidation could not be employed, and the majority of the employees could control. It might even be wise to require that more than a majority be required in voting for a strike, that it be two-thirds or even three-fourths, thus insuring that the grievance was so strong as to be entertained by a greater number of employees than a majority only.

It is apparent that much of the recent labor agitation is not participated in by all the employees of the various corporations who are having strike trouble. From the best reports, the original sit-down strikers in the first General Motors sit-down strike were a relatively small proportion of the employees. This indicates that the strikes are fomented by the agitators and the more restless employees, and that the more stable element did not consider them justified.

Resort to strikes by labor unions and picketing by such strikers bears too close a relation to racketeering to be permitted. Substantially, the racketeer demands that some business man pay him tribute in some form to avoid injury or insure protection. When labor unions go on strike and picket, they are demanding that the employer accede to their wishes, and are using physical force to require him to do so. If the employer were always wrong and the labor unions always right, it would be less obnoxious, but anyone knowing human nature will realize that one party to a controversy is as likely to be in the wrong as another, and that settlement must be made by an impartial agency.

When labor disregards the law and attempts to intimidate by employing violence, it is proving itself worse than the employer it is attacking. This is not the way to a solution. It prevents the harmony essential to a prosperous community. When you employ violent methods you prevent the exercise of sound judgment. Violence is not a method resorted to by those of good character, and its employment should discredit those who use it. They who resort to violence shift the responsibility to others, but that is by way of justifying their acts.

The action of our labor unions in endeavoring to obtain their ends by violence is reminiscent of the actions of the French Revolutionists, who discredited democracy and were superseded by a military dictator finally. The violence of the French Revolutionists did much to retard the development of wholesome democracy in other nations. Many friends of democracy were horrified, shocked, by the extreme violence displayed by its adherents in France. Mob action controlled by hatred and prejudice will not solve difficult economic problems. On the contrary, the very violence exhibited will discredit those employing it regardless of how good their intentions may be.

The use of violence by labor union men, in forcibly expelling nonunion employees from a plant and preventing them from working as they wish, infringes on the personal liberty guaranteed each individual by our constitution. Labor is playing a high hand in using violence, disregarding the rights of the public, accepting only such laws as meet with its approval. Such action is the reverse of that consistent with orderly government.

Granto, Grievo, Closo, and Presento are large factors in our existing labor unrest. The labor unionists stress their grievances, take the benefits for granted, think only of the present, not of the future. They are incapable of a sound, wholesome, outlook. Add to this infantile tendencies, pure stupidity, and the influence of agitators arousing such feelings that the workers cannot see good in anyone or anything opposing them, and you have the answer to the causes of the present unhealthy labor situation.

One of the most serious objections to strikes is the fact that they usually cause innocent people to suffer. A small group of employees will go on strike, either sit-down or otherwise. This may result in stopping work for many times as many employees who have no concern with the question at issue. The longshoremen's strike on the Pacific Coast damaged many innocent business men and injured our merchant marine; Hawaii was badly affected. A similar strike in Puerto Rico caused like hardship.

Friends of labor defend the strike even though harm is done others by saying it is the only weapon which labor can use. Any weapon that is unjust to others, to innocent people, is not a fit weapon to employ. The true solution to labor difficulties is in raising the individual standards of conduct of citizens throughout the nation, the employees, the employers, and of the government, so as to avoid the need for resort to strikes.

If all employers consider the welfare of their workers, strikes will be unnecessary. If we have an able efficient government protecting innocent parties, fair to capital, fair to labor, strikes will be unnecessary. Thus the true solution to labor difficulties is not in collective bargaining or in vast labor unions which of themselves tend to create friction and ill-feeling; it lies in all citizens co-operating to attain higher standards of conduct on the part of all, re-enforced when necessary by able, efficient government.

One who sincerely has the best wishes of labor at heart can give little support to some of their strikes. For instance, strikers in Seattle demanded that a ship be unloaded on a dock and the merchandise again loaded into another vessel. The employers wished to unload one ship directly into another; a sensible, efficient thing to do.

When labor unions resort to strikes to create work for themselves with utter disregard of the interest of the employer, they are undeserving of consideration or respect. It is a short-sighted policy on their part. They eventually will lose the support of the fair-minded. The unnecessary expense they cause will damage American shipping, driving it to foreign ports or other places where it receives less abuse.

We have had similar difficulties with longshoremen's strikes in San Francisco, the Hawaiian Islands, even against our own government sending supplies to Alaska. The suffering of the public is not considered. The unions demand that their demands be met in full. Then when these demands are met, they later impose additional ones.

Such conduct not only affects the interest of labor, but threatens the downfall of democracy. Under a democratic form of government, the wishes of such large groups of voters as labor unions must be considered. The politicians lack the strength to enforce the law. Eventually some more forceful person or persons will establish a form of government that will prevent abuse, and by virtue thereof receive the support of all those whom labor is unjustly treating.

When strikers put a picket line about a plant, armed with clubs, and refuse to permit law-abiding American citizens to enter the plant and go to work, these law-abiding citizens have but to organize under competent leadership, arm themselves with guns, and fight their way in. When our government stands by and does nothing about a situation like this, the law-abiding citizens in time will have to take the law in their own hands. A relatively few men under capable leadership can control large masses, as history has shown. We may yet expect to see this attempted by some determined citizen refusing to have his life ordered by irresponsible agitators indirectly supported by our government at Washington.

Thoughts

One can sometimes obtain some very profound information from those not commonly considered great thinkers. For instance, today a girl made what I considered to be a profound observation. She was born and brought up in a coal-mining locality. In some discussion regarding labor, she made the statement that labor is more inclined to strike, to resort to violence, when well paid and prosperous. When suffering from deprivation it is less likely to resort to violence. That labor generally is governed more by feeling than by reason and that the labor leaders reflect the feelings of the members of the labor unions at a particular time.

This observation is quite true as far as it goes. We know that in times of depression there are fewer strikes. In boom times labor is very willing to go on strike. In a larger aspect, we can explain the long suffering of Oriental peoples by this. They are accustomed to suffering and willing to make the best of conditions.

This action of labor is caused in part by human nature; man does not thrive as well on prosperity as he does on hardships. When he is subjected to trials his better qualities are more commonly brought to the fore than when he is prosperous. Those who have little are thankful for the little they can obtain, whereas when they have much they tend to take it for granted and demand more.

To insure better conduct on the part of labor, we must educate it. Instead of having labor prihuman in outlook, make it adhuman. The public will be greatly benefited by this development and labor will not only be made more worthy but benefited as well.—*January 9, 1938*.

Strikers who see no virtue in those desiring to work, who break windows of cars and factories, are not men in the highest sense. They are just overgrown, badly trained children who should be spanked.

Strikers are but little more than frantic horses. Soothe them, give them a square deal, but let them know there is a master whom they must obey. Do not let them believe they are master. Such conduct is fatal to the control of a horse. Do not permit yourself to be intimidated by their violent actions or give in to unjust demands. Use horse sense.

Continuous disregard of law by strikers will in time result in similar action by others and may cause nation-wide civil war.

XXXVII

LABOR COSTS

WE CAN WELL USE THE TERM LABOR COSTS IN DESCRIBING THE costs of labor. Labor costs are increased by shorter hours, higher wages, benefits, government regulations, the interference of the labor unions with work, inefficient labor, or any action which tends to increase the actual cost of the labor itself.

When labor costs become so high as to render the operation of a business unprofitable, it will be discontinued, thus causing unemployment. Great care must be exercised in regulating wages. There is as much possibility of causing harm by extremely high labor costs as there is by permitting labor to be exploited. Interference by the government should be reduced to a minimum and efforts made to encourage natural economic forces to maintain wages at the highest level consistent with the greatest degree of prosperity.

Extremely high labor costs force employers to employ as few men as possible and utilize labor-saving devices to the maximum. When, however, labor-saving devices are introduced in order to meet the demand for increased products, they stimulate employment by increasing the demand for material, thus increasing employment in other industries. You have here a contradiction that is both easy and difficult to understand. Extremely high labor costs cause unemployment when they force the employer to introduce labor-saving machinery to produce the same quantity of goods. When labor-saving devices are introduced to increase plant capacity, they lessen unemployment by increasing the demand for labor in industries from which their material is obtained.

When labor costs are only ten per cent of the final selling value of the product, it is relatively easy to increase wages. When labor costs represent fifty or seventy-five per cent of the value of the product, it is almost impossible to increase wages without destroying the market for the product. Thus labor-saving devices, by lessening labor costs, actually permit higher wages. Labor unions, in opposing the reduction of labor costs, are prejudicing their own interests. The soundness of this view is shown by the fact that wages in the United States are higher than wages in any other country. This is a direct result of the greater use of labor-saving devices.

High wages exaggerate a period of great business activity. Business is then enabled to pay these wages. The workmen then have more money to spend. This creates a greater demand for goods and stimulates business activity. The opposite condition, however, prevails in a depression. High labor costs discourage industry from embarking in new enterprises and cause it to seek labor-saving devices and any means at hand to lessen labor costs.

We often hear the argument put forth that high wages improve business conditions. This is true when the conditions are good, in which case the high wages are themselves caused by the period of prosperity. High wages of themselves will not improve the welfare of the wage earner. They are produced by good business conditions. They themselves do not produce prosperous conditions.

Maintaining high wages and short hours does not always benefit labor. The wage earner pays for them in concealed, obscure ways such as higher taxes, higher prices and fewer jobs. Unduly high wages discourage employers from starting new industries or enlarging those already existing, thus causing unemployment. Labor may be able to intimidate capital into raising wages, but it cannot require capital to embark upon new enterprises. This is a fact labor unions have yet to learn; it is obvious to the sensible, but not to the labor leaders.

There is a point at which wages are of the greatest benefit to the wage earner. When they are raised beyond this point, he suffers. Let us call this point the maximum wage. When wages are raised beyond this point or hours unduly shortened, which is the same in their ultimate effect, the employer must increase the price of his product in order to cover the increased cost. This tends to lessen the demand for it because people will be less willing to pay the increased price. This lessening of demand results in the employer producing less and requiring fewer employees.

From the standpoint of the employer, there is a minimum wage, reduction below which works to his injury. If he has skilled workmen and reduces their pay below this minimum wage, they will leave his employment and obtain work elsewhere. As the result he will have an inferior working force which will result in an inferior quality of goods and higher production costs.

Thus we have a maximum wage for the employee and a minimum wage for the employer. These are natural economic laws which prevent the payment of too low or too high wages. Unwise and arbitrary interference will result in harm to those who hope to be benefited by it.

Labor costs can be reduced by the employee without sacrificing pay. He can give more efficient service, making it possible for his employer to give him greater pay. As opposed to this, the worker who attempts to do as little work and get as much pay as possible tends to increase labor costs. He himself suffers from this conduct, as he becomes a less and less efficient worker and a less desirable person generally.

Labor itself should co-operate with the employer in reducing labor costs. The most unsound feature of present-day policies of organized labor is the fact that they increase labor costs. Organized labor today demands as much as it can obtain and gives as little as possible. It should give as much as possible and should demand only what is fair. This policy would be both intelligent and just; in the long run, labor would benefit far more in a material way than it will under existing policies.

The effects of minimum-wage laws are less pernicious in a period of industrial activity than a period of depression. During a period of activity, work is plentiful and jobs easily obtained. In a period of depression when jobs are few and obtained with difficulty, a minimum-wage law tends to increase unemployment. The employers themselves are making little profit or operating at a loss, and must cut expenses. If they can reduce wages they might be able to avoid reducing their employees. If a minimum-wage law exists, they may have no other alternative.

The true solution to unfairly low wages and the exploitation of workers is not by the passage of laws to prevent it. The true solution is to establish an environment so high that employers will voluntarily treat labor fairly and unfair treatment or exploitation will be so condemned by public opinion as to be nonexistent. If the efforts now being devoted to protecting labor's interest by statute were directed toward creating an ascendent environment of this nature, far better results would be obtained.

We have been so accustomed to the abuses of the past as to feel that repressive measures are necessary to correct them. But we have been trying repressive measures for many years and the situation is worse in many respects. Let us now change our policies and adopt expressive measures instead. Instead of prohibiting employers from abusing their workers, let us encourage them to treat them fairly and with consideration.

Repression is not good for the development of the individual; it is not good for the development of considerate employers either. The development of the individual demands the utmost freedom of expression. Likewise, the development of considerate employers demands the utmost freedom of expression on their part and encouragement to perform their duties to themselves, their employees and society.

When an employer abuses his power, he should be dealt

with so effectively as to prevent further abuse by him. We should consider such conduct to be an offense against society. For many years we have been repressing business and trying to reform the criminal. Let us reverse this policy. Let us reform business, and repress the criminals and those who prey upon others.

Developing an economic structure that will pay the highest possible wages to all is a task requiring the greatest of ability. Arbitrary increases of wages or legal enactments establishing minimum wages can be productive of more harm than good. The wage earners are not the only ones to be concerned. The interest of the public must be protected as well as the employers.

Economic laws cannot be defied with impunity. When we arbitrarily raise wages, far-reaching effects will ensue throughout the entire economic structure. When conditions justify such action, it may be wise. When conditions do not justify it, it may be productive of great harm to those whom it is intended to benefit.

We have had some five years of efforts to improve the condition of the workingman or workingwoman. Yet today I notice here in the city of New York a headline regarding demands of laundry workers for a minimum wage of fourteen dollars a week for women and minors. This is an extremely low wage. It is remarkable how some people in large cities like New York manage to live on the small wages they receive. They must pay high rents, buy food and clothing, meet innumerable expenses—and yet, somehow, many survive on a mere pittance.

The problem of increasing the general well-being is one that should be approached sympathetically and intelligently. Our methods heretofore have included too much denunciation of capital, of the wealthy, and too little understanding of the complex problems involved. If we cease the denunciation, cease to create ill feeling and endeavor to improve the general well-being of all, it can be accomplished.

Not, however, by the passage of wage laws, increasing the

powers of labor unions and similar measures. We will have to go far deeper into the causes of unsatisfactory conditions. If intelligently approached over a long period of many years a vast improvement can be effected. This must be accomplished in accord with economic laws. We must employ positive acts of a helpful nature, not negative acts of a harmful nature.

XXXVIII

LABOR MISLED

A FACTOR WHICH LABOR AS A WHOLE FAILS TO CONSIDER IS that workers vary in their ability; some are efficient, others inefficient. The natural tendency is for the efficient worker to be penalized by the inefficient when subjected to labor rules. When you establish rates of pay that give the poorer worker the same pay and consideration as the efficient one, you discourage the development of efficient workers.

Many attempts have been made by well-meaning men to establish communities in which the injustices of the capitalistic system would not exist. These communities invariably failed. The primary cause of their failure was the establishment of equality of pay for the workers, with no means of insuring equality of performance. That is to say, it is very easy to fix the pay, but it is far more difficult to require the individual to earn it.

When the pay is fixed, and there is no incentive to better performance, the abler workers are discouraged and tend to go elsewhere, where they can obtain better pay. The idlers, the inefficient, the incompetent, do little or nothing, but are willing to draw their pay. It is for this reason that labor unions are fast becoming the greatest menace to our country.

They demand many fixed benefits and they have no means of making all workers worthy of the benefits. Their tendency is to give the same reward to the indifferent, incompetent, and lazy as to the able, efficient, deserving, conscientious worker.

The average American laboring man has a good fund of

common sense, a good sense of justice. When a labor union is dominated by average American workmen it can be a constructive force. They are willing to do their part in bettering the condition of the country. They, like other citizens and interest groups, are the victims of conditions. They have felt it necessary to organize unions to protect their interests, and it is but natural that they would be inclined to favor their own interests.

I have talked with several splendid types of American workingmen, good mechanics who do their work well. They have no sympathy with the violent labor agitators. They realize the difference in the quality of work done by different individuals. They feel that workingmen should unite to protect themselves, but they also see problems too difficult for the labor unions to solve.

An intelligent workman in sympathy with labor admitted his inability to see how labor unions could solve the problem of rewarding workmen in accordance with their ability. Take a group of a dozen carpenters. They will vary in ability and in energy. The very best one is probably worth twice as much to the employer as the poorest one, and yet the labor unions arbitrarily establish a fixed scale for all carpenters. How can this be met by labor unions? They cannot meet it, and give each what he deserves.

A painter who did small jobs in plastering, paperhanging and painting, necessitating the employment of a few workmen, mentioned an illuminating instance. He put two men to work painting ceilings. At the end of the day's work one of these painters came to him and said, "This fellow you've got working with me is no good. Take him away and let me do the job myself. I can get along better without him." This was done, and the one man painted all the ceilings in that building by himself.

How would your labor union meet this problem? In their demands for work for all employees they require the employer to take any number of men and pay them alike. The general effect is to penalize the most efficient workmen for the sake of giving the poorer one a chance. If the labor unions did not exist, a more ready application of the principle of the survival of the fittest would take place. This would result in more readily rewarding the efficient, who would not then be burdened by the inefficient.

This is a problem which labor unions do not face frankly. All too often the most worthless workmen are the biggest agitators. They obtain control of the union and dominate its policies by violence and denunciation.

Our social legislation has the same effect. It attempts to help a lot of people in need of help, but why do they need help? Is it not their own fault? Unquestionably in a great many cases it is the fault of the individual. He is often incompetent, lazy, and unwilling to exert himself.

We hear little of this from the social workers but it is a practical fact which should not be overlooked. The criticism of our social reform and labor legislation is that it is insufficiently practical. It should endeavor to assist where necessary, but not at the expense of penalizing intelligent efforts and promoting parasitism.

The members of our most violent labor unions are not all bad men by any means. This is shown by the fact that many of them take excellent care of their families, assist their friends, and possess, in general, many of the fine traits of normal human beings. They are brought into an unfortunate state of mind by environmental influences conducive toward it.

On the whole they have not trained minds; their mental processes are simple, primitive, and infantile. They are inclined, like the child, to be dominated by Granto and Grievo. When to this be added some real injustices and continued association with fellow workers having the same views, then finally, inflamed by agitators, the men are brought to a state of mind where they are not controlled by justice or sound thought.

They are governed by their feelings. It matters little whether the injustices they complain about are real or imaginary. The effect upon them is the same. An imaginary injustice will affect the individual just as strongly as a real injustice. The intensity of the feeling is far more influential in determining his conduct than its actual merit.

Thus we see members of labor unions on strike violate the law, intimidate law-abiding citizens, and use physical force toward others who oppose them. They are in effect a large group of men who could be decent but who have become a mob of law violators. These men cannot be entirely blamed for this condition.

They would cease to be so if we had a wise government, if we had able thinkers in control who would solve economic problems to the best of their ability. Able leaders at the same time would explain to the workers the difficulties of economic problems. They would encourage them to be thankful for what they have instead of taking all for granted and harboring grievances.

The power of free speech is badly abused in permitting agitators to arouse members of labor unions. Subject average men to the influence of a forceful, strong agitator, and he will soon arouse them to violence. On the other hand, subject these same men to the influence of a really strong forceful character—an able orator who knows men, who can talk to them, who will explain the problems and the need for restraint. If these men could have confidence in this thoughtful man, he could control their action and guide it toward constructive channels.

The bad feature about labor unions is that the thoughtful men do not become leaders. Able, thoughtful men do not like the discord of labor agitation. They direct their gifts into other channels. The natural result is that those men who do attain leadership in labor unions are the agitators who make themselves popular by continually stressing the grievances under which the men are working. They continually promise more benefits, and stir up ill-feeling, in much the same way that our politicians obtain votes by promising anything to the voters.

These violent striking laborers are the victims of vicious circumstances more than of inherent viciousness themselves. They become law violators because of the politicians, our liberal thinkers, their own agitators, unwise government policies, and a great many other influences that could be corrected by the wise action of wise men. Not the least of these factors is that our schools, which are supposed to educate youth, fail to promote good citizenship. Labor problems cannot be solved unless we have leaders in the nation who inspire confidence in their ability and character.

At this time it seems probable that eventually extreme force will have to be used to insure the survival of civilization in our country. When this force is applied it may result in killing a great many of these deluded men who are less guilty than their leaders. As in the past, they will be the ones to suffer, while the guilty men will escape.

All the men composing the violent labor unions who behave so badly in strikes are not hoodlums. They have been subjected to the influence of hoodlums, of agitators, and to a combination of environmental influences that have for the time being caused them to place some of the less desirable traits in their make-up in control. They are to all intents and purposes, for the time being, hoodlums, not by real intent, but by force of circumstances.

These men would respond to sensible means to improve their condition if able leadership existed to obtain their confidence; if they could have explained to them a reasonable understanding of the economic conditions so they may realize they are not being persecuted or unjustly treated by everyone; that there is another side to the question; that if they themselves are willing to co-operate, those whom they are now opposing can likewise be brought to co-operate. A solution can be accomplished by means of harmonious co-operation, whereas today a solution is being prevented by misrepresentation, violence, and continued ill feeling.

Among the men taking part in strikes armed with clubs and using violence, are many who, judging from their features, are strong characters, capable of great development, mentally and morally. They become violators of the law as the result of the environmental influences in which they were brought up.

Many were born into families which suffered abuse from employers in the past and had difficulty in making a living. As a child such a man hears much criticism of existing economic conditions and much denunciation of the wealthy. He naturally believes that he is being badly treated. He attends school, learns to read and write, but is taught little about human nature or how to develop himself fully. He receives little assistance from the church, merely being asked to worship God and pray and live a good life, but not being told just how to do so in a practical way.

Now let us take this strong individual who really has a basically good heritage. Suppose he is brought up in a community where the economic problems are being solved in the best way, although his family is poor. A better spirit prevails, an efficient government exists. The parents realize that the government is doing its best to correct conditions. The employers, capital, churches and schools are all doing their best to bring about an environment conducive to the best in all. Education stresses Ascendency, and it is in the environment. The young boy is taught about the basic principles governing human acts, taught to develop Primo and Co, and is not subjected to the influence of labor agitators or politicians.

Can you visualize the difference in this man? Instead of being what he now is, a violator of the law and an aggrieved person using violence to obtain justice, he is a desirable citizen and a good worker. He considers the rights of others, appreciates the difficulty of solving economic problems, and is doing his duty.

This is what we should aim for. It is the vicious existing environment that causes our terrible condition. When we attempt to accuse any one class of being entirely at fault, we are in error. It is a combination of all circumstances, all existing people, all influences. All alike are failing to do their duty as they should.

We must take special care to be very fair to labor and avoid permitting its unlawful, violent acts, and selfish, prejudiced leaders to cause us to overlook the fact that there is a side to its case. Employees have been, and in many cases still are being, unjustly treated, even though they are too prone to blame employers and see no fault in themselves. This is a somewhat universal human trait which they are far from being alone in possessing.

Labor leaders and labor unions vary in their conception of public duty. Some have regard for others. They do not cause so much trouble. They are rewarded for their consideration by receiving consideration. We have more violent leaders, more violent unions, that are but little removed from racketeers. Labor itself should eliminate its racketeer leaders and racketeer unions, as they tend to discredit all labor.

Members of labor unions should themselves analyze critically all action taken. They should ask themselves whether it has been well thought out, is fair to the employer, considers the interest of the public, and will in the long run benefit them. Has the action of the union been determined in a spirit of thoughtfulness and consideration, or has it been done in a spirit of anger, stressing the grievances and overlooking the benefits?

The short-sighted policies of labor unions are displayed by the condition of building construction. Labor unions demand high wages and short hours; jealousy exists between various unions as to the right to do certain types of work. This results in building construction being so costly as to be prohibitive. As there is little construction going on, much unemployment is caused to members of the building-trades unions. They, however, are not the only sufferers. If the restrictions imposed upon the building industry by the labor unions were removed, a great building boom would ensue and a great demand for building materials would be created. All members of the building-trades unions would have employment and the demand for building material would create employment for many others.

The action of organized labor often results in hardships upon other labor not organized. As illustrative of this I may mention a young married couple with a child who were earning a living from a business not connected with building trades and not paying high wages. They were penalized by high labor costs in building their own home. Here is a fine young family, one of many, upon whom the nation's future rests, being penalized in establishing a home of their own as a result of the selfish action of building-trades labor unions in making the cost of construction so high as to inflict a hardship upon them. Labor is not only causing the wealthy to suffer but it is causing other workers to suffer. The latter's suffering is the more severe.

The sit-down strikers are not suffering from long hours or insufficient wages. They are misled by unwise leaders stimulating them to continually demand more, regardless of others. Yet we find other workers suffering want, lauding them. Labor's worst enemy is indeed labor itself, not capital. If labor would co-operate with capital, work could be found for all, and suffering would diminish.

The depression was greatly lengthened by unwise interference with the functioning of economic laws which, if permitted to function unhampered, would have lessened the severity and shortened the period of depression very materially. The action of labor unions is bad in this respect. Strong unions, such as those of the railway employees, were able to maintain relatively high wages throughout the depression. Those railway employees who, by virtue of their seniority, were able to obtain constant work during this time, were rewarded to the prejudice of others.

Maintenance by strong unions of extremely high wages and short hours works against the interests of the ununionized depressed classes of labor, in that they must work for less pay and longer hours. Industry has just so much money to expend for labor, and the strong unions, by getting more than their share, are taking it from the ununionized workers. This tendency is hard to trace through all its manifestations, but it is a real condition and functions just this way. This illustrates again that unwise interference with economic laws by people not understanding them causes hardship while they flatter themselves they have been accomplishing great good. The best interest of all labor should be directed toward obtaining fair pay and fair play for all, whether union or nonunion, strong or weak, prosperous or depressed.

If the employers were free to act, they would get labor at the cheapest place, tending to level off wages throughout the nation, raising them where they were low, and lowering them where too high. This, if carried out, would result in more employment; greater demand for raw materials, thus stimulating industry; and finally, absorption of all the unemployed, causing all to benefit.

Our labor policies are suicidal in persecuting capital and preventing it from developing new industries and solving the problem of unemployment. We have more labor agitation, more labor legislation, and more reform legislation now than at any time in the past—and with it all, more unemployment.

We have unemployed parading the streets demanding benefits. Why are they unemployed? Largely because the threatening policy of organized labor is preventing capital from expanding and absorbing the unemployed. The more labor agitation, the more demands the labor unions place upon capital, the less willing will capital be to undertake new enterprises.

These unemployed who are demanding benefits do not see this. They do not blame other labor unions; they blame capital alone. These men are not intelligent. They are poor ignorant men led by agitators. It is a crime to be successful in their eyes, and one lacks merit unless he has nothing.

The action of the labor unions and of the unemployed is a positive demonstration of the existence in adults of infantile traits and a low standard of intelligence. Yet it is these people whom we are permitting to dictate the conduct of our affairs.

They have been stimulated to this activity by our own leaders, the men who are supposed to govern the country, the politicians.

American labor is today the best paid in the world, and yet we have more labor troubles than any other nation. In China, where labor is paid very little, there is no labor trouble. The people are glad to work for the merest pittance. This, in itself, should cause labor to think. If the American workers are better off than labor in other countries, why should they cause so much labor trouble? The natural result will be, if labor agitation continues, for industry to go to the cheapest labor. Bad as conditions are in our own country, they seem to be worse in other countries. Capital cannot seek refuge elsewhere with any certainty for the future. If sometime some other country offers security, it will go there.

The economic affairs of countries having a relatively low standard of living as compared with our own are now having a great effect upon our own industrial life. This will increase with the passage of time, as they become industrialized and more able to compete with us. Much of the economic unsettlement in the United States and other countries possessing a high standard of living is caused by competition with countries having lower living standards. The general tendency of foreign trade, if permitted to operate unchecked, is to raise lower standards of living and lower the higher standards of living until they are equalized. We are being faced with this problem today. No sensible effort is being made to meet it. It is a problem which our labor unions never consider and one which is but little discussed.

The excessive demands of organized labor cause unemployment and higher taxes and will bring about more unsatisfactory conditions in the future in which they will suffer along with the rest of the country. In attacking capital they are attacking themselves in the long run. Common sense should tell us that violence, prejudice, and stupidity will not improve economic conditions. These are the measures that labor is resorting to. If we permit this to continue, conditions will grow more and more unsatisfactory and labor agitators will still find means to blame others than themselves. We should face the facts and solve our economic problems in accordance with them.

Labor unions oppose the efficient operation of industry and business by placing restrictions upon the reduction of the working force. They endeavor to require the employers to employ as many men as possible, thus interfering with efficient management. The labor unions take a short-sighted view because they feel that their interests will be better served by having more jobs available. They fail to see that unwise interference of this nature hampers industry and prevents the development of new industries which would require more employees and increase the national wealth, thus bettering working conditions.

Organized labor does not see that it is forcing inflation and that its high wages will in time buy less and less. The net result will be that all will lose. Labor will suffer with the rest. The very measures it is advocating will result in less actual pay because of the decreased purchasing power of wages as the result of the inevitable inflation if the extravagant policies we now tolerate are continued for a sufficiently long time.

Capital and employers generally are constructive. They are engaged in activity that produces wealth. By contrast, our labor unions and our government hamper constructive activities. Both our government and our labor are receivers from others. The government receives vast sums of money in payment of taxes, the labor unions receive vast sums from the employers in the form of wages. Our capitalists and employers pay out money to others.

Of these three groups, capital is the only constructive one; it is serving society. Honest workmen who give fair value in services for wages received likewise are contributing to society. They could do still more if unhampered by labor unions and the government.

Agitators in labor unions protected by our government make greater and greater demands against which the employers are helpless. Discharge one of these agitators and immediately a whole union goes on strike because they claim he has been discriminated against for union activity. If the same agitator were in a Civilian Conservation Corps camp and did the same thing, he would be very promptly discharged.

Civilian Conservation Corps camps have been conducted by army officers who have had much experience in the handling of men. They deserve great credit for maintaining discipline under difficult conditions. They find these measures necessary. It is likewise necessary that the employers have similar disciplinary power and have the right to discharge from their employ any individual who is a bad influence.

Groups of men working together are influenced very readily by the various members composing the groups. One agitator can influence a large number by magnifying their grievances in much the same way that a rotten potato, if permitted, will cause a whole barrel to rot.

Handling men is a difficult task. It is an ability that few possess. We have corporations employing over a hundred thousand men. In handling these large groups efficiently and maintaining order, rigid discipline must be maintained. When we take the power of discipline from the employer by refusing to permit him to discharge undesirable elements, we are bringing about the downfall of American industry.

A clipping I just glanced at from a newspaper mentioned the stoppage of work in one of the General Motors plants as the result of certain employees on the assembly line refusing to work. The paper mentioned rather casually that this was the fortieth time stoppages of a similar nature had occurred since the General Motors agreement with the Committee for Industrial Organization settling the sit-down strike.

This illustrates the difficulty of a corporation conducting its affairs when the power of maintaining discipline is withheld. If the corporation had full power to hire and discharge whomsoever it wished, these men would have been discharged upon having refused to work the first time, and the ridiculous situation of having forty incidents of work being interrupted would not exist.

This shows the viciousness of permitting labor unions to dominate the control of a corporation. When work is stopped, financial loss results to the company. The labor union is unable to control its own members and to insure good behavior. Doubtless the men causing these stoppages are among the least desirable employees whose services could well be spared.

In one of our large city hotels during a period of labor unrest and strife, considerable feeling existed among the employees with no great justification, but they brooded and talked about the matter and believed they had quite a grievance. The situation was felt by the hotel management; they were very careful to avoid any acts or say anything that would tend to aggravate the trouble. If a waiter neglected to attend to his duties properly, rather than precipitate a strike, they would ignore it.

No organization can be managed efficiently if able managers are not permitted to select the ablest employees and place them where their services will be of the greatest use. When a small group of agitators are enabled to dictate to the manager policies regarding labor relations, the efficiency of the service will deteriorate rapidly. If this condition is permitted to continue American industry will rapidly pass from the most efficient in the world to one of the most hopelessly inefficient.

Thoughts

What incentive, what encouragement, does an able business manager have in extending his enterprises? Under labor domination he has neither. Such being the case, why should an able, industrious, ambitious man subject himself to insults and humiliation, by continuing to strive for achievement? Why should he create industries if he will be unable to control them? If the employees assert the right to set the wages, hours and the conditions of labor?

Add to this the many other restrictions the government places upon him in the way of taxation and supervision. The chances of success are materially decreased, and there is no reason why a sensible man should undertake the risk with the cards stacked against him. We shall soon begin to feel the effects of this situation.

Our country achieved a marvelous development largely as the result of noninterference on the part of the government, permitting each individual to exert himself to his utmost, assured that he would derive the full benefit of his efforts. Our present rulers reverse that system, discouraging anyone from undertaking any enterprise because of the obstacles put in their path. If they should by any chance prove successful, they are subjected to humiliation and taxation by the government and domination by irresponsible labor unions. Continue this policy and your unemployment will increase beyond anything that has heretofore existed.

Give the employers full power to control their employees, but see that only the deserving are permitted to become employers.

Members of labor unions should be thoughtful, reflect over their acts and see if they have been benefited by strikes or by the resort to violence and abuse of their employers. How much better off today, for instance, are the automobile workers of General Motors? Just about a year ago they were on a sit-down strike. Not because of overwork, harsh treatment, low wages, or long hours. They were on strike simply to obtain the right to dictate certain matters of policy to their employer. Are these same men better off today than they were a year ago? They are worse off. They are being punished for their own violence and disregard of the law. If we can educate our common citizens to realize this truth, we can discredit violent labor leaders and obtain harmony in our country.—*February 19, 1938.*

XXXIX

GOVERNMENT AND LABOR

ONE OF THE BASIC REASONS FOR THE EXISTENCE OF ANY GOVERN-
ment is the function of settling disputes between its citizens.
Our government is failing to perform this most basic duty
of all governments when it proves unwilling and unable to
prevent strikes and labor disputes. It admits its inability to do
justice to both capital and labor and protect the public, and
by so demonstrating its inability has forfeited the respect and
support of decent citizens.

The apathy of the people in the face of this is amazing.
It is somewhat similar to the decadence of Rome. Yet they
respond to an emotional appeal, a sentimental occurrence,
such as a kidnaping, a murder or a speech promising to correct all ills. Why is this? Because our environment stresses
this sentimental development and inhibits mental clearness
and understanding of what is mentally and morally sound
and right.

When labor unions go on a strike, place pickets around
a plant, and use forcible means to prevent other workers not
in sympathy with the strike from working, they are violating
the liberty guaranteed by our constitution. It is a vicious
procedure when any interest group is permitted to determine
the righteousness of their measures. It indicates the utter
breakdown of our government if permitted to continue. Illegal action arouses resentment and will bring about retaliation.

If the strikers are justified the government should give

them justice and avoid the need for their placing pickets about a plant and using force to prevent others from working. If the employers are justified in their contention and the strikers are abusing the employers, the government should protect the rights of the individual citizen in his desire to work, and insure him protection while so engaged.

Sensible action by the government will avoid the need for strikes and will avoid violence in connection therewith. This action would be living up to the purposes for which government is intended in preserving order among its citizens and preventing such a condition as exists in the jungle, where the strong may despoil the weak at will.

The interest of labor would be better served by directing that effort now spent toward increasing the power of labor unions toward promoting an efficient government capable of safeguarding labor's interests, preventing labor's excesses, and giving the welfare of all citizens equal consideration. Capable, efficient, honest government would benefit labor as fully as it would benefit any other deserving class. The prosperity and general well-being of all deserving groups will be more benefited by seeking the prosperity and general well-being of all individual citizens than by having a particular group or combination of groups attempt to obtain benefits for themselves to the prejudice of other groups having opposing interests.

The tendency of any interest group when it becomes powerful, is to abuse its power. This gives rise ultimately to the creation of resentment among other individuals and groups and eventually causes them to combine to control the aggressive persecutor. This results in a continuous series of conflicts between interest groups. This is a primitive way of conducting affairs. The intelligent method is to consider the interest of all and promote harmony. With harmony there will be greater possibility of considering difficult problems in a calm manner with far less of anger, prejudice, and denunciation.

Labor unions or other interest groups designed to protect themselves from abuse should not exist in democracy. All citizens should constitute one interest group to strive for fair dealing for all. Interest groups within the nation only cause ill-feeling and harm when they assert themselves in furthering their own interests, disregarding the interests of others.

If we had an able, efficient government that would correct all injustices, that would protect the interests of all its citizens, labor unions would have no grievances and no need to organize to defend themselves. Thus, the true cure for labor problems is in high standards of citizenship and efficient government. The organization of labor unions is justified when they must defend themselves against injustice but from this point, they rapidly develop bad features.

The worst sufferers from labor union excesses are its own members. Banded together to defend themselves, it is natural that they exaggerate grievances and blame all but selves. Such an attitude is destructive to character development. The principles of Ascendent Psychology teach that each individual must develop Primo and be cognizant of his own faults in order to correct them.

Labor agitation offers a too ready means for the weakling to thrust the cause of his failure upon his employers, upon capital, upon anyone but himself. The biggest labor agitators are those men who have permitted Eato to become a dominant drive. They entertain a perpetual grievance against capital, employers, and successful people generally.

The literature of labor and the speeches of its leaders condemn it. They are one-sided and untrue. They never admit doing anything wrong. It is always the employers who are vicious and abusing them. Anyone having knowledge of the working of the human mind realizes that men in large groups, by talking over their troubles and exaggerating them, can easily reach a state of mind bordering on insanity, unable to act fairly. When this state of mind exists, some impartial agency should intervene.

Organized labor is being deluded by its leaders who have created the belief that in order to get what they are entitled to, they should resort to violence. If someone in whom these men had confidence would explain the economic problems to them they would not be such ready victims to agitators. It is here where our schools and politicians fail miserably.

Regardless of what we may say about the politicians being merely a reflection of the environment and as good as the people that elect them, we must hold them responsible for much. In their efforts to obtain office and defeat the opposing political party or other opponent, they have continually made promises utterly impossible of fulfillment. This action of the politicians, combined with labor agitators and reformers whose intentions are better than their understanding, has brought about the present unfortunate state of affairs.

Both our politicians and labor leaders represent the poorest quality of men. Politics is too dirty a game to encourage men of high character to enter it. To become a successful labor leader one must be an agitator, use force, unethical methods, conciliate the violent elements within the union and appeal to many infantile minds. No able man will undertake such a calling, no man of character will enter it. Therefore we have today among our labor unions and politicians men of poor character and ability. Their efforts and associations have resulted in their attaining some degree of ability in handling and appealing to their followers, but this has prevented their development into individuals of good character or of broad viewpoint capable of helping labor, in the case of labor leaders, or of governing efficiently and honestly in the case of politicians.

Our politicians and labor agitators, who are having more to say about our affairs than other persons, are the direct opposite of what we would expect in men of high character and great ability. They create a very bad atmosphere throughout the nation and are a lowering influence upon the environment. They have not developed Primo. Neither one ever admits making mistakes. Labor leaders are good examples of the development of Granto and Grievo to extremes. They have nothing whatever to be thankful for. They take every benefit they possess for granted and have many grievances.

Everything in the world is wrong but themselves. They are the only virtuous people. All others are vicious.

Look back over history and let us see what men live in memory today for their high character. Take Robert E. Lee, for example. He lived in a time of great disturbance and finally of civil war. He had no part in bringing it about. It was his opinion that it could have been avoided had wise counsel prevailed. Forced into a difficult situation not of his own making, he went through four years of war caused by the very same type of radical agitators we have today.

Whom do we respect the most, the radical agitators who brought about the Civil War or Robert E. Lee? They do not compare with him from the standpoint of moral character or ability. If Robert E. Lee had been high in the councils of the nation before the Civil War started and had been supported, it would never have been fought.

We can well apply this example to our present-day conditions. We are following, in our labor leaders and in our politicians, the very same class of men corresponding to the abolitionists and politicians of the Civil War era. We should seek among our people for Robert E. Lees, put them in control, and put the agitators under their control. Robert E. Lee was not continually telling the world that he was without fault and promising people free benefits or constantly airing personal grievances. He lives today, the leader of a lost cause with character undimmed. Were he with us today he would have the same opinion of the politicians and labor agitators now as he had of the agitators of his day. He said but little but we know he disapproved of them.

The mere fact that labor must organize to defend its rights against employers is in itself evidence that our government and our politicians are inefficient. Instead of finding a solution and leading the way toward it, they must be pushed into action by labor organizing itself into strong groups having great voting power, and by its exercise trying to force the politicians to grant them reforms or special benefits. This is a very illustrative example of the fact that our leaders are incapable of leading but must be driven by those whom they claim to be leading. Great leaders cannot be produced by this means. They cannot be driven. They display ability by exercising it, and become leaders by virtue of their very strength which is recognized by others willing to trust their interests in their hands. We elevate incompetent men to be leaders because they can flatter and promise. Then we wishfully sit on the sidelines and hope that they will be able to carry out some of their promises.

The weakness of our politicians in following the popular clamor and attacking capital shows their utter unfitness to be entrusted with the destiny of our country. If they were statesmen they would tell about the economic laws, would point out the difficult problems to be solved. Do they do this? No, they follow the crowd, pleasing those who have the most votes and attacking those who have the least.

Labor disturbances have been fomented by our government. When the New Deal administration took office there was little labor agitation. With the passage of the N.R.A. and with the encouragement of the administration, labor unions launched a great drive for increased membership. Later on, when the original sit-down strike occurred, it received indirect support from our government. Many men joined labor unions believing the administration desired them to do so. The postoffice department has refused to deliver mail to plants surrounded by striking pickets.

Labor agitation has had the direct support of the administration since the entry into office of the New Deal. This administration has persecuted capital and the employers legally by the passage of whatever measures it could, and has resorted to indirect encouragement of violence through labor unions. It seems inconceivable that the American public would submit to such misuse of their government. They would not, if they understood. They have placed their confidence in men whom they expect to be deserving of it.

This persecution by the government of capital and employers can have no good results. How sensible men can embark on such a policy, with any hope of obtaining results, surpasses belief. The way to bring about prosperity in the country is to stimulate industry, protect it, encourage it, help it to find jobs for the unemployed and get them off relief by giving them constructive work. This increased work would cause increased demand for raw materials, and work would soon be found for everyone.

The policy of the government in persecuting industry stops it from expanding to absorb the unemployed. Our whole system is wrong when we hope to obtain prosperity by denouncing those who are successful, persecuting them and making promises of better days to come. Promises and wishful thought will not bring about better days in the future. Careful planning and helpful co-operation would. When we have a government that adopts sane policies, protects capital, encourages it and restrains law violators, we may hope to solve economic problems.

When labor uses violence that violates the rights of others and the government proves unwilling or unable to control it, a reign of lawlessness will be bound to ensue in time. Citizens whose rights are abused by labor will themselves resort to violence to protect their rights. When the aggrieved parties resort to violence in their turn, they will be stimulated to greater violence than that of the labor unions. This is a condition that well deserves careful consideration. When the government is unable to guarantee freedom and the right to work to individual citizens, they some day will resort to violence to protect themselves. This violence may become very severe and seek revenge on those who have attacked them in the past.

Incompetent government is at fault in permitting economic conditions to get so bad as to require labor to use violence in the first place, and is further showing its incompetence in being unable to protect others against violence, whether from labor unions or any other source. The basis of all government is to protect the citizens. When it fails to do so, it becomes unworthy of surviving as a government.

Tolerance by the government of law violations by labor unions will result in other groups following the same example. When a sufficiently large number get together they will say, "Why should we obey the law? You don't make the labor unions do it!" This will bring about a reign of lawlessness, following the example of others.

It is only the thoughtless who approve sit-down strikes. The thoughtful can see the probability of the same violence and disregard of law being shown by others. When government permits violence by certain privileged groups, it invites attack itself by other groups. Those violently assailed will be driven in desperation to employ like methods. Violence breeds violence. When it is tolerated in one group it invites retaliation from others. Our short-sighted rulers in tolerating such a condition are encouraging civil war, which will result in their overthrow. Those unable to prevent violence are clearly inadequate to the task of government.

What is the cause of all these strikes in the country when our labor is the highest paid and best treated of any nation in the world? It is the result of a mental condition. These workers have been told by our government, by the politicians and by their leaders that they are being unjustly treated. They have talked about this among themselves, have brooded on the matter, have overlooked benefits, have dwelt on grievances, and have reached an unhealthy state of mind incapable of seeing the situation in its true light.

If our politicians were statesmen equal to the task they would point out some of the benefits which labor is deriving and bring about a more healthful atmosphere. Instead of doing this they continue to denounce capital. Many support the strikers in flagrant disregard of the law. These strikes are a direct result of our government's activities. Not a word comes from Washington to bring about better understanding —only continual denunciation of capital, the very capital that pays these workmen and supports them.

The existence of a National Labor Relations Board for the purpose of hearing grievances of employees will, unless carefully administered, actually create grievances. If the employee feels that this labor board will favor him, he magnifies grievances or even sometimes creates them, feeling that when his case appears before the board he will be able to obtain something.

This is practically a subconscious reaction of the unreflecting. A man with a grievance is not a good worker. He is more concerned about his grievances than in earning his pay or considering his employer's interest. As a result he fails to do his work well and does not earn his pay.

Why should we permit a few men to tie up the work of many and cause suffering to many firms and people not even concerned with the controversy? The longshoremen's strike in San Francisco caused great suffering to innocent individuals and great injury to American commerce. Men who had nothing to do with the issues involved in the strike were the ones who suffered most by it.

When we permit this to go on we are being unjust to decent citizens. Regardless of the controversy between labor and capital, a decent government would see that the public was protected and that innocent people were protected. There are any number of instances recently where strikers have intimidated citizens not concerned in the strike and have prevented them from enjoying the liberties which our Constitution guarantees to all.

Strikes are caused not by labor itself but by inefficient, incompetent government. When the government is unable to solve economic problems, the sufferers will take the law in their own hands to correct the evils from which they are suffering. This tendency is further strengthened by a weak government unable to enforce existing laws. The strikers realize that they may act with impunity, disregarding any laws that oppose their desires. We pass laws limiting capital and corporations, but no regulation of any kind has been passed limiting labor unions. They do as they please, spend their money as they see fit, and nothing is said.

Conflicts between capital and labor are not limited to these two, but they include and affect the public, which is by far the most important. The public through its government must control both capital and labor, giving both a square deal, thus insuring its own best interests and that of all concerned.

The violence of strikers in assaulting those who wish to work is a manifestation of the primitive. Ignorant savages displayed the same use of force against those who did not believe as they did. These strikers are far more to be censured than the ignorant savage, for they attempt to justify their violence by claiming it is for the benefit of the downtrodden. When our civilization—our government—is so weak, so incompetent, that it is unable to protect the downtrodden and permits its citizens to engage in violence to protect what they call their rights, we are but little removed from unthinking savagery.

Our government has indeed fallen to a low estate. It is now the big corporations that are supporting the law and sticking up for what is right. It is the labor agitators and our government who are oppressing them, fomenting violence and breeding disrespect for the law because of their disregard and failure to enforce it.

The question now before the law-abiding citizens of the country is whether they will submit to a government of weak politicians dominated by the lowest element in the country, or whether they will assert their manhood and refuse to be so dominated. They may as well combine now. Putting the matter off, hoping for a turn to the better, is more likely to result in things getting worse. The politicians must be removed from the control of the government, and the vicious element in the country must be placed under control of the decent element.

Labor activity, as displayed in the form of collective bargaining, strikes, and demands for the closed shop, receives its strength less from the merit of these objectives than from the fact that no other methods have been suggested to improve conditions. If we had a government deserving of confidence, if the labor problem were being frankly faced and attempts made to solve it in a sensible way, ample support would be received, not only from men not belonging to labor unions, but from a large number of those now members. In the absence of leaders in political life capable of solving the problems of labor, the natural recourse of the workman is to unite in labor unions to protect himself and to gain whatever benefits he can. In doing this he is but following the example set by the politicians themselves and by other interest groups.

The action of labor unions in strikes is very similar to the conduct of children who have discovered that they can intimidate their teacher without fear of punishment. The labor agitators stimulate their not very intelligent members into believing they have wrongs, and knowing that they will not suffer any punishment for their misdeeds, they do not hesitate to violate the law and the rights of others in their efforts to intimidate their employer into acceding to their will. Children would not get out of hand when in the control of a capable teacher, neither would the labor unions get out of hand if we had a government. The cure in both cases is simple. Put in a teacher who can handle the children, and put in a government that can handle infantile human beings.

The great number of strikes, the wide prevalence of lawlessness and disregard of police officers and other representatives of the government whose duty is to maintain order, is a direct result of our governmental policies encouraged and supported by impractical reformers. When groups of citizens such as our W.P.A. workers can spit upon and call policemen vile names at will, we have brought about a situation that will result in the eventual use of crushing force. Payment of benefits to adults spoils them just as readily as children are spoiled by fond parents. When the benefits are withdrawn, the former recipients have a grievance. The attacks by politicians and government officials generally upon employers have further resulted in spreading a general feeling that the unemployed are being badly treated by someone.

A strong government using force to maintain law and order would be severely criticized by many sentimental people. Our present government should be severely criticized if it were to use force. It has promised the people to bring about an era of prosperity to all. When its insane policies have failed and it is called upon to use force to repress those who have been disillusioned, it is justly subject to criticism, not for using force, but for the unsound policies which it has inaugurated, bringing about increased distress. It will soon be apparent to all that it has failed miserably to fulfill its promises.

The policy of our government regarding labor is different in the conduct of its own affairs than in the requirements it places upon employers. This is well exemplified by the C.C.C. When this was organized, many undesirables were enrolled. The officers in charge of the various camps found that the best way to maintain peace and order was to discharge the undesirables. What success the C.C.C. has achieved is in large part due to the elimination of the undesirable element from it. This elimination is still going on. Each year many thousands are discharged for disciplinary reasons. The government thus arbitrarily discharging these boys reverses its own policy and requires corporations to retain such workers by supporting labor unions. It is the same element that is undesirable in the C.C.C. that becomes the agitators in labor unions and dominates them.

From the standpoint of psychology, labor leaders are the victims of a narrow type of specialization causing them to magnify the abuses under which labor is suffering and to fail to see the benefits. They have dwelt upon the problems of labor for so long as to have developed a very narrow outlook, unable to see that raising wages too high and shortening hours to too great an extent will cause unemployment, in addition to causing higher prices which will use up the additional gains they attain from higher wages.

The labor problem must be solved, not by labor leaders, but by men having sufficient knowledge of economic laws to apply them practically. We must have a government controlled by men able to do this. When we permit labor agitators to dictate the policies of our government by fear of votes, we are placing our economic affairs in hands unqualified to handle them.

With the government attacking capital and with labor dictating the hours, the wages, the conditions of employment, and who shall be hired, the owners and managers of property have all the responsibility and labor all the privileges. This is a short-sighted policy for labor because under such conditions no sane-minded capitalist will invest money in new industries. Existing labor policies will create more unemployment and more suffering. How can we expect capital to embark on new enterprises if it is attacked on all sides, unprotected and at the mercy of ignorant employees stimulated to unwise action by agitators?

We attempted to prohibit the consumption of liquor by law. That failed and was given up. We attempted to regulate industry by means of the N.R.A. and it was on the point of collapse before declared unconstitutional. These attempts to regulate all things by government regulation are bound to fail. Sensible moral people do not need to have their affairs regulated by the government. Their own code of what is right and proper is sufficient. The passage of many laws harms the virtuous.

We have passed many laws attempting to regulate wages and hours. Let us think a minute on the effect of this. To be extreme, suppose we passed a law and rigidly enforced it, establishing a minimum pay for all of ten dollars a day for a six-hour day. What would be the result? You would immediately have the greatest era of unemployment the country had ever seen. Employers unable to pay these high wages would immediately release their employees. As there would be so many unemployed, business in all lines would suffer. This is the very effect our labor legislation and labor unions are producing. High wages are a benefit, within limits, but when they go beyond a certain point, they cause unemployment. Capital will not embark on new enterprises when labor conditions are uncertain. They will be unprofitable. Therefore new industries are not started and the vast army of unemployed increases.

The increasing number of unemployed youth constantly being added to each year from school and college is a problem which all far-seeing men should seriously consider. It is a direct result of our foolish policies regarding labor, industry, and social welfare. If labor unions were abolished and wages and hours allowed to find their own solution through the functioning of natural laws, the problem of unemployed youth would cease. This may be a drastic statement, but look back several years. Did this problem of unemployed youth exist to such a great extent before this era of social-reform legislation and labor activity? It did not. When we defy natural economic laws by arbitrary reduction in hours of labor and raising of wages, we contribute to unemployment. Those who suffer most from unemployment are not the labor unions who are strongly organized. It is the young people of the coming generations who are the greatest sufferers.

Instead of prohibiting child labor by laws, we should concentrate on raising the environment to such a high standard that such laws would be unnecessary. It should not be necessary to have laws to prevent children from being abused. Few people will abuse them, and those that do so are unfit to be at large in society. Let the children work as they will, and when someone abuses them, punish that particular individual. Remove him from the environment. The aim of those favoring child-labor laws is good, but the measure is unsound. Teaching children to be idle does not build their character. They should be encouraged to work so as to develop themselves. Work is not harmful to them but idleness is.

Much support for child-labor laws comes from organized labor under the general theory that if children are prohibited from doing work there will be more work left for the members of the organized labor unions. This is unsound. When you prohibit people from working, you lessen the demand for the material which they would use in their work, which lessens the demand for other labor. The more people at work the more wealth is created, the higher the standard of living, and the better off all are. Prohibiting labor has just the opposite effect.

A statement made by one of our prominent economists in a position to know was that sixty per cent of the income of business went to the wage earners before the depression and that they received eighty per cent of it during the depression. So many factors enter into the computation of wages and profits that sufficient information does not exist to state just exactly what percentage of profit is being given to wage earners, and how much goes to stock- and bond-holders. The fact that suitable information does not exist shows the utter incompetence of our politicians. Before attacking capital, they should endeavor to get at the facts and find the relation between wages and profits. It would be relatively easy for the federal government to do this with the facilities at its command.

It is expecting too much for capital management to look beyond their immediate field of activity and see all the problems connected therewith. It is equally unfair to expect labor to meet all the problems arising from their relations with capital. We should establish a government capable of doing so, a government controlled by master scientists who can see the relations of capital and labor in all their ramifications and do justice to both.

To Labor

The more you persecute and abuse your employers, the more unemployment and harm you will cause. The employers are supporting practically all citizens in the nation. The more they are handicapped, the less willing they will be to start new enterprises or expand, and labor will suffer because unable to obtain jobs. The true solution is to support a government that will do justice to all and promote sound economic measures so all may have a decent living. You will not get this by violence and creating ill feeling. It will require the full co-operation of all, each doing his best to advance himself by his own efforts and assisting others to do so.

XL

LABOR ENVIRONMENT

THE INFLUENCES MOLDING OUR ENVIRONMENT ARE STRESSING the development of Granto and Grievo to the exclusion of thankfulness and an appreciation of the good things we have. We are more comfortable than past generations, but we fail to appreciate our increased comfort and luxury. Less dwelling upon grievances, less taking of benefits for granted, and greater appreciation for the good things we now enjoy will be a far sounder influence.

We hear much denunciation of capital and industry. There is a general tendency to blame them for all existing evils and a failure to recognize that they are doing much good. When we attack them we are attacking the very institutions that support the people. The effort devoted to attacking them could better be used in assisting and stimulating them to greater efforts.

Adapto functions in the development of grievances on the part of labor as it does in all other ways. When a workman hears agitators stressing his grievances, broods over them, thinks about them, discusses them with his fellows, when his whole environment contributes toward making him believe that he is being badly treated, he develops in just that particular way. Even though he has not been badly treated, he is firmly convinced he is a badly treated individual. He is confirmed in the habit of seeking his demands by violence and intimidation. He ceases to think of others or the effect of his actions on the future. He is a spoiled child led to exaggerate his grievances and to see no merit in his employer.

We hear much said of the enormous profits capital makes from overworking labor. It is believed because it is so easy to believe. Investigation would show that the average return on capital is not exorbitant. Vast fortunes have been made by able individuals under a happy set of circumstances. Vast fortunes have been lost under adverse conditions. Labor agitators overlook the losses and try to make all believe that all capital makes enormous profits at the expense of labor.

We have farmers, housewives, and small employers working a hundred hours a week or more for little, yet our labor demands a thirty-hour week, with high pay and many other benefits. These same men cry out about the repression they are receiving from their employers. Never in the history of man have hours of labor been so short and the pay so high. Yet labor claims to be abused and demands more. We may as well face the facts and realize that there is no limit to the demands of childish groups of adults inspired by agitators to believe that they are being wrongly dealt with. Give them thirty hours a week now and they will demand five hours later. Eventually they will demand that they be supported in idleness; in fact, many are doing so today.

We have employees on strike who are receiving the highest pay and work the shortest hours of all time. They demand the right to dictate certain policies to their employers. At the same time we have throughout the country vast numbers of unemployed unable to get jobs, prevented from going to work by these selfish labor unions who claim they are working for the best interests of the laboring man.

We see W.P.A. workers parading and demanding more benefits. We see any number of strikes in the country in which the strikers demand not so much increased pay and shorter hours as the closed shop, the check-off, control of hiring halls, and more or less control over the conduct of the corporation's affairs. Neither the strikers nor W.P.A. workers are entirely without some modicum of justification.

They are the victims of circumstances, of incompetence, of the inability of those in control of the government to anticipate evils and correct them.

We have had so much agitation, so many attacks on individuals, so much abuse, as to create great ill-feeling and prevent sound action from being taken. What we must do is to bring about a better feeling on the part of all, blame all citizens for the existing unfortunate condition of affairs, and have all contribute toward rectifying it. Politicians have made impossible promises to the downtrodden, have acted unwisely in efforts to help them, have talked too much of the abuses they were receiving and not enough of the benefits.

All labor leaders fail to look abroad and see the ultimate consequences of their acts in extreme demands for short hours and high wages as compared with what other countries are receiving. Compare the standard of wages and living conditions in our country with China and the Orient, or even with European countries. We are far ahead. One would think that there would be great labor agitation in China, where conditions are so hard, and none in the United States where they are relatively good. But it is just the opposite. The better conditions are, the more labor has, the more it demands and the more agitation it creates to substantiate its demands.

The ultimate consequences will be bad when we view them from the standpoint of foreign trade. We cannot keep our industrial technique secret. Other countries will learn our methods, adopt them, manufacture the same products we now manufacture, and undersell us because of lower labor costs. Our foreign markets will in time cease to exist because of our high wages, short hours, and high cost of labor. This can be met for the time being by efficient management, but there is a limit to efficient management. The policies of our labor unions are preventing efficient management.

We are suffering from a great amount of reform legislation and labor agitation in which people are impatiently taking action to correct many evils. We would be better off if nine-tenths of our laws were repealed and labor unions abolished. We should direct our efforts toward raising the character and intelligence of the individual citizen and establishing a public opinion so high that it would not tolerate abuse or evil. Instead of being ruled by agitators, impractical reformers and politicians, all of whom contribute to class feelings, we should be ruled by men who will lessen ill-feeling and who are an example of virtue themselves.

What politician, what labor leader, could we point to as an example for our children on which to model their own lives? Not one. We cannot expect a solution to our problems when we permit the very environment to be dominated by the most vicious element in it. We must repress the vicious people, put the virtuous and intelligent in control. Have them as an example toward which youth will strive.

A politician to obtain the Jewish vote made belittling remarks about a foreign ruler. His action was widely applauded by many Jews. If educated men can be led by their feelings to applaud such acts we can easily see how less educated men can be incited to almost any belief by favoring circumstances.

The Jews who applauded so publicly do not realize that by so doing they are creating ill-feeling on the part of law-abiding American citizens against Jews and are doing their race great harm. If the average American citizen gets to believe that the loyalty of Jews to their race is greater than the loyalty of Jews to America, he is bound to resent it, and efforts to disfranchise Jews or expel them from the country will receive support. Some Jews accuse Christianity of attacking the Jews. If they continue to make such statements they will be instrumental in bringing about such attacks. So far few Jews have been persecuted in this country as Jews.

Labor organizations are adopting an equally short-sighted viewpoint. They do not think of the possible consequences of their actions. Let them continue to disregard the rights of the public and violate the law, and they will bring about similar violations of law and similar violence directed against themselves. What is fair to one party of a controversy is fair to another. Labor should realize that its trials and troubles are more the result of incompetent government than any other cause. Instead of attacking capital and requiring it to give in to them, they had better exert their efforts toward bringing about a wise government that will do justice to all, insure harmony, and improve economic conditions.

Take an average group of a hundred people, roughly illustrative of existing conditions in our country. Of this hundred, forty will be too old, too young, or too feeble to work. Twenty will be engaged in the performance of home duties, caring for the family and the home. Ten will be unemployed. This leaves thirty who must support the other seventy. To lighten the burden on these thirty and insure the greatest prosperity, all should work. The old and feeble should assist in ways suited to their abilities and strength. The young likewise may assist in ways that will not harm them, and at the same time will prove strengthening to their character and development. If everyone is helping, the burden is lightened on all concerned. In order to insure prosperity to all, everyone must contribute toward it.

Our economic life should be so ordered as to permit of work being found for everyone. When we see the vast numbers of people living in inadequate houses, see the vast improvements that could be made in making this country of ours a garden spot, we can truthfully say that ample work exists to employ the energies of everyone. It is a matter of proper organization only.

We are working in the opposite direction when we unwisely limit hours of work and arbitrarily raise wages. This increases unemployment and lessens the demand for work. We must educate our workers so as to have them understand that when unemployment exists it is caused by far-reaching factors and that the best means to alleviate it is to reduce wages and lengthen hours in order to stimulate work, thus creating additional jobs and reducing unemployment.

The greatest objection to labor unions is the bad effect they have upon moral character. In lowering the moral character of the workers and the citizens, they will ultimately cause a general lowering of economic standards. Industry, particularly under modern conditions, demands able, intelligent workmen of good character. We should resort to all means to encourage the development of these qualities, and at the same time endeavor to remove bad influences preventing their development.

One of the most vicious effects of labor agitation is its effect upon the young. They hear in the family and on the street much denunciation of other people, and feel that they are being unjustly treated. When a person develops a grievance of this kind and finds ways and means to blame others, the tendency is to seek no fault within himself. If this be continued it will destroy all possibility of developing sound understanding or good character. It is a sign of weakness to constantly blame others for your misfortunes. The true method to build character is to analyze yourself, shoulder the blame, and then exert yourself to overcome your deficiencies. Only after you have honestly removed all blame from yourself have you the right to blame others.

The atmosphere of many of our backward industrial districts is very depressing. The people are rude, crude, unable to find anything to criticize in themselves and blaming all their misfortunes upon their employers. They are the victims of vicious environmental influences which have brought them to this most unhealthful frame of mind. One can understand why they feel so, but one can also see that no action of any kind will help them until they are willing to correct their mental outlook, admit some fault in themselves, and endeavor to correct it.

The belief on the part of any person or group of persons that they are victims makes them unable to take a sound view of their problems. They must be brought to recognize the fact that all the virtue and right is not on their side and that by preserving such an attitude they are forever condemning themselves to their present low estate. If they were to spend as much effort in correcting their own shortcomings as they do in denunciation of others, the atmosphere would very quickly reflect this, and they would soon improve their environment. Calling upon others to solve their problems for them is harmful. They must do it themselves.

We must bring about on the part of each and every citizen in the country a realization that existing conditions are the fault, not of any one group, but of all citizens, and that all must work together harmoniously if matters are to be improved. We must so reconstitute the economic order that all can find employment. We must lessen attacks, violence, and misrepresentation.

Those who talk the most and claim to be abused are the ones who are least abused. Our democratic institutions unfortunately pay too much attention to those who talk much. There is ample work in the country for all. It requires but wise handling, the co-operation of all, and a determination to solve the problems, not in a spirit of violence, but in one of helpful co-operation.

The more power a person possesses, the greater is his need for developing Co in order that he may treat those under him with fairness, consideration, understanding, and sympathy. The very possession of great power and authority on the part of an individual has demoralizing effects upon his character unless he is strong, realizes this, and guards against it. Kings, emperors, and rulers of the past often became callous to the suffering of those with whose welfare they were entrusted.

A similar criticism can be applied to business men having many employees under their control. We pass from one extreme to the other. Some years back, the employers, reflecting the conditions of their times, considered their rights and privileges more than their duties to their employees and treated them, in many cases, with extreme lack of consideration, if not injustice. This naturally aroused resentment on the part of both the employees and the public, resulting in the organization of labor to protect itself. Organized labor grew stronger with the passage of time; so strong as to compel the politicians to listen to them instead of to capital as previously, making the politicians the creatures of labor.

With this great increase in the power of labor, they have been persecuting capital which is now being caused to suffer, less for its own misdeeds than for the heartless attitude of the employers of a less socially conscious era. Labor is abusing its power. It persecutes all employers and offers no encouragement for an employer to be considerate.

This attitude must be corrected by the direct intervention of the public through the action of their government. Labor on the one hand must be required to live within the law and not be permitted to persecute anyone. Capital must be protected in its rights and encouraged to fulfill its responsibilities.

Each citizen should carefully think over the statements made by the employers and by the labor leaders, analyze them coldly, and see who is the more consistently sensible and in the right. He will find that of recent years employers have been sensible and understanding. From the labor agitators there has been little but abuse—lack of understanding and consideration.

Whenever you persecute a group of people you arouse their resentment and cause them to endeavor to defend themselves by whatever means are available. This is true of capital. We are persecuting it today and it is defending itself as best it can with whatever weapons it has available. The efforts now being spent in persecuting capital, and the efforts spent by capital in defending itself, could be utilized to better advantage.

The evils under which we are living today are derived from the past. Many people of wealth and power abused them. This abuse caused resentment. The injustice of many people having so much and others so little gave rise to social feeling and reformers to correct the evils. Liberal thinkers the world over attacked the many evils and injustices, labor organized to defend itself, received the support of the public and much social reform legislation was passed, the politicians following the lead of the liberals in their efforts to effect reform.

An employer may sometimes be able to abuse his employees and get away with it. Such abuse, however, is a sign of poor character. The best way to correct this is not to pass laws to control the bad employer and thus penalize the employer who has the interests of his employees at heart, but to create an ascendent environment so that no such abuse of power will exist. We should develop such a fine moral sense among the people that anyone who abuses his power would lose the approbation of deserving people.

Abuse of power should be considered a very serious crime, and be as harshly condemned as any criminal act. We make a serious mistake, however, in attempting to handle abuse of power by employees as an economic question. It is a moral question, one requiring the use of moral reform. Employers employing large numbers of men have a great responsibility which they should not abuse. The development of a highly moral environment would prevent the existence of abusive employers. The condemnation of the public would be sufficient deterrent. The passage of restrictive laws and attempts to regulate and interfere with the management will then be unnecessary and their harmful consequences avoided.

Industry, which is condemned so unreasoningly, is carrying its burden better, more efficiently and more loyally, than those who attack it. How it can survive under the constant stream of attacks it receives from all sources is a marvel. It shows on the part of industrial leaders the greatest of ability to adapt themselves to such abuse and struggle on, supporting the people in spite of themselves.

However good the intentions of capital may be, it cannot

carry them out if it is attacked by the very men it is supporting. We must bring about on the part of laboring men a better understanding of the problems with which capital is faced. Cause them to see that by unwisely abusing capital they prevent it from developing new industries, from reducing prices, from creating a greater demand for goods and from reducing unemployment. Labor must be brought to support capital fully in an effort to reduce unemployment and suffering. Fighting capital will never accomplish this. The effort which capital may have directed, if unhampered, toward contributing to the welfare of the nation is directed to defending itself against attacks.

The sound solution of economic problems demands careful thought, free from prejudice, to the end that capital, labor, and the public alike are fairly treated. All must work together without friction, misunderstanding, hatred, or any other feeling that will prevent calm reasoning and just action from prevailing.

Solution of labor problems will not be reached by labor organizing and attacking capital bitterly; it requires the development of high standards of citizenship which will support a government that will encourage business and industry, protect labor, and protect the public; that will function for the greatest good of all.

The very organization of labor unions to defend their own interests, to secure shorter hours, higher wages, and benefits from their employers results of itself in creating friction. We should concentrate our efforts upon improving the employers and the standards of citizenship. Have everyone strive for Ascendency. Have all realize that their own interests are best served by performing their duties well. With the nation consisting of citizens all striving for this end, no conflict between employers and employees will exist. Harmony will prevail, the employee will receive better treatment and better wages, and the employer better service.

The true solution to the labor problem is to have employers of such high character and sense of responsibility that they themselves will safeguard the interests of their employees. This would render labor unions unnecessary. They could then be abolished. With their disappearance the greatest cause of friction between employers and employees would be eliminated.

The solution of the labor problem lies not in labor unions or collective bargaining or efforts to intimidate the employer. It lies in establishing such an era of prosperity that there will be insufficient workmen. The employers will then voluntarily cater to the employees to obtain their services. This era of prosperity can be made enduring if we take means to decrease the number of men seeking work by eliminating the most useless, undesirable elements. This can be accomplished by birth-control methods over a long period of time, by segregation of the most undesirable individuals, and through the functioning of economic laws which, because of increased prosperity, will elevate the environment and the people.

This solution will also include education in citizenship to cause each citizen to consider the rights of others and be willing to serve—not demand service. It will also include an efficient government that will restrict governmental activities to a minimum and lessen the burden of regulation, heavy taxation, and debt.

Thought

Stop a moment, you who blame all ills of man upon capital or the wealthy. Communistic Russia has neither. Should they not be better off? Their land one of happiness, peace, contentment? But it is not. We must seek elsewhere. In man himself.

XLI

SOCIAL REFORM

GOVERNMENT RELIEF AND SOCIAL BENEFITS CONTROLLED BY A democracy such as our own will assume unhealthful proportions. Demands for benefits are too closely associated with votes. As a result the politicians attempt to conciliate all groups demanding benefits. This results not only in penalizing the deserving citizen to reward the less deserving, but in placing such great burdens upon the government as eventually to result in the crash of the entire system. Those who are really in need and deserving of assistance will then suffer want.

The worst effect of relief is that upon the character of the individual citizen. Instead of devoting his efforts toward self-development and the solution of his own problems, his efforts are devoted toward making excuses for his failure and toward substantiating increased demands upon the government. Associated with this is the development of hatred and ill-feeling toward those who, for any reason whatsoever, are in more prosperous circumstances.

We must recognize that nature is merciful in being ruthless and that we, in our attempts to be merciful, may be cruel. Reasonable assistance and consideration for the helpless and all those needing help is desirable. The great difficulty is to prevent good intentions from being abused by the undeserving and to avoid making deserving people undeserving. They will be badly influenced by the environment and the example of others.

In an environment built upon a system of government relief there is little encouragement of strong characters. They are penalized. The man who has nothing, who continually demands from others, is the man who is rewarded under such a system. A far more sensible method would be to devote the effort toward the elimination of the weaklings. Our relief and reform measures are making a bad situation worse. They will bring about still worse conditions in the future.

Almost all ideas of our helpful reformers call upon the government for money to shoulder the cost. How long can this continue? Where does the money come from? Someone must work to create it. The more money you call upon the government to spend, the more you are penalizing the man who works. What fools men can be! Reforms as the result of government spending are not reforms. Reform must go deep into the heart of human beings and touch feelings that money alone cannot touch.

Our country became great because built by men who did all for themselves and families. It is now becoming puny because our government not only does not encourage its citizens to care for themselves but penalizes those who attempt to do so. Let us preserve the strong qualities of our ancestors and apply them to meeting today's problems. Let not our present-day luxuries soften us. Let us be men, like the early settlers. Did they ask for help? No. They merely wanted freedom, the right to live their lives, to work and to profit from their own efforts. They demanded freedom from the government control that is now being forced upon us.

People demanding benefits do not stop to think that they must be obtained from some other source in order to be paid, and that when the demand for benefits becomes extreme they cannot be continued. Sound economic policy demands that the government pay no benefits to anyone, but utilize its efforts toward encouraging all to get along without the need for government benefits. If all the efforts now spent in demanding benefits from the government and from business were devoted by those concerned to their own development and to efforts to support themselves, many of today's problems would not exist.

We should face facts and realize that the common citizen pays for all social legislation. The means by which he pays are often concealed from direct view and difficult to trace, but he nevertheless pays. Our politicians cater to the voters by levying taxes against the well-to-do, but these heavy taxes are passed on to the average citizen by increased prices, unemployment, and unsatisfactory economic conditions.

When the government pays large sums of money for the relief of unemployed, many devote much effort to obtaining these benefits; whereas if the government paid no benefits whatsoever, their efforts would be directed toward means of sustaining themselves by their own efforts. They would seek the assistance of others, friends, members of the family, who could assist. When the government attempts to give them relief, their friends are willing to place the task of assisting them on the government.

The deserving unemployed suffer by the payment of doles and benefits which all too often go to the undeserving unemployed. The money to pay these benefits must be raised from some source, which results in more taxation upon industry, creating additional unemployment and rendering it impossible for the deserving to get jobs because the undeserving demand benefits. Let us cease to have our economic policies determined by those who are constantly demanding benefits. Let us have control by and in the interest of those who neither ask for, nor receive benefits.

Government relief appeals more to our good intentions than to our judgment. The very fact that it is now necessary shows the existence of other problems requiring solution. Our efforts had better be directed toward the solution of these problems, rendering the need for relief unnecessary. A bad feature of the relief policy is that it builds up a vast bureaucracy and gives additional strength to the politicians in obtaining jobs for their adherents. This may become so extreme in time as to prevent the existence of a sound economic structure.

When you start giving government benefits, you are starting something that democracy is ill-fitted to deal with, that is destructive to character, that undermines the economic structure, that increases government inefficiency and bureaucracy; it encourages the politicians to make greater and greater promises of more and more benefits in order that they may obtain office. Truly a most vicious development.

Government cost and extravagance penalize the deserving people of the nation because they must pay the taxes which furnish offices for politicians and their adherents and build up giant bureaucracies to support those unable to support themselves.

Our politicians receive sympathetic attention and applause when they advocate welfare measures. For instance, they will demand heavy government expenditures to improve housing conditions for the poor. The public applauds these measures because they are intended to help the poor. What the public does not see, however, is that they are basically unsound. The fact that private industry does not build suitable structures for the poor shows the existence of a basic fault in our economic structure. Building government structures on borrowed money and taxing other capital aggravates this situation.

It is in problems of this nature that democracy is meeting its test today. Unworthy politicians advocate popular measures to obtain office. The public supports the politicians for the reason that they are trying to help the poor. Higher standards of statesmanship and citizenship would demand sound measures to correct the causes of economic ills.

We will find that the men causing the most harm are those occupying the highest positions in the nation. It reflects little credit on the intelligence of the American public to fail to demand the greatest reform of all, without which all other reforms will be useless; namely, a means of putting able, honest men in control of the affairs of the country.

Stressing by leading politicians of the fact that one-third of our people are ill-housed, ill-fed, and ill-clad, and promises to do something to correct the situation may indicate worthy motives. The unworthy feature appears when the government attempts to shirk the responsibility for this condition and blames it upon the common scapegoats, capital and big business. Refusing to face facts, shirking responsibility, and blaming others will never solve this problem. Such action will, in fact, aggravate it.

Our very government is supported by taxes from business profits. What relief is now being afforded to those suffering want is raised directly or indirectly as a result of business profits. Attacks upon business will lessen these profits, discourage business development, and reduce tax receipts, rendering the government itself unable to afford further relief.

Attacking and discouraging business will also result in more unemployment and therefore in greater demands for relief. The American public has yet to realize that the enunciation of good intentions is insufficient to correct existing evils. The cause of these evils must be pursued to their source in an honest endeavor to correct them. When we see government officials refusing to face facts, denouncing capital and other scapegoats, we see officials who are being dishonest in attempting to transfer the blame for existing ills from themselves unto others.

The citizens should demand results from their politicians. They have heard denunciation of capital for a sufficiently long time to become utterly disgusted with it. Any person with common sense should realize that continual denunciation will not accomplish beneficial results. We hear statements from our leaders, intended to appeal to popular prejudice, regarding the enormous profits of capital and the abuse of labor, that are misleading and in many cases false. It should be easy for a proper survey to be made of all profits received in the country by all people from all sources, and present the facts. Do the politicians do this? They do not.

They prefer to conceal some facts and exaggerate those that arouse public feeling and keep them in office.

When we have public men attempting to mislead the people, we cannot expect sound governmental action. We attack the criminal and punish him, but is not the crime committed by our public men in making false statements, in spreading class hatreds and ill will, far more harmful? The criminal is not dangerous because public opinion is opposed to him, but our public men are dangerous in that they claim to be serving the public, to be doing any number of things for the good of the country and for the underdog. The methods they advocate, their speeches and acts, tend to perpetuate existing conditions and prevent sound solutions.

To carry out adequate reforms requires able men who will not abuse their power. The use of birth-control methods to reduce the undesirable element, the adoption of an improved method of crime prevention by keeping individual records of all people and removing the undesirable from contact with the desirable, requires that great power be placed in the hands of officials. We could not place such power in the hands of the officials we have today.

Vast social reforms cannot be accomplished unless we produce master scientists, men of such character, such ability, that they will not abuse their powers and will not advance faster than their knowledge permits. They will gradually, by wise action, eliminate the evils from which we are now suffering by treating the causes, in contrast to the present methods of treating the effects and perpetuating the ills into the future.

Unemployment is increased by unwise social legislation and the payment of benefits by the government which raises taxes and the cost of doing business. Requiring the employer to grant greater wages, shorter hours, and benefits to his employees, raises the cost of his doing business. Both together raise prices, which lowers the demand for goods and lessens production thus increasing unemployment. Truly a vicious circle. Why not encourage natural laws to take their course, permitting them to reduce unemployment and trust to the solution of our economic problems by concentrating our efforts upon moral development? Unemployment can always be reduced by reducing wages. Why not do it instead of having a great many other worse abuses?

Our laborers are higher paid, we spend more for education, give more to ex-soldiers, distribute more for relief, than any nation of any kind. But labor unions, teachers, American Legionnaires, people on relief, all alike demand more. There seems no limit to human rapacity once it becomes fashionable. Unless we change our outlook, we are headed for disaster. A civilization based on penalizing thrift for charity cannot endure, nor is it worth enduring. All these demands will defeat themselves, for a day will come when increased demands will not and cannot be met.

In viewing the activities within our nation and seeing the vast sums spent on education, social welfare, attempts to help everyone and correct all evils, one cannot help but arrive at the conclusion that the heart of the nation is inherently sound and good. The people are striving to do their very best, but unfortunately their efforts are not well directed. The leadership adequate to directing such a fine race of people does not exist. If the ability of those having good intentions equaled the quality of their intentions, our country would be a heaven indeed. The unfortunate part about this lack of ability is that the very cost of all these worthy moves is putting such a crushing burden upon the finest people in the land as to render them unable to bear up under it, and undermining the economic structure.

The people controlling our institutions are penalizing those who are able to sustain themselves by requiring them to support a great number of unfit, morons, vicious, and lazy. The true method should be to reward the deserving and eliminate the undeserving by birth-control methods or other means. Persecuting the fit, rewarding the unfit, is leading to disaster.

Our rulers are conducting a policy much similar to that

of Louis XV of France, which in substance was "after us the deluge." In the meantime the situation gets worse. It is lack of understanding, lack of thinking on the part of the citizens of our country, that is bound to destroy us if continued.

There was much wholesomeness in our early institutions. We should preserve the goodness of those institutions. Instead, we hear much criticism and ridicule of those days. Yet from the standpoint of common sense and performance those men did a far better job than we are doing. They made the nation and we are pursuing a policy that will destroy it.

A great contributing factor to our inability to solve present-day problems is the development of specialists in their particular field to such a degree as to cause them to overemphasize their importance and demand increasing amounts from the public for support. We see this in our school system. Vast amounts are being paid for public education, and yet the teachers' associations demand more and more. They claim and believe they are teaching youth.

The entire educational system must be revamped if we are to obtain our money's worth from what is now being spent. Instead of appropriating more money as teachers desire, we need more efficient teachers and more efficient methods of instruction that will teach citizenship and moral character, teach the student how to think and to be an asset to the community.

Doctors demand increased amounts for their hospitals. Those interested in criminals demand more money and bigger prisons to care for and reform public enemies. Throughout the whole country we hear the constant demand of reformers and well-wishers generally for more money to help further their good intentions. The more money they receive, the worse the situation gets. They apply the efforts toward perpetuating existing evils instead of eliminating basic causes.

Our government, our entire environment, our entire society, is far more unsound today than it was a hundred years ago and is constantly getting worse. Yet to hear our educators and welfare workers talk, they are accomplishing great things. Whatever may be the merits of our educational system, it is making people increasingly unable to think, to look to the future, or to understand the consequences of their acts. Ninety per cent of the problems today are created by the muddling efforts of well-intentioned people to improve conditions or to help someone. A little consideration, a little thought, would show this. Bad conditions alone do not create the demand for reform; the reforms themselves often create bad conditions.

Psychiatry was unknown as a profession not many years back. Today psychiatrists are very active. We have great numbers of hospitals for mental disorders and have more mentally disordered patients than ever before. Our reformers have brought about the passage of more reform laws than any nation has ever before seen, and yet we have greater unrest. Our labor is the highest paid and best treated of any labor in the world, and yet we have more labor agitation than any other country. We hear much talk about crime, improving the environment, reforming the criminal, and we have more crime and more criminals than any other country. Our politicians make more noise and pat themselves on the back for more virtues than any other class of politicians in history, and we have the most inefficient and most wasteful government. We have more doctors, more surgeons, more hospitals, and more sick than in the past.

All these activities demand increasing amounts of money; all these specialists demand support for their efforts. If we judge by the results, they accomplish little good, or make matters worse. The American citizen can well take time out and think over this strange situation. There is something wrong. There is a sound solution if it be sought for; cease being sentimental and cease to be guided by those people who make the most noise. Establish an environment that will encourage each individual to make his own way in the world and be of good character. Establish an economic system that will contribute toward this, and remove all weaklings, all agitators, and all who are a bad influence, from the environment.

The increasing prevalence of mental disorders is contributed to by the stress of modern civilization, but the greatest single factor contributing thereto is the reversal of the laws of nature in providing for the elimination of the unfit. The efforts devoted by society to perpetuate and care for the unfit results in a consistent lowering of the mental standard.

The elimination of criminals, mentally disordered people, and the poor elements generally in modern society can be effected without difficulty when our society is equal to it. These incompetent people are less of a threat at this time than is the apathy, prejudice, and lack of understanding of our highest intellectual types about modern problems. It is the better type in our society that is holding back advance. No one willingly follows the more undesirable types. It is the influence of those who preach reform, who would like to accomplish good, but who are unequal to the task.

All alike are the victims of the environment. Our politicians are products of the existing environmental influences, which encourage exaggeration, attacks on capital and reform measures to help those who have little. We must elevate our environment, build citizens who will require the politicians to appeal to their minds.

In a country as large and wealthy as ours there is no excuse for unsound economic conditions to exist. When they do exist, they may rightly be attributed to inefficient government. If the effort devoted to attacking capital, promoting relief activities and getting benefits, were devoted to helping capital, reducing unemployment, and stimulating industry generally by wise measures and helpful co-operation, the need for relief measures would cease to exist. Everyone would have jobs and industry would be in such a sound condition as to support all reasonable demands with ease.

The most desirable class of citizens within the country

are those really good workers among both rich and poor, and
it is this class that should be protected and encouraged. All
others failing to belong within this classification should be
eliminated, whether they be wealthy or poor. The advantages of belonging to the desirable class of citizens are so
great that all would so belong once we used proper educational methods to cause people to understand their duties to
the nation and to others. The essential thing to develop is
Ascendency. Those people who strive for Ascendency are
desirable citizens; those who make no attempt to attain Ascendency are undesirable and are the ones to be segregated
or eliminated.

The man who is willing to solve his own problems will,
by uniting with other like citizens and eliminating those
who demand that he support and serve them, have less burdens and increased prosperity as the result of their elimination, and the society of which he is a member will be worthy.

The great reason for the striking lack of progress in the
solution of today's difficulties lies in man's inability to think.
The average man has good intentions, but is confused by the
many conflicting ideas of those who should lead the way to
solution. The result is that any number of laws are passed
intended to help others or improve conditions. They have
good intentions behind them, but they are not soundly
planned. We should exhaust all efforts to bring about on the
part of every citizen the ability to think better, to understand. He will then be less willing to support unsound measures with good intentions, and more willing to support
measures sound in their final effect.

To develop the ability to think soundly, one must acquire
objectivity, must be able to place their conscious mind in
control of the subconscious by logical reasoning uninflu-
enced by personal feelings, previous beliefs, environmental
influences, or anything that tends to inhibit the truth. Primitive man was largely controlled by his subconscious mind
and desires. Present-day men are similarly controlled. Their
psychona has developed without intelligent direction. As a

result it is more primitive, more infantile, more concerned with pleasing whatever the individual may desire than with obtaining facts. An intelligently controlled and developed psychona will realize this tendency. Instead of being dominated by primitive desires, it will be dominated by intelligent, conscious mental efforts seeking the truth and what is best for the individual's happiness and development.

The savage, the ignorant, the abused, the dull have a certain limited Co for their immediate family, associates, and fellows. Only the enlightened, educated, and intelligent are capable of a Co which takes in all men as well as their own limited circle. It is in furthering this development that efforts should be concentrated, for only by so doing can man's problems be solved.

Co is very strong in our country and the civilized world generally, as is shown by the many efforts being made to help the poor and downtrodden. The pity is that an equal amount of intelligence does not exist to direct it. Co can be made so sentimental and impractical as to cause great harm. It should be used with scientific accuracy with regard to future effects to insure the promotion of Ascendency. Men capable of doing this are not now in control of the affairs of nations. Man permits himself to be controlled by mere noise. He has yet to learn that real ability more often exists without noise than with it. He should separate the noise and his personal amusement entirely from the serious problem of thinking, and seek for the solution of difficult problems by quiet earnest research.

A bad feature of social-reform measures is their influence upon the environment. When well-meaning reformers attack existing institutions and evils, they stress grievances to the exclusion of thankfulness. We should recognize that life is hard. Instead of continually calling attention to the grievances, we should take them as a matter of course. We should not talk about them, brood over them, creating a mountain out of a molehill. If we recognize that injustices and evils have always existed, that innocent people have suffered in the past and will suffer as long as man exists, we will be establishing a philosophical attitude that will contribute toward a more wholesome environment. Let us stress the good things of everyday life, make more of them and make them better. At the same time let us minimize the grievances and reduce their harmful effects to a minimum.

Thoughts

Not only do we have citizens unwilling to serve the government without pay, but we have many demanding that the government maintain them. This bodes ill for the future. To reform our government we must improve the standard of citizenship so that our citizens will be willing to serve their government without demanding compensation. We must create such a public opinion that anyone demanding benefits from the government will be so severely censured that it will be unheard of.

What is at fault? Whom or what should we blame? Stupidity, incompetence, lack of moral character and courage to face the issues squarely and solve them.

Gripe

As long as we are attempting to reform everything else in the country, we should include our publishers in this universal reform movement. An excellent means of education and reform for publishers would be to sentence them to write books to meet with the approval of those writers whose material they have rejected or refused to consider. Perhaps in time they will learn to appreciate real merit in literature.

Apparently their standards of worth are reversed. They publish what should be rejected and fail to publish what is of merit—or else nothing of merit is written. In any case they should first develop the ability to produce some thought of their own before they take it upon themselves to reject something produced by others that may be of value.

Our present-day publishers are just like our reformers and politicians—trying to decide things of which they themselves are examples of what not to be. The failures are governing those capable of succeeding. Those without worth are condemning those possessing worth. The vicious are denouncing the virtuous. The insane are calling the intelligent insane.—*February 19, 1938.*

XLII

THE DEPRESSION

Business booms and depressions are the product of unsound economic conditions associated with unsound mass psychology. When business is good the public tends to become overconfident. When business is depressed, the tendency is to become overpessimistic.

The 1929 boom and the resultant depression were world wide. The origin of both can be traced to the World War. During and after the war the governments created enormous national debts, increased expenditures and taxation. Additional burdens were assumed by most governments in enlarged programs of social welfare. International trade difficulties and high tariffs contributed to unsound world wide conditions. Each nation attempted to serve its own interests and in so doing disregarded the interests of other nations. Many countries borrowed heedless of the future, creating uncertainty by the threat of future inflation. Thus conditions were unsound within our own country and in most European countries. When this became generally apparent the boom collapsed.

The boom of 1929 was in large measure due to the overextension of credit. Farmers borrowed on their farms, the average citizen made installment purchases, and business concerns generally borrowed too extensively. Vast sums were loaned for stock-market operations. During the height of the boom, there was a great feeling of optimism and a somewhat generally prevailing belief that we had established a new system of economic security in which neither booms nor depressions would occur.

The boom was stimulated by the action of our bankers in loaning money to foreign governments, thus permitting them to make purchases in the United States and further stimulating our own industries. When conditions abroad became so unsound as to prevent further loans their purchases ceased, tending to depress our industries.

The action of our bankers turned out to be unwise, but it would have been a wise measure had their efforts to assist foreign nations resulted in bringing them back to financial stability. In looking back after the event we can see that our bankers erred in their willingness to make foreign loans, but at the time there was some possibility that these loans would help stabilize international conditions.

The expansion of bank credit in 1927 in our own country was the result of efforts of the Federal Reserve System to support the weakened financial conditions in foreign countries. This action contributed to the boom of 1929 and the resultant crash. Thus to a great extent, our financial fiasco was in part due to unwise but good-intentioned measures to help foreign nations. This goes to show the intimate relationship between nations and the need for sound international policies on the part of governments and international banking concerns.

Stock-market activity was a considerable factor in developing the boom to unwise proportions. Many people ignorant of stock speculation, made large sums of money by buying stocks; others were encouraged to follow their example. This increased the demands for stocks and forced them up far beyond their worth. A contributing factor toward enhancing stock values was furnished by our income-tax laws. Many wealthy people would undoubtedly have sold their stocks for high prices if they had not been deterred from doing so by the large income taxes they would be called upon to pay therefrom.

A wise government could have taken measures which

would have prevented the boom of 1929 from reaching its extremely high stage and could have similarly avoided having the depression reach such extremes. Natural laws should have been allowed to function. Had this been done, the depression could have been greatly lessened by encouraging the back-to-the-land movement from the city, the enactment of legislation which would have permitted the cleaning up of insolvent firms without unnecessary litigation, and other constructive measures to assist natural laws.

Labor had great influence in forcing the depression to extreme lows by opposing wage cuts. Had employers been free to reduce wages in accordance with the demands of their industries, the unemployment problem would have been less because more people would have been retained on the payrolls. This in itself would have stimulated consistent demands for goods and would have prevented the depression from declining to the extremes it did.

Unwise measures of the government served both to accentuate the boom of 1929 and the resultant depression. For instance, after the stock-market crash the president, Mr. Hoover, called a meeting of the big industrial leaders of the country and induced them to agree to make no wage cuts, hoping thus to forestall a business depression. This step would have been a wise one had the economic situation not been world-wide and so bad. Actually, this measure was the very opposite of what should have been done. A twenty-five percent wage cut at that time upon all employees, government and otherwise, would have been a wise step. As the depression progressed, the problem of the corporations was to reduce expenses. Not being able to reduce wages, they reduced the number of employees, increasing the number of unemployed, whereas had wages been reduced, they could have retained the same number of men in their employ.

The public does not have a sound understanding of economic problems. A drastic wage cut would have been opposed, and could not have been carried out. As the depression progressed, the employers were finally compelled to re-

ASCENDENT GOVERNMENT

duce wages, and eventually the government resorted to the same means.

Had this policy been inaugurated at first, many corporations would have been saved from bankruptcy and many bond issues from repudiation. There would have been less unemployment, less distress, less need for relief, and a general lessening of the severity of the depression. Thus we see that action undertaken by the government, and lauded at the time, only served to make matters worse.

XLIII

THE NEW DEAL

ANY DISCUSSION HAVING TO DO WITH THE POLICIES OF THE New Deal, of politicians, of labor unions, of today, is not discussion of a positive nature from which we can learn anything. It is education of a negative type which shows us what we should not do. To sound unspoiled minds of the future, trained to good behavior and good thought, the policies of these people will seem more like the antics of inmates of an insane asylum than of normal human beings.

We deprecate and ridicule many of the acts of man in the past. His acts today will receive the same attention from future generations if they succeed in elevating themselves to high standards of thought and conduct. Progress has been made from savagery to a certain degree of civilization. This civilization must now be perfected by the elevation of the individual to higher mental and moral standards.

The New Deal contains two elements which give it great strength: demagoguery, which appeals to the ignorant, and sentimental efforts to help the downtrodden by governmental action. Its efforts will in the end defeat their aim because they are unsound. The education of the citizens will be promoted by letting their plans continue unhampered and prove their unsoundness. Once public opinion realizes this, it may be possible, if efficient leadership appears, to bring about sensible government.

The New Deal administration tried to do many things that were popular with the so-called liberal element. None of the measures were aimed to correct the causes of existing unsound economic conditions. They tended to perpetuate existing evils and their final effects will be harmful. Many things attempted served to oppose one another, such as reclaiming arid lands in the West and at the same time paying farmers to reduce cultivation.

Had the administration devalued the currency and stuck to a sound policy of thrift, assuring business of no tampering or experiments, the resultant effect would have been much better than so much tinkering. This would have been the sensible measure from the practical political view. Devaluing the dollar sets a bad example and should not have been done. However, there was such a great amount of indebtedness in the country as to require some scaling down. Wages were too high to encourage the absorption of the unemployed. By devaluing the dollar the effect would be to lessen the burden of indebtedness and reduce wages, thus stimulating business activity. This would have absorbed the unemployed, stimulated all lines of endeavor, and would have afforded a quick popular means of escape.

In reducing the value of the dollar, the administration was actually giving a forty per cent cut in wages to the workman. The forty per cent cut in the gold content of the dollar was immediately felt by government employees abroad. In their case it amounted to a forty per cent pay cut. This was due to the fact that the value of the dollar was immediately affected with relation to foreign currency. Within our own country so many other influences operated as to prevent the wage earner from realizing that he had actually received a forty per cent pay cut.

Its effect was canceled through the N.R.A. to some extent by raising wages and shortening hours. The net result was much talk and little real improvement in the condition of the working man. When you undertake to improve conditions, it must be paid for in some other way. Industry, if left alone, will adapt itself to the changed conditions. The tendency always is to work back to what they were before the change was made.

All these attempts to help the workingman have not helped him. The benefit he has received is not the result of the action of the government. It is the result of other causes which government policies have prevented from developing as they normally would in giving the working man greater returns.

Unsound economic policies will fail if persisted in. The New Deal administration has no definite policy and has done many things that oppose each other such as raising wages and devaluing the dollar. The country can survive a long time even under harsh regulation as long as the public submits and as long as capital is able to carry on.

The vast sums which our government has been spending were obtained from the savings of the much abused thrifty and wealthy. If they were unwilling to give their money to the government, the government would not have it to spend. What a strange contrast! The government obtains money from the very people it denounces as being the vicious element in the nation. Without their support it could not exist.

From whom do most of our people obtain wages? From the corporations and employers. Who pays most of our taxes? The wealthy people, capital and those who have been successful in life or have the capacity to earn. From whom does our government borrow the money necessary to carry out all its relief measures? From the people who have saved their money. Who receives the benefits our government is giving? The poor, the undeserving, those who have nothing and those who have failed to provide for the future.

Capital receives none of these benefits. The deserving citizen capable of taking care of himself receives none. Who is being persecuted by our government today? Capital, the wealthy man, the successful man. Who is permitted to violate the law with impunity? Sit-down strikers, those who have votes, income-tax violators whose policies are in accord with those of the administration.

We hear the president ask for a tightening of the income-tax laws against the wealthy. This is popular. He thinks that an attack on wealthy income-tax evaders will meet with popular response, but he is afraid to attack sit-down strikers. He ignores that. A riot occurs in which strikers attack police-men, resulting in the deaths of a half a dozen people and in-juries to many others—ignored by the administration. Yet this very strike, this very attack, has been stimulated by its own agitation in constantly attacking wealth and employers, and by promising benefits and higher wages to the employees.

Government depends upon the enforcement of the laws. If the laws are unjust, they should be made just, but they must be enforced. If they are ignored or violated, the tend-ency will spread. A government that permits the laws it has sworn to support to be violated by those in sympathy with its measures thereby makes itself the fomenter of law viola-tions. Carried to a logical conclusion, it will result in the law-abiding citizens combining against their own government. When this is done, civil war is bound to ensue. We have this dread thing creeping as unsuspectingly upon our politicians of this era as it crept upon the politicians of the Civil War days.

The politicians survived the first civil war, but it is un-likely that they will survive the second. The very fact that they have permitted a civil war to be inaugurated while they control the country proves their worthlessness and demands that somehow, somewhere, some way, capable leaders be found equal to the task of governing our great nation. The place to seek for these men will not be among the politicians who have failed. It will have to be from men who do things; not from those who talk and promise.

A policy of paying farmers not to produce crops and paying men on relief not to work is the reverse of sound action. The more products produced, the higher is the standard of living and the greater is the per capita wealth. When we pay people not to work, not to produce, the money for this purpose must be raised by charges upon those who are working, who are producing. Thus we are penalizing the worker, the producer, and rewarding the nonproducer, the nonworker. This is the policy of our New Deal, short-sighted, insane, and disastrous.

When the New Deal policies are about to fail and their failure becomes apparent to all, the logical weapon in the hands of the politicians will be to bring about inflation. This has been talked about so much that people disregard the threat. When, however, the government treasury is exhausted, when the great burden upon the government in paying benefits is too great, when much agitation and criticism exist against the government, when bonds cannot be sold at a reasonable price, the resort will be to inflation. This will be blamed upon the capitalists, upon the bankers, upon everything but the politicians and the New Deal. It may delude the public. An era of more or less prosperity may ensue. When the inevitable crash comes, anything may happen.

As regards the welfare of the country, it is unfortunate that the courts existed, to attempt to require compliance with the law and constitution. The mere fact that they have done so has resulted in their becoming scapegoats. Naturally those concerns and people who were being unjustly treated by the New Deal policies would go to the courts for protection. This gives the New Deal grounds for blaming the failure of their policies upon the courts. Had the courts not existed, and had the New Deal been able to pursue its policies without restrictions of any kind, it would long ago have discredited itself and would have no one to blame but itself.

The so-called reforms of the New Deal are limited entirely to attempts to answer economic problems and improve the economic well-being of those who have little, or what the New Dealers consider to be insufficient to live the fuller life. While they stress the economic problems, they contradict themselves by the expression, "Human rights versus property rights." Thus while their reforms are limited to economic ends, they endeavor to give the impression that they are accomplishing far-reaching social reforms, the betterment of humanity and protecting human rights.

Never in the history of the world has a government existed

crying its virtues aloud so strongly and by very contrast pursuing policies far more vicious in their effects than if planned. They break down the very character of the citizens by giving them benefits and encouraging them to demand more. They persecute those who do not demand benefits but who must pay for the benefits given the undeserving.

We may talk of the cruelty and short-sightedness of governments of the past, but we have established within our own country a glaring example of all that a government should not be. Yet it is supported by many and receives the applause of liberals throughout the world.

When such utter incompetence can be considered ability, when actions destructive of the virtues of citizenship are commended as elevating them, we have not far to seek in looking for the reasons for man's inability to solve his problems of government: incompetent leaders qualified only to smile, talk well, and promise, who peddle their own merit and virtues while denouncing those who oppose them; ignorant short-sighted people led to believe they are being unjustly treated and demanding benefits. But it will pass. Let us hope it will be an example for the future of what to avoid.

Any person who continually extols his merits shows by such action that he himself is doubtful. Subconsciously he realizes that he does not possess them. He endeavors to overcome this feeling of inferiority by telling both himself and others just how good and virtuous he is. The same observation applies to a government. When it continually extols its virtues and denounces its opponents, it is trying to accomplish by words what it is unable to accomplish by deeds.

Efficient government acts, governs efficiently, and accomplishes results. An inefficient government will talk much about accomplishment and will accomplish little except talk. Is it not a sign of weakness for our government continually to denounce capital and big business? If able men are conducting the government, why can they not control capital or anybody in the country who does not behave properly? Quiet measures would accomplish this far more effectively than denunciation.

Thoughts

I can see no example to good citizenship, no good for the future, no sensible action in the New Deal, its policies, or its personnel.

The New Deal is merely bribing the "have-nots" by taking from the "haves."

The New Deal has reached a maximum high in promises, incompetence, and extravagance. It has created an awful mess to be cleaned up before our government can be put on a sound basis.

XLIV

ROOSEVELT

I AM DISCUSSING MR. ROOSEVELT VERY FRANKLY NOT BECAUSE of personal animus but as a public duty. To my mind he represents in his person those influences that are threatening the destruction of our institutions and of the best that America has produced. I consider Mr. Roosevelt to be an excellent example in himself of the average politician of today. Therefore, when I discuss him cooly and objectively, and point out the reasons for his acts, I am in large measure discussing the qualities possessed by the average politician. I am using him as somewhat of a guinea pig, as a symbol òf political viciousness.

We must educate the public to select and support good leaders, to understand what good leaders are, to enable them to avoid following herd reflectors. Unpleasant as the task may be, it is necessary that Mr. Roosevelt and his policies be exposed to the light of day in order that the public may understand why he is as he is and that future generations may avoid following similar leaders.

While I am attempting to do this with a view of educating the public of today, my statements are made with a view to what generations a hundred years hence will think of them. My statements regarding Mr. Roosevelt are based upon what knowledge of human nature I possess.

We cannot well free ourselves from personal feeling. Many people are ardent followers of Mr. Roosevelt. Many others hate him intensely. The former are governed more

largely by their feelings than by sound logic. The latter are
often governed by their feelings but they sometime employ
much sound thought. I have tried to avoid giving undue
expression to my feelings, to present the facts in accord with
truth, and have tried to avoid denunciation. It is, however,
difficult to avoid the use of strong expressions when discussing viciousness.

Unpleasant as the task of exposing Mr. Roosevelt may be,
it will be fully justified if we can make him immortal for
all time and have his place in history established as being
the "last of the demagogues."

Mr. Roosevelt is able to obtain a wide following for many
reasons. The prestige of his office is helpful in obtaining the
support of many Americans wishing to be proud of their
country. A common defense of Mr. Roosevelt has been,
"Well, he tried to do something, anyway." Many well-
meaning, well-intentioned good citizens feel this way about
Mr. Roosevelt's efforts. They realized that much was wrong.
Therefore, anyone who attempted to correct the wrong
obtained their support. Whether the action taken was wise
was less important than that action of some kind be taken.
Very few people are qualified to determine the wisdom of
social reform. The good intention alone enlists their support
and they hope and wish that successful results will be obtained.

Mr. Roosevelt's radio voice has been a great asset to him.
His pleasing personality has attracted many. His constant
denunciation of wealth and oppression has obtained support.
The people are good sports. They wish to help the underdog
obtain his rights from the powerful wealthy class. This is
always a strong drawing card in any demagogic appeal. The
inability of our churches and our schools properly to teach
citizenship, to teach the individual to think and to see the
shortcomings of democracy, has assisted in the creation of a
citizenship responsive to leaders of Mr. Roosevelt's type.

Lack of effective opposition has contributed to Mr. Roosevelt's strength. No leader of equal appeal has appeared to

oppose him. Mr. Roosevelt or men of his type will control the country until they meet the opposition of men able to attract a following, and who in addition possess practical ability and are able to grasp the complex factors entering into modern conditions and effect a workable solution.

The people who have attacked Mr. Roosevelt, have often helped him more than harmed him. When a wealthy business man attacks the New Deal policies, he has little influence. Public opinion condemns him at the start. He is merely attempting to protect his own interests. The opposition must come from someone who has no personal axes to grind, who is sincere in furthering the prosperity of all, whose motives cannot be questioned and whose character is unimpeachable.

The ability of Mr. Roosevelt to obtain the support of the American public proves conclusively the widespread prevalence of Infanta in the average adult. We may liken Mr. Roosevelt to a schoolteacher who promises his children recesses, play, candy, many other little things of which children are commonly deprived and which they intensely desire. Of course they would support him, think he was a great fellow. He would be more popular with them than with their parents or other teachers who call for hard work and preparation for the future. Mr. Roosevelt does not call for hard work from the public. He does not call for preparation for the future. He does not consider the welfare of future generations. He considers the welfare of Mr. Roosevelt. He wishes to promise, to please, and to smile. He is as much a child as those he undertakes to guide. If he were a sensible man he would see that his present policies were bound to end in disaster and that he will go down in history as a contemptible failure and a discreditable demagogue.

Probably the best means to educate the American public to sound sensible economic measures, is to permit Mr. Roosevelt to finish his present term of office. It may even take another term under his direction to show the unsoundness of his policies. Many influences have existed to prevent disaster to the New Deal. For one thing they have been able to draw upon the vast wealth of the country and the accumulated savings of many.

As long as citizens will contribute money to the government for this purpose, it can gloss over its errors by government expenditures. There is a limit to this, even in this wealthy country of ours. Mr. Roosevelt's promises, his strength with many classes, postpones this inevitable day of reckoning. But if his policies are continued it will some day arrive. Unquestionably he and his adherents will then blame capital, big business, anyone but themselves.

We should appeal to the more sensible American citizens and show them that a government that occupies office for several years, is unequal to the task of controlling capital when it continually denounces it. Further, that a government in office several years should be able to carry out some of its glowing promises.

Mr. Roosevelt has made any number of promises. He promised to reduce government expenses twenty-five per cent and instead increased them. He has been promising for many years to balance the budget and it is still unbalanced. He has been promising security to every person in the country, promising the fuller life.

We must strive to make it apparent to the most stupid that when these benefits are not forthcoming, they are due to his incompetence and unsound policies. We should not permit him to blame big business men or any other person. We must develop a public opinion that will condemn those that are guilty. This condemnation will include Mr. Roosevelt, the New Deal administration, the politicians and the many selfish interest groups who support present policies because of special benefits received by them.

Mr. Roosevelt claims that when he took office in the spring of 1933 both the profit system and the social system were in a state of collapse. This statement has been so constantly repeated as to receive the belief of many. The truth is that the rock bottom of the depression was reached the year previously—in the summer of 1932. The unsatisfactory condition existing when Mr. Roosevelt took office, with reference primarily to the bank panic, was due to political uncertainty to which he himself was the largest contributor.

The Hoover administration was no great success. It nevertheless did adhere to some sound policies. If Mr. Hoover had been re-elected in 1932 and continued his policies, conditions would have steadily improved; we would be in far better condition today as a result.

The great difference between the Hoover and Roosevelt administration is the difference of economic conditions. Mr. Hoover became president almost at the height of the biggest business boom the country ever experienced. His term of office occupied that period during which the boom declined to a drastic depression. Mr. Roosevelt entered office when this depression was at its lowest; it could go no lower.

All he had to do was to permit natural economic laws to function and conditions would improve of themselves. Instead of adopting this wise policy, he attempted to do much by direct government interference. He then claimed that his acts improved conditions, rectified evils and accomplished much good. The acts of his administration only retarded recovery and built up a vast national debt. They have caused the existing decline in business. They are the cause of future uncertainty.

The lack of intelligence of our American public almost convinces me of the utter futility of attempting to accomplish anything. Here we have a president entering office at the bottom of the depression with all conditions favorable to wholesome improvement. He denies this, claims that our institutions are threatened with destruction, that he and he alone has saved them; and many believe him.

One can search in vain in Mr. Roosevelt's speeches for a definite policy or definite action to correct evils. His speeches contain much denunciation of malefactors of great wealth or similar people and contain many expressions designed to appeal to the public. An expression such as, "I will not let the American people down," is meaningless. An able man would not repeat such futile expressions as that. He would take for granted that the people would believe in him. When a man constantly reiterates his intention not to let the people down and similar expressions, he is trying to convince them by words; he shows somewhat of a guilty conscience feeling within himself that he actually is letting the people down. He is employing the Defenso measure of saying to the public very convincingly that he will not let them down.

Another inane expression commonly used by Mr. Roosevelt in his speeches is, "You and I know." From a practical standpoint, suppose Mr. Roosevelt and his hearers know that such a thing is a fact—why constantly repeat it, why punctuate the speeches with such inane punctuations as, "You and I know"? Actually this is somewhat of a demagogic trick by which the hearers are flattered by being told that they have something in common with the speaker; that he, a great, intelligent man, is patting them on the back for possessing an intelligence and understanding somewhat approaching his own in that they understand things in common. It also tends to build up a sympathetic oneness of common interest, of feeling, in that the speaker is at one with his audience and is defending them in what they already possess and denouncing those who threaten their possessions, interests or oppose their beliefs.

Mr. Roosevelt has what we may call a flighty mind. That is to say, his attention flits from one thing to another in accordance with whim or chance or whatever influences are brought to bear to attract his attention. He lacks ability to view many things with relation to each other. This is a result of Infanta, immature mental development, of uncontrolled Wisho, lack of mental ability and unintelligent use of such mental ability as he does possess. Mr. Roosevelt also apparently is very readily influenced by the last person who talks to him. Inconsistent, illogical, swayed by the influences of the moment.

An examination of his policies since he has been president,

shows no definite consistent aim of a practical nature. He believes he is the great leader of democracy; believes he is controlling wealth and helping the poor; believes that he is an efficient administrator. All these beliefs are mere personal conclusions not founded upon fact.

An able man would not only believe; he would seek sensible measures to carry out his beliefs. Here is where Mr. Roosevelt is lacking. He lacks the ability to formulate measures that will further a definite aim. He also lacks the administrative ability to carry out sensible measures if such were presented to him. Mr. Roosevelt also is unwilling to admit fault in himself, which is a real bar to greatness.

Before election he promised to reduce government expenditures. Since he has been president he has made any number of predictions about balancing the budget. He did the opposite of his promises. He increased government expenditures and he has not yet balanced the budget. The policies he is carrying out will prevent this entirely. Thus we can also say that Mr. Roosevelt does not fulfill his promises and that predictions by him of future accomplishments are more likely not to be fulfilled than lived up to.

Under such an administration it is not difficult to see why business is uncertain and hesitant about planning for the future. Mr. Roosevelt does not know what he is going to do. If he does promise definitely to do something, his promise is more likely to be unfulfilled. Business and industry must have certain definite conditions upon which to base sensible action. If conditions are likely to be changed at the whim of the president, or by the influence of a person or group, no continuity of policy exists. To attempt to surmise what conditions will be a year hence is utterly impossible. Yet we have many who consider Mr. Roosevelt to be a great man. Those who so consider him are not thinkers; they are governed more by Wisho and by their feelings.

William Jennings Bryan was instrumental in bringing about our present unsound condition in affairs of government. Roosevelt is continuing his efforts. Our public men

of today are of less character than at former periods, if we
except the period just after the Civil War. This loss of character and greater incompetence is due to the fact that they
have accepted the popular belief that capital is responsible
for all ills, labor for all virtues, and have capitalized this
because popular and giving votes. They resort to the actual
bribing or buying of votes by means of government benefits
or subsidies. This may last for some time, but its own viciousness will discredit it and lead to far worse conditions than
they try to correct. Incompetence is not so harmful when it
adheres to a let-alone policy where matters are adjusted to
existing conditions. When it interferes it will be bound to
expose itself to the discerning. But few are discerning.

The influence of men lives after them, whether it be for
good or ill. Mr. Roosevelt is a direct product of Mr. Bryan's
impressions on the American public. He is the logical successor of Mr. Bryan's ideas. It would be interesting to note
just how much his own thought is derived from Mr. Bryan.
As one looks at the two, there is a very great similarity between them. Mr. Roosevelt has appropriated for his own use
all of Mr. Bryan's means of attracting votes, has modified
them to suit his own personality, and added some of his own.
He is a Bryan in an era of advanced Bryanism. Mr. Bryan
attacked the wealthy, but took good care to look after his
own material gains. Mr. Roosevelt denounces the wealthy,
but likewise sees that Mr. Roosevelt has plenty. These people
who denounce wealth so vigorously could well set the example by giving their wealth to the poor and sharing the
poor's poverty.

Mr. Roosevelt combines in himself two commonly existing environmental influences: the politician able to flatter,
please, promise, and obtain votes, plus the Wisho liberal
reformer who desires to reform existing institutions but
does not know how. He has combined his political astute-
ness with Wisho liberalism, taking those reform measures
that are popular with the masses as his own. He has thus
become in his own eyes not only the great leader of democ-

racy itself but also the great leader of all reform measures designed to help the forgotten man and crush the malefactors of great wealth.

There is a great similarity between Mr. Roosevelt and Louis XVI; both unequal to the task, both products of institutions placing them in positions for which unfitted. Louis XVI inherited his position, Mr. Roosevelt was put in his present position by democracy. The fact that democracy cannot get a better man for such a high office as president of the United States proves that it is as little fitted to survive as an institution of government as were the ancient monarchical institutions which produced Louis XVI. It will be recalled that they collapsed with him. It is not unlikely that the democratic institutions of the United States will collapse with Mr. Roosevelt.

Roosevelt represents the culmination of American democratic institutions just as Louis XVI did the feebleness of ancient royalty in France. Both weak, futile, useless; preventing solution of problems of government. Both represent the ills of their times; sound government required the removal of Louis XVI, and will require that of Mr. Roosevelt.

Mr. Roosevelt's action in giving away government money reminds me of royalty distributing largess. It was not uncommon in the days of absolute monarchy in Europe for the king or queen to drive through the streets in an expensive coach with outriders, receiving the applause of the multitude and graciously casting coins to them.

There is a very great similarity between Mr. Roosevelt and Mr. Buchanan. Both were weak, both lived lives of promises in order to obtain high office. When they obtained the office, they were specialized politicians; unable to administer efficiently or establish sound policies. Both were products of their times and both failures.

Roosevelt will ultimately discredit himself, for people like their leaders to be strong men who will lead, not wait for public sentiment to show itself and then follow it under the pretense of leading. They want a leader who will lead so well as to form a strong public sentiment to follow and sustain his acts.

Soldiers respond readily to a leader who is fair, strict and considerate. They resent injustice and lack of consideration. The same holds true of men everywhere. Once convince them that you have their interests at heart, and they will loyally support you. This is the reason for the great strength of Mr. Roosevelt today. He has obtained this from groups benefited by his measures, by flattery, promises, and demagoguery. His measures are unsound and finally will harm those now benefited. But it takes real understanding of many involved economic problems, greater than we can expect of the average citizen, to see this. His hold on the people is not sound in that it is not based upon justice or consideration to all. Flattery and promises will succeed for a time, but something more solid is needed to establish lasting reforms.

Mr. Roosevelt himself believes he is saving democracy, that his measures are the only ones that will do it and he the only man capable of accomplishing it. All who oppose him or his measures for any reason are doing so for selfish motives. He has been greatly inflated by the applause he received from the unthinking multitude and his courtiers. His smile, his promises, his attractive personality, his high position, the belief he has created that he is accomplishing wonders for the downtrodden, have all tended to inflate him. This is evidence of smallness of mind and character. A big man could not fall into such a childish belief.

Mr. Roosevelt claims to be fighting the great battle for the people. In reality he is saying and doing whatever will get votes, regardless of merit, although he doubtless believes that he will really do more for the people than anyone else. He foments class hatred, makes impossible promises, uses many words, is unsound and incompetent; just a politician. His mission is to destroy democracy in this country. If he actually planned to do so he could hardly plan better than he has done and is doing. He will have an effect on history for a different reason than he hopes. His unsound measures will eventually lead to a revolt against them and cause sound measures (we hope) to be adopted.

Mr. Roosevelt knows just enough about economics to believe he knows much, so much as never to err. A most dangerous condition for anyone, especially when the knowledge is superficial, permitting them to see the effects readily, but the causes with difficulty.

Mr. Roosevelt has a pleasing manner, voice, good intentions, talks well, flatters well, appeals to the sympathies of the voters by promises to help the underdog, but is impractical, unsound, thinks only of the present, not of the future. He is a great fomenter of class feeling, his utterances are a parody of popular measures. He illustrates in himself the breakdown of what would have been a decent character had it not entered politics.

Instead of balancing the budget and decreasing expenses, he has pursued the weak policy of using government money to satisfy the demands of any group sufficiently powerful to make them. There is nothing frank, simple or direct in his methods. He cannot be believed. He exhibits deceit, treachery, and double dealing in his transactions.

The New Deal has no plan. It tries out any measure that has possibility of popular favor. There is nothing deep about it, no effort to get to the real cause of existing problems. It embarks enthusiastically on projects without thought; the Florida ship canal and the Passamaquoddy tide project were undertaken energetically, pursued with much activity for awhile, and then abandoned. These two projects in themselves illustrate the futility of the New Deal: much activity, much excitement, much accusation, but eventually failure and oblivion. It requires no prophet to foresee this; only a little common sense and a little knowledge of man's past history.

It is strange that the New Deal, despite its cry of "human rights versus property rights" does nothing to improve the moral atmosphere, although it claims to have done so. It gives only economic benefits, disregarding the bad effects on the character of individuals becoming mendicants dependent upon the government for support. Mr. Roosevelt made the statement in his second inaugural that there was a better moral atmosphere in the country. One could look about in the months following seeking in vain for this—sit-down strikers, agitators, wild accusations, anything but what one could call a good moral atmosphere.

Mr. Roosevelt obtained his great strength with the people largely because they believed in him. He has the faculty of saying things very convincingly, saying the very things the public would like to hear, and naturally they believe them. There has been so much talk of the abuse of labor by capital that they are only too glad to follow someone who holds the club over capital and supports labor. He is appealing to prejudiced feelings, self-interests, to anything but character and intelligence.

Mr. Roosevelt voices attractively what the public would like to believe, with many fine, high-sounding sentiments, much flattery and promises. For how long will it last? Until his policies result in the failure their unsoundness will insure. But this may take a long time, because his power by virtue of control of the government is great. When they do fail, he can probably pass the blame on capital to the satisfaction of himself and his supporters. It will not be he who is at fault but the vicious capitalists, the courts, all those who have opposed him.

A cold analysis of Roosevelt's speeches and remarks shows the predominance of platitudes, wishful thinking, leading a great fight for the lowly, much that sounds well but exhibits little real thought and promising no sound action. A pleasing voice, pleasing personality, an incompetent, mediocre politician—only he and those who follow him are right; all others are not only wrong but inspired by vicious motives.

Mr. Roosevelt would be a good doctor for a patient who only needed to be told convincingly that he is well. In this case he has taken a fairly healthy individual, told him that he was sick, and by his efforts has caused him to become sick.

His promises so far have caused the patient to believe he is getting well, but some day the patient will realize that he is getting worse, and lose confidence in his physician.

Mr. Roosevelt takes credit on his administration for all benefits or anything that has happened to make things better. He blames all evil and all harmful occurrences on his enemies and on capital. Our people swallow this. Truly they are receiving just as good a government as they deserve.

The wage increase and hour decrease by steel, automobile, and other concerns has caused credit to be claimed by Mr. Roosevelt. Many believe this. What they do not see is that labor is only getting back what he took from them by devaluing the dollar in 1933. They may think they are getting something, but they will find they are no better off than they were before, and will wonder why.

Mr. Roosevelt is the victim of the existing environmental influences. Wisho liberalism, the capitalism complex, the reform madness, the high position he holds, the applause of his followers, have caused him to believe that he alone is right and that his measures are the only correct measures. There has grown up within him a great resentment against the big business and industrial leaders of the country, inspired by an inferiority complex of which he himself is ignorant.

This has become an obsession with him and he is determined to bring these big leaders to their knees, using the power of his high office to accomplish this. It is a state of mind not different from religious fanatics of old who denounce and persecuted all who failed to follow them. Strange how history thus repeats itself; we have a leader elected by popular vote who has permitted himself to become as mentally unsound as the fanatics of the Dark Ages.

There is no reason why the American public should suffer from the insane viewpoint of one man, no reason why we should stand by and permit him to abuse the powers of his office to persecute those with whom he disagrees. This situation holds possibilities for disastrous consequences. Unfortunately he has a vast following among the ignorant, among the Wisho liberals, among the reformers and impractical busybodies who can mind everybody's business but their own.

The measures he advocates are unsound and their unsoundness will be increasingly apparent with the passage of time. We may then expect the same violence the sit-downers displayed in their violations of law to be exhibited toward our federal government as represented by Mr. Roosevelt. When this occurs, it will take an abler man than he to straighten out the mess.

The epidemic of strikes we had during the year 1937 was a direct result of Mr. Roosevelt's attempt to bring capital to its knees, by using the prestige of his office to force General Motors to confer with sit-down strikers in possession of their plant and further using his influence on the governor of Michigan to cause him to follow the same policy. As a result of this effort on the part of Mr. Roosevelt to employ his office to satisfy a personal grudge against the wealthy, he has directly caused labor to get out of hand and caused the decent people throughout the country much unnecessary annoyance. He has further shown himself unequal to the position he fills and has convinced the patriotic citizens who wish to be proud of this country that his government is too weak to preserve law and order and too inefficient to solve the economic problems that cause labor to resort to violence.

Mr. Roosevelt made the remark, one time, when there was considerable advance in business and that he had planned it that way. When the epidemic of sit-down strikes, and the steel strike, was at its height, he did not admit that he had planned it that way. Sometime later, in response to pressure, he made the famous remark, "A plague on both your houses." His actual remark should have been reversed. The advance in business was made in spite of the actions of the administration, and the labor trouble was caused directly as the result of the support given the C.I.O. by the administration.

President Roosevelt's speech today, (January 3, 1938) is

a discredit to himself and to the country. One would gather from his speech that he is infallible, makes no errors and that all who do not admit this infallibility are impelled to deny it by selfish motives. This is the opposite of sensible action to solve the country's problems. If he would devote the same effort he now spends in justifying his acts and denouncing opponents, to seeking the errors of his administration and correcting them, his efforts would be of a more constructive nature.

Some of his statements are directly misleading. One which I object to, for instance, is a statement that the national income has been increased from thirty-eight billions in 1932 to sixty-eight billions in 1937. The natural presumption is, of course, that his administration has brought this about. If we analyze this closely, even accepting his own figures, and take into consideration the depreciation in the dollar from the original hundred-cent dollar to the present sixty-cent dollar, we will find that the apparent increase in national income is so slight as to be negligible. We can hope for no alleviation of our difficulties under such leadership, a leadership that misleads, sees no fault in self, no merit in those who do see fault in its policies.

Mr. Roosevelt has something to say about sectional and class animosities yet it is to class animosity that he has been the greatest contributor. He displays the utmost concern over the plight of the ill-fed, ill-housed, and ill-clad, and constantly finds fault with certain wealthy individuals who are abusing their privileges. He disclaims any attempt to condemn all of capital, saying that only ten per cent of business men are the violators. If he is to be honest, he should point out specifically by name the guilty people and the offenses of which they are guilty. Unless this be done, he is guilty of inciting feeling against one class by other classes.

In his Jackson Day speech Mr. Roosevelt obtained quite a laugh by referring to the concentration of power of public utility holding companies as four inches of tail wagging ninety-six inches of dog. Of course this is a demagogic appeal to arouse the public against the big utility magnates. If we try to analyze what could be meant by such a statement, it has no meaning. For instance, the past history of man has shown that a single able leader has effected great reforms. Mr. Roosevelt's own administration is far less than four per cent of the people. His policies are established by himself and a relatively small number of advisers. The people have no choice except to reject or support them.

We may liken the policies of government, of utilities, of business and industry generally, to the small rudder which establishes the course of a gigantic ship. Efficient management, efficient control will always be exercised by a single leader or a relatively small group. The true virtue of democracy is to have intelligent citizens select able leaders to administer their affairs. Similarly with utilities; able managers should conduct them.

Mr. Roosevelt received much applause in a recent speech by saying very eloquently, "I will not let the American people down." To the unthinking this brings about a great response. Actually it is evidence of weakness, uncertainty, Wisho, and demagoguery. An able leader would not resort to saying so convincingly that he would not let the people down. He would already have demonstrated by his acts that he would not do so. This is largely where Mr. Roosevelt gets his strength. He says the things that people would like to have him do or refrain from doing but he is unable to perform the acts that people would like to have him perform.

It is remarkable that he has been able to exist for five years by talk and promises. There is an explanation for this however. He occupies such a strong position that loyal citizens naturally support him. The prestige of his office has great power. He has the vast resources and wealth of the United States to call upon to pay for his blunders. The foolish attacks made upon him; the general feeling against capital and hatred of oppressors; his role of defender of the people, of the downtrodden; his claim of waging war for democracy; his denouncing of capital and malefactors of great wealth—all have given him support.

He also obtains support from many interest groups because he favors measures which they demand. Many purely selfish people like him as president because of his weakness. They can obtain things from the government by threatening attitudes, can violate the law and resort to violence, without interference by the government.

Despite all this, however, it would seem that there would be sufficient intelligence in the country to point out the harmful effects of his measures. There is sufficient ability in the country to realize and to understand, but this ability is not united with other qualities that would attract public following. Many, able to recognize the harmful effects of Mr. Roosevelt's teachings, make such bitter attacks upon him as to strengthen him and discredit themselves.

We are today the victims of a vicious system of poor standards of education, of poor conduct, and of inability to think. Such a man as Mr. Roosevelt would be unable to obtain office in a community of sensible virtuous citizens. Yet he has obtained office, has been re-elected, and obtains sufficient support to pursue his policies.

Men generally like a strong leader. Why should they follow a weak one? The primary reason is the very human drawing quality of Mr. Roosevelt's disposition and intentions. All sound well. He expresses them well. We, in effect, are following a leader who smiles, promises, and endeavors to please everyone; a herd-reflector who tells or shows us what we would like to see, hear, or believe. He promises to do what we would like to have done and a vast majority of the people follow him. His opponents generally lack human appeal and feeling and, it must be said, have failed to intelligently present their case. They have been as stupid as Mr. Roosevelt has been incompetent.

But the populace is fickle. I wonder if Mr. Roosevelt has ever heard of the incident of Aristides? The Greeks had a very commendable institution of writing the name of those whom they wished to ostracize from their country on a tablet. One day a Greek citizen, unable to write, asked Aristides, upon meeting him, to write the name Aristides on the tablet. "What have you against this man?" said Aristides. "Nothing," replied the citizen, "but I am tired of hearing him called Aristides the Just." Not a very nice trait, but human nature, and we may yet see it displayed in a desirable form. Instead of being used to expel a just man from his country, it can well be used to overthrow an incompetent government. People will get tired of hearing about the great war for democracy, the great infallible leader who is leading this fight; the vicious interests combined together to oppose enlightenment. All who oppose lack merit. All under his leadership are God's chosen. When the most stupid see that the fine promises are not being fulfilled, and that some of the benefits to which they have been accustomed are being withdrawn, their resentment will be aroused and they will scorn the very administration they previously supported and praised. Public opinion swings to extremes, much as the pendulum of a clock; now in the throes of the most extreme worship and applause, then swinging suddenly to the most violent extreme of denunciation and hate.

Quite sometime back I observed two notices on the front page of the same newspaper that, to me, described the Roosevelt administration and policies very conclusively. The one notice described the activities of Mr. Roosevelt in calling a conference to reduce automobile accidents. The other notice had regard to the arrest of one of his sons for being involved in another of several automobile accidents.

We have another example of lack of thought in the remarks of Mr. Roosevelt, constantly being the leader of democracy, leading the great fight of the people against the wealthy capitalist, uttering the most puerile statements, showing an utter inability to grapple with the problems of the day. On one occasion, enthused by the dedication of a dam, he extolled the country for refusing to pay vast sums of money for armaments. A few days later he made a speech about war, intimating that the country and the world faced destruction. If we are so near destruction, it would seem that the money spent on the dam could well have been used toward preparing the adequate defenses for which he belittles foreign nations. If the war comes which he predicts, and we are inadequately prepared, we are bound to suffer. It is strange that hardly anyone analyzes the statements of this man, points out their faults. He is denounced by many, but often the denunciation is of such a partisan character as to discredit itself; is often as bad, or worse, than his own statements.

The unsoundness and impracticability of Mr. Roosevelt's policies are well shown by the Florida canal and the Passamaquoddy project. He embarked upon these projects, spent much money upon them, and then finally abandoned them uncompleted. A great impetus in the inauguration of the construction of the Florida canal was a storm that did some damage along the Florida coast. Mr. Roosevelt expressed great concern over this and said a Florida canal was necessary to avoid such hazards. What an inane viewpoint! Ships have been sailing the seas for untold ages. They cannot always have protected canals in which to navigate.

Political expediency was involved in the Passamaquoddy project. The political situation in Maine was such that the expenditure of large sums of federal money on the Passamaquoddy project would obtain votes for the Democratic party. Is this not a vicious system—our national administration spending vast sums on a useless public work for the purpose of obtaining votes to maintain itself in office?

Mr. Roosevelt embodies in his own person practically all the components of Today's Extet. Of them all, Traffico is the one least applicable to his case, although he is a great influence in stimulating it in others.

Mr. Roosevelt exemplifies in his own person that side of present-day American institutions that threatens to destroy them by efforts to improve but at the same time safeguarding self interest. Like so many American reformers, Mr.

Roosevelt advocates measures that will require others to perform their duties and fulfill their obligations. He fails to see the need for himself setting an example of that unselfish conduct without which no enduring reforms can be accomplished.

I have attempted to seek the basis for Mr. Roosevelt's policies. He has no policy. Like all human beings, he has been influenced by his environment and by all past experiences. Certain definite impressions will naturally exert an overpowering influence upon his acts. There are several such influences that seem to dominate. I would list them as:

1. Fear of communism
2. Equalizing Wealth
3. Political Expediency
4. Animosity to Big Business

Mr. Roosevelt apparently has fear of the growth of communism, the Left or the United Front, whatever we choose to call it. We see this demonstrated by his willingness to conciliate those who have little or nothing. Closely associated with this fear of communism is his desire to equalize the distribution of wealth and to punish the malefactors of great wealth. He, like most Americans, can see the injustice of some having little and others having so much. He would like to correct this situation but lacks the ability to do so.

Inasmuch as Mr. Roosevelt is a product of politics, political expediency and the desire to obtain or retain office and promote political self-interest are among the paramount interests controlling him. Practically all measures he supports are dominated by political expediency. Will they enhance his personal fortune? Will they attract votes? At no time has he advocated any measure, however sound, that conflicted with political expediency. This is a short-sighted viewpoint. No amount of political expediency will prevent the failure of unsound policies. When they fail, the political expediency employed will be discredited.

Mr. Roosevelt seems pleased with his expression regarding

the Minimum Wage Bill, "establishing a floor for wages." Any floor you build must rest on the ground, which is a firmer, far more enduring foundation, which will exist long after whatever floor you build has gone. It will adapt itself to changing conditions. Why build a floor over the entire country? Let those who want a floor for a special use build their own floors. Why have the government prevent those people who prefer the firmer foundation of the ground from having it? If the floor is not well built, if it is too high, if it is unstable, it will collapse anyway, and those who trusted to the artificial floor will have to rely upon the natural ground foundation.

This idea of Mr. Roosevelt building a floor just about expresses his policies. He is building a floor so high of such unstable material that it will collapse. It will make a few dents in the ground in doing so and the people will be just where they were before the floor was erected.

Mr. Roosevelt is a president sworn to enforce the law who promotes lawlessness on the part of sit-down strikers, who lent the prestige of his office to force law-abiding employers to confer and compromise with lawbreakers who had seized and occupied their property.

Mr. Roosevelt denounces crime and criminals harshly. Yet he himself cultivates friendly relations with crooked political machines. The associates and associations of Mr. Farley are of such a nature as to discredit him in the eyes of any respectable citizen. Yet he is Mr. Roosevelt's political manipulator. Many local political machines supporting Mr. Roosevelt are a discredit to our democratic institutions. Yet Roosevelt is willing to accept their support and conciliate them while denouncing the viciousness of his opponents.

Mr. Roosevelt is very willing to denounce wealthy tax evaders. He, however, takes great care to find no tax evasion in the adherents of New Deal policies. People who continually denounce others for offenses are more likely than not to be guilty of the same offenses themselves. The income-tax law is so complicated that fault can be found with any income-tax report dealing with profits from many sources. If the income-tax returns of all supporters of the New Deal were scrutinized as closely as those of its opponents, just as great a percentage of evasions would be found.

According to this morning's paper (March 8, 1938), Mr. Farley emerged from a White House conference with President Roosevelt and announced a far-reaching revision of presidents' pictures on postage stamps. Washington to go on the one-cent stamp, Jefferson on the three-cent stamp, Coolidge on the five-cent issue, and so forth. This is doubtless part of Mr. Roosevelt's far-reaching campaign to improve the lot of those who are ill-fed, ill-clad, and ill-housed.

One of the far-reaching reforms Mr. Roosevelt undertook early in his administration, was to modify the military salute given to governors of the state. I forget the exact number of guns they were receiving or are to receive under the new order. Mr. Roosevelt felt that increasing the number of guns in their salute was justified. I do not know the exact reason for this. It doubtless has far-reaching consequences upon the welfare of the forgotten man.

A statement by Mr. Roosevelt, in which he says substantially that he would show capital who was their master, is very illuminating as showing his character and ability. It indicates an inferiority complex, perhaps not consciously known, a feeling that the able industrial leaders are superior to him. It shows Infanta, the spirit of getting even, of showing that "I am better than you." It shows a grudge, a determination on his part to use his high office in a grudge fight. It shows lack of real manhood because real men do not indulge in threats; they act. It shows demagogic appeal in that by consistently attacking wealth, he draws applause and brings the poor to look upon him in the rôle of protector.

The willingness of the great number to follow Mr. Roosevelt shows that the average man's feelings are generally not intelligently controlled. Mr. Roosevelt, as a leader, appeals to many human qualities except those having to do with intelligence, the exercise of Primo and deep thinking. If he himself possessed great ability, all would be well and the support he is able to attract from the public would be harnessed for constructive achievements. If the public possessed this quality of intelligence, Mr. Roosevelt, as he now is, could not be their leader.

Mr. Roosevelt displays Infanta by his desire to be the center of attraction, to make some startling announcement to attract attention. He displays the antics of a child in much of his conduct. We see this demonstrated very often in his press announcements. Invariably, when anything of importance is to be announced, he is there to announce it. This is the retention in Mr. Roosevelt of childish characteristics. How often have we seen children resorting to whatever acts would make them the center of attraction and would enhance their feeling of importance? Notice a picture of Mr. Roosevelt sometime, with some of his courtiers about while he is signing something. He shows evidence of Infanta, of boyish enjoyment of power, glorying in the adulation of his creatures. When Mr. Roosevelt makes startling pronunciamentos he does so more for self-glorification than because of reasoned conclusions. Naturally before he makes the startling announcement in public, he thinks it over. Will it strengthen his political fortune; will it make him the center of attraction? He does not look to the far-distant future for the ultimate consequences of his acts. He does not possess the ability to do so. We are witnessing the government of a great nation conducted by a man dominated by Infanta, the desire to be the center of attraction and to make unusual announcements; dominated by political self-interest and the present; but unable to reason soundly, to form accurate conclusions, or to consider the future effect of the policies he announces.

Mr. Roosevelt is an excellent example of the display of Wisho. He states very often as facts things which he would like to have exist. He states them in a very convincing manner, convincing both himself and the uninformed. This is very common in his speeches. At one time, for instance, he spoke of the improved moral atmosphere existing in the country. He wishes that such was the case and he belives it. By his mere announcement he expects others to believe that this great moral improvement has been brought about by his efforts during his administration.

Today, (August 19, 1937) I read an account in the paper of Mr. Roosevelt's speech at the celebration of the three hundred and fiftieth anniversary of Virginia Dare's birth. A line that caught my eye was a subhead reading, "People back him, he asserts." Then he went on to say he pictured the people as standing behind him in, "my opposition to the vesting of supreme power in the hands of any class numerous but select."

A few words like this can be very illuminating. They show several things; that Mr. Roosevelt possesses much Wisho and makes this statement wishing it were so. His wish is so strong that he believes it. In his subconscious there exists considerable doubt as to whether the people back him. His emphasis on the statement that they do is a direct admission of his lack of certainty that they do so back him. He says things here, as he so often does, as positive statements, as existing facts, which actually are untrue. He says them so persuasively and emphatically that he convinces himself of their truth. Being thus convinced himself he sees no reason why others should not also be so convinced.

Another illuminating thing is that he exhibits the weaknesses of so many leaders, when they succeed, in identifying his own personal views and interests with the poor classes of the country against what he calls "the numerous select classes." We should endeavor to develop more intelligent citizens capable of understanding human nature and reading between the lines. With more intelligent people able to do this, politicians such as Mr. Roosevelt would be unable to make their weaknesses convincingly appeal as strength.

In addition to being afflicted with a cause complex, Mr. Roosevelt is also the victim of obsessionism. This is not an unusual combination. It is quite common among leaders of a somewhat weak type who think well of themselves, who lack Primo and common sense, and are dominated by egotistical Wisho. An able leader will realize that however great his gifts, he is also successful as a result of favoring conditions. The victim of the cause complex commonly fails to realize this and is prone to believe that the cause he is leading was created by himself, that he is ordained by God to lead it, that all people or things who for any reason do not credit his sincerity or honesty of purpose, are enemies of the cause, without merit and therefore personal enemies.

Mr. Roosevelt clearly displays Infanta and Wisho by refusing to face facts. He convinces himself by saying everything is all right, that it actually is all right. He has spent many billions of dollars, added many billions to the national debt. A sensible person would see that such a policy will inevitably lead to disaster, yet he believes that everything is all right. He expects to go down in history as the great friend of the forgotten man, the plumed knight defending democracy against the vicious capitalist.

It is to be hoped that Mr. Roosevelt represents the final development of attempts to appeal to flattery, class feelings, and self-interest and that by his failure he discredits the employment of such methods in the future. By contrast he should show that sound thought will have to be employed and sound action carried out. No one who is faultless or without error can accomplish great projects. His inability to see the errors in them will result in their inevitable failure when put into practice. As long as Mr. Roosevelt has ample federal credit and money to call upon to make up for his blunders, he can survive, but when he has exhausted the federal treasury, he will crash.

Mr. Roosevelt says many things he does not really believe, just to please his audience or score a point. This is a dangerous procedure which tends to divert one's development from real facts and truth, to a hope, a belief, that the good wishes will come true.

Mr. Roosevelt is sincere in many of his beliefs, but lacks

Primo, objectivity, sound knowledge, thought and reasoning power. He is always leading crusades for the people and democracy, against evil and their enemies. He creates false hopes on the part of the poor. It is this policy that is directly responsible for labor disturbances; for W.P.A. workers occupying legislative halls and demanding tribute.

Mr. Roosevelt would not have his present unsound mental condition if he had developed Primo from an early age and realized how unsound an attitude is, that one can do no wrong and is always right. This attitude has perpetuated his faults, and his surroundings have been such as to contribute further toward it. If he was a really able man, he would not permit himself to get in this condition. Adapto has been brought into play, and his condition now is practically hopeless. He is not a bad fellow; his intentions are good. He means well. He lacks the ability to carry out sound measures to put his intentions into practice. He would not be a bad person if he lived the life of a common citizen and had not undertaken to correct all the ills of man. He forms an excellent study from a psychological standpoint as showing how a really decent man can be developed into a bad influence on his times by lack of understanding of the principles governing human conduct and by permitting unsound thoughts and acts to develop a psychona that prevents sound thought or action. Truly, nature revenges itself upon those who violate or disregard her laws.

Mr. Roosevelt has the faculty of accomplishing those very things he tries not to do. At the beginning of his administration he opposed the payment of the veterans' bonus, yet he was the man who brought about its final enactment into law. The large sum spent by him on various relief expenditures gave the American Legion the excellent argument, "Everybody else is getting government benefits, why shouldn't we? We're far more entitled to it than those other fellows that didn't serve during the war and risk their lives in defense of their country. The government has spent billions on everybody who asked for it, why shouldn't the

American Legion get a share?" This argument prevailed with Congress, and Mr. Roosevelt took great care not to endanger his political future by opposing it too strenuously.

A recent remark made by him about not leaving this country in the condition in which Buchanan left it to Lincoln causes one to believe that he is unconsciously pursuing that policy, with the difference perhaps that he will not turn his government over to a legally elected successor, but to someone who will overthrow his administration by force. He has now been in office about five years, and it is very unlikely that the sensible, decent, element of the country will submit to further misgovernment for two and a half years more.

His policy of taking from the Haves to give to the Have-nots, at the same time praising all the Have-nots for all the virtues in existence, promising them more and persecuting the Haves, draws a sharp line of demarcation between the conflicting elements in a future civil war. Those who are successful in life, who are able to care for themselves without government benefits, will be arrayed against those unwilling to care for themselves and demanding support by the government.

The line of demarcation between these two elements is far sharper than that separating the opposing forces in the Civil War. Then it was a problem of opposing sectional interests. In this case it will be the capable against the incapable, the intelligent against the stupid, the decent against the indecent—all brought about by incompetent politicians promising anything so long as they manage to obtain office. Can anyone say that a system such as this is deserving of survival? Let us determine to reform our institutions in such way that they will be a credit to us and a help in solving the problems we are suffering from.

Mr. Roosevelt has himself created the relief problem. He has a great faculty of creating problems himself and then treating and perpetuating them. The expression he so often uses, saying in substance, "Let no one starve," is pleasing to the sentimental unthinking public. Why do not they be sen-

sible and ask why this is? We had no such relief problem
before the New Deal administration. The answer is simple.
Mr. Roosevelt's measures have themselves created the relief
problem; his floor for wages, his ceiling for hours, the uncertainty of his policies, attacks on business, and stifling
regulation have prevented industry from functioning naturally. The unsound policies of the New Deal are reflected
in unemployment and demands for further relief.

A sensible economic policy on the part of our national
government would abolish the relief problem entirely. If
capital were given a chance, it would soon find work for all.
Not only would the need for relief cease, but there would
be a vast increase in the production of wealth and in improving the standards of living. But according to Mr. Roosevelt
he has made no error. His policies are sound. The vicious
capitalists are the ones at fault. When will the American
public demand results instead of denunciation?

Mr. Roosevelt's foreign policy is in keeping with the weakness of his domestic policies. Many foreign nations are controlled by ruthless nationalists seeking to advance their own
interests by brute force if necessary, regardless of the interests
of other nations. Mr. Roosevelt has denounced these ruthless tactics and has suggested a quarantine of the offending
nations. He expresses fine sentiments but it will take more
than this to control aggressor nations. They know that Mr.
Roosevelt will not resort to force. Therefore, they pursue
their ways without fear of interference by the United States.
Mr. Roosevelt's attacks upon them have only served to arouse
their animosity. They will be only too willing in the future
to combine against the United States if such action will advance their interest. It would be far better for Mr. Roosevelt
to keep quiet. The foolish American public heeds talk but
foreign rulers require something more substantial.

The most trivial incident in life may be a vital influence
toward success or failure. Sometimes a commonplace occurrence may, through chance, fate or circumstances, be the
impelling force toward success or failure. We all possess a

name which in the average case is of little importance upon our fortunes. Yet in the case of Mr. Franklin D. Roosevelt, it has been the direct cause of his becoming president. If his name had not been Roosevelt, he would probably never have been appointed Assistant Secretary of the Navy, would probably never have obtained the public consideration he has, and would never have become president.

The name Roosevelt was one to conjure with after the retirement of Theodore Roosevelt from the presidency and its possession on the part of Mr. Franklin D. Roosevelt was a distinct political asset. He possesses many other good political assets such as pleasing personality, a pleasing voice, the ability to make friends, and other attributes. These would have been insufficient if his name had not been Roosevelt.

We may even continue the speculation as to chance farther back to Mr. Theodore Roosevelt. Suppose that some intelligent person had been with President McKinley at the time of the fatal attack upon him and prevented his murder. Mr. Theodore Roosevelt would not have become president and the name Roosevelt would not have been one to conjure with later as an asset to political success.

As a matter of fact there was some such series of chances involved in President McKinley's murder. I read sometime ago an account of a man who sometimes guarded Mr. McKinley. Due to some trivial occurrence he was not present at the time Mr. McKinley was attacked. This man believed that had he been there he would have prevented the fatal injury to the president.

And so we go through life patting ourselves on the back for our success, not realizing that we have been assisted by chance and that those who have promoted our advance have themselves likewise been assisted by chance.

Chance has favored Mr. Roosevelt in many ways. He has simply been lucky. For instance, if the more level-headed leaders of the Democratic party had, at the nominating convention in 1932, considered the future of their party or their country, they could have controlled the convention so as to have insured the nomination of a reasonably sensible man who would have been elected president. But again, fate, chance, or luck favored Mr. Roosevelt. His unskillful opponents caused him to be nominated and made him president.

But perhaps it is not all for the worse. Possibly he is the instrument to insure man's progress, not by positive efforts, but as a negative example embodying in himself unsound doctrines that will effectively point out the evils of our institutions and cause an entire reconstitution of our political, social and economic order. Such a drastic change in man's institutions could not possibly be effected quickly unless the previous ones were so thoroughly discredited as not only to demand sound measures, but to afford both the leadership and the popular support to carry them out.

In all discussions given by Mr. Roosevelt, somehow all great men of the past had his same viewpoint. He is the inheritor of all their goodness and is perpetuating it today. He has never admitted making an error in anything. He believes he possesses such great ability as never to err. Others lie but never Mr. Roosevelt. This attitude on Mr. Roosevelt's part shows the retention of much Infanta in his make-up, an inability to see wrong in self, a willingness to interpret all things to substantiate existing conclusions and to further personal aims.

A sensible man knows that he is not always right and will admit it. He will endeavor to profit by his errors and avoid repeating them. No sane man would continually state that all great men of the past were working to achieve the aims he also is advocating. Neither would any sane man claim that he was greater than all great men of the past; that whereas they only tried, he actually was going to succeed; in effect that he is the greatest man of all time.

The weak part about this argument is that great men do not devote continual effort toward extolling their greatness. They act and let their actions speak for themselves. Mr. Roosevelt is unquestionably a great man in extolling his own merit and in obtaining a public following. He is a great man for talking, for promising, for smiling, for spending government money, for buying votes, and for denouncing all who oppose him. This type of greatness, however, is that employed by the child.

When Mr. Roosevelt is given his final place in history a few generations hence, it will be determined by his acts. Saying himself that he is a great man will not convince impartial historians. They will seek for something more tangible to justify claims to greatness. Mr. Roosevelt may have a great effect upon the future; not by positive action but by action of a negative nature. He may discredit democracy in this country. He may discredit demagogues. He may educate the unthinking public not to be deluded by demagoguery but to seek able men.

We can often learn far more from our enemies than from our friends. For the same reason we can very often learn more from the blunders of others than from their constructive achievements. If we can educate the public to see Mr. Roosevelt's true nature, we may convert him into a constructive force. Not by what he has done, but by being the greatest herd-reflector of all time.

At times I have a somewhat hopeless feeling regarding man's future. Despite the great effort I have spent in evolving a philosophy to bring out the best in man's nature and social institutions to further it, I am faced with a practical demonstration of the difficulty of insuring sensible action. Mr. Roosevelt is a glaring example in himself of the inability of man to think or to select leaders of worth.

When a man such as he can obtain control over such a great nation, secure the enactment of laws and possess the power to execute them, we may well feel hopeless as to man's future. It seems impossible to develop a government adequate to further Ascendency, when we contrast what such a government would have to be with our present one.

On the other hand there is a slight glimmer of hope. Mr. Roosevelt by his utter incompetence and his inevitable failure may so firmly impress upon the public the need for thinking, the need for good leaders, the need for sound policies that a drastic revolution in thought, in conduct, in government, in social institutions generally will be effected. So suddenly, so drastically as to be beyond belief.

This is possible—but after all, one must face facts. The possibility is slight. The probability is slight. But let us not be pessimistic. Let us plan and endeavor to accomplish this. Let us not throw up our hands and resign our fate to incompetence. Let us show why they are incompetent and let us show why and how it is possible to develop competent leaders, sensible policies, and public support for them.

Thoughts

Judging from Roosevelt's speeches he is on the right road to all that is good, and all who oppose him are vicious.

———————

Mr. Roosevelt is mentally warped and mentally unsound. He has promised so much and has received so much flattery and adulation, that he believes he is deserving of it.

———————

Roosevelt is a good-intentioned, well-meaning fellow elevated to a position beyond his ability; it demands more than promises, smiles, pleasing personality and good intentions.

———————

About the most generous thing you can truthfully say about Mr. Roosevelt is that he is a Badsamaritan.

———————

As Louis XVI represents the nadir of the old regime in France, so does Roosevelt represent the nadir of democracy in the United States.

———————

Mr. Roosevelt is always good, and right in any shape or form he cares to choose to execute his measures; a noble character without mistakes, incapable of an unjust thought, bitterly oppressed by the vicious capitalists.

Roosevelt is the possessor of a great unrecognized incapacity to comprehend sound measures or carry out sound action, but he possesses a great ability to say nothing most convincingly.

Nero fiddled while Rome burned. Roosevelt is fiddling but does not even know there is a fire.

A short time ago Mr. Roosevelt in a speech extolled America for spending money upon national public works of enduring value as compared to many other foreign nations wasting their money in preparations for war. Now he is advocating appropriations for a large navy as preparation for war. There is nothing consistent about his actions.

—January 5, 1938.

Gripes

Again Mr. Roosevelt is the great leader of the people against those opposing democracy, fighting the big business malefactors of great wealth. Why does he not curb them? He has been in power five years. Why does he not name them, point out the individuals guilty of such heinous conduct. He cannot do it for the simple reason that his appeal is a demagogic one. Those whom he hates so bitterly are far more meritorious citizens than he.

As long as he claims to be leading the great fight, let's give him one. When a man asks for a fight, why not accommodate him? So far his enemy has been an imaginary one, self-created, denounced and belittled as he wished, the poor capitalist who is not able to fight back. Let us give Mr. Roosevelt someone who can fight back. Just see what sort of a leader he is. Possibly, he will not be so successful against a real enemy as he is against imaginary ones.

If Jefferson, Jackson, Lincoln, or Theodore Roosevelt could have heard his speech yesterday, they would have been somewhat startled by the interpretations he gives their acts. He has called other people liars. When a man misstates facts in such way as to further his own aims, he is a liar. That is what Mr. Roosevelt does consistently. Unfortunately, there is always sufficient divergence in interpreting history to substantiate in some degree almost any viewpoint. The ignorant masses are willing to accept any plausible story that appeals in some way to already established conclusions.

The attitude of Mr. Roosevelt would be laughable if it were not for the position and power he possesses. Here is the greatest democracy in the world, a great nation, having great influence upon world affairs and upon the future of man, almost under the entire control of a man of unsound mind. His mental unsoundness is a form of obsessionistic insanity. He and he alone is the great leader of democracy. All things he does, nurture and protect democratic institutions.

If one analyzes this viewpoint, one will readily see a contradiction. Democracy is a government of many. When we have a leader who dominates all, we have something more nearly approaching a dictatorship than a democracy. Substantially Mr. Roosevelt is a demagogic politician seeking power for himself but at the same time convinced that he is furthering the welfare of mankind and democracy. It is impossible to reconcile the statements and actions of the insane. The type of insanity possessed by Mr. Roosevelt however, that of obsessionism, does provide certain definite aims.

He is convinced he is a great leader, a great man, the servant of democracy and advancing the welfare of the human race. This is an obsessionistic belief. The measures he advocates from time to time to further this aim and promote his popularity, are beyond explanation. They are utterly inconsistent, as much so as the acts of an insane person. And this is the man who is governing our country today.

—January 9, 1938.

Mr. Roosevelt himself is an invitation to civil war. By virtue of his position, the side which he is on will be under his control. He will be the leader. Any cause led by Mr. Roosevelt will be poorly led. The greatest injury an enemy could wish upon his foes would be to have them led by a man like Mr. Roosevelt. Civil war will require drastic, definite action. This is the very quality that Mr. Roosevelt lacks. Wars will not be won by smiling, talking, and promising. They must be won by fighting a tangible foe.

If the selfish few Mr. Roosevelt so harshly condemns are preventing prosperity after five years of his rule, will they not continue to do so? This statement of Mr. Roosevelt is a plain admission of his inability to control the selfish few and further, that he cannot bring about that prosperity that he so glowingly promises. Why doesn't someone expose this fellow? Check his accomplishments with his promises. They are as far apart as the federal income and outgo has been during his administration—and like them, will never meet.

Mr. Roosevelt claims to be the leader in a great fight against the selfish wealthy but by his own admission admits that he cannot control them. They are still preventing his much promised prosperity. Throw the talking, promising, fool out and put someone in who will act sensibly; someone who, instead of denouncing a selfish, vicious group, will take steps to control selfishness and viciousness. If such steps were undertaken by a sensible person, the operation would begin with the New Deal administration itself.—*March 26, 1938.*

XLV

MUDGY, PUDGY

Mr. Lewis and Mr. Roosevelt are very interesting speci-
mens for the study of human nature and conduct. Mr. Roosevelt is a specialized politician; everything he says or does is
dominated by its vote-catching ability. Mr. Lewis is a stronger
person in certain respects and a cruder one. He harshly denounces those who oppose him with little regard for the
public opinion of the entire nation but with much regard
for the opinion of the members of his labor unions who,
being composed of men brought up under much the same
environmental influences as himself, have very similar beliefs. In addition he has a great desire for personal power.
His outburst sometime ago against Mr. Girdler, calling him
a megalomaniac, is but the reflection of Mr. Lewis' own desire for personal power, his resentment at having suffered a
defeat, and an attempt to make up by denunciation and noise
for what he could not do otherwise.

Both Mr. Lewis and Mr. Roosevelt are products of their
particular times, environments, and forms of activity. Both
believe they are great leaders, that their cause is just, that all
who oppose them are vicious and inspired by ignoble motives. It speaks poorly for our times when two men of such
characteristics can have the great power and influence they
possess.

Mr. Lewis is the worst enemy of the laboring man and
Mr. Roosevelt of the man in the street. Both claim to be
serving the poor worker. Instead, however, of delving deeply

into underlying causes, both Mr. Lewis and Mr. Roosevelt repeat prevailing thought. By this means they actually prevent the solution of pressing problems and cause harm instead. The American public has yet to learn that noise, bluster, denunciation, promises, and the expression of good intentions are insufficient to solve the problems of the day. It will require earnest effort on the part of men of ability.

Roosevelt, Lewis, and Farley are excellent examples of the influence of the environment in producing men reflecting it. All three flatter themselves that they are controlling many present-day forces. As a matter of fact they have been molded by these very forces.

Mr. Roosevelt and John L. Lewis are both excellent examples of the fact that as you think and act, so will you become. They both lack Primo and never admit making a fault. Both are seeking justice for the downtrodden and bringing about an era of good. Mr. Roosevelt, the smooth politician, looking to the herd for what will be popular, promising all things to all people, smiling pleasantly, talking sweetly, the great leader of democracy against all enemies. He has said this so much that he believes it himself.

Mr. Lewis is the product of violent labor agitation and an unhealthy labor atmosphere. He has undertaken to solve labor's problems by appealing to violence and by asking all laboring men to organize under his leadership. By intimidating capital he has sought to compel the payment of high wages and other benefits.

He has grown up in a vicious labor atmosphere and is unable to be fair. He knows little of economic laws and does not realize that the more he attacks capital the more unemployment he causes with more suffering to the laboring man. He is without fault.

We should give a little thought to these two men. They are the ones controlling our country's destiny at the moment. They are not men of high type or great ability. They are the product of forces which they believe they are controlling. They both attack wealth, create much ill-feeling and prevent the solution of the problems which they think they alone are capable of solving.

It is to be hoped that these two will be the last men of their types to become prominent in our country's affairs; that man's knowledge will soon be too great to permit mere herd reflectors to control their destiny; that man will realize that those who claim to be without fault are faulty and that only fools are always right.

Mr. Lewis is a product of conditions. He is not inherently a bad man. He has been made so by unsound social conditions. Mr. Lewis is punishing society for tolerating and permitting them to exist. Like so many misguided people he is bringing about greater ills than the ones he believes he is correcting.

Mr. Lewis shows evidence of personal feeling rather than union interest. He is envious of the big industrialists. He wishes to humiliate and make them grovel before him and thus exalt himself. He has the desire to be a big man and be looked up to.

To the close observer John L. Lewis has conducted himself in such way as to show, and has practically said on several occasions, that he is striving more for his own power than for the interests of labor. He is suffering from an inferiority complex and takes great pleasure in making the big industrial leaders humiliate themselves before him in asking his help in labor problems. It is pleasing to his childish desire for power to have able men consider him in the conduct of their affairs. If he is the best man labor can find to represent their interests, then God help labor. Truly labor unions are in a bad situation. The leaders of any movement are living examples by which it should be judged. Our labor leaders are a discredit to themselves and to the labor unions.

From the psychological standpoint, Mr. Lewis is a very interesting subject. A man's past experiences and desires tend to build up a mental set in a definite fixed direction. One can almost predict the response of the individual to these acquired beliefs, which may or may not be true. If he is subjected to true influences throughout his life, his beliefs will be true.

Mr. Lewis has been brought up in a labor atmosphere; his outlook is limited by his past experiences and the set which his mind has taken is rigid. He can see virtue in no measures other than those he advocates. He himself is unwilling to modify his beliefs. He is certain in his own mind that they, and they alone, are the correct ones.

Man today the world over is being governed by just such beliefs; beliefs established that are in accord with the individuals' personal experiences, wishes and likes. He establishes that which is congenial to him or to his class and condemns that which he does not understand or which contradicts. If we can impress this fact upon all and establish an environment that will be conducive to truth alone, we can have all acquire beliefs based upon truth. We can have all establish a mental set that will further truth.

This set viewpoint established by Mr. Lewis is a common thing in human affairs. Mr. Lewis has been brought up in an environment of labor activity. He has seen much of the abuses suffered by his fellow workers. He has talked with them, has read labor literature, and has absorbed the labor atmosphere of labor unions. He does not consider all other complex economic and social problems bearing on labor. He considers only the organization of laboring men into unions which will compel capital and their employers to serve them.

This viewpoint is unsound because of failure to consider many things far remote from the welfare of labor to the casual glance but imperative to its prosperity. Mr. Lewis is no more at fault in establishing such a viewpoint than are many others.

Our religious leaders earnestly endeavoring to serve man have developed such great regard for the Bible, Christ, Christianity, and their church as to prevent understanding of the causes of human ills. One who attempts to improve social conditions based upon positive knowledge would have to attack the church and its teachings ruthlessly. He would be bitterly opposed by most of the church people who are themselves striving for the same aim. The church leaders, like the labor leaders, are short-sighted, lack understanding, and are harming man.

If we develop a mental set based upon truth and develop the ability to see the remote causes producing our ills, we can bring about a more wholesome viewpoint. It should be apparent to any sensible person that neither labor unions nor present-day religious teachings have solved our problems or will solve them.

A solution must be obtained from an unprejudiced disinterested viewpoint, an earnest seeking for the truth, a willingness to sacrifice present interests for the future, a willingness to serve man and not demand service. Here again we notice the similarity between Mr. Lewis and the average minister. Mr. Lewis claims to be serving man, the average minister claims to be serving man, yet both demand that they be served.

Labor Royalists

Labor royalists are those people who worship labor and the laboring man. They believe he can do no wrong under any consideration. They do not believe that sit-down strikers who convert private property to their own use are violating either legal or moral rights. They do not believe that anything done by labor unions on strike can injure the public or that the public should object to any conduct, however vicious, on the part of labor unions. Labor royalists have no regard for others. They are themselves their own greatest enemies, fighting against their own best interests, by employing measures which will harm them in the long run. They think it perfectly right for strikers to put a picket line about a plant, arm themselves with baseball bats or clubs, and beat back law-abiding citizens who wish to go in to work, denying them the rights guaranteed by the Constitutions. Labor royalists believe that any labor union has the right to vio-

late all the laws of the country for any reason or no reason.
The mere name of labor gives it a holy sound which should
cause all to fall down on their knees and worship it.

Labor Serfs

The efforts of our reformers, our politicians, and our
Wisho liberals have resulted in making capital and the employers serfs to labor agitators. Past history shows that persecution and the production of serfs entails bad consequences
to a nation permitting them. They break out in rebellion
sometime against unjust treatment. The existence of serfs
whose sole duty is to serve others in an unthinking, blind
way, with no right to control their actions, is destructive to
the development of healthful institutions within that nation.

Whether these new-type serfs that labor has created will
submit forever remains to be seen. Unlike the serfs of old,
they have ability and intelligence. The old governments
could ride roughshod over their ignorant serfs unless an
able leader could bring about intelligently controlled action
on their part. It is not likely that our ablest citizens will
blindly submit to permanent serfdom without protest. If
they do, they deserve to remain serfs.

Gripe

A society that creates and permits itself to be controlled
by such creatures as Farley, Roosevelt, and Lewis is not deserving of survival.

XLVI

GRIPES

A BRIEF NOTICE IN ONE OF OUR WEEKLY NEWS MAGAZINES illustrates clearly the type of men who conduct our government. In one case the lieutenant governor of a state during the absence of a governor, called in the governor's secretary and ordered a conference of the state utility companies' magnates. When both the secretary and the utility executives declined, he denounced the state governor for lack of cooperation and jealousy.

The other case was also that of a lieutenant governor creating an uproar over the difference in salary as lieutenant governor and as acting governor for several periods during which the governor of the state was absent from state territory.

One constantly sees similar exhibitions on the part of our politicians. Sometime ago there was a miniature civil war in New Orleans because of a controversy between the governor of the state and the mayor of the city. Quite recently there was a controversy in Rhode Island in which the governor of the state proclaimed martial law on a race track, and turned out state troops to advance personal aims despite decisions of a state court.

We see our politicians discrediting themselves in a infinite number of ways, allied with criminal gangs, abusing anyone or anything that will attract votes, yet claiming to serve the people. How long will the American public stand for this? This is not democracy. It is not decent government.

They do not furnish an example of good citizenship. Let us eliminate these unworthy men and demand that our public servants be men of character and ability, worthy of respect and confidence.—*January 7, 1938.*

Whenever I pass an elderly scrubwoman, scrubbing stairways and floors in the hotel, I am impelled to do something to express my appreciation of her courage, and her willingness, to perform unpleasant menial tasks to support herself. A poor old woman, striving with her feeble strength to maintain herself by her own efforts.

By very contrast, the thing that most maddens me today is the unscrupulous efforts of our politicians to obtain this poor woman's support by denouncing the wealthy and telling her that they and they alone are endeavoring to lighten her burden. To me it is self-evident that they have not lightened her burden. There she is, scrubbing, expending her puny, feeble strength to obtain a mere existence.

At this very moment politicians are smoking fine cigars, denouncing the wealthy, enjoying government salaries and service; paid for in part by taxes which in their final effect press down upon the poor scrubwoman. If the politicians were accomplishing what they say they are, that poor feeble old woman would not be scrubbing.

It is not capital that is exploiting labor in our country today. It is these low, vicious, loathsome demagogic politicians who are exploiting the poor scrubwoman. While doing it they try to convince her that they and they alone are her benefactors. This thought so maddens me that at times I feel inclined to get a gun, get such men as I can to follow me, and start a wholesale slaughter of politicians. Not a pleasant thought for a plain citizen; not idealistic; just pure savagery. The savagery of the jungle aroused by a still more vicious savagery cloaked under the guise of good intentions.

—*January 8, 1938.*

I am utterly disgusted by continuous denunciation emanating from members of our national government. They have been in control of the affairs of the country for five years. If conditions are bad, unquestionably they are to blame in some way. Do they admit this? No. They denounce the bogey-man, capital, the wealthy, in an endeavor to distract public opinion from their own shortcomings.

—January 3, 1938.

Continuous denunciation of capital is very similar to continuous and prolonged advertising campaigns. When convincing talkers extol the merits of Tums, Carters Little Liver Pills, and Lydia Pinkham's Vegetable Compound, they influence a certain number of feebleminded people into believing that there is merit in these products. This belief is established by convincing and repeated extolment of them. Our consistent denunciation of capital and big business has the same effect. Many feebleminded people believe it, because of constant repetition. This is further supported by a willingness to have a scapegoat upon which to blame one's own failure in life.

Members of the administration have recently been accusing big business of a capital strike. They blame business for the existing recession. Whenever I see people blaming others for poor results and assuming no blame themselves, claiming that all merit, all intelligence is on their part, I very promptly and properly conclude that they are distorting the facts. In the absence of further information I would be inclined to believe that the accuser is more guilty than the accused. The administration has been attacking capital for the past five years, calling big businessmen names, levying heavy taxes upon them, restricting their activities by government regulations, and has failed to protect them against labor agitators.

If I were a businessman or a business manager, I would withdraw from all participation in business. That is my own personal feeling. Last spring for instance, when sit-down strikers had possession of General Motors plants, had I been Mr. Knudsen I would have promptly resigned my position with the General Motors Corporation. My feeling would be that if I am entrusted with the management of a large business, I will perform its duties to the best of my ability. I would consider that fair treatment of employees is essential to efficient management. When, however, employees supported by the government violate the law and forcibly occupy the plant under my jurisdiction, I would consider that it was unfair to me to have anything further to do with a business, or government, or strikers who assume to dictate my policies by intimidation; who assume no responsibility for their acts whereas I was supposed to be responsible but had lost power to control.

Our big business men have a far higher sense of public duty than I have but they are also short-sighted. They possess a desire to keep industry running in order to keep people employed which is commendable. On the other hand, their efforts permit an incompetent government to exist. The sooner this government is discredited, the sooner it will be possible for sensible men to obtain control and carry out sensible measures.—*January 12, 1938.*

Most of our labor leaders, politicians, and American Legionnaires are racketeers laboring under a cloak that conceals their object. They are legal racketeers, whereas criminals are not. They claim good motives which the criminals cannot well do. Who is the most dangerous? They are all alike in their general aim to get all they can for themselves regardless of the rights of others. How can we control or

even censure legitimate racketeers when so many of our
people have similar motives and tolerate them in others?

The low estate of our politics is shown by the class of
people who assemble as delegates to the national conventions
of both parties. What terrible creatures! If our country depends on them for guidance, may God help us! They are
far below the average of any group of self-respecting workingmen in their conduct, standards, and intelligence. The
antics they display on the convention floor would be a discredit to schoolboys at play. They resemble the orgies of
savages. Canned applause for their candidates, yelling, crying, screaming for hours at a time, making much noise in an
endeavor to make up for lack of character and ability. An
able man does not have to employ noise to convince others
that he is able. On the contrary. Have we had able men
come from a nominating convention? Just ballyhoo artists,
good at promising everything to everyone, spending money
that they do not own, the while condemning those who made
it. And we stand for such creatures controlling our affairs!
One may well wonder if there is any manhood in America.
I believe, hope, it is slumbering in disgust and will yet assert
itself.

Observation of the conduct of representatives and senators inspires one with disgust and the feeling that democracy
is a failure when it cannot find better men to conduct its
affairs. They all seek popular applause, demonstrating on
the floors of the House and Senate their interest in the
common man, their desire to help him, and be his friend.
They show the greatest enthusiasm for measures that redound to their glorification. The publication of the Congressional Record, with the insane remarks contained
therein, is a discredit to the country.

The congressmen and senators act more like schoolboys

than sensible men. Strangely enough we hear little criticism of them. Their most inane remarks are published in the newspapers, scattered broadcast throughout the country, and given serious attention. They contain promises for the under-dog, denunciation of the rich, a determination to persecute the wealthy tax evaders—just a lot of demagogic appeals to the voters.

When we see the low standing of intelligence in the coun-try, the poor environment, the labor troubles, the relief, the distress, we have not far to seek to locate the cause. It is in the halls of Congress. If these men were as able as their promises, these conditions would not exist. No effective re-form of any kind can be made in the United States with such men in control. We must find men with brains and character to direct our government.

When these politicians have made a failure of things, they will admit no error on their part. It will still be the wealthy men and capital who are at fault. Think this over a minute. They control the government, control the country. Should they not be able to control capital? Denouncing capital is a means of using it as a scapegoat, trying to conceal from the voters their own incapacity by blaming others.

Anyone with any understanding of human nature knows that it is the weakling, the incompetent, who is always ready to blame others for his errors. Only a fool never makes mis-takes. By this line of reasoning all our senators and congress-men are fools, and we are being governed by fools.

One wonders whether our politicians are not riding for a great fall. The prestige of the administration, of Congress and the Senate, is great. The patriotic citizen does not care to attack his own government. He wishes to be proud of it. He has heard much talk from reformers and well-meaning people about the evils of the day, and is led to believe that his Congressmen and government are taking steps to correct them.

When, and if, he realizes that they are just a lot of muddlers making bad matters worse, his resentment is likely to be aroused in a very angry form. So far he has not shown the intelligence of the average hog. You cannot feed a hog on promises. He will come to the trough if there is food there, and he may come a few times if he is just promised food and does not find it. Unlike the American public, he will not believe promises without tangible results. Some day, it is to be hoped, the American public will attain equal intelligence.

What a disgraceful exhibition when our president, cabinet, senators, representatives, and high-salaried government officials get together to praise a political manipulator to the skies because he has put them in office and assists in maintaining them at the public expense; a machine politician paid by the public but serving the politicians. What a low institution democracy has become in our country!

We are being ruled by those who can holler, scream, yell, and create the most noise. They are so successful in this as to convince themselves that they are great men. They prevent others from seeing their blunders because of the noise they make. They drown out all opposition, less by logic than by mere volume of ballyhoo. Meanwhile the problems they claim to be solving remain unsolved; their efforts to solve them are creating new ones that are worse. They, the virtuous politicians, are leading the fight against the vicious capitalist, who is the cause of it all. The poor capitalist! What a vicious person he is! No friends, no virtue, nothing to do but support those who oppress him, pay the taxes, shoulder the abuse, be the scapegoat for the blunders of the politicians. Should we not give the poor fellow a chance? If the public must hate someone, why not hate the politicians and let the capitalists go on with their labor of feeding and supporting the nation unhindered by the politicians?

Democracy in the United States has reached an all-time low. Politicians who control the government retain themselves in office by exchanging benefits for votes. This burden has reached a critical stage and will soon crash. It will take a far abler government to meet this crisis than our present-day politicians can furnish.

A gathering of farmers has expressed its disapproval of the expenditure of public money to increase the navy. They object to this not with regard to the measure itself, but for the reason that they fear that if the government spends so much money on armaments, it will be unable to continue the payments now being made to them. If we could have a much lower standard of citizenship, I do not know just what it would be.

The most alarming fact to me about this situation is that no one raises his voice to point out the viciousness of such conduct. Not only does it lower the standard of citizenship, but in the long run, short-sighted, selfish policies will exact their revenge. Does anyone try to tell the public this—our educators, our scientists, our politicians, our leaders anywhere? Not one.

Why try to do anything for such people? Let them go their way, suffer from their ill-advised acts. See what becomes of our much lauded democratic institutions. They have clearly proven their unworthiness when they have produced the standards of citizenship we now have in our nation; when they have produced such an utter lack of leaders of character or ability. Let the democratic institutions perish. Why save them? The people themselves are unworthy of the effort. They demand service but with equal vigor refuse to serve. America, you are doomed!—*January 29, 1938.*

If our politicians were statesmen they would delve into economic problems, acquire a thorough mastery of them,

pass legislation that would ensure obtaining adequate reports from all firms so that profits, wages, and taxes would
all be clearly shown. By this means it would be possible to
determine whether labor was being abused; whether capital
was taking more than its share. It would not be difficult to
do this; a simple matter of business.

By having reports of the same nature, all essential facts
could be embodied in very simple form. If this were done,
and the facts presented to the public, it would show that
labor was receiving its full share of the profits of business
and industry and that capital was not receiving more than
it should. It would show, however, that enormous sums were
being paid by capital and the well-to-do to the government
in the form of taxes.

Economic problems are not difficult to solve if an effort
be made to solve them. They are made the football of political controversy. The capitalist is the universal scapegoat at
all political gatherings. Labor leaders join in to substantiate
their demands for benefits, the simple minded liberal talkers
and writers join in because they do not have brains enough
to know any better. The situation is muddled up beyond
understanding simply because no one adequate to the task
and able to command the resources of the government has
appeared to work out a solution.

We cannot hope to solve our economic problems with a
lot of low-grade politicians more interested in office than in
the welfare of the country. They have not the ability to solve
the problems anyway. We must have men of brains and
character to govern this country if we want to have it well
governed. If you expect to have an operation you select a
good surgeon. For the conduct of our government, instead
of able honest men, we get fellows who can smile, promise,
alibi, and denounce capital.

The inane news items seen in our newspapers disgust me.
This morning for instance I see a headline reading, "Lewis

declares Dubinsky acts like Lot's wife." This is the man who is directing the destinies of labor. That is the sort of headlines our newspapers put before the public. Either we will have to establish higher standards among our citizens, find worthwhile leaders, prevent the circulation of such inanities, or in time all civilized men will be morons.

—January 13, 1938.

There is a great similarity between politicians, labor leaders, and the Japanese military. All alike exhibit primitive thought which sees merit only in themselves and viciousness in all who oppose. Public opinion condemns the conduct of the Japanese in China. We would do well to place our own house in order before condemning others. Contemptible as the Japanese militarists are, they are no more contemptible than our own savages. Both threaten man's future. Both must be curbed if decency and order is to prevail in the world.—*December 28, 1937.*

I am tired of hearing the same old platitudes, the constant repetitions from all sources of a lot of fine intentions. Why don't these people tumble to the fact that this has been done for a long enough time to prove the futility of their efforts and that someone must do some real thinking and work if any improvement is to be made? While disgusted at the apathy of the common citizen, I sometimes feel that he is displaying great intelligence in ignoring the ballyhoo and tumult stirred up by a lot of people who don't know what they are talking about. There is a great opportunity for someone with brains to do some real thinking. He will just about have a corner on the market and be able to do about as he wishes in the world. There would be practically no competition. Whatever our civilization may be accomplishing, it is failing to produce sensible people within it.

George III was a piker as compared to our present-day rulers. Our forefathers rebelled against his action more for an abstract interference with their liberties than actual oppression. Today we are permitting our liberties, our rights, to be taken from us by our own elected officials. George III never interfered with the right of a man to work. In our country today that right is being consistently interfered with. Men are not permitted to work unless they obey the dictates of labor agitators seeking personal aggrandizement. Truly the government of George III, against which our forefathers rebelled, was conducted upon a higher degree of regard for the individual than our present one.

I am just a common ordinary citizen aroused to the most extreme disgust by the conduct of those men who are now entrusted with the leadership of the nation. They can only denounce and belittle others and exalt themselves and their measures. They do not solve today's problems. They spread ill-feeling, encourage violence and class hatred. They spread before the public inane propaganda clothed in an attractive form which prevents understanding of the issues. It is not the nation who should be quarantined. The people as a whole are sensible and will respond to able leadership. It is the insane leaders of the nations who should be placed where they can do no harm. Let the people follow a leader who knows where he is going.

Rarely does the ability to think exist in conjunction with noise. The noisy people who have been talking for years can do naught but talk. We should cease to listen to their chatter and find doers capable of doing something of value. Find thinkers able to think. If we desert the noisy and seek capable doers and thinkers they can be found. They exist, but are obscured by the fog of existing noise, denunciation and insane vaporings generally.

Our ministers, our reformers and our politicians are similar in many ways. All alike are crying for benefits for man, extolling their own virtues, telling others to worship them and do as they wish. What we want in our religion is people who will set an example in their own lives and will assist others in getting some joy out of life, not denouncing or belittling.

We have ministers who denounce war. At the same time they try to disarm the nation and thus make war inevitable. They also denounce foreign rulers and stir up ill-feeling abroad. The utter stupidity of such methods is beyond belief. Suppose they did disarm our country and continued to denounce foreign rulers. These foreign rulers would send troops over here and require them to get on their knees and worship them. These are the men who are trying to teach our young generation how to live.

I lose all patience with these fellows who are running about demanding that the world follow in their footsteps and do as they say. The people we should follow are those who mind their own business, who live a decent life, have a little fun and do their duty. These people who go about shouting their virtues, attacking all the evils in the world, telling everybody to follow their methods and do as they say are the ones we should lock up in an insane asylum. We should prevent them from polluting the atmosphere with their crazy teachings. Turn the present inmates of the insane asylums loose; they are relatively harmless.

To effect practical sensible reforms in our social institutions will require the use of intelligent physical force. It will require substantially the exercise of something approaching dictatorship. While this force will be necessary to restrain the ignorant, the vicious and those who wish to resort to violence, it is far more essential that it be used to restrain the infinite number of pseudo-reformers continually advocating measures that require the expenditure of money. They place burdens on the country and industry, and cause harm generally. These sentimental impractical people must be suppressed by force.

Not the least are the sky pilots who claim to be serving God and demand that man follow them. When we permit our public opinion and policies to be created by such fools it is hopeless to expect sensible action. Their insane meanderings have so permeated public opinion generally that nothing less than brute force can eradicate it.

The need for this appeal to physical force has been brought about by these fools who worship democracy and free speech; who wish to reform the vicious, help anybody and anything. Their foolish ideas are just the opposite of nature's laws. Nature eliminates the weaklings. Our reformers demand that the strong carry the weakling on their backs. The sooner the strong rebel and refuse to carry the weaklings, the better for man's future happiness and development.—*January 12, 1938.*

XLVII

JEWS

JEWS ARE RECEIVING PERSECUTION IN MANY COUNTRIES TODAY. There is some feeling against them in our own country. This somewhat universal feeling against Jews indicates the existence of certain qualities in them as a race that cause friction. The Jews will advance their own interest if they seek their own shortcomings and endeavor to correct them. The friends of Jews will be rendering them a great service if they point out tendencies that arouse ill-feeling.

It is in this spirit that this brief discussion of Jews is given here. To cover the Jewish question in detail would require a very extended discussion which would include their past history and religion. This discussion is intended to point out certain obvious unwholesome tendencies without going into detail in tracing their development.

A serious criticism against many Jews in this country from the standpoint of citizenship may be expressed by saying they are Jews first and Americans second. Many Americans, whose outlook is entirely American, feel, and with reason, that many Jews are not as whole-heartedly American as they. When justification for this belief ceases, and all Jews are as whole-heartedly American as are other Americans, much of the feeling against them would cease to exist. All individuals of the Jewish race would do well to develop Primo and Extro; strive to see what is going on in the minds of non-Jews. They could readily see why many Jews give rise to ill feeling

and criticism, and that the Jews themselves are the ones who
can do most to correct this situation.

Feeling against the Jews is in part one of resentment
against those who take, keep, and fail to give to the community a fair return for value received. The Jews' Co is for
his own group, not outsiders. This is only natural. Many
other groups have the same quality, but because the Jews
are of a different religion and possess somewhat similar
racial characteristics, feelings of all other groups can more
readily be aroused against them. The Jews would be far better citizens in a country of their own than they now are as
members of a minority group among other nationalities.

Many highly desirable citizens among the Jews in the
United States unwittingly contribute to racial feeling. It is
natural for the Jews to place their race before the country they live in, and natural for Americans to resent it.
Jews as a class lack Primo somewhat more than the average American. They fail to see the viewpoint of the other
person. When a Jewish leader makes belittling remarks
about the American public and the persecution the Jews
are receiving, it cannot be well received by American citizens. When the Jews raise this question they are creating
it themselves. It is very short-sighted for a racial minority
to blatantly denounce the majority in a country which has
given them the privilege of shelter. They will endanger the
privileges of citizenship by abusing them.

When it becomes necessary for candidate for the office of
mayor of the largest city in the United States to conciliate
the Jewish vote by denouncing those who oppress the Jews,
we are introducing the racial element in American politics.
This is a cheap political trick. It is a very natural instinct
of any race to support those who attack their oppressors.
Nevertheless the Jews are being very short-sighted in permitting their racial feelings to be appealed to in politics. If
the Jews are such poor citizens as to give their adherence to
politicians who appeal to racial feelings having no bearing

upon conditions in the United States, they demonstrate their undesirability as citizens.

They are a very slight minority in this country although strong in New York City. It would be a relatively simple task to disfranchise the Jews. The Jews are now receiving equal rights with all other citizens. They should carefully avoid taking action, however slight, that presents them in an unfavorable light, that will arouse prejudice, that may involve the loss of these rights and perhaps persecution. Race feeling can very easily be aroused and those groups likely to receive it who are in a great minority show good judgment in carefully refraining from any action tending to arouse it.

The unwillingness of Jews to admit faults in themselves and their great willingness to charge undue persecution and discrimination is unquestionably developed from their past history, religious teaching, and environmental influences generally. Their religion quite commonly devotes much attention to their history and the oppression and persecution they have suffered at the hands of other races.

An enlightened viewpoint would realize that there are two sides to this question, that the Jews have not been without fault, and the other races have not been without virtue. If the Jewish religion, the Jewish people, the Jewish institutions, would adopt this broad, healthful viewpoint, encourage their people to seek faults within themselves, to find virtues in other races and other religions, they would be greatly improved in conduct. There would then be less complaint about Jews considering themselves before the rest of humanity regardless of merit. If the Jews themselves seek faults in themselves and correct them, they will be far finer individuals. They will then cause less friction and there will be less justification for discrimination against them.

It is very ungenerous for Jews to attack American institutions, to claim persecution, unjust discrimination, and other mistreatment. Worthy Jews are not discriminated against, and have achieved wealth and success in this country. The Jew himself, by his hypersensitiveness, creates the very thing he denounces.

Much feeling against Jews in this country has been aroused by the conduct of recent immigrants who have been the victims of persecution. These Jews have consideration for their immediate circle but they do not have proper consideration for those outside their circle. They do not adequately appreciate the free asylum granted them in this country. They are too willing to make money by unfair trade practices.

The most obnoxious Jews lack sensitivity. They lack the ability to understand the feelings of others. These Jews are notoriously discourteous. This results in the entire Jewish nation being penalized for their misconduct.

General Grant was so incensed at the conduct of Jewish cotton traders during the Civil War that he promulgated an order expelling them from the territory under his jurisdiction. General Grant was a very fair man. Such conduct on his part shows that these Jewish traders were guilty of practices justifying his action. This criticism is not necessarily limited to Jews alone. Any race that has been persecuted will, of necessity, resort to all means to protect itself. We see any number of foreigners abusing the freedom granted in America. They seek personal gain only. They see no obligation to the community.

There are very poor-type individuals among Jews just as there are among other nationalities. We should not condemn Jews as a race. We should condemn the undesirable of all races. The standard of citizenship and conduct among American citizens is not so high as to justify us in condemning other races or nations for their shortcomings.

The feeling against Jews is less because of their race of itself than the combination of race with culture, religion and language. When a distinct racial group perpetuates a culture, religion, and language different from that of the country in which they reside, they will arouse some feeling against them. This feeling will depend in great measure upon their merit and the extent to which they permit their interests to prejudice those of others.

The existence of Jews as a separate racial group in the nation, perpetuating culture, religion, and language of their own is reminiscent of the loyalty of primitive tribes. Like the Japanese, the Jews are not as good citizens of other nations as they would be for their own nation. But unlike the Japanese, this condition could be corrected with relative ease. If the Jews would abandon their culture, religion, and language, their racial differentiation would soon disappear. This could be accomplished quite readily if a universal religion in accord with science and appealing to the better human qualities were developed. Causes for friction would then cease and they would become as one with other inhabitants of the country. This condition is approached now by the higher-type Jews. Those who arouse the greatest feeling are the ones who pursue self-interest to the prejudice of the rights of others.

XLVIII

NEGROES

GOOD-INTENTIONED PEOPLE ARE OFTEN CRUEL IN SOME OF THE reforms they bring about. For illustration—it is very cruel and inconsiderate to take a backward race living simple lives and educate the young children to have desires impossible of fulfillment. As the result, instead of living happy, carefree lives they live resentful, unhappy ones. In their simple way of living they did not know enough to be dissatisfied. Now with the education that has been thrust upon them they are discontented with their lot, but they do not have the opportunity to improve it. These are practical conditions which should be faced in dealing with human affairs.

We have this very situation in the United States in attempting to educate and elevate the negro race. Many negroes are responding and achieving a certain amount of success, but on the other hand, the conduct of the average negro is worse than in the slave days. They would be better off as a race under the control of an aristocratic form of government dominated by white people. If negroes were not educated they would not be discontented with their lot and, as a race, would be happier.

The bad feature of educating colored backward races is psychological. They feel marked off by color. When they acquire knowledge they all too readily demand association on equal terms with whites, and insist that whites take them up socially. From a practical viewpoint, both races would be better off if the negro remained uneducated and ignorant.

He would then cease to aspire to social equality and would not create social problems.

The worth of a man should not be his color or race but his just deserts, his real worth, moral character, and intelligence. Unquestionably many negroes are far superior to many of our white people. We must, however, take a practical viewpoint of this matter, realizing that the Anglo-Saxon does have race feeling against negroes, and does not care to be intimately associated with them. He should be protected in this right.

In seeking the solution of the negro problem, we should be guided by intelligence and the laws of nature. Present-day civilization was entirely created by the white man. The negroes have contributed little to civilization. The fruits of civilization should be enjoyed by those producing them. Attempts to educate and elevate the negro to the white man's stature are opposed to nature's laws. Instead of providing for the survival and development of the fittest, we are devoting much effort to the development of those whose past history has shown them to be unable to produce a civilization of their own. Having thus failed themselves they should not be permitted to become a burden upon the white race. They should not be permitted to demand the benefits of the civilization they themselves were unequal to the task of producing.

Negroes when living among fellow negroes fail to contribute a great deal to civilization. Some, under an environment dominated by white people, make fine citizens largely because of the uplifting effect of association with the white race. As a race the negroes have not contributed to the advance of man, and should not receive more consideration than they merit. In evaluating races, those who have contributed most to man's advance should receive first consideration, those who have done little should receive little. This would result in the worthy becoming more worthy. They should not be held back by foolish efforts to raise backward races. Let each raise himself, not penalize the abler by requiring that they raise others. Many well-meaning people desire to help the negroes by laws.

Let them help themselves, care for themselves. If they are deserving, let them prove so.

The negro problem in the United States is an entirely different one from that in Brazil. I am informed that there is no feeling whatever against negroes in Brazil, and that they are received among the white people without discrimination. This is not true in the United States. Therefore the handling of the problem in the two nations should be entirely different. A racial problem of this kind is very difficult of solution and requires great ability. In the United States we should consider the white race first, as they are the controlling element and the one that has built the nation up to its present greatness.

Educating the negro and giving him all the advantages for self-improvement and development prejudices the interests of the white man. For every negro advanced to a high position, a white man is penalized. Sentimental attempts to correct all ills and do justice to all men will result in creating more and worse ills. The future of this country is in the hands of the white man. He should not be thrust downward by any race, regardless of the high motives of those advocating such action.

It is in the solutions of problems of this nature that our sentimental well-meaning reformers are inadequate. They wish to help but always at the expense of those who will not need help if permitted to work out their own destinies. The white man throughout the United States is being held back, his development retarded, by the presence of negroes within our borders. However nice it may sound to elevate them, it is done at the expense of the white race.

The large mass of negroes in the country lowers the standard of living of the white man. Negroes have had a very bad effect upon the poor white man of the south, both in slavery days and at present. Their gradual emigration to the north is bringing about similar conditions there. The negro has the same effect on American labor standards as the immigration of several million Hindus or Chinese would have. Because of their lower standard of living and willingness to work for less, they would compete with the American worker and require him to work for less, thus lowering his standard of living. The full effect of the negro in lowering the standard of living of the white man is not shown to such a great extent because of the activity of the labor unions and of our social reform legislation in establishing minimum wages and hours. The general tendency is to cause more unemployment, but the effect is the same.

The vast majority of negroes are engaged in work of the simplest kind. This brings them in direct competition with the most poorly paid white workers. It is the poor classes of white people who are most severely penalized by being required to compete with the negro. The existence of so many negroes results in keeping wages for unskilled labor very low. Chambermaids, scrubwomen, must compete with negroes engaged in the same occupations. White men employed as ditch diggers and laborers must compete with negroes. As the result their wages are made far lower than they normally would be. If we could remove all negroes from the country, a great shortage of labor would result in the more unskilled classifications. As a result, a great increase in wages in the less well-paid callings would result. The well-to-do white people can avoid contact with the negro. The poor white people must compete with them and have their wages and standard of living reduced as a result.

As long as we have negroes in the country there will be a considerable amount of miscegenation. This occurs not among the best elements from both races but generally among the less desirable elements. The offspring are often undesirable, although there are some very splendid types of mixed blood. Just what the final outcome of this racial mixture will be, has yet to be determined. On the whole, it seems better for the white race to remain a pure white race—not absorb all racial groups with which it may come in contact, thus resulting in a mongrel race. A great nation should consist of one people,

with the same feelings and ideals and without racial animosity.

Absorbing people of less developed races by a highly developed race helps the less developed but tends to hinder
the progress of the highly developed race. This includes standards of living, of thought, culture, religion and behavior.
Efforts to raise all submerged peoples and races puts too great
a burden on the advanced race, tends to lower their standards,
and may prevent the highest attainable standards from prevailing.

Comparing New York with what it was some twenty years
ago, the thing that impresses me most is the changing character of the citizens. There are far more negroes and colored
people generally. One sees negroes everywhere. The attitude
of the average citizen toward the negroes is in general that he
should be treated fairly. They do not devote much thought
to the subject or ask why he is there. They accept the fact
of his being there and try to treat him fairly. They do not
care to associate with him while perfectly willing to permit
him to live his own life as long as he does not annoy them.

This influx of the negroes is bringing about many problems
and it would be well if the American citizen would pause and
think of the future. It may sound well to talk about giving
the negroes the rights of everybody else and assisting them,
but how about the white people who need assistance, who are
forced to compete with the negro?

Races that differ much in structure, outlook, had better be
segregated and kept to themselves. No friction or ill feeling
will then arise. It is expecting too much when we ask them
to live side by side without friction or ill-feeling of any kind.
There are enough difficult problems in the world to be solved
without unnecessarily creating others, such as racial hatred
and rivalry. The best way to avoid friction is to remove
contact.

The best solution to this problem, to my mind, is in the
removal of the negro from the country. Negroes by nature
are a tropical race. The very color of their skin was developed

as a means of resisting the Sun's rays. Therefore they belong in the tropics and should not infringe upon the white man's area in the temperate zones. While a costly process, emigration should be employed to remove the negroes from this country. Vast unsettled areas exist in the Amazon Valley, in Colombia, Venezuela, the West Indies, and Yucatan, readily accessible to the United States.

Another solution would be to place the negroes entirely under the domination of the white people, establishing in the southern states in the cotton belt an aristocratic form of government in which the white people are the overseers and the negroes the workers, much similar to what the conditions in the old slave days were except that slavery would not be tolerated and the negro would be fairly treated.

The negro is far better off and happier in a condition of simple ignorance, doing as the white man tells him, than he is made by education and social welfare legislation designed to raise him to social equality with the white man. The best friend the negro ever had was the better-class white planter of the south who knew him, cared for him, controlled him, and utilized his services to advantage.

The advance of negroes since the abolition of slavery has not all been for the better. Some of the finest type darkies I have known were the old slaves. They were courteous and well behaved in contrast to the aggressive, self-assertive young negroes of today who demand full equality with white people.

One solution of the negro problem would be afforded by one hundred per cent birth control by negroes. Permit them to have no children. As the present negroes disappear, their race will not be perpetuated by offspring. This will be attacked bitterly by well-intentioned sentimental people, but who in the United States will not admit that the country would be better off without the negro? The removal of the negroes would better the economic status of the white man. While there are some able negroes, on the whole their standard of living is below that of the white people. Their elimination would increase the per capita wealth and general prosperity of the nation.

Elevating the inferior tends to lower the superior. It is better for the superior to strive alone without this handicap, and let the inferior raise themselves by their own efforts. Giving the negro full rights, votes, and other civil privileges tends to lower the white man. No legislation that does this should be tolerated. The future of America depends on the white man, not the negro. Where their interests conflict, the interests of the white man should prevail.

The marked reluctance of Anglo-Saxons to associate with negroes should be considered as a practical matter. Opposition by liberal thinkers to disfranchising the negro does not consider the harm that is being caused to the white race by giving him the vote. If he did not vote, much cause of friction would be removed, and racial animosity would be less.

When, after the Civil War, the negroes were given the right to vote and a large part of the white people of the south were prevented from voting, resulting in the carpetbag governments, the south got a demonstration of what negro government could be. When they managed to get control of the government again, they took steps to prevent negroes from voting. This has had a bad influence on the south. The relations of the two races would be much better if the negroes had no right to vote. Giving the negroes the vote adds another group to be conciliated and adds nothing to the strength of the voting public.

The negroes are now becoming a strong voting minority in the northern states, so strong as to require the politicians to consider their interests. The Democratic party has been courting the negro vote very assiduously in the North of late, and the negroes hold the balance of power in many states. This is very likely to be turned against them some day, resulting in race feeling. We have many other interest groups in the nation, but racial interest groups are far more vicious than others. Resentment is more easily aroused against them.

Negro politicians and white politicians alike are being very short-sighted in permitting this situation to develop.

That the dread in the South of negro domination has sound basis is shown by the large negro minorities in Chicago and New York City. Both these groups demand legislation to benefit their race, and are not wholesome influences in either locality. Negro communities in our large cities, or in any locality where negroes congregate in large numbers as a solid group, are not a contribution to society.

Negroes differ in ability and character just as do any other race. The finest type negroes are the equal of white men, and the lowest type negroes are very poor indeed. To what extent negroes possess the abilities to carry on a civilization of their own without white support is debatable. As a race they are not equal to the average American mentally, are less inclined to provide for the future and are more primitive.

The negro has not yet governed any country in an enlightened manner. It is a question whether he can do so. It would be an excellent experiment to establish a negro country in some part of the world causing the ablest negroes the world over to emigrate there and see if they can contribute to civilization under their own leadership and control. On the whole they are not a contribution to this country. Their presence here has a bad effect in causing a racial problem and complicates many other problems. The white man is adversely affected economically and morally by the presence of negroes. The sole benefit is to the negro. He is being elevated by living among people of a higher culture, inheritance, and standards of living.

Negroes generally display the qualities of a more primitive race. They are more infantile, given to impulses, and less considerate of the rights of others when their feelings are aroused. This is true despite the fact that there are many splendid negroes who are fully considerate of other's rights. When we consider negroes as a race we must consider the general average.

The crime ratio for negroes is four or five times as great

as that of white people. Regardless of how fair we may desire to be toward the negroes, we are bound to conclude from this that they are not a desirable element in our population. Those familiar with conditions in slavery days as compared with the present will see that the cause of this crime increase is directly due to attempts to educate the negro.

Negroes as a race are more gross than the white race, more inclined to seek physical pleasure. The very high rate of venereal disease among negroes is a serious condition. This is one of the very undesirable features about the race and shows them to be less desirable citizens than white people.

The majority of Americans do not wish to associate with negroes or have their young girls attend schools or social functions with negroes, and justly so. The wishes of the majority should be respected, for they are the nation. The emigration of the negroes to the north and their settlement in white residential districts results in a loss in property values and causes the more respectable white people to move therefrom.

The many laws passed preventing the segregation of negroes in residential districts or public conveyances, and generally supporting them in forcing themselves upon white people in white establishment, are wrong. The better behaved negro does not care to force himself upon white people. Means should be employed to control those negroes who do not have much consideration for others and who assert their right to be with white people. The best interests of all will be served in recognizing the practical fact that the negroes are a separate race and should be prevented by law from annoying white people.

Negroes should not be permitted to force themselves upon white business establishments, places of amusement, or otherwise, when white people object. The owner of the business suffers by being required to serve negroes, as he loses the trade of his white customers by receiving negro patronage.

Protecting negroes in getting service in white establishments is unconstitutional when a man's business is thereby injured. This is a means of depriving one of property without due process of law. It has not been so interpreted by our courts. From the standpoint of equity and justice a man has the right to exclude negroes from being served in his establishment if by admitting them he loses his white clientele. Any business should have the legal right to limit its service to its most valued customers.

Negroes are presuming too far on the spirit of tolerance of the white people, many of whom feel it is unfair to discriminate against the negro in any way. This feeling is largely academic and applies more to white people not in touch with the negro problem and not required to associate with negroes. The vast majority of white people wish to treat the negro fairly, but his demands will inevitably turn feeling against him.

During the war, negroes brought pressure upon the War Department to prevent segregation of negro and white patients in army hospitals. This was even carried out in army hospitals located in southern states. What right have negroes to insist that white men occupy the same ward in a hospital with them? There is no justification for such action. They are demanding not fair treatment but intimate association.

Only recently negro organizations have been bringing pressure to bear on the Navy Department to have a battleship manned entirely by negroes. They advance the argument that there are twelve million negroes in the United States and that they should be given full representation in the navy. Their consideration for the navy is less to have it an efficient agency of national defense than to convert it into an agency for the glorification of the negro race.

Why should negro congressmen endeavor to force negroes upon the Annapolis Naval Academy and negro officers upon the American Navy? They do this claiming equality of rights. A more sensible viewpoint would be to recognize that they are arousing feeling against their race by such action and that negro officers in the American Navy are not wanted by the navy and would be an element of discord. Instead of increasing the efficiency of the navy, they would lessen it.

There are many fine, courteous, considerate negroes who would be a credit to the citizenship of any nation. If all negroes were of the same character as Professor Carver of Tuskegee, they would indeed be worthy of the highest respect. This man devotes his efforts toward constructive achievement. He does not demand social equality with white men. He does not consistently stir up agitation. He quietly works among his own people. He is deserving of the utmost respect just as negro agitators are deserving of the utmost contempt.

We also have many negroes who are continually asserting their equality with the white man, who demand the right to attend white universities and go to school with white people. We have negro women who demand service in white beauty parlors and negro politicians who secure the passage of laws in northern states preventing discrimination against negroes. These are the ones who create feeling against their race.

We have had negro politicians as members of Congress who spent most of their efforts to secure jobs for negroes and advancing negro interests, showing that their racial feeling is ahead of their duty as citizens. When they willingly foment class feeling and receive the support of other negroes, they will ultimately cause persecution of negroes. This will not be brought on by the white people, but as the result of the demands of negro agitators. The average white man has no objection to the negro going his way, making a living, but he does object strenuously to having negroes force themselves upon him.

XLIX

PACIFISM AND FORCE

THERE HAS DEVELOPED, IN THE MORE HIGHLY CIVILIZED countries having free institutions in the last few decades, a greater sympathy, a greater understanding, of human suffering and a desire to alleviate it. This feeling may be productive of much good if properly used. Its use requires, however, the employment of force in order that those people or those nations having less sympathy or understanding may be controlled. Many of our finest well-meaning people fail to recognize this. They wish to give the savage the same treatment to which they are accustomed, hoping and wishing that he will respond in kind. The savage must be treated as a savage. That is the only treatment which he understands. When we try to control him by sentimental, well-intentioned efforts, we will do more harm than good. We must face this fact frankly and treat less civilized people with the consideration their degree of civilization permits.

Pacifists are the worst enemies of world peace. The methods they advocate are sure to bring about war. People often have good intentions and, in attempting to carry them out, defeat their aim.

The horrors of war, the killing and maiming of millions, justify pacifists in attacking it. They could be a great influence for good in promoting sensible thought to prevent war if they were equal to it. Their methods are more harmful than if they did nothing. They treat effects, not causes. The problem will have to be solved by practical, sensible means. Paci-

fists are like our other impractical reformers who are bringing about future ills far worse than those they are trying to
correct. It is easy for any person to denounce war and its
horrors, to say it is cruel. We know that; talk does not help.
What we want is sensible action that will lessen the possibility of war.

Feebleminded Wisho liberal thinkers do more harm than
good in spreading doctrines such as passive resistance and
disarmament. They have good intentions but their measures
would be suicidal if carried out. We must recall that man
raised himself from savagery by the intelligent use of force.
We today must repress criminals by force. If we disarm our
own country, savage foreign nations may conquer us and
destroy our institutions.

Pacifists who demand that our army and navy be abolished
and denounce foreign dictators are protected by the very
army and navy they wish to abolish. Those who attack Hitler,
for instance, are protected from his returning the compliment
by our navy. If it did not exist, if he decided to hang them,
who would defend them? Their defense is the very men whom
they attack, men behind guns trained to obey, willing to die
upon the call of duty. It is not the soldiers or sailors who bring
about war. They give their lives. It is the incompetent rulers
whose orders they obey that have caused all wars.

Pacifists would do well if, instead of attacking that which
they do not understand, they would set a good example of
individual conduct and restrict their activities to those things
they do understand. These same pacifists object to the use of
force in restraining lawless elements in our own country.
Apparently any group of hoodlums has great virtue and
should be left to do as it pleases. They are stupid men claiming to be doing good for man, telling him how to behave
himself yet advocating measures that will destroy the very
civilization in which they live.

Substantially the attitude of many well-meaning pacifists
is, "War is evil. Better any kind of peace than war. Endure
anything rather than resist. The use of force in resistance

brutalizes. Civilization must be defended with the instruments of civilization. Resort to the instruments of barbarism makes you a barbarian." Let us think over these conclusions. If we adopt such a policy what should prevent the Japanese from conquering our country; crushing our free institutions; requiring us to worship the Mikado; requiring that the white race be subjected to miscegenation with the Japanese? The pacifists themselves would be ruthlessly destroyed and their policies with them. Our nation would then be required to serve and further Japanese conquest.

It is such insane policies as these that threaten future civilization. We have any number of people who have good intentions, who wish to do something to improve the common lot, but the methods they advocate are commonly fraught with the most serious consequences. Some sensible means should be found to curb war between nations. Methods that advocate that the finest, most civilized nations refuse to defend themselves are not sensible. It means that they will be conquered by the barbarians and converted into barbarians themselves. The opposite would be the more correct solution. Meet force with more force. Suppress violence with the use of greater violence. Let the civilized sensible nations cooperate and crush the uncivilized barbarians. Let us have peace, not by destroying civilized nations but by destroying barbarism.

When we adopt the policy of nonresistance to savages, we are reversing the advance of evolution. Instead of utilizing the agencies of civilization to perpetuate and further advance it, we are permitting savages to employ the agencies of civilization for the perpetuation of savagery. In effect, a policy of nonresistance to aggression will result in the domination of the adhuman by the prihuman, through the use of scientific instruments of destruction developed by the adhuman. Instead of using them himself, however, to subdue the prihuman, the pacifist refuses to adopt this sensible policy and permits these scientific agencies of destruction to be turned over to the prihuman for the destruction of civilization and progress. Instead of permitting the prihuman to dominate us, we should become adhumans in the fullest sense and dominate the prihuman by the use of methods capable of controlling him, brute force.

Our misguided but well-meaning pacifists advocate many ridiculous ways of preventing war. You will hear such expressions as, "We should defend our country only against attack, only use guns on our own territory to repel an enemy, and not permit our soldiers to be sent abroad on foreign land." To those not well versed in the military art, this sounds like a reasonable policy. Merely defending yourself against attack is not sufficient. Very often the best defense is an aggressive attack. If you remain still on your own land awaiting attack, the enemy can attack you in unexpected places. He can assemble his resources at will. He can strike at the heart of your strength while by the strictly defensive attitude on your part his territory is protected. When you get involved in war you must use all your power to crush your opponents, or be destroyed yourself.

Pacifists who callously look on while the Japanese kill, rape, and plunder in China, would feel differently if they were receiving the same treatment. Suppose that instead of the Japanese violating the Chinese girls, their own wives or daughters were receiving the same treatment? Yet that is the inevitable result to their children's children if their views prevail. How short-sighted and cruel!

There is a great difference in the heartless killing of innocent Chinamen by the Japanese and the summary action of Mussolini in Ethiopia in executing disturbers of the peace. Since Italy has conquered Ethiopia, she must maintain law and order. To do this among primitive people requires that brute force be employed against those guilty of offenses against constituted authority. The Japanese, however, have resorted to promiscuous mass murder against the most innocent Chinese. This is truly deplorable. Yet many liberals have condemned Mussolini for executing Ethiopians and express the wish and belief that the Japanese will civilize

China. And these are the people who claim to be serving man's future welfare!

As long as nations exist in the world possessing strong armies and navies governed by leaders only too willing to display their power, we must retain means to defend ourselves. Our efforts should be devoted toward bringing about a better understanding of the mutual interests of man, and only when the possibility of aggressive attacks upon us be lessened would it be permissible to reduce our power to repel them.

Not only should the individual develop Profito that he may profit from the past and avoid committing like errors, but civilization likewise should profit from the failure of past civilization. Unless this be done we will commit the same errors and may ourselves be destroyed. Because of failure to exercise Profito, civilizations have perished in the past, and unless we profit by their experience we ourselves will perish.

The tendency of ancient civilizations was to settle down, to lose their warlike spirit and, as the result, often to be overthrown by people less civilized but more savage and warlike. We have this same tendency in modern life in the form of pacifists opposing preparation for war on the part of our country, thus rendering us helpless when attacked by savages.

These well-meaning pacifists fail to visualize the effect of their acts. If they could exercise their pacifism on the savage races they would be doing some good, but the savages do not heed them, and many sentimental civilized people do. If their policies were carried out, we would not only be rendered unable to defend ourselves, but would invite attacks by our weakness, thus permitting ourselves to be destroyed, as many nations of the past have been.

We teach the savages to use the latest scientific weapons of destruction, rendering them more able to accomplish our destruction at a future date. We are giving them the benefits of our scientific knowledge in the control of disease, which results in an increase in their numbers. At the same time luxury is decreasing our own numbers, thus tending to place the savages in a position to overwhelm us both by numbers and by the use of the scientific weapons which we have given them and taught them to use. How stupid man can be! And yet the people advocating these measures are sincere in their beliefs and feel they are serving man. Their intentions are better than their intelligence.

The claim of many pacifists that disarming this country would help pacifism by encouraging other countries to disarm is an erroneous assumption under existing conditions. It would weaken the real interests of world peace by giving us less influence in international affairs, where the real influence is still force, and would be more likely to cause war. The short-sighted pacifists, by their very efforts to prevent war cause it to be inevitable, showing again the mischievous effect of busybodies trying to direct affairs with which they are incompetent to deal.

The true answer is to raise man to a higher conception of his duty, to realize that he is a citizen of the world and should consider all other men in the world as well as his own country. Let us not delude ourselves that this will be brought about by Wisho thinking. It will require the development of a higher conception of duty to our fellow man than has yet existed in the world.

In the meantime our efforts had better be devoted to solving the problems within our own country by bringing about a feeling of co-operation among our citizens. Conditions in our own land are so bad that we should remain quiet on international affairs until we have displayed capacity to keep our own house in order.

L

THE RACE PROBLEM

WE SHOULD LOOK AT EXISTING INTERNATIONAL CONDITIONS AND consider just in what direction we are drifting. The problem that is being most inefficiently handled and is most threatening for future war, is that of race. Well-meaning people the world over have thought it desirable to promote democratic government among all races and elevate the colored races. These people are not practical. They do not look to the future to see what the final result will be.

Efforts made to educate the backward races and elevate them are at the expense of the white race. The development of the world has been by the white man. Therefore he should rule and benefit from his efforts. Instead of this we have many well-meaning people who wish to convey the benefits of civilization to the backward races; and finally, after they are elevated, the white races will be destroyed. Most of the colored races are living within the tropics, and they should be required to remain there. Instead of encouraging them to establish their own governments and educate their own citizens, they should be ruled by the white man.

If the white people would get together and establish a sensible form of world government, an aristocratic form of government could be established in the tropical countries, in which the white man would be the ruling class and property owners. The colored races would be the workers, well-treated, but occupying a distinctly subordinate position. This would enable them to be controlled and prevent the development among them of agitators creating discord.

The efforts we are making to educate the colored races do not arouse gratitude on their part. They have a feeling of inferiority and wish to show their equality with the white man. We have examples all over the world of any number of agitators striving to stir up their people to oppose the white race.

This problem could be permanently solved now if wise action were applied. Treat the colored people well, but let them know that this world is for the white man and will be ruled by him, and permit no further racial problems to arise. The colored races and white races should not be required to live and work alongside of one another. We have an example in the United States of negroes, a tropical race, infringing on the white man's temperate zone, where they do not belong. They are intended by nature to live in the tropics; therefore put them there and keep them there. To insure against disturbance, place them under the wise rule of able white men.

The colored races will be far happier under wise white rulers than under the rule of their own agitators. The idea so many superficial people have, that the democratic form of government is the ideal of all and should be practiced universally, is an error. Experience has shown that primitive people are happier and better satisfied, under a wise, strong ruler who tells them what to do and sees that they obey.

Many in the United States, familiar with the democratic form of government, think it should succeed all over the world, and even among the most backward races, because of its having had a reasonable success here. It is failing in our own country at present. The reason for this failure is due to low standards of citizenship. We have too many not very intelligent people who are ready clay in the hands of political agitators. If democracy cannot succeed in our own country, it is far more certain to fail in more backward countries.

We have a problem in our own country of lessening the

number of weaklings and of raising the standard of citizenship so as to insure sound democratic government. This can best be done by reducing the number of unfit citizens and increasing the number of good ones. A great step toward this would be the removal of the negroes from the country. They are now creating a political problem and their influence is not being directed toward the support of sound government. We must be practical and plan for the future, trying to solve tomorrow's problems today.

The white race has in many respects pursued, and is pursuing, a policy toward the colored races that is both foolish and suicidal. The white race by its own action is committing ultimate race suicide, decreasing their own numbers and increasing the numbers of the colored races. The opposite policy should prevail. We have it within our power now to determine just what the racial origin of the inhabitants of the world a thousand years hence will be. Our failure to face this problem and solve it will result in the virtual extinction of the white race and the ownership and population of the world by the colored races.

The white race is also teaching many of the colored races the art of war, furnishing them both with the implements of war and with traditions that incite them toward war. In a great many cases colored nations exhibit a determined effort to show their equality with, or superiority to, the white man. They fail to appreciate what the white race has done for them, which is only natural, and are absorbing from the white civilization examples and beliefs that stimulate them to war and nationalism.

If world peace is to be attained in the near future it must be attained under the supervision of the white race and as a result of the white races co-operating with this object in view. The white races should inaugurate a policy of discouraging preparations for war among the colored races and should restrict their emigration. They should remain in their own home countries and exercise birth-control measures if necessary. Such measures would avoid the need for conquest to obtain more territory to care for an increased population.

If we try to elevate all the backward races to the standards of our own, we will be holding back our own progress and will be contributing toward the destruction of the white race by promoting the increase of the backward races at the expense of the white race. Any effort spent in elevating the backward races is used at the expense of effort that could well be more intelligently directed toward advancing the white race.

Scientific racial improvement demands the elimination of the more primitive, more unfit, more undesirable, and the promotion of the most fit, most advanced, and most desirable. Thus from every viewpoint except a sentimental one, we should devote our efforts toward promoting the advance of those most deserving and who themselves contribute toward the advance. When we penalize the most deserving, the most able, by requiring that they help the less deserving and less able, we are discouraging intelligent enterprise and entrusting the future welfare of man to those least capable and deserving.

The Anglo-Saxon element in the United States is being gradually superseded by a mixed race containing elements from all races of man in existence. This development is slight but continuous. The actual percentage of people of pure white blood is decreasing yearly with miscegenation and the higher birth rate of those of mixed or colored blood plus some immigration, both legal and bootleg.

This is an inkling of the racial changes awaiting the future world if racial mingling is permitted to continue unregulated and unrestricted. The white race will gradually disappear and be replaced by a mongrel one containing mixtures of many races. The final type may be no worse in character than that we now have, but it will retard man's higher development for centuries.

Quantity should be limited now and quality encouraged. Miscegenation does not come generally from the best stock of the races participating, but usually from the less desirable types. Free mixing may raise the standard of living of the more backward races, but will lower that of the higher races and thus retard advance.

Let us make this a white man's country. The white man built it up, made it what it is. Why should he share his achievement with other races? We should consider this more from the viewpoint of our children than of ourselves. We have many problems to solve, and their solution would be facilitated by racial homogeneity.

To abolish war we must create an interest group of the most progressive white nations who will create a government of their own and control the colored races. Civilization has been brought about by the white nations, and they are therefore more entitled to the control of the world's affairs. In addition to this, they are by far the most enlightened, and in fact the only race capable of conducting the affairs of the world.

Of all colored races the Japanese are the most advanced, but because of their form of government they cannot be a great contribution to world civilization. They believe in the godlike qualities of the Mikado. They are insane nationalists. All nations opposing them are vicious. They themselves possess only virtues. They are a disturbing factor in international affairs and have forfeited all right to a voice in the conduct of world affairs. This despite the excellent qualities of the Japanese people as a whole. They are far superior to their government.

One constantly hears on the part of various members of the colored races, particularly Japan, of an intention to overthrow white supremacy and to liberate the colored races from the dominance of the white race. This is inspired in part by feelings of inferiority, partly by the desire to further national aims or political motives and advance self-interest.

Many well-meaning white people have endeavored to elevate the colored race. From a practical standpoint the effort had better be directed towards lessening the number of colored people, restraining their activities and limiting their development to their own countries. The white race is foolishly educating and arming the colored races and creating race hatred on their part.

Eventually, if existing trends are permitted to drift as at present, we may expect many wars between white and colored races. How much more sensible, how much more simple it would be for the white races to assert their dominance over the world now, disarm the colored races, and maintain white supremacy and white civilization throughout the world.

The Japanese are living examples of the short-sighted policy of the white race with regard to colored races. White races have given the Japanese their civilization and taught them to make war. The Japanese have now developed a vast army and navy and are a constant menace to world peace. Their leaders frankly announce their determination continually to extend their domination. They seek to ally other colored races against the white race. They continually stir up racial discord. They are still savages with a primitive mental outlook. They are inspired against the white races by intense feelings of racial inferiority.

No well-intentioned foreign policy can get around this fact. It is a practical impossibility to make the Japanese nation a wholesome international influence. To do so would require an entire recasting of their social and political institutions; of their religious and personal outlook. They must be restrained by brute force; the same agency to which they are appealing themselves. They are savages and must receive control by the only weapon savages acknowledge—brute force.

It is possible to establish a world government but it must be done by the white race. The colored races must occupy a subordinate position. We should discourage education among the colored races. This only tends to create unrest. It is cruel to educate them without providing means for improving their economic condition, and when we do elevate members of the colored races, we prejudice members of the white race. In this particular instance, the interest of world peace, and the welfare of the white race, are in harmony.

There are many conflicts of interest between white nations. They are permitting these present-day problems to obscure the great problem of the future, that of racial strife. They should compose their difficulties, cease to fight among themselves, and agree upon a form of government that will place them in control of the entire world and prevent the development of colored races threatening the white civilization. The progress of the world has been brought about by the white man, and he should enjoy it. There is no reason why he should transfer these benefits to the colored man and eventually permit the colored man to destroy his benefactor.

Thought

Unless the white races unite they are doomed. The black, brown, and yellow babies will smother out the white ones. Act now before it is too late.

LI

SAVAGES

ONE WHO SURVEYS THE CONDITION OF MAN THROUGHOUT THE world today and has hopes for an eventual better world, cannot help but be discouraged. Contrast the action of Great Britain and the United States in protesting vigorously to Japan against harm to their own citizens, but standing aside, callous onlookers, when innocent Chinamen are murdered in cold blood under conditions of the most heartless cruelty. If we are ever to have a better world, savagery must be suppressed. The nations must not only suppress it within their own borders, but must unite to suppress international savages as well.

The existing civil war in Spain and the unjust invasion of China by Japan shows the utter incompetence of the present rulers of nations to deal adequately with international problems. Each nation primarily is so interested in its own selfish interests, its domestic politics and in present benefits, that it fails to look into the future, to consider the rights of others and to realize that the best interests of each can be best served by insuring the prosperity of all. The nations stand by, callous onlookers, while the most ruthless killing proceeds in Spain and China. This situation is greatly contributed to by the sentimental impractical well-meaning people who abhor the use of force, who pursue a peace at any price policy. While deploring the slaughter in Spain and China they oppose the use of the only method that will correct it, overwhelming force.

What would be your opinion of a strong healthy man who remained a disinterested onlooker while a brutal bully attacked and tortured an innocent child? You would denounce such a person with the utmost vigor. This is substantially the attitude the United States has taken as a nation in permitting Japan to brutally attack China. Just as each individual has responsibilities to his community to set a good example himself and to prevent abuses to others, so has each nation the duty to set an example of good conduct and to prevent cruel nations from abusing helpless ones.

While the United States is not directly responsible for the existing hostilities in China, she could have prevented them. Had the Japanese known that the United States would fight to insure the territorial integrity of China, they would not have proceeded to extremes. This is particularly true if the United States fleet had been maintained in a condition fit for use. Our well-meaning pacifists are largely responsible for bringing disaster upon the Chinese.

Our weakness itself may invite attack. The speech of Mr. Roosevelt in Chicago denouncing aggressive nations aroused the sensitive Japanese military. When they saw that no action would be taken of a positive kind, as shown by the failure of a conference of the peace-loving nations sometime later, the Japanese were encouraged to believe that they could retaliate upon American forces without danger.

The attack on the *Panay* was unquestionably stimulated by this belief, associated with the general desire to inaugurate a campaign of terror in the Far East and expel all foreigners from China. Cruel, ruthless force such as the Japanese are exhibiting cannot be met by the pacifists' expression of good intentions or similar devices. It must be met with greater force, greater ruthlessness.

Eventually this situation will result in war, probably after Japan has become increasingly powerful and the United States somewhat weaker, rendering a successful conclusion more difficult for our country. It would be a relatively simple task to crush the Japanese if we had on our side the whole-hearted assistance of the Chinese nation. This could readily have been done had we sensibly moved when opportunity offered.

The aggressive and unjust conduct of Japan offers an excellent opportunity for the United States, Great Britain, and France to definitely settle the Far East problem for all time with little risk. The entire American Fleet should be sent to the Far East to base upon Singapore and Hongkong. They should be reenforced by suitable vessels by the British and French navies. This could readily be done without endangering the strength of these two nations in home waters. Accompanying this fleet should be a vast force of aeroplanes. The Japanese empire is very vulnerable to naval and air superiority.

The great distance from our shores to Japan and the vulnerability of the line of communication extending from our Pacific Coast to the Far East can be corrected by establishing a line of communication through the Mediterranean to Singapore and Hongkong. Thus our bases and line of communication will be closer to ourselves than to Japanese attack. It will only be necessary for this fleet to assert its superiority and cut off communications between Japan and the Japanese forces on the Asiatic mainland. These will soon be utterly destroyed by the action of the Chinese, Korean, and Manchukuoan forces.

We should be as mercilessly calculating as the Japanese. They initiated their attack on China to prevent her from developing the strength necessary for self-protection. Had the Japanese delayed their attack a few years more, in all probability the Chinese would have been able to resist successfully. We should attack and destroy Japan now while it is a task of relative ease. Every year of delay adds to her strength and lessens our own. The longer the task is put off, the more difficult it will be to accomplish it successfully. War is inevitable anyway. Why not do it now and get an unpleasant job over with?

The attack of the *Panay* was unquestionably contributed to by the widely distributed remarks of many peacefully inclined American citizens to withdraw all Americans from China from the time the Japanese first started aggressive measures, constantly repeated after each aggressive act of the Japanese toward Americans. These irresponsible people actually convinced some Japanese army officers that if they would kill a few Americans, American forces would be withdrawn from China and American interests there abandoned to the mercies of the Japanese.

When one reflects upon the harmful consequences resulting from remarks of irresponsible but prominent people, one is confronted with the limitations of a democracy and of free speech as opposed to an autocratic government which prohibits free speech and permits only the circulation of that which it approves.

The abuse of free speech by so many contributes toward the overthrow of democracy in our country and to the curtailment of the privilege of free speech. When any privilege is so exercised as to be converted into an abuse causing harmful consequences, the inevitable result will be an attempt to control the abuse. If we can prevent the abuse of free speech, we can avoid its curtailment. If we permit its abuse, we will soon cease to possess it.

If we pursue the policy advocated by our well-meaning pacifists, we will stand on the sidelines, permit Japan to conquer China, then to require the Chinese to serve in her armies, then to conquer Asia, and eventually to take the world. Our country will be included in this world conquest. The freedom of thought that is being preserved in those countries controlled today by democracy will cease.

The Japanese will require all to worship the Mikado. They will ruthlessly destroy the unselfish thought of great thinkers; the efforts of these men will then have been in vain. Those who extol the merits of free speech, of the right to think, had better combine while there is yet time, and suppress the savages who threaten its destruction.

What a sad fate to befall the unselfish efforts of great men of the past, to permit savages to destroy forever high-minded seeking for the truth by the adoption of a policy which permits the circulation of only such knowledge as is in accord with their beliefs. Savages can contribute nothing to civilization. They can, however, if permitted to employ the agencies of civilization, perpetuate savagery forever and destroy in this perpetuation all the work of the greatest thinkers mankind has produced.

A nation whose citizens worship their ruler as a heavenly being, which permits itself to be dominated by a military oligarchy who murder prime ministers and high officials of the government, who kill innocent victims in time of war, who intentionally sink foreign warships and fire upon foreigners without provocation, is not a nation that will contribute toward the advance of civilization. Neither is it a nation that is fit to exist in a world which claims to be civilized. The denial of facts by the leaders of Japan, attributing false motives to Americans, the refusal to permit truth in their press, is convincing evidence that the Japanese leaders are unworthy of respect. A nation that permits itself to be controlled by such leaders, is also unworthy of respect.

The intense propaganda of Japanese militarists and nationalists among their people to the effect that the world is their enemy, seeking their downfall, and that they must arm themselves against it, will make itself a fact—with the difference that they themselves have created it. Its final consequences remain to be seen. The Japanese people at home are a fine race of people, a credit to themselves and to the world. We should have no quarrel with them. But one can only have a feeling of disgust for their leaders who are continually spreading ill feeling.

One would gather from the Japanese outbursts that all countries in the world are vicious except the Japanese, and the only virtuous government in existence is the Japanese government. This is a common failing of all incompetents. The more incompetent they are, the more vicious are their opponents, and the more virtuous are they themselves.

The attitude of these insane Japanese leaders is one with

the feeling of our own government in Washington today. The difference is that the Japanese leaders pursue this propaganda to arouse the feelings of their people against foreign nations; in our own country the feeling is aroused against our own citizens.

Study of the Japanese from the standpoint of psychology is very instructive. Travelers going to Japan and visiting the Japanese in their homes comment upon the fine people, their courtesy and many good qualities. The same travelers seeing the Japanese in Peking comment upon their overbearing manner, their failure to consider others or be courteous. This may be attributed to the environmental influences, but it also shows what we may call a national inferiority complex. At home the Japanese is a fine fellow, abroad he wishes to impress his importance and ability upon foreigners.

Unconsciously they realize that their present civilization, their recent great progress and modern development, have all been copied from foreign nations. This causes their subconscious to feel secretly that they are inferior to foreigners. Added to this is the matter of difference of race, physical appearance, and size. Feeling this way, it is only too natural for the Japanese abroad to endeavor to conceal this feeling of inferiority by going to the opposite extreme, being bullies, intimidating, threatening, and trying to impress others.

The Japanese in general are good people in their own country but far from desirable elsewhere. Wherever Japanese exist outside of Japan, friction develops. They cause trouble on our Pacific Coast. They are encroaching upon our fisheries in Alaska threatening their destruction. Native fishermen in Panama have objected to the unscrupulous methods of the Japanese in using dynamite in fishing grounds. Complaints are received of unscrupulous Japanese methods in business such as mislabeling Japanese goods of an inferior quality to discredit merchandise of other nations.

Regardless of the merit of the Japanese people, international harmony demands that they be required to remain in Japan. They possess merit when among themselves but lack it when associated with other races, nations or people. This Japanese characteristic is caused by the fact that they are primitive in mental outlook. They are considerate only of their own tribe. Those who are not Japanese are to be plundered, exploited, discredited; and when they oppose Japanese aggressions, they are to be killed.

In the last century, civilized public opinion abolished human slavery throughout the world, at least to the extent of prohibiting barter in human flesh in those countries under the control of civilization. We today are standing by callously permitting a far more injurious type of slavery to exist. I refer to the mental slavery in Russia in which a large population is being required to worship communism, to submit to the harsh rule of a ruthless dictatorship, to submit to having their mental activities prescribed by the government, thus preventing the development of the finer human qualities. The Russians, as a people, are as deserving as any other nation if subjected to proper environmental influences. We are callously permitting them to be subjected to a form of mental slavery far more injurious to future generations than the physical slavery of the past. If this is unchecked our children may be subjected to a similar form of slavery.

Russia affords much light on the psychology of man, showing how he will respond readily to beliefs and how such beliefs can influence the thought and conduct of an entire nation. Resentment against the old Russian regime, capitalism, and the wealthy resulted in communism getting control. Partly as a result of feeling, partly by design to insure the perpetuation of the new regime, all things opposing communism were bitterly denounced and its own merits exalted. The faults or deficiencies of communism were generally overlooked. Great developments in the educational field stressed this viewpoint, with the result that the younger generation in Russia are now communists, are unable to visualize other forms of human institutions, do not realize the faults of communism, and have a one-sided mental development.

No great benefits will be obtained by man from Russia.

Inquiring minds are throttled in their infancy. Instead of being able to question, to inquire, to seek the basic causes for all things, they are required to worship what is now established. This is the most vicious, cruel method of crushing mental development possible. This is true despite the fact that there is a little merit in some of their present institutions. No really great civilization can develop that does not promote and encourage the freest expression of thought and investigation into all phases of human activity.

There is far less liberty under communism than under any other form of government. We see this well exemplified in Russia whose rulers can arbitrarily kill at will those who oppose them. The fact that the government is the sole employer and that the individual citizens are entirely dependent upon the government for jobs results in giving even small government officials great power over the average worker and a small government official is entirely within the power of higher ones. Thus in Russia you see little or no criticism of whatever action the government may undertake. There is no free discussion, no free public opinion, no mental development. Yet we have many in this country advocating communism or doctrines closely allied thereto.

Both Russia and Japan exhibit what we might well call mass insanity. It does not differ in principle from similar conduct on the part of other nations. The interesting and instructive thing to note here is that the same principle applies in the insane conduct of nations as it does in the individual lunatic. The insane person lacks Primo and Co, the very same qualities lacking in mass insanity.

Neither the Japanese nor the Russians analyze themselves closely as a nation or as a people. They do not seek for and criticize their faults and errors and attempt to correct them. They consider themselves to possess many virtues of which they permit no questioning. Inasfar as the spirit of Co is exercised, their interests as nations are paramount to those of any other nation. No feeling of consideration or co-operation is really entertained. Nice-sounding words are frequently expressed but not meant.

Russia and Japan are the two governments that are doing the greatest harm to future world peace. These countries are controlled by oligarchies who control the press, speech, and education, and who teach all their citizens to believe certain established and accepted beliefs. They prevent the circulation of any truth that may be considered opposed thereto. There are many fine individuals in the Russian and Japanese nations. The civilized nations of the world should act to rescue them from mental slavery in order that they may be a contribution to civilization.

LII

AMERICA AND THE WORLD

THE FOREIGN POLICY OF THE UNITED STATES TODAY IS DIS-
creditable. War is in progress in Spain, war and violence in
China. A great threat of world war exists in Europe. What
does our government do to improve conditions? Those entrusted with the conduct of our foreign affairs have much to
say about America's traditional foreign policies and about the
aggressions of other nations. They have no conception of the
difficult problems facing many nations.

Because we, of the United States, have vast areas of undeveloped territory and natural resources, we fail to appreciate the situation of many nations crowded within narrow boundaries with but limited resources; so limited indeed
as to provide only the barest sustenance for their people. At
the same time we possess untold natural resources.

Rather than denounce other nations for aggressions, we
should appreciate our own good fortune. We should sympathize with them and seek for a correction of the underlying
causes of war and international conflicts. Claiming that we
are a virtuous nation and that those resorting to violence are
vicious helps no one. It shows callous indifference on our
part to the suffering of the citizens of less fortunate countries.

Our leaders are very skillful in finding means to justify
their polices and extol the virtues of their conduct. At the
same time they admit that the international situation is so
bad as to threaten the destruction of civilization. This is an
admission on their part that their measures and policies have

failed. They refuse to accept the blame for their failure; instead they denounce other nations. Unquestionably other nations are at fault in resorting to aggressive action but the United States is equally at fault in refraining from sensible action.

Instead of employing sensible measures or resorting to sensible action, we have resorted to words. The aggressive foreign nations realize that we will not support our words with action. Therefore, they do as they will. The disinterested altruistic attitude of the United States, as the result of our remoteness from foreign quarrels, would give us a great voice in international affairs. We should exercise this great influence to preserve international harmony. At present, we do nothing to preserve it. We denounce those who disturb it and they know only too well that we will do nothing else.

If the United States would take a strong stand against criminal nations, ample support would be forthcoming from other worthy nations. The criminal nations would not dare to resort to actions violating the dictates of humanity if a sufficient number of worthwhile nations were prepared to repel violence with greater violence.   .

Discreditable as our present foreign policy is, it is fortunate that no aggressive action is being taken while we have Mr. Roosevelt as president. He is clearly unequal to the task of directing the operations of a great war. A war conducted under the direction of Mr. Roosevelt would be very likely to result in disaster. We have many able officers in both the army and navy. The ablest ones among them would probably not be of the type that would appeal to Mr. Roosevelt. He is insistent that he have yes-men to serve him. Able generals or admirals cannot be yes-men.

Even if Mr. Roosevelt were fortunate in his selection of able admirals and generals to direct the armed forces, he lacks the ability to co-ordinate the civil and military functions of the government to insure success. Our general staff has prepared plans for the mobilization of the nation in the event of war. Some of these plans are ridiculous. They provide for placing the industries of the nation under the control of the army general staff. God help our nation when our general staff undertakes to conduct its industries! The general staff does not possess the ability to do this.

However capable an army officer may be, he has grown up in an environment far removed from knowledge of business and industry. We cannot expect the average army officer to possess the knowledge and ability required to supervise the business life of the nation. This should be the task of the president and his cabinet, and this is the ability that is so much wanting in our government today. Rather than risk war under such direction, we had better submit to any humiliation that any nation chooses to inflict upon us.

The remarks of our senators, representatives, and others in control of our foreign policies display incompetence, ignorance, and failure to understand their duty. Somehow they feel that Americans are not to blame in the slightest degree for conditions in Europe. They have no understanding of the vast problems awaiting solution in Europe.

The United States is separated from the rest of the world by vast oceans and has developed free from many influences retarding the development of Europe. We should appreciate our good fortune and assist in lessening national animosities between other nations. Our country alone is capable of taking the lead in improving international conditions.

The attitude of our leaders does not assume any international duty, no responsibility to the world to improve conditions. A narrow-minded, isolationist attitude is as harmful to world peace as is the attitude of the most vicious nationalists in Europe and Japan. We cannot expect a solution of international difficulties under the guidance of such men. We must remember that international problems in this day of ready communications have a vital effect upon our internal prosperity. We must develop leaders with an international outlook, men who will seek to advance the welfare of the world.

We must not continue to follow men who denounce the rest of the world and claim that America alone is without fault. I get disgusted hearing people denounce others and pat themselves on the back for their superior intelligence and worth. People who do this are neither intelligent nor worthy.

The unwise handling of our foreign affairs prior to and during the World War was instrumental in causing the World War. If our country had been governed by able men, the World War could have been prevented. The same holds true today. If we had able men in control of our nation, they could prevent what threatens to develop into a World War in the near future.

Our rulers in denouncing European nations are but repeating the prevailing thought in our own country. This is very similar to what the leaders of European nations are doing in their countries. They are stressing the grievances of their people and promising to do something about it in efforts to obtain their support. If the United States was a small European country and had the same leaders we would be just as great offenders as many European nations are now.

We must develop leaders with an international outlook who will be above and beyond the narrow-minded feeling now common in our own country. We must develop throughout the world in all nations leaders who will consider the welfare of man throughout the world including future generations. We must establish an international atmosphere, an international citizenship that will permit the growth of international feeling, that will encourage all leaders of all nations and all citizens of all nations, to realize that the interests of all world inhabitants are best served by mutual co-operation. They are not served by an isolationist policy which denounces other nations as being unfit for association.

There is a distinct danger in Americans denouncing foreign nations so liberally. They may arouse considerable resentment on the part of European nations and magnify ill feeling. Some day it is not impossible that Europe may be assembled under one government. When that is accomplished, it will be a powerful nation indeed. If it then chooses to punish the

United States for past insults, it could do so with little danger to itself.

Not only is it our duty to adopt a sane international policy and develop sane leaders, but it is likewise a matter of self-interest. Spreading hate and contempt for other nations is but perpetuating existing international hatreds. We are sowing the seed for the same aggressions against our children that we so generally deplore in Europe today.

Must man be forever governed by fools? Can he not develop sufficient intelligence to find able leaders? Man has always been governed by fools. They govern our own country. They govern most of the nations of the world. They talk, denounce, and spread ill feeling—and the poor, ignorant man in the street suffers. But are they ever at fault? Not they. It is always the vicious people who are opposing them.

We must be fair, impartial, and realize that those who choose to speak for our own country are as good at crying and screaming as the representatives of foreign nations, and as little capable of sound thought or action. There are a few countries in the world, however, where higher-type men are in control, supported by a citizenship of a higher type than we possess, or than the average nation possesses. These countries are Norway, Sweden, Denmark, Switzerland, and Costa Rica, small nations with smaller problems, but nevertheless setting an example of efficient conduct of affairs and of high standards of citizenship, that all other nations can well profit by.

We hear much talk of the evils of war and much talk of world peace. Just what is being done to prevent war and promote peace? Nothing but talk. Cannot our nation act in such way as to further world peace? Can we not do something more valuable than threatening to quarantine nations? Can we not establish an international policy that will be deserving of the respect and emulation of all nations? Instead of denouncing other nations, let us show, by words and deeds, that we appreciate their difficult problems and are doing our utmost to assist them and promote world peace.

Let us take a stand for the freedom of mind and thought the world over. America should break off all diplomatic relations with those nations that censor the press and give false accounts of foreign nations. No world-wide education to insure international peace can be carried out in countries that denounce other nations and perpetuate hate, at the same time prohibiting the circulation of the truth.

Why should we receive the diplomatic representatives of a nation such as Japan, for instance, and treat them with courtesy? The Japanese government is not deserving of such consideration. They control their press at home and permit the circulation of the most outrageous lies against the American government, people, and policies.

If we were to adopt the policy of breaking off diplomatic relations with any nation that failed to permit its citizens to hear the true facts of international disputes, we could bring about the gradual development of an international atmosphere that would insure a lessening of racial and national animosity. It is useless to attempt to prevent war unless the citizens of all nations have free access to the truth concerning international affairs.

An attempt to build up an international citizenship, a loyalty to all men above national loyalty, will be bitterly opposed by selfish dictators or oligarchies controlling selfish nations. By prohibiting the circulation of truth concerning the causes of war, they will perpetuate it. They, however, would have a difficult time explaining to their citizens why the United States broke off diplomatic relations with their government.

We could, in addition, appeal to the people of these nations themselves, by means of the radio or whatever facilities are available. The bandit leaders of nations would be placed in a delicate position. It is questionable whether they could long continue their present policies. It is quite possible that many would be overthrown. If a majority of the nations of the world determined to maintain this international freedom, they could compel all others to do so likewise.

By receiving the representatives of such people as those now governing Japan, Germany, and Russia, we are supporting their policies—policies which prevent the development of wholesome international feeling and will inevitably produce war in the future. If we refuse to have anything to do with these international bandits, we can, in time, create throughout the world a public opinion that will condemn them. This condemnation will be so strong as to result in their overthrow. If we can accomplish this, the cause of international peace will be advanced toward solution.

From a psychological standpoint the same basic human feelings are involved in international war as are involved in labor conflicts or any other conflicts between interest groups. The approach to war will vary with the intensity of feeling aroused and the degree of violence employed by the different interest groups in attaining their desires; likewise the amount of opposition that is opposed to their success. If the opposition is overwhelming they will be less prone to resort to extreme violence, just as a small weak nation will not attack a large powerful one.

Opposing interests between groups within a nation, with propaganda and many environmental influences contributing toward ill feeling, results in a feeling very similar to selfish nationalism. We had an example of this in our own Civil War when, because of the agitation over slavery and conflicting interests, two parts of the nation, essentially the same in racial origin, developed great feeling against each other and eventually fought a bloody war. The same feeling is exemplified in the existing labor agitation in the nation, when organized labor unions are considering their own interests regardless of the rights of all others not belonging to their unions, thus creating intense class feeling.

There is some actual foundation for this, but the contributing environmental influences have transformed organized labor from organizations intended to protect the laborers' rights into organizations which are actually persecuting all opposing groups but firmly believing that they are protecting their own rights. This is much the same as the feeling of nations at war, when each nation fully believes that it is in the right; all or most of its citizens believe likewise and are unable to see any fault in their country or its policies.

The situation within our own country is much similar to the international situation. Our government is conciliating strong voting groups by acceding to many of their demands. This results in the rights of many others being prejudiced. In the international field the various nations are doing the same thing, each striving to protect its own rights at the expense of others. There is no international government bringing this about. It is the short-sighted view of each individual nation striving for survival. Within our own country we have this situation brought about by our own government. That is to say, our government is creating within our own nation as unsatisfactory a condition as exists in the international field.

Economic conditions within each nation are much influenced by international conditions, and each nation should strive toward bettering them. We could render our greatest contribution to improving international relations if we regulated affairs within our country so that internal conflicts did not exist. Then with our vast wealth and prestige we could have a greater voice in world affairs and could point the way toward sound international action.

Let us solve the problems in our own country first, and when these are solved we will have proven to the world that we are worthy of being heard when we attempt to inaugurate sound international policies. Vicious nations as well as vicious individuals must be controlled and prevented from injuring decent nations, but before we can classify them as being vicious we must prove that we ourselves have elevated our own nation to high standards of conduct.

To insure harmony within our own country we must create on the part of all citizens a desire and willingness to work for the welfare of all. In securing international harmony we must likewise have the various nations modify their institutions, especially the educational ones, in an endeavor to encourage their citizens to consider the interest of all men in the world, not only their own nation. The great Civil War in our own country would not have occurred had this matter been understood at that time and lived up to. Our leaders then should have created a willingness on the part of the abolitionists, the slave owners, and conflicting commercial interests to advance the best interests of the entire nation. We are today faced with this same problem in having many interest groups within the nation developing loyalties more to themselves than to the nation as a whole, thus again bringing about the threat of civil war.

Domestic harmony and prosperity, will be assured throughout the nation when no selfish interest groups exist within it and all are members of one interest group working for the benefit of all. The same applies to the international situation. One nation, one world, one interest group will prevent conflicts or wars and promote international harmony.

We cannot hope to stop wars until we stop strikes. They are essentially the same: interest groups striving for their own interests regardless of others, using force and intimidation to attain them, but failing to use intelligence or righteousness.

We, as a nation, must set an example of peace and harmony within our own borders before we can expect to have our opinion respectfully considered in international affairs. The development and growth of selfish interest groups within our country, fighting, demanding benefits and creating discord, is a portrayal of international conditions. We must crush the vicious interest groups, cause the others to become more conscious of their duties, establish a harmonious feeling within the nation, and then endeavor to bring about better international feeling.

Thought

We should do our part as a nation in international affairs to the same extent as a conscientious citizen should in national affairs.

LIII

THE NATIONS' LEADERS

WHEN ONE LISTENS TO THE RECENT STATEMENTS MADE BY THE different governments relative to the aggressions of Japan on China, the denunciations of the so-called democratic governments by the dictators, and vice versa, one is forced to the melancholy conclusion that the men entrusted with the conduct of the affairs of nations are not able and not even gentlemen. They are children, crying, screaming, fighting among themselves, denouncing those who disagree with them.

These men display no evidence of the ability to think, make no attempt to solve the problems facing the world, and yet the people of all the countries submit to them and do not question their acts or seek for abler men. When such an atmosphere exists, the able, thoughtful men can have no voice in the conduct of affairs.

These crying, screaming, spoiled children who are now governing the nations are creating an environment which permits them to remain in power. It is to be hoped that as time passes, when these people and their policies have been discredited, that sensible men and measures will be given a chance to correct the havoc they have wrought.

It is hopeless to expect any solution to international affairs or sensible action toward the prevention of future wars as long as we have governments of the present types in the various nations of the world. All alike are intense nationalistic interest groups controlled by politicians or leaders who resort to all possible means to obtain popular support.

Because of the heritage from the past, the most ready way to appeal to the masses in certain nations is to stir up the old racial animosities which, being continually revived, militate against international harmony. They are of use in maintaining politicians in office or in maintaining existing leaders in control of the institutions of the nations, but they do not contribute toward international harmony or to the best welfare of the nations themselves.

This is a problem that must be approached by the able thinkers in each nation not allied with any government, in carrying out a program of education among the masses, showing them that there is no need for intense national hatreds and that all people and countries in the world must work together if they are to thrive.

The situation in the international field, with so many conflicting nations each intent on pursuing its own interests, is very similar to that of the American colonies before the adoption of the Constitution. Each colony pursued its own interest to the exclusion of the rights of others, and endless confusion was caused. The colonists solved that problem by the adoption of the federal Constitution, the far-sighted men of that day taking sensible action to solve a pressing problem in the interest of all. But their problem was simpler than the world problem. The colonies were inhabited by men of the same race, same language, very similar interests, on the same continent. They had no past heritage of racial hatred.

The problems in the international field are far greater, more complex, and will require the ablest leadership, the greatest thinkers we can produce, to solve them. The problem is further complicated by one that did not exist in our colonies. We have a great many Wisho liberals and pacifists who wish to do something to help improve international conditions. They are mere theorists unable to compose a practical solution of international problems.

The problem of insuring international harmony is not beyond solution. It is being made worse by unwise efforts to help as much as it is by the intense nationalistic agitation of politicians and rabid nationalists. Those whom we consider the friends of international harmony are its worst enemies, and these are the ones we must guard against. We expect them to help and they are hindering.

World peace cannot be brought about by the existing leaders of nations. They are politicians of the poorest type, stirring up war rather than preventing it in order to have issues to attract votes and remain in power. A new type of leader must be found if we are to improve international relations— able men with an international outlook. We must put master scientists in control of the nations who will serve man the world over.

The World War was brought on by the incompetent leaders of the nations. The British statesmen of the last century were among the greatest offenders. Their efforts to perpetuate the old Turkish Empire, refusing to strengthen the Balkan states for fear that Russia would become dominant, their desire to further British interests at the expense of all others, were some of the greatest contributing factors. Had the British statesmen of that day been enlightened, had they stimulated the formation of strong independent Balkan states, it is possible that a more healthy situation would have prevailed in Europe and that the World War would have been avoided. It would surely have prevailed if a better understanding had been created among statesmen, with more consideration for other nations. In looking back on history we can see the great harm done by leaders of preceding generations by their failure to solve the problems of their day in such way as to prevent them from being passed on to others in a form requiring a resort to arms.

Anyone having faith in the future of man can arrive only at a pessimistic viewpoint in viewing the situation in Spain: two parties bent on exterminating each other, each one half right, half wrong, the victims of unsound institutions and incompetent leaders. They are unable to find able men to adjust their affairs. They permit them to be determined by force and appeals to ignorance, prejudices, selfish interests of individuals, class hatred, viciousness and ignorance. While this situation goes on in Spain, the powers of the world look on hopelessly and helplessly.

If the nations were governed by able leaders and had the true interests of the world at heart, they would find means to compose the differences between the Spanish parties and bring about peace. Direct intervention might be necessary. A capable man should be found to conduct the affairs of the country for a brief period and restore law and order. But many other nations are just as incompetent as the Spanish people, and are near the same situation.

Looking over the policies of the nations of the world for the past hundred years, one cannot help but arrive at the conclusion that they have been conducted by crazy men. A nation would ally itself first with one nation, then another, in trying to serve its own interest. As a result of this short-sighted policy they created ills for the following generations. The nations are friends today, enemies tomorrow, friends again the following day in accordance with the most trivial conditions, trying to maintain the balance of power, trying to look after what they consider to be national interests, and as the result all suffer.

Thoughts

Today in the newspapers mention was made of plans by France to build two large battleships in order to counteract Italy's armament program. The same paper also announced that Great Britain is building a vast air force sufficiently large to exceed that of several other probable enemies.

How long will man submit to this madness? Can they not see that their destinies are in the hands of madmen, that vast sums of money, much human effort, and much scientific knowledge is being directed not toward advancing man but toward destroying him?

Can we not by some means reach the common citizen who will suffer by war, have him cast aside these madmen, stop killing other men, solve today's problems in a spirit of fairness and justice to all, not permit madmen to destroy civilization and permit the world to be dominated by savagery?—*January 12, 1938.*

Sound solution of world economic problems requires the conduct of the affairs of nations by the ablest men having regard for the future over the present, and considering international good will and welfare above selfish national interests.

If the world statesmen were actually planning for everlasting war and torment for man, they could hardly plan any better than they are now doing.

Fine sounding phrases are not enough to abolish war. It will require sensible action on the part of sensible men.

Woodrow Wilson made war against the German government and made peace against the German people.

We can hardly be civilized when we have legalized mass murder, war. Yet what are our leaders doing about it? Nothing. Is this not convincing proof of their incompetence?

Killing, brutality, and denunciation throughout the world must stop. Our present-day leaders are unable to stop it. They must be cast aside and replaced by a man or men who can stop it.

LIV

WORLD PEACE

WE CAN EASILY FIND FAULT WITH THE FOREIGN POLICIES OF all nations. On the one hand they lack able leaders and on the other they lack citizens sufficiently informed on international affairs to support able leaders if they existed. International affairs will continue in their present hopeless muddle until the leaders of the nations prove adequate to handle them and until they have developed a citizenship intelligent enough to support wise measures. This, of course, applies to democratic countries only. In countries governed by dictators, the dictator himself is able to establish the policy and obtain the necessary support. Thus, a dictatorship has a marked superiority over a democracy in the conduct of foreign affairs.

The great friction and clash of interest between Great Britain and Japan in the Far East today is an example of a short-sighted foreign policy. About thirty-five years ago British statesmen were courting the Japanese and had an alliance with them. Great Britain's very own policy has built up Japan into a powerful enemy capable of threatening British interests. Under existing international conditions Great Britain is practically helpless to defend herself against Japanese aggressions.

Great Britain and France are as much at fault for the unfortunate condition existing in Spain as are Germany or Italy. If they had conducted their foreign affairs with intelligence and thought for the future, they could have arranged for military intervention in Spain when the civil war first started. They could have prevented the extremists of either the Right or the Left from prevailing and could have assisted the Spanish nation in establishing democratic institutions founded upon the support of the intermediate body of the Spanish people. The civil war in Spain is a conflict between extremists on each side. Both these extremists could have been discredited if support had been extended the middle classes.

Neither Great Britain nor France saw the need for inaugurating this wise policy at the outbreak of the Spanish civil war. Even had the leaders of these two nations seen this need, it would have been impossible for them to have carried out such a policy. It would not have received support from the citizens of their respective countries.

It is easy for citizens of the United States, Great Britain, and France to denounce the aggressions of Italy and Germany. The three democracies have by fortunate circumstances obtained control of an undue proportion of the world's natural resources. Germany and Italy have but little of the world's natural resources. Thus these three democracies are in the position of possessing great wealth and preventing poorer nations from obtaining it. If this disparity in wealth did not exist, there would be less danger of conflict. It is the existence of this condition that enables the dictators to arouse their people and obtain their support against the wealthy democracies.

This is a fact we should recognize in doing justice to both parties. These wealthy democracies should be willing to share their wealth with their less fortunate brethren. Unless they do so, this injustice will be capitalized by dictators controlling the destinies of the impoverished nations, causing a resort to violence to obtain what they believe is justice. It would not be necessary for the democracies to share their wealth with the poorer nations. They should merely render it possible for the poorer nations to have an opportunity. Considering the vast amount of undeveloped natural resources in the world, this would be a relatively simple task to bring about.

The democracies should appeal to the people of these impoverished dictatorships. The people of all nations should work togther with a firm endeavor of advancing the interest of all. Denouncing those countries under the control of dictators and extolling the merits of democracy but tends to aggravate existing grievances. We should recognize our good fortune and admit our faults. We should see the merits of these other countries and obtain the whole-hearted co-operation of their people—not denounce them and create more friction rendering a solution of international difficulties impossible without a resort to violence.

The present unfortunate condition of affairs in Europe can be attributed in large measure to the opposition by Great Britain and other nations to Mussolini's conquest of Ethiopia. They took the view that Mussolini was an aggressor and that the uncivilized people of Ethiopia should be protected from civilization, should be condemned to exist as an independent nation in a state of savagery.

European nations should not have opposed the advance of civilization. They should actually have co-operated with Mussolini. Instead of this, he was bitterly opposed. The opposition to him was largely influenced by internal national politics and the influence of impractical sentimental people. They felt they were discouraging war by opposing Italy's conquest of Ethiopia. Their short-sighted viewpoint insured that Italy would be antagonized. This would result in her supporting Germany against France, Great Britain and other nations. This is substantially what has resulted.

The present conditions in Europe can be directly attributed to incompetent leadership and the influence of well-meaning people advocating unsound measures to improve international conditions. Ill-advised measures have brought about a condition of affairs more threatening in certain aspects than the conditions existing before the outbreak of the World War.

A war in Europe would be a most heartrending catas-

trophe. Modern weapons of war, the closeness of the countries to each other, and their defenselessness against attacks
from the air will cause great suffering to innocent people
and destroy many of the finer things of modern civilization.

The present community of interest between the three dictatorships of Italy, Germany, and Japan is founded upon a
shaky footing. It cannot and will not last. The leaders of
these three nations are seeking to further their own interests.
They have allied themselves with the other two for the time
being to further these interests. Later, they will be only too
glad to ally themselves against them if they conceive such
action will benefit them.

We can see examples of conflicts between them in the
past. Italy threatened war on Germany a few years ago, in
order to maintain Austria's independence. Japan and Italy
were at outs when Ethiopia was invaded by the Italians. At
no time in their past history have these three nations been
great friends. They differ in too many respects. Their present
support of each other is an expedient into which Italy and
Germany are, to some degree, forced. Make it worth their
while and they will only too willingly fight Japan or fight each
other.

Those who are friendly to democratic institutions and bitterly oppose the policies of Hitler and Mussolini should not
lose their perspective. Dislike for a nation's ruler should not
permit denunciation of the entire nation. Rulers will change,
but nations will endure. International harmony demands
that the individuals of all nations try by individual efforts to
promote it. Far greater regard should be given to the future,
many years hence, than to the present. Hatreds that we create
and encourage today will exist tomorrow to plague our children.

Dictators are not necessarily a great evil. It depends largely
upon the man himself and the conditions under which he
became dictator. Mussolini has been a great contribution, a
great constructive force, to the Italian nation. It is unfortunate that, as the result of unwise opposition by other

European nations, he has adopted a foreign policy opposed to international harmony.

Hitler has not been a constructive force for Germany. Just what degree of success he obtains in carrying out his present policy remains to be seen. His success so far is due more to the weakness of the opposition than to his own ability and strength. While Europe is threatened with a great crisis, we see France torn with internal conflict. Other European nations, relying upon France for support, have lost confidence in her stability. This, in conjunction with the short-sighted opposition to Mussolini's annexation of Ethiopia, has given Hitler an opportunity to carry out selfish measures with but little opposition from other nations.

We can draw an instructive comparison between Mr. Roosevelt and Hitler. Both represent in themselves undesirable elements in each nation that have obtained control of the government. Because the Germans are more accustomed to dictatorial rule, Hitler has crushed all opposition to himself and his policies. Mr. Roosevelt has been unable to do this in the United States. Our free institutions prevent such action. He has in large degree obtained a following by extolling democratic institutions. He, therefore, cannot suppress free speech. In this respect the American people are more fortunate than the Germans. We can eventually get rid of Mr. Roosevelt. It is doubtful if the Germans will be able to get rid of Mr. Hitler. From the standpoint of individual conduct and intelligence, the average German is fully the equal of the average American. Both are unfortunate today in being under the control of incompetent rulers. Bad as Mr. Roosevelt is for the United States, Hitler is far worse for the Germans.

This comparison of Hitler and Roosevelt is interesting as showing one of the greatest merits of democracy and one of the greatest faults of dictatorship or absolute monarchy. A democracy can remove its incompetent ruler. A dictatorship or an absolute monarchy is very often unable to do so. The dictator ruthlessly crushes all opposition to his rule and, at the same time, appeals to the prejudices of his people to strengthen his position. As the result, it is practically impossible to build up the necessary opposition within the nation to remove him from office.

This is especially true when the dictators make use of ill-feeling against foreign nations as one of the principle means of arousing the feeling of their own people. This is one of the strongest forces giving Hitler his great power in Germany today. Germany has been unjustly dealt with by foreign nations. Hitler capitalizes this and stirs the feelings of the Germans to support his policies.

The short-sighted policies of the foreign nations of the past have brought this about. It is questionable whether it is not now too late to adopt a more sensible policy. However, the attempt should be made. We should approach the German people, in an endeavor to enlist their whole-hearted co-operation in the solution of man's problems.

It is a reflection on the German people to submit to a ruler of such poor qualities as Hitler. It is a reflection upon the other nations of Europe to permit Hitler to create so much fear and suspense without being able to control him effectively. The various European nations are considering their own interests, the immediate present. Many have internal conflicts. Even those with the best of intentions do not know what to do. There should be enough ability in Europe to evolve a sane continental policy and require that all nations conduct their affairs in accord therewith.

The policy of European nations in fighting and annexing their neighbor's territory has existed for many centuries. It has caused untold suffering. Those who benefit today suffer tomorrow. Common sense should tell all that they should abandon this suicidal policy and seek for the underlying causes of unsatisfactory conditions and determine upon a definite policy to correct them. With all nations working together in this spirit, it would be easily possible to solve all existing international problems. In bringing about the solution, the interest of no one particular nation need be prejudiced. The interest of each would be served by the prosperity of all.

There is a very weak feature about the intense nationalism of Germany and Japan. Of necessity, these two countries consider their own interests and do not consider the interests of the world or other nations. Other countries in general recognize the cruelty, the uselessness, and the injustice of war. The tendency throughout the world is toward international citizenship, a world society in which all nations have equal rights, have their interests protected, and in which war does not exist.

The intense activity of the Germans and the Japanese will, in time, arouse against them the united opposition of all other nations of the world. They will unite to protect themselves against attack. The aggressive policies of Germany and Japan are more the policies of aggressive leaders or groups than of the common people. In each country there is generally a group of intense nationalists, prejudiced against other races and nations. It is this group that at present is dominant in the affairs of these two nations. But there is still a larger group within each that is less interested in nationalism than in life itself. A wise international policy can obtain the adherence of these groups against the intense nationalists now controlling their policies.

The aggressive policy of Germany can be checked in Europe by simple sensible action on the part of the smaller nations on the continent. If they would unite they would form such a strong aggregation as to intimidate Germany. They would be so strong in fact that they could compel Germany to join their union rather than permit itself to be conquered by them.

Europe can profit by studying our own experience during our struggle for independence. The expression, "In unity there is strength," is still sound. The symbol of a bundle of staves being strong and powerful even though composed of relatively weak units, is an exemplification of conditions in Europe today. If these weak units unite, they become strong and powerful. They are then able not only to protect themselves against aggressors but also to intimidate the aggressors themselves.

Their interests are not opposed to each other. Primarily such a union is prevented by existing animosities stressing nationalism and racial feeling. Wisdom could be employed in teaching the inhabitants of these countries that the interest of all would be better served if they were united under a strong government.

Again we are confronted with the lack of a leadership adequate to effect this consummation. The existing leaders of these nations, instead of furthering such an aim, are intensifying national feeling and existing animosity. How stupid and short-sighted! The long-suffering inhabitants of all these nations will suffer from the incompetence of their leaders.

A sensible solution to existing animosities in Europe would be for all European nations to unite together and conquer Russia and Western Asia. Instead of one nation trying to plunder the territory of another, let all concentrate upon sharing the vast Russian and Asiatic territory. If communism could be overthrown and superseded by a government composed of the ablest thought of Europe, a great advance would be made in man's affairs.

There would be as great an economic development in this combined European-Asiatic empire, as there was in the United States in the past century. It would result in the gradual disappearance of racial hatreds. All races would see the need for mutual co-operation. By each one considering the rights of others, all would benefit. Certainly, all are suffering intensely under the existing era of intense selfish nationalism. This change to co-operative internationalism is the true solution.

We, in the United States, are reversing this process. Although we do not have the racial ill-feeling and nationalistic traditions of Europe within our country, we are building up artificial animosities between conflicting interest groups. Our present unsatisfactory condition will constantly get worse as long as we permit this suicidal policy to continue. When we require all citizens, all interest groups to consider others, our condition will be vastly improved. Why cannot the sensible people of Europe and America recognize simple truths? Or are there no sensible people?

To insure universal peace, we must be practical. Fine words and expressions of good intentions will not insure peace. The most practical means is to secure co-ordinated co-operation by a group of nations sufficiently powerful to impress their will upon the rest of the world. To do this they must themselves benefit. This can be insured by providing that they share the possessions of those nations who do not belong to this alliance and who oppose the abolition of war.

To accomplish this requires a higher standard of leadership than has yet prevailed in international affairs. If the leadership be forthcoming, a form of international citizenship can be created in which all citizens of all nations will be loyal to the world as well as to their own nations. In order that this international citizenship may be established, it is essential that it be combined with self-interest.

Idealism alone when opposed by self-interest will be severely handicapped. Combine idealism and self-interest with able leadership and ruthless force, and world peace will be established. The abolition of war will not be the greatest benefit. Great as this boon will be to mankind, it will be exceeded by the creation of higher standards of individual character and international conduct.

It would be sensible for the altruistic nations of the world to compose their difficulties and require all selfish nations to disarm—by sheer force, if necessary. The altruistic nations could then reduce their armaments, thus lessening the great burden they impose upon taxpayers and industry generally. Maintaining vast armaments to protect oneself against attack indefinitely is far less sensible than assembling an overwhelming force and crushing those who threaten to attack. We should face this problem and meet it now—not put it off for an indefinite day of reckoning, not shirk our task and pass on to generations as yet unborn problems we should solve today.

The action of nations, in going to war to deprive other countries of territories or for national gain, is organized brigandage on a large scale, and just as much of a crime as brigandage on any scale. Individual criminals must be suppressed in the interest of the individual citizen, and likewise individual criminal nations. To do this will require an international agency, powerful, able and respected, that will give justice to all.

It is not necessary for the rest of the world to submit to the dominance of dictatorships or oligarchies that assume to direct the thoughts of the people of their countries and pursue policies detrimental to international harmony. Their people can be appealed to through the radio in a language they will understand.

Regardless of how powerful any oligarchy may appear, the very fact that it suppresses questioning and free thought, is an indication of instability and weakness. The proper place to attack is at this weak point. Educate the people under the dominance of a vicious oligarchy to see its viciousness. Expose it. Not by means of vile propaganda, but by positive truths that cannot be refuted.

Such action need not necessarily be taken by a government. Those interested in international harmony and man's future welfare should be willing to lend their efforts and ability in such a campaign of international education. Contributions could be accepted from all sources to finance the undertaking. Money spent in this way would be far more effective in preventing future wars than any other method if well directed.

From the standpoint of psychology, war is more akin to the activities of criminal gangs than any other form of social activity. Criminal gangs are inspired by lack of Co, Primo, and Extro, and dominated by descendent Groupo. They do not analyze their own acts. They do not consider the sufferings of others outside their groups. They only seek to advance their immediate self-interest. This is substantially the attitude of nations involved in war.

War, in fact, is worse, because each nation can impute noble motives to itself and bad motives to the enemy, by this means obtaining the support of good people. The criminal gangs cannot impute noble motives to themselves in such way as to obtain the support of fine people. Their selfish aims are apparent to the intelligent.

If we have a universal high standard of intelligence, a knowledge of Ascendent Psychology and an international outlook on the part of all men to strive for the benefit of all, we could transfer their loyalty from a national basis to an international one. This would prevent selfish nationalists from leading this fine quality of loyalty into waging war against one's fellow men.

A nation having this fine international viewpoint, might find it necessary to war against the criminal nation opposing the development of an international outlook. The criminal must be controlled by force. Criminal nations opposing the interests of man must likewise be restrained with force.

We can classify war by criminal nations as being descendent and war on criminal nations as being ascendent. The latter type war should be supported by all people having the future welfare of man at heart. If all support such efforts intelligently, descendent war can be abolished from the earth.

Sensible methods of prevention against crime would not be limited to arming oneself as a protection alone. If intelligent methods were employed force would be used to eliminate the criminal entirely. We should employ force to eliminate international gangster criminal nations. Let us cease to arm ourselves against their attacks. Let us instead destroy them and avoid the need for constant vigilance and the maintenance of expensive armaments forever.

He who gives no heed to the future, living only in the present, is prihuman. So likewise are nations who, in the conduct of both their internal and international affairs, fail to consider the future intelligently. Applying this thought to existing governments, we are bound to conclude that practically all are prihuman in nature. They consider the present without regard for the future. They are concerned with obtaining present benefits, unaware that evils are developing that threaten the destruction of the better elements of man's nature in some future day if they are permitted to develop unchecked.

A most discreditable exhibition for powerful civilized white nations is displayed by Italy and Great Britain in radio broadcasts designed to appeal to Arabs. This has gone to the extent of presenting free radio sets in order that the broadcast may be received. It is a sign of weakness on the part of these powers to court semisavage tribes by propaganda. Each power endeavors to obtain their support, at the same time discrediting opposing powers. Why cannot civilized nations agree upon a policy, a definite aim, and work together to advance civilization rather than stir up strife among semi-savage tribes in an effort to obtain their support to harass and injure the interests of each other?

Japanese expansion is defended for the reason that they have insufficient territory in their own country for the rapidly increasing population. They should therefore be permitted to expand into other countries to relieve congestion at home. This is a good policy for the Japanese but bad for the white race and the future interest of man. Under no condition should colored races be permitted to expand into territory suitable for settlement by white races. In fact, we should reverse this process. Encourage their emigration from white territory to lands unsuited for white settlement.

An excellent illustration of this condition is afforded by our negroes in the United States. Vast territories exist in the tropics suitable for the negro race. They should be caused to emigrate to these vast unsettled tropical areas. Their departure from the United States would render it possible for us to relieve the congestion of some European nations. We could then permit some of the most desirable people from Europe to emigrate to the United States.

A great deal of the intense national rivalry and friction in Europe is caused by congestion. The countries are small and overpopulated. The problem of living is so difficult as to prevent high standards of living or an advanced degree of development. Any measures we can employ that would render territory available for settlement by the white races should be employed. It would not only relieve congested conditions and improve their economic well-being; it will also prove sound for the development of future generations.

It is very unfair for the races of continental Europe not possessing colonies to be denied expansion, when there are such vast amounts of undeveloped territory in the world. One of the great virtues of a world government would be to correct this injustice. Europe is the home of the white people. The future interest of man demands that the white race be permitted to develop, populate, and control the world. We should therefore render all suitable territory available for settlement by Europeans.

The belligerent attitude of present-day German leaders will turn the world against them. There is an increasing liking for fairness in all men. We can sympathize with Germany's wrongs but we cannot sympathize with the aims and methods of her present rulers. Germany was unjustly treated after the World War. Now having become strong again she seeks revenge and will be unjust to others in her turn. Let us all be just to each other at all times. Then no one will suffer injustice and later be tempted to exact revenge for past sufferings.

Germany's leaders are products of environmental influences. They have brooded upon the injustices done Germany upon the conclusion of the World War. They have again revived the dream of Germanic domination that was instrumental in causing the World War. They have sought to appeal to the German people by waving the bloody shirt much as our northern politicians did after the Civil War. The bloody-shirt policy was unsound then. It is unsound today.

We must find means to enlist the co-operation of the

German people in advancing their aim and the aim of civilization. We can appeal to their own self-interest in carrying out such a program of education. They would be sensible enough to see that waving the bloody shirt is opposed to their own best interests. If we extend to the German people an invitation to co-operate in the promotion of world harmony, if we associate with it a program that will serve German people and all white people, their support can be obtained.

Germany's leaders are not international-minded. They continually stress the virtues of the Germans and assume an extremely truculent attitude toward other races. In this respect the German leaders are as short-sighted as the Japanese leaders. Both unnecessarily antagonize other nations and races. If they are opposed with any degree of skill whatever, such policies will defeat themselves. No nation is willing to be conquered by another nation.

What we need is an international government that will serve all races and nations. The aggressive actions of the Japanese and Germans may stimulate this development. Other nations should be sensible enough to refuse to continually live in fear of attack. They should combine and subdue these aggressors. They should establish a world free from war in which the rights of all are fully respected.

The attitude of the rulers of Germany and Japan is very similar to the attitude of our labor leaders. They are never satisfied with what they obtain. They will consistently and continually demand more. Further concessions granted them are opposed to international harmony. They militate against it. Germany cannot expand any further without causing other nations to suffer. Her present rulers do not consider the rights of other nations. Germany's policies today are not conducive to international harmony. They should be opposed. The Germans are trying to carry out the same policy that failed so hopelessly in the World War. They have less chance of success today than at that time. Yet their leaders foolishly pursue the same policy and are inviting further suffering upon their people.

Disregard by one nation of the rights of others will eventually lead to mass action to subdue the offender. Criminals are deterred from crime by fear of punishment. Nations likewise can be deterred from offenses against other nations by fear of punishment. It is a relatively simple task for the well-behaved nations to band together against nations disregarding the rights of others and suppress them for the common good.

The demagogic propaganda during the World War, particularly in our own country, of waging war to end war and saving democracy, is having a bad effect on international thought today. The failure in the World War to save democracy or to end wars has given many the belief that it cannot be done. Further, when measures are advocated to end war by means of another war, the public very naturally thinks of the propaganda of World War days and vociferously objects to any such action.

We must correct this unfortunate state of affairs. We must teach the public that most men, particularly politicians, are all too willing to clothe their policies in the most glowing colors and highest ideals. Because incompetent men have obtained support by the abuse of good intentions in the past should not prevent support being given able leaders today who will carry them out.

There is a little ray of sunshine for the future that may bring about the solution of international problems. The terrible wars in Spain and China; the constant threat of war throughout the world; the military, air, and naval rivalry among the nations, of Europe particularly, bring forcibly to the attention of all thinkers the horrible threat to all people which exists in such an international atmosphere. This should result in earnest seeking for a solution to international problems and should produce able leaders capable of carrying it out. It should prove so welcome to all nations and people as to insure hearty and universal support.

Thought

Let us abolish war. From a purely business standpoint alone it would be far cheaper to destroy war now than to continue to spend millions each year for armaments.

LV

WORLD SCIENTISM

THE MENTAL OUTLOOK AND HABITS OF PRESENT-DAY MAN, which cause him to look to the present, his own interests and his own locality rather than to the future, the interests of man and the world, are the great difficulty in bringing about sane international policies. If problems between nations were decided with a view to the welfare of all and the future, sane action would be forthcoming and war would be abolished.

Nationalism is the product of environmental influences. The people of a nation very naturally form an interest group. Their institutions are molded so as to strengthen the feeling of nationalism, causing the citizens to support their own nation against others. The feeling of nationalism in Europe was relatively slight before the era of the French Revolution as compared with the present. Its development is due to environmental influences favoring its growth. These influences can just as well be directed toward world peace. To do this requires, on the part of those controlling the nations, a willingness to permit the development of an environment conducive toward world peace. This would require the development of understanding and appreciation of the fact that all men are members of one worldwide interest group and should co-operate harmoniously in order that the best interests of all may be served.

There is a marked relationship between child gangs, nationalism, and war. Why should the Balkan peoples, for instance, hate and hurt one another when they are so similar?

It shows a combination of childish traits, ignorance, the short-sighted view of self-interest, inherited animosities, and re-taliation. The real way to international peace is not to judge people by race but by their service to humanity. This group insanity or group infantilism is commonly seen in our own country in adults when the most trivial incidents sometimes cause one group to ridicule, to threaten, or to attribute false motives to another.

Other factors are often involved, such as feelings of in-feriority, jealousy, envy, and self-interest. It is displayed in our labor disputes, politics, and religion, and is something that can well be eliminated from our life. There is also a considerable amount of boasting similar to that of young children boasting of the prowess of an elder brother. In some minds it becomes an accepted fact after enough repetition. The more one studies man, the more one is forced to conclude that he has not as yet grown up. He remains but a child, and not a particularly intelligent or well-trained one. Let us grow up.

One of the most encouraging hopes for future world peace, and at the same time one of the most depressing spectacles at present, is afforded by the children of all races and nations. Look at them in all countries where they are not too severely repressed, whether negro, Oriental, European or American. If given a chance and brought up in a wholesome environ-ment they are all basically sound, cheerful, and fun-loving, and all enjoy their play. They absorb national hatreds en-tirely from their elders.

It is horrible to think that these innocent youngsters are living in a vicious environment causing them to think ill of children in other nations. When they become adults they are encouraged to denounce each other and have death-dealing weapons placed in their hands to slaughter and kill. They have their very beliefs influenced by vicious thoughts of others who are no more vicious than they.

We may compare this with the condition in our own country today. I saw a picture in a paper recently of some children parading in support of a sit-down strike in which their parents were engaged. What chance have these children, brought up in an atmosphere encouraging them to believe they are being unjustly and harshly treated? What good will they be if they believe that they alone are in the right, and that the employers and those who oppose them are in the wrong? This is identical with the influences brought to bear upon children in the different nations, causing them to hate the children of other nations. They hate others not as the result of inborn hatreds but as the result of the environmental influences brought to bear upon them.

If the wealthy, if the employers in our country are so vicious as to abuse their employees, for God's sake let us do something about it and stop spreading hate throughout the land! Let us not have this continual agitation of sit-down strikes; of children parading in support of parents on strike; of picket lines thrown around factories and places of work, with strikers using clubs to repel anyone attempting to enter.

You cannot blame this situation upon capital or the employers alone. Labor is equally at fault. The one most at fault is our own federal government. If our leaders are incapable of handling such a situation, put men in charge who can handle it. The same applies to international affairs. We do not have an international government to control vicious nations. If we can establish within our country a government capable of governing, we may set an example of efficient government to the world. Then we may hope for the creation of a government for the world equally competent.

The European peasant is the finest of men, hard-working and long-suffering, asking only for a square deal, the right to work, to be happy, to enjoy life, to pay taxes, and to support the world. False, selfish, incompetent rulers and leaders have proven inferior to him and unfit to rule him. They have not entirely destroyed his virtues. He will retain some always in spite of them. But if he only had a chance! Let us give him one. Suffering suppression and abuse, slaughtered on the battlefields for centuries by the millions, giving up his life to his rulers at their bidding, believing that in doing so he was helping them—oh, the tragedy of it! If only the rulers were even in slight degree as good as the ruled! Can we not give him the rulers to which he is entitled, and which he has earned by centuries of service? The answer to this should be Yes, but look where we will, all indications point to No. His rulers are again about to have the peasants slaughter each other. How terrible! If only they could be made to understand!

National rivalries, war, and preparations for war press heaviest against the very poorest classes in all nations. Rivalries between nations result in interference with foreign trade which seriously hampers internal trade. As a consequence, the poorer classes are penalized by paying higher prices for goods purchased, by lower wages, and by unemployment. Under modern conditions, the maintenance of armies and navies is very costly. This money must be raised by loans or by taxation. Either of these devices imposes a burden upon the most poorly paid.

National rivalries and preparations for war have a still more harmful effect in preventing the wholesome development of industrial life. When industry is developed with a view to preparedness for war, it is seriously restricted in advancing higher standards of living. The interference by the government seriously restricts the development of individual initiative. It prevents business from developing to meet the social problems of the day.

The heavy taxation, in European countries especially, prevents internal development. For instance, there are relatively few automobiles in Europe. The heavy taxation and poverty of the people prevents wide ownership. Great possibilities exist for an era of prosperity in those countries under competent government with less militarism, less nationalism, and less taxation. People the world over have just cause to feel resentful of the way they are treated. The resentment should be directed toward their own government and incompetent leaders. These leaders are unable to improve the

welfare of the poor man. They obtain his support by denouncing some other nation or class, blaming them for the
suffering of the workingman.

What a great development would take place in Europe,
Asia, and Africa if they were all under one government,
controlled by able leaders! Roads could be built from Con-
stantinople to Shanghai and Capetown with hotels lining
the routes. Tourists and automobile trucks could drive all
over the three continents without hindrance.

To bring about better understanding between people of
the nations, facilitate commercial relations, and lessen the
possibility of international conflict, we should establish an
international language. The easiest way to do this would be
to take the English language as the basis upon which to work;
it is nearly an international language now.

We should establish a phonetic alphabet, using the most
commonly accepted symbols of the English language and in
foreign languages that would be most familiar to all. The
number of distinct sounds in English is around fifty or
sixty, the total number of sounds in all languages around
three hundred.

To this phonetic English alphabet should be added the
necessary letters to provide for writing all languages in the
world. We should then bring about its adoption as the
international alphabet, and all people should use it in writing. By thus having all languages using one alphabet, the
tendency with use would be to select and use those words
that most clearly express the meaning. In time a truly international language would be evolved in much the same way
that our present languages have developed.

If this program would meet with the co-operation of all
countries, they could provide for compulsory education in
their own language and, in addition, the compulsory teaching of English, thus making it possible for the traveler to
travel throughout the world and transact his business in one
international language. This would be a great boon to
commerce, would promote sympathetic understanding of

the people of one country with those of another. It would be a great move in the interest of world-wide peace. It would further the spread of scientific knowledge by facilitating its communication in ready form to all people. From the standpoint of man throughout the world, this would be a most beneficial measure and would cost little.

There are several thousand different languages in the world. Each of these languages has many different individual sounds, anywhere from one to several dozen. The international phonetic alphabet would use only necessary letters. These identical letters would be used in all languages. We would then have several thousand different languages each containing many different sounds, all of which could be indicated by the use of about three hundred letters and symbols.

The natural tendency over a long period of time would be to develop one language for all men the world over, if we could overcome the spirit of national rivalry and other opposing influences. This development would save very much in the interest of efficiency. It would permit effort now spent in mastering many different languages to be directed into more constructive channels. It would facilitate the ability of any one person to master any other language.

The European languages lend themselves to development of a phonetic alphabet based upon the English language today. There are some thirty or forty European languages, all intimately related. They have grown away from each other by lack of association and opposing interests. They can grow together by harnessing today's present facilities for ready communication and substituting, instead of opposing interests, a common interest.

The greatest philologists and language authorities of the world should be assembled on the task of building up this international alphabet. A permanently constituted board should be established to supervise the preparation of international dictionaries and generally further the development of the alphabet. Simplicity, use, and practical application should be stressed. Theoretical linguists will have to be associated with practical men in working out this solution. Some simple means of printing to show the accent and pronunciation, may be helpful at first, to be eliminated as the pronunciation becomes readily understood. It is possible to show the finest shades of enunciation by the use of standard letters and simple symbols of pronunciation.

With the adoption of this phonetic alphabet for the English language, simplified spelling would naturally have to be a part of the program. This in itself would be a great boon to our educational system in educating the young, saving years of wasted effort, and lengthening the individual's life by that amount. It would facilitate the mastering of the English language by foreigners, saving them much effort.

We should look upon the establishment of an international phonetic alphabet and language as being a move in evolutionary progress. To insure harmony throughout the world, we must have all men so taught that they may understand all other men. This is best accomplished by all speaking one language.

The object of establishing an international phonetic alphabet would be to provide for the eventual establishment of one language throughout the entire world. By adopting a universal phonetic alphabet and having all nations employ it in their present language, an international language will be eventually developed by absorbing into itself the best and most expressive words and terms of all existing languages.

If we could secure the whole-hearted co-operation of all races, nations, and people to bring this about, it could be accomplished in a relatively brief period. Present-day facilities in communication, education, and spread of the printed and spoken word, all favor such a development. If we could divert the effort now being used by intense nationalists to spread their own culture and language to contribute toward an international language and culture, the task would be very simple.

Man is foolishly spending much effort in war and nationalistic propaganda that prevents his own future advance. If we can bring about, throughout the white race, a willingness to cooperate and establish a universal European culture throughout the world, all nations sharing and contributing of their best, we will have a wholesome international atmosphere that will insure the success of the aim.

The attainment of international peace, amity, and good will, requires intelligent effort directed toward:

1. The development of a world-wide religion stressing individual Ascendency and contributing toward man's mission as being the duty of all.
2. Alleviation of racial animosities by making the white race paramount in world affairs and beneficiently controlling other races.
3. The development of a universal language so that all may readily understand one another.
4. The creation of one universal interest group inspiring the loyalty of all men.
5. The molding of all national cultures into an international culture absorbing the best from each.
6. The use of publicity, the development of education and all environmental forces to further the attainment of man's mission.

Christianity is the religion of the white race. We can develop it into a world religion conducive to harmony and world peace. We have but to associate Christianity with Ascendent Psychology to make it an ascendent religion contributing toward the attainment of man's mission and furthering individual Ascendency.

In establishing a universal interest group of all men the world over, we must consider practical application, human nature, and the future. To meet all the requirements, this universal interest group must be composed of races sufficiently harmonious among themselves to prevent racial antagonism. Thus this interest group must be the white race. To insure both the present and future good, it must be based upon a selected group within the white race—those of high moral character and superior intelligence. We should consistently endeavor to raise this intelligence and character by improving the culture and environment. We should also encourage the increase in numbers of this selected group by positive means, and by negative means decrease those of poorer quality.

We observe in different nations a great deal of activity toward natural development and the training of vast numbers of men in the army and navy for the purpose of serving their country. The citizens of each nation believe they are doing this for the best. It is but natural that this feeling should exist. All world-wide environmental influences tend to intensify nationalism to make of each nation an intensified interest group seeking salvation by its own effort.

With such an international and national viewpoint there is no other channel in which really fine citizens can direct their activities to advance their nation's interests. By creating a white man's interest group throughout the world we can obtain the loyalty of all the white nations, placing international loyalty above national. They would then have the redemption of man and the solution of man's mission to work for. As great a loyalty could be obtained toward advancing man himself as is now being obtained in advancing the interests of each particular nation.

This is approaching the solution of war and international harmony in a scientific way in accord with human nature. To accomplish this great undertaking will require great practical ability and the ablest of leadership. Many difficult problems exist between the white nations themselves; but they can be solved if sufficient effort and ability is directed toward their solution.

Enduring world peace will be practically impossible as long as the individual's loyalty is to his nation. National loyalty prevents an international outlook. The nations are then primarily selfish interest groups seeking their own advantage without regard for the welfare of all. To insure enduring peace, we must establish the individual's loyalty toward the world, toward man as a whole. We must establish an international government that will receive this loyalty direct. The various national governments then, instead of arousing national feeling as they are now doing, will be subdivisions of this world government. They will have, as one of their primary reasons for existence, the promotion of international citizenship. Their efforts will then be directed toward international harmony. Instead of placing national interest before international, they will place international interest before national. This will insure world peace.

A very efficient type of international government could be established by having the affairs of the world controlled by a selective senate of twenty or thirty master scientists. If they were the ablest men in the world, well-qualified for their positions, they could control all affairs of man throughout the world, prevent war and insure harmony.

It is useless to attempt to establish such a world government until some large nation such as our own has established one of a similar kind and has it in successful operation. Then, having proven a success, it may be adopted as a form of government for the world. .

To insure the satisfactory solution of international affairs requires that all citizens in the world consider themselves members of the vast interest group of man the world over, that they strive for the interest of all men and not for particular nations. This view cannot well be established as long as we have many separate nations dominated by leaders who appeal to national feelings to maintain themselves in office. Their loyalty is to their nation, not to the world. To insure international harmony we must establish a citizenship whose loyalty will be to the world, not to the nation only.

A selective senate of master scientists controlling the world and appointing the rulers of the various nations would make these rulers internationally minded, instead of nationally minded as at present. That is to say, they would have an international outlook, their loyalty would be to the international government. They would promote measures to advance international harmony. At present the great bar to international peace is the activities of the rulers of the nations, in advocating measures designed to enhance national self-interest regardless of international interest. Scientism will insure the prevalence of the sensible broad viewpoint that the interests of all nations are dependent upon furthering international interests.

In order to establish a sound international government we will have to proceed very slowly. The spirit of nationalism cannot be abolished at once. Economic questions must be handled with great skill and existing barriers gradually eliminated. Existing barriers have resulted in the various industries in different nations adapting themselves to them. Great harm could be done by sudden drastic action. All problems, no matter how difficult, can be solved if the solution be earnestly sought. The most essential thing is to obtain on the part of all human beings a realization that they are citizens of the world. Then build upon this foundation a determination to solve man's problems.

Scientism is not only the most efficient form of government for any one nation, but it is the only type government that will prove adequate to the task of governing the entire world. Scientism is based upon the basic principles of human nature and nature itself. It will apply these principles in an endeavor to develop social institutions appealing to the best within the individual human being. In time it can bring about a world utopia.

Thought

What the entire world wants is a revolution against the Right and the Left, a revolution against extremists. Let the decent, hard-working, level-headed middle-class people assert their power and control all insane agitators.

LVI

BY THE WAY

Health, Wealth

WHAT PERSON IN THE ENJOYMENT OF EXCELLENT HEALTH would exchange it for feeble health and sickness accompanied by wealth? We all too commonly take health for granted and do not appreciate the great boon it is. We are continually striving to accumulate wealth. We stress economic difficulties to the exclusion of other interests. Any person possessing excellent health possesses something far more valuable than great wealth.

The Simple Life

We have a vast number of environmental influences opposing the simple life. For instance, many commercial agencies advertise widely to sell their products. We hear much declamation regarding the merits of Coca-Cola, chewing gum, and similar items. It is questionable whether we should permit unlimited advertising of this nature. Neither Coca-Cola nor chewing gum are essential to life. They oppose living a simple life. We should eat simple foods, drink simple things, dress simply, use those articles that are natural and wholesome. We should discourage the use of the artificial and the unnatural. Instead of having so much advertising extolling commercial products, we should have advertising to encourage the simple life.

I have heard much over the radio of the merits of Carter's

Little Liver Pills. Almost all human ailments and spells of poor disposition are attributed to a liver condition which Carter's Pills can readily correct. If, instead of buying liver pills, these people would indulge in a little more exercise, do more work, and develop a healthful mental attitude, they would be in far better condition. I doubt whether Carter's Little Liver Pills can improve one's brains. Intelligent use of the brains, however, will accomplish this. This must be done by the individual himself. A good start on his part would be to disregard advertising attributing marvelous virtues to medicinal pills.

I have heard much discussion over the radio regarding the merits of Tums. It is claimed that they correct the acid condition of the stomach resulting from overeating. Their sponsors actually encourage people to overeat to obtain the pleasure derived from it and then use Tums to prevent harmful reactions. Here we have the producer of a product actually encouraging harmful acts in order to sell his product. The stomach will be benefited by eating simple foods. Most of us would be better off if we ate much less than we do at present. When an advertiser encourages people to overeat and then urges the purchase of his product to prevent ill effects, he is contributing toward ill health. Advertising of this nature should be utterly prohibited.

Today (March 30, 1938) on the radio, I happened to hear a portion of some propaganda to sell products that arouses my ire. The announcer represented a company handling food products. He cited an incident in which a backward child, dull, uncertain, hesitant, was given this particular product and, in a short time, ceased to be backward and became intelligent, active, and alert. I object strenuously to such misrepresentation of any product. I also object to appealing to a mother's finer feelings. If a child is backward and stupid, it is very unlikely that any article of food will remedy this condition. There are usually a great many other factors involved. Such advertising will cause many mothers having backward children to purchase this product, hoping to benefit them. In many cases, the hope is without foundation. In some cases, the child's case is beyond remedy. Yet these radio salesmen stress the benefits their products will accomplish by its use. Unquestionably a good diet will help children but it cannot achieve miracles. All too often products of little merit are extolled far beyond their worth. Publicity and advertising agencies often endeavor to arouse whatever feelings they can to sell their products. We must bring about higher standards on the part of advertisers and commercial firms. They must be required to sell products of proven merit. They must be prevented from selling poor products by means of false representation.

Herdé

The human mind is incapable of realizing the Herdé effects of infinitesimal acts or things. We cannot see the influence of the relatively insignificant upon the vast universe. Because we are unable to do so we are unable to understand everything. We can, to some degree, visualize the overpowering effect of the sun upon the earth in some of its simpler manifestations. We are utterly unable to visualize the effect which the activities of a single ant will have upon the sun. Yet it is the activities of millions of antlike creatures and things, associated with larger objects such as the sun and with still larger objects beyond our comprehension, that perpetuate the universe. They produce continued change and adaptation to this change; the constant evolution of life, of matter and of force. The most minute affect the most mammoth; the most mammoth affect the most minute. The sun and all large things in existence are aggregations of an infinite number of ant like elements.

Mass Emotions

We can readily account for mass emotions by attributing them to the influence of Spirito and Herdo. That is to say, a group of human beings of somewhat similar tastes and likes can be emotionally aroused by the same conditions.

Practically all human feelings can be harnessed to further an emotional state of this kind. It has occurred to me, however, that some part of this emotional condition may be attributable to herdé influences. The many individuals composing a group would tend to create somewhat of a herdé affinity among themselves. This could react upon herdé influences existing without the individuals of which we have no knowledge. Herdé exforces, we might call them. We can neither prove nor disprove this possibility. There does seem to be somewhat of a relationship between mass emotionalism and some of the manifestations of herdé consciousness. It is very likely that the same or similar forces are employed to some degree in each.

Brain Research

Pursue suggested ideas from a book previously read regarding used and unused brain cells. The writer advanced the theory that certain brain cells having had cell imprints created within them and having been assembled in nerve paths with other brain cells, become working cells. These seemed to be sharply differentiated in the brain from unused cells. The latter show signs of lack of use, of not being developed.

Carrying this theory to a logical conclusion, it would seem that the brain has a vast store of cells for future eventualities. As the child develops, the most conveniently located cells have impressions made upon them and are associated with other cells being similarly developed. Depending upon the activity of the individual the number of used cells increases and the unused ones decreases.

Unquestionably, fine distinctions of location and ideas will exist in different individuals. This will be influenced by heritage and by use throughout their lives. The brain is constructed on such a delicate scale that we are prevented from observing these fine shades of differences.

No two human brains are entirely alike at birth. A difference exists even though it be so fine as to prevent detection by the finest instruments. As the individual grows older, the variations will increase. The influence of his environment, of the use to which his brain is subjected, will all tend to cause it to still further differentiate itself from all other brains.

The aim of Ascendent Psychology is to master the principles governing this brain development; to assist each individual to developing his brain to be an efficient instrument. This development must be in accord with inherited gifts and acquired desires. One of the objects of establishing an ascendent environment is to promote the development of institutions furthering the aim of Ascendent Psychology.

The above was a personal note to insure further research into the functioning of the brain. Inasmuch as this series of books is intended to stimulate thought, particularly among young inquiring minds, I include it herein. If many fresh young minds devote their efforts towards perfecting Ascendent Psychology, mastery of the brain, human nature and man's problems, a consistent advance will be made in man's affairs. We must stress not only material advance, not only mental and moral advance, but also make life itself more worth living. Those who contribute toward this noble endeavor will themselves obtain the greatest of pleasure from pride of achievement, deep interest, and unselfish efforts. —*February 27, 1938.*

Mental Conditioning

An excellent example of mental conditioning is afforded by noise and distraction. Ordinarily thought is best conducted in solitude, in a quiet place, free from noise or distraction. Thought conducted in the presence of distractions or noise requires increased energy. This is caused by the fact that energy is being employed to conduct thought and is also being employed to overcome the effect of the noise and distraction. One can, however, become conditioned to the presence of noises or distractions, becoming utterly oblivious of them and able to conduct thought very nearly as efficiently as if they did not exist.

If a person accustomed to thinking in a quiet secluded nook is placed where there is much noise and distraction, his efficiency as a thinker suffers. If, however, he continues his efforts, in time he overcomes the influence of the noise and the presence of distractions. This, however, will apply only to accustomed noises or accustomed distractions. After a person has been accustomed to these, they are ignored. Noises or distractions of an unusual type must be conditioned by familiarity in order to be disregarded.

In this process of conditioning noises and distractions, a most complicated series of factors is employed. The intense desire of the individual to accomplish certain things results in the subconscious endeavoring to further his desire. The entire system automatically endeavors to adjust itself to the desire. In this case the desire is to think. Therefore, as thinking cannot be done efficiently in the presence of noises and distractions, the subconscious mind automatically builds up a specialized form of inhibition which disregards those things tending to interfere with the pursuit of thought.

We can liken this conditioning to noise and distraction to the functioning of Granto. A person taking benefits for granted simply ceases to think about them. His attention is concentrated upon other things. Similarly, a thinker, having overcome the interference of noise and distractions, simply ceases to note them, refuses to recognize their existence, and at the same time directs his energy toward thinking.

This illustration also points out how in one case normal human qualities are ascendently employed and in the other case descendently employed. Conditioning to disregard noise and the distractions hindering constructive thought is an ascendent development. A person, however, who refuses to note the many benefits he receives, is guilty of descendent conduct. It is by intelligent understanding of these basic principles of human nature and their sensible employment that future generations will attain high standards of thought, conduct, and achievement.

Mental Functioning

We may liken the functioning of inhibition during the process of thinking to the resistance of electricity. If we vary the physical structure of a wire, we vary its resistance. This is substantially what takes place in the nerve cells of the brain. It is done automatically in order to guide nerve impulses to the appropriate brain cells. Coupled, of course, with the functioning of inhibition is excitation. An impression received arouses excitation which is positive action, the opposite of inhibition.

Excitation causes a relaxation of inhibition, lessening the resistance of the physical structure of the nerves, in order to permit freer flow of nerve currents. Recent experiments to test the resistance of nerve fibers of plants demonstrated that this resistance is reduced two hundred times at the point of activity. That is to say, the nerve impulses of the plant increase the conductivity of the nerve fiber two hundred times by lessening the resistance normally existing to their passage in an undisturbed state.

This same development occurs in the human brain in a higher degree. Applying the force-adaptation principle we see that an impulse or series of impulses will leave permanent impressions upon the brain. This will result in definitely establishing the inhibition or resistance to guide similar or related impulses to their proper destination. This destination will be that part of the brain best fitted to handle the message. These impulses, or nerve messages, work in conjunction with Survival, the instinct, the senses, and the entire body structure. All by virtue of force-adaptation are being constantly modified to permit more complex activities.

Dreams

Dreams will often afford us a ready means of observing the mental functioning of hunches, premonitions, and precognition. Dreams are produced by mental activity. So likewise are hunches and similar phenomena. If we understood the functioning of the brain thoroughly, we could explain each satisfactorily.

The interesting feature of dreams in regard to hunches is that they anticipate future happenings by past experiences and knowledge; by past feelings of anxiety, dread, or desire. To these elements the brain often adds little embellishments of its own which may be untrue, impossible, or ridiculous.

Such embellishments are illustrative of primitive thought. During a dream the seat of consciousness is slumbering in whole or in part and the instinct brain, the primitive mind, is in control. This has been the origin of many religious beliefs. It is an example of the way many men actually reason today. They believe what they wish to believe or what they fear, finally accepting such beliefs as being positive facts. The able thinker will consistently seek for the truth and develop his brain to contribute toward this, the opposite of primitive methods.

Past thoughts of the most trivial nature or transient events may be interwoven in dreams. These trivial thoughts or incidents may even extend back into babyhood before conscious recall. This is due to the fact that, as a baby, certain impressions were registered upon your brain. Your conscious mind had not yet sufficiently developed to recall these consciously. They are therefore in your subconscious mind. When, during a dream, these impressions are stirred into activity, they will appear in the dream, often in the most grotesque way.

During dreams some brain cells are activated by what closely approaches pure chance. There will be a lessening of the inhibition of certain brain cells. Also as the result of past mental activity, some will have a greater responsiveness to certain other cells. When, during a dream, certain cells are activated, they tend to activate others that are most responsive to them or are in a disturbed condition. This disturbed condition may be the result of bodily activity such as overeating or disease. This is why we sometimes have such grotesque dreams.

Things happen in dreams that are absolutely impossible because of what we can well describe as a conglomerate jumble of brain cells. We might liken this condition to that of having a well kept set of files placed in a jumble of confusion by dumping them together and mixing them up generally. As a result of this activity many unrelated items will be in close proximity to others with which they are not normally connected.

We can visualize this condition to some extent in dreams. A very similar jumble of thought may become definitely established conclusions. As a result of pernicious activity, the brain paths are adapted to this particular jumble. The very natural human trait of thinking well of oneself causes the possessor to believe he has something of merit. This confidence develops into a strong belief and prevents him from putting his thought jumble back into an orderly file from which sensible information could be obtained.

This thought jumble may result in complete insanity or in an infinite number of degrees between the sane and insane. When the individual accepts certain things as being positive facts, his entire brain structure is adapted to this all-absorbing belief. With the passage of time and the indulgence of similar activity, it becomes still more firmly established.

It is for this reason that we should encourage children at the tenderest age to exercise Primo, to question their beliefs. If they establish beliefs founded on facts, on the truth, their entire mental development will be wholesome. If they establish false conclusions, refuse to question them, their entire brain development will be built around erroneous assumptions. It will be utterly impossible to establish a sound working brain after this condition has existed for a considerable period.

Mother Hostility

Today's (March 1, 1938) paper published the result of an interview with a prominent psychiatrist regarding mother love. Substantially this psychiatrist said that mother love is just a myth and that his experience indicated that most neurotic children suffered from parent hostility. He further stated that many incorrigible or mentally ill children brought to his attention, were suffering from psychiatric states induced by maternal hatred rather than love. He cited numerous cases of mothers' cruelty, such as sprinkling cayenne pepper on children's tongues to prevent lying, catching their fingers in rat traps to conquer stealing habits and prolonged beating for petty misdeeds.

This expert failed to explain just why mothers treated their children so. This is an example of present-day psychiatry. Our psychiatrists talk a great deal but they do not know what they are talking about. Naturally a man who devotes his life to a profession will acquire some knowledge regarding it. Our psychiatrists know just enough to prevent sensible action. They employ vast numbers of technical terms which sound impressive but are meaningless. Why doesn't this psychiatrist explain why mothers abuse their children? Why doesn't he assist mothers in controlling themselves and avoid committing cruel acts?

Mother love is a basic force, one of the strongest human feelings in existence. When a mother treats her child cruelly, it is the result of many other influences. A cruel mother is invariably unhappy, dissatisfied, and discontented. Very often when the mother does abuse the child, both are to blame. The child is sometimes wayward, unruly or thoughtless. The mother may abuse the child because she has no other outlet upon which to vent her displeasure. This abuse is the result of lack of Primo, Extro, and Co.

When the mother is confined in the home subject to many annoyances, if she is not a strong character, she tends to brood over them, magnifying their importance. She fails to see faults in herself and is all too willing to blame others. If her child misbehaves it is very possible for her to develop the child into a scapegoat for all things and punish him needlessly.

Abuse of children by their mothers is not the result of lack of mother love or its nonexistence. It is the misuse of Responso to such an extent as to overpower the normal feeling of mother love. To this degree it approaches a state of mental unsoundness; not insanity in the full sense but somewhat of a descendent obsession.

Each case of cruelty by the mother would require knowledge of the mother's entire life. If she permits circumstances to control, her acts will be a process of development influenced by all experiences of her life. When a person misuses Responso, they may harness all psychas to support harmful acts. Continual brooding on unpleasant things will build a molehill into a mountain and in the process of building draw upon all human feelings.

Very often the mother's abuse is caused by resentment of repression and injustice, stored up within her. This resentment may readily be expressed when the child commits some small offense. The mother then, her feelings and emotions aroused, resorts to drastic action to punish the child, believing she is doing it because of the child's wrongdoing. Actually this is a means for her to obtain expression of repressed feelings and a relief of inner tension, and also a means of exercising Migro.

The mother's abuse of the child may also be an Expresso, Glance over the different Expressos and note how many could be concerned in abuse of the child by its mother. Many can be so employed. When we combine with these Expressos the many other feelings of which a human being is capable, we can satisfactorily explain any act of cruelty by a mother. Just as many womens' normal sex lives have been thwarted by the artificial conditions of civilized living, so has the normal instinctive expression of mother love been thwarted by harmful mental attitudes.

Abuse by the mother may be occasional, spasmodic, as the result of moods; it can also be more or less consistent. It may even be directed mainly toward one child to the exclusion of others. It is very easy to visualize a situation in which the mother has had a severe quarrel with her husband, putting her in a bad mood. Some slight infraction by a thoughtless child would then be likely to receive more severe punishment than justified.

When we consider lack of Primo and Extro, coupled with somewhat of a martyr complex, we can readily visualize a condition in which the mother will vent her ill-feeling upon thoughtless children. Her action, instead of improving the conduct of the children, very often makes it worse, thus bringing further action of a similar kind.

Cases of cruelty by the mother to her child are relatively rare. Those mothers who consistently abuse their children are a very slight percentage. They are the victims of unwholesome mental conditions but not more so than the average politician or agitator who claims to have a cure for social problems.

The agitator's cure will always advance his own interests and express his own feeling. Similarly the mother who mistreats her children is permitting moods, frustration, irritation, or unhappiness to cause her to be unjust. She wishes to punish them for wrongdoing, not realizing her own shortcomings. The agitator also usually has a scapegoat whom he wishes to overthrow or punish for the unsatisfactory conditions of himself or his group.

Training Children

In training children be fair to them, share the hardships, the struggles, the deprivation of pleasure. You must be generous in sharing suffering with them. If they share agony and suffering, they are sharing something which wealth cannot buy. They are having built within them a greater understanding of agony, of adversity, of thoughtfulness, and are being made strong worthwhile persons. Give them the full share of those things that torture the very soul of man. Then they will be better able to appreciate the suffering of others. They will be more worthy as a result of understanding what suffering is. If they never experienced anguish of soul, they have missed something that will strengthen the strongest character.

Friends, Children

Real friends make life worth living. One of the finest pleasures in life is to have the friendship of fine deserving people. One should seek to obtain worthwhile friends in order to live a successful life. For this reason we should have children of our own; true friends created by ourselves. God created man. He has given to us the ability to create other men and women after our own image. Is it not godlike to create another being to perpetuate yourself? How much pleasure and joy there is in bringing a fine fresh mind into the world, setting a good example, watching the young being develop into maturity. Children make us more unselfish. They can be our truest friends. We should not forego this highest pleasure of life. We should indulge it to the fullest, both as a matter of personal gain and of duty.

Personal Evolution

Do you realize that during your lifetime you pass through an evolution not unlike that of man himself? You came into this world a small helpless babe. You grew rapidly, learned to walk and talk; you became conscious of your surroundings; then you learned to read and write; to observe and reason about what was going on about you. Then you reached adolescence, thought of love, high ideals, and great achievements. Then manhood. And finally complete maturity.

Unlike the evolution of man, which is controlled by the forces of nature, you can to a great degree control your own evolution. You can direct your activities into constructive channels. You can develop good character and improve your intelligence. You should seek within yourself for knowledge regarding your gifts and your shortcomings. Look upon yourself as being a mechanism of marvelous construction. Take pride in using this mechanism so as to develop it into a still greater marvel.

Self-development, whether it be mental, moral, or material, demands the development of Primo. It requires the meticulous cultivation of reflection and of thoughtfulness. When you seek unremittingly for your faults, you become cognizant of their existence and can take measures to correct them. This healthy communing with yourself, this healthy exercise, gives you greater understanding of yourself. Once you inaugurate the habit of reflection and of being thoughtful, it will grow with you.

If man is to advance to high estate, it will be accomplished through the existence of vast numbers of thoughtful reflective individuals. It is this very lack of thoughtfulness and reflection that prevents the solution of present-day problems. Individuals, groups, and nations are all too willing to resort to action without reflection or thought. The result is their action is unwise and does not take into consideration the ultimate consequences. If their acts were carried out after due reflection, the harmful aspects could be eliminated. If great intelligence and consideration for others were developed in addition, they could insure that their actions would be constructive in all respects. Let us be thoughtful and reflect before we act.

You should each day upon arising, upon going to bed, or at any suitable time, say to yourself, "John Doe, you're a fool. Get next to yourself and do something about it. Find out what makes you such a fool and see if you can't overcome this shortcoming." Practice this mental exercise for many years thoroughly, honestly. You will become familiar with your shortcomings and will be able to correct them. This will improve your intelligence and ability to think and make you a more likeable person.

On the contrary, if you form the belief that you are nearly

perfect, that your failure in life is caused by somebody else or that you are the great leader fighting the battle of the forgotten man, you are unable to see faults in yourself or your methods and will not be able to correct them. You become further confirmed in this unwholesome mental attitude with the passage of time. Superficially you may be a pleasing character if your development has taken the direction of pleasing others, but your inherent worth will be slight.

The reason man's affairs are in such sorry state today is because they are being conducted by men unwilling to be honest with themselves, unwilling to seek faults within themselves or faults in the measures they advocate. They have developed a specialized ability to present things in a light to favor their false conclusions.

We must develop leaders who will take the opposite course, who will seek for positive answers, seek constantly for the faults in suggested solutions; men who will not permit personal feelings to cause them to form erroneous conclusions. Let us cease to be governed by obsessionists. Let us be governed by arthoists.

Introverts, Extroverts

To some degree we may consider the introvert to be somewhat further advanced in the evolutionary scale than the extrovert. Of necessity, the introvert uses Responso to a very high degree and Responso is one of the most recent developments in man's evolution. When we associate the introvert with abstract thoughts of an original nature, the comparison with evolutionary advance is more apparent. Many of the lower forms of animal life display activities of a nature resembling the conduct of an extrovert to some degree. But none of the lower forms of animal life exhibit the higher mental attributes of the introvert.

The highest development of the individual demands that he be an invert to some degree Our entire body is a delicate machine which will respond to the use it receives. It will develop as desired, as used and as trained. For the individual to develop himself to the highest degree demands that he possess a knowledge of himself. This requires the ability to look within oneself constantly. This enables one to become cognizant of one's good and bad points and employ measures that will promote constructive development.

The reason so few men today are well developed is because they are largely extroverts. They live outside of themselves and seek the approbation of others. They fail to look within and build up a strong desire to develop self-approbation for one's good qualities.

The introvert has been discredited to some degree because there is danger in abusing concentration upon oneself. It must be of a healthy constructive nature. If it is abused it can lead to mental conflict and even insanity.

We must be introverts to the extent of insuring communion with ourselves, obtaining understanding and furthering self-development. We must not be introverts causing mental conflicts or unhappiness. We must also be extroverts to the extent of seeking the approbation of worthwhile people and enjoying the many things life has to offer outside of ourselves. We must not become extroverts to the extent of living entirely outside of ourselves in the futile pursuit of pleasure or in seeking the approbation of idle people.

The Bloody Shirt

Our labor leaders are bloody-shirt wavers. By this I mean that they appeal to the grievances of the members of their union. They denounce the wealthy and all who oppose them. They accuse them of being enemies endeavoring to enslave the workingman. One who waves the bloody shirt sees no fault in himself or his measures. He sees only merit in himself and his followers and only vicious motives in those who oppose. We see this bloody-shirt waving going on throughout the world. The Japanese militarists and Germany's leaders make use of it. The communists in Russia find the bloody shirt a most effective weapon in controlling the masses. Our own politicians employ it as one of their favorite weapons. They denounce the wealthy, the capitalist, and exalt those who have the most votes. Let us cease to be ruled by those who wave the bloody shirt. Let us cease to have our opinions formed by them. Let us cease to have the environment poisoned by the waving of the bloody shirt.

Waving the bloody shirt is very similar to waving a red flag in front of a bull. The bull is angered, enraged. The appeal of the red flag is not to his brain, it is to unreasoning animal feelings. When our labor leaders or politicians wave the red flag or the bloody shirt, they are appealing to audiences having the mentality of an enraged bull. They are appealing to unreasoning feelings, based not upon intelligence but upon prejudices and grievances. The communists are great wavers of the bloody shirt, of the red flag. The red flag, as being the symbol of the Reds, is very appropriate indeed. They cause their audience to see red, if possible. They appeal to the most despicable feelings of their followers. They appeal to anything but intelligence and consideration for others.

The Selfish Few—The Many Laws

Mr. Roosevelt has recently again denounced the selfish few. This despite the fact that he has been in office five years and has secured the enactment of many laws. Why, may we ask, do not these many laws control the selfish few whom he denounces so freely? The many laws he has brought about are, by his own admission, unequal to the task of controlling the selfish few. Is it not time for a change in government policies and leadership? We would do well to remove the selfish few now controlling our government and repeal the many laws handicapping honest business and industry. Five years of promises and denunciation should be enough to convince even the stupid American public that he who denounces so freely is unable to do anything of a constructive nature.—*March 28, 1938.*

Economic Education

I just glanced over the report of one of our medium-sized
corporations for the year 1937. It is a fair sample of corporation reports and is very interesting for many reasons.
It shows that sales in 1937 were about the same as in 1930
but that taxes were twice as great. Sales during the year
amounted to forty-four million dollars. The net profit was
slightly over three million dollars and total taxes paid
slightly less than two million.

The fact that this corporation paid twice as much taxes on
the same amount of sales as seven years ago sheds light upon
where our present-day government and financial policies are
leading us. These constant attempts to help somebody cost
money. This money is being raised in ways that penalize business, rendering the plight of the country worse as the result
of reform measures intended to improve conditions.

The government receives one-third of all profits without
investing in the company or assuming risk or responsibility.
The government is more certain of obtaining its taxes than
the stockholders are of obtaining dividends. A reduction in
business can wipe out the profits very rapidly. This would
reduce taxes levied upon net income but those taxes levied
on sales and fixed property values will not be subject to
reduction by a reduction in profits. Our government is
actually a preferred partner in all business. One would
think that the government would encourage business in
order to receive greater returns. Yet our government severely
attacks business.

This company's report fails to go into detail regarding
wages, the amounts spent upon research, and similar charges.
This is a criticism we can apply to practically all corporation reports. They fail to take the public into their confidence and adequately show the operations of the corporation. They should, for instance, show the salaries paid to the
management in great detail. They should list, by name,
those who receive considerable sums.

The corporations throughout the country would be advancing their interests if they established a somewhat uniform type of financial statement. This would be an excellent means of educating the public and showing just how business is being handicapped by unwise government and labor policies. A concern that derives a profit of three million dollars from sales of forty-four million is certainly not making undue profits.

The ignorance of the public as to economic matters is the fault of many people; our educators, our politicians and many others. The managers of the corporations are likewise guilty. They should resort to such means as are readily available to educate the public. They should prepare their reports with this object in view.

Thoughts

Visit some of the most backward communities in the country. If you are able to establish friendly relations with these backward individuals and become as one with them, you can readily understand why and how they perpetuate their backward condition. They ridicule outsiders and innovations in order to hide feelings of Inferio. Advance is utterly impossible to people possessing such a state of mind. This primitive outlook can readily be observed not only in these backward communities but among groups claiming to be intelligent as well. Our labor unions form an excellent example of this. They ridicule all who oppose their beliefs. Such a state of mind prevents the solution of the labor problem. If they had the solution, the problem would be solved. When they refuse to heed others, they prevent the development of constructive thought, upon which the solution of labor problems depends.

A strong inner urge to improve one's condition supported by intelligent effort will overcome the handicap of the worst environment. It will even overcome the handicap of a poor heritage provided the mentality is sound.

――――――

We must not permit our emotions to control our sympathy for the underdog. We must be intelligent and recognize the fact that many underdogs are unworthy creatures. Let us give all underdogs a chance. Then we need not waste our sympathy upon those who insist upon remaining underdogs.

――――――

Let us try the honor system for business for awhile. Let us give it a period of, say, five years of the utmost freedom. Put it on trial to redeem itself. Business will then be enrolled on the side of labor to give the laboring man a fair deal in advancing their welfare voluntarily. This would be just the opposite of the present situation in which business is defending itself against unjust demands. Business is today using its efforts in defense against attacks. Why not permit it to direct its efforts into constructive channels?

LVII

CONCLUSION

The Primary Virtue of Democracy

THE PRIMARY VIRTUE OF DEMOCRACY IS INDIVIDUAL FREEDOM of expression. Democracy itself is of little value without individual freedom of expression. Any form of government that promotes, conserves, and protects individual freedom of expression, is a superior form of government. Not only is individual freedom of expression the primary virtue of democracy, it is the primary virtue of all constructive government. It is essential to the development of man as an individual and as a collective group. Democracy exists to nurture and protect individual freedom of expression.

When we hear friends of democracy encouraging multiplicity of laws, government regulation, and the restriction of individual liberty, we should condemn them outright. They are endangering democracy. The true method is to appeal to the individual, master the laws of Ascendent Psychology, and give each individual the greatest freedom of expression. We should have our government directed by those that are worthy of individual expression. Because some abuse individual freedom, we should not penalize those who are worthy. Let us protect the worthy and remove the unwholesome influence of the unworthy.

We should condemn our democratic institutions for the reason that we today are permitting those unworthy of individual freedom of expression to control, regulate, and restrict the freedom of those who are worthy. Our unworthy politicians obtain support from selfish, unworthy citizens, and are denouncing, regulating, and abusing the deserving citizen. To save our democratic institutions, we must place worthy leaders in control of them, and have the policies of government dictated by an earnest desire to grant the greatest individual freedom and to reward the worthy.

The Democratic Principle

There are certain principles underlying the universe. There are certain definite principles underlying human nature. There are certain definite principles insuring the success of democracy. The one principle that transcends all others is the democratic principle itself—the principle that successful democratic government demands a minimum of government and a maximum of freedom of individual expression. As government activity increases, individual freedom decreases. Individual freedom is the essence, the vital spark of democracy. A democratic form of government cannot survive if it overexpands. The very act of expansion contracts individual freedom. Ultimately it will cease to be a democratic form of government.

An administration attempting to increase the functions of government, the while posing as a defender of democracy, of the people, is an enemy of democratic institutions. This is substantially what the New Deal administration is doing today. We have an example in Russia of the violation of the democratic principle. Communism is not and cannot be democratic. The vast extension of government activities results in regulating the most minute acts of the citizens and prevents the development of that individual freedom of expression which is essential to the existence of democratic institutions. In Russia today we do not have freedom of expression for the individual and we do not have democratic institutions.

So far the New Deal Administration in our own country has not destroyed all of the essentials of democracy. We still have freedom of speech and many other benefits remaining to us from our past democratic institutions. The existing administration is able to survive because it is able to obtain money from those it is attacking. It actually buys the support of many citizens by the payment of benefits, to the prejudice of the best interests of the nation. When it remains in office a sufficiently long time, the increased demand for benefits will consume the wealth accumulated by individual efforts.

When this occurs, we will be faced with two opposing developments—either the government will expand and become somewhat as Russia is today, making all citizens serve it or those citizens still demanding individual freedom of expression will reassert democratic principles. If, at that time, the government itself is in the hands of an administration similar to the New Deal, civil war may result. We may witness the anomaly of sincere democrats fighting for individual freedom under an able leader, against a government that claims to represent democracy but is actually destroying it.

Citizenship Standards

The progress of man has been brought about by the efforts of able individuals working more often in opposition to the wishes of their government than in accordance with the government's desires. Institutions controlled by many individuals are not equal in efficiency to the ablest individually conducted activities. More often than not, success in governmental policies follows great leaders. The less burden we put upon the government, the less we restrict the individual, the more opportunity will be given for great men to arise, solve the problems of their times, and lead the government toward the soundest measures. The increasing participation of the government in the private affairs of the citizens is lessening incentive and lowering the quality of citizenship.

The liberalism dominant in the beginning of our national government wished freedom, liberty, as little government as possible, and the right of the individual to do as he wished, with reasonable regard for the rights of others. Present-day liberalism is demanding that the government interfere with the liberties and rights of all individuals in order to guarantee certain economic benefits to them. It is easy to understand how this development occurred. The increasing consciousness of the fact that it was unjust for many people to be suffering want while others had great wealth resulted in the gradual development of means to curb the wealthy and benefit the poor.

Liberalism which demands that the government do much for the individual, and in so doing deprive him of much of his liberty, is unsound. The government should restrict its activities to essentials. The less governing it does, the more efficient it should be. When liberals demand that the government do something to benefit the poor, they are inaugurating a policy that results in vast masses of people demanding further benefits from the government, whereas a policy in which the government does not give direct economic benefits results in this effort being directed toward actually solving their own problems themselves.

It is the latter which the government should promote, endeavoring to see that all have a fair chance and are encouraged and protected in their rights. By encouraging each individual to solve his own problems and having a nation in which each person does solve his own problems, the need for government interference will cease to exist because the problems requiring it will not exist.

It is not the wealthy whom I fear; it is the poor character of the average citizen himself that constitutes the threat to the future. When the wealthy are denounced, the unfairness of so few having so much is the principle grievance emphasized. Carrying this view through to a logical conclusion, brings to light a weakness which those who denounce the wealthy have not thought of. It is this—if the wealthy are so few they exert but a slight influence upon moral character. What harm, for instance, could sixty families have upon prevailing standards of conduct? They are but sixty families among twenty million or so. These sixty families are not the cause of all our ills. The causes lie in the average citizen himself. Rather than denounce these sixty families, he had better devote his efforts toward making himself worthy. Then, when he is a worthy person, he will be fit to criticize others less worthy.

The great lesson we learn from the downfall of ancient civilization is their failure to establish a government which raised the standard of the individual citizen. Applying that test to the present day, let us ask ourselves, "Does our existing government contribute to the moral advance of the individual citizen?" My answer to this is, "No, it does not." On the contrary, it reflects the moral atmosphere of, not the better class of citizens, but the more undesirable class. Therefore the men who at present control our government must be removed and replaced by men deserving of respect by the better class of citizens and capable of contributing to the elevation of moral character.

We must make knowledge of Ascendent Psychology so universal that all citizens will have a fair understanding of themselves. We must stress the fact that man is of animal origin and of necessity retains within himself prihuman attributes. One of the great threats to existing democracy is the fact that man's prihuman nature, his undesirable qualities, are being constantly appealed to. It is a relatively simple task to inflame men by constantly stirring up their grievances.

We must develop citizens who will not permit themselves to dwell constantly upon grievances and will not heed those striving to stir them up. We must develop an environment that will appeal to man's better nature; that will discredit and disapprove of attempts to appeal to his poorer nature.

Much of the existing labor agitation and denunciation of capital is harmful for this reason. It appeals to man's poorer qualities. When grievances exist, the citizens as such should demand constructive action to correct them. They should not support mere denunciation which does nothing to improve matters and serves only to create ill-feeling.

Enlightened citizens in a democracy should have sufficient understanding of human nature and the human mind to know how they form their opinions. Ask the average person for his views on any subject and he will usually have an opinion to express. You can ask opinions on the most difficult problems and obtain ready answers. To acquire the knowledge necessary to properly answer these questions would sometimes require years of painstaking effort. Yet our citizens willingly answer them and are convinced that their opinions are correct. Just how do they arrive at these opinions? They absorb them from whatever influences they are subjected to. They accept those opinions that are most pleasing to them. The calm objective thinker seeking for basic truths upon which to form a conclusion is practically nonexistent. We must endeavor to model our institutions so as to develop citizens of this type.

After the citizens have formed their opinion they will follow those leaders who most nearly express what they would like to have expressed. If their leaders have great personal appeal, they will follow them with the utmost loyalty. A truly great man, able to inspire the support of vast numbers of followers, can accomplish great achievements. To do this he must have ability, character, human feeling, and other qualities which will inspire the loyalty of intelligent citizens. A democracy lends itself readily to the leadership of demagogues who appeal to the baser feelings. We should guard against demagogues and anything that tends to lower the standards of citizenship. We should strive to produce high standards of citizenship and worthy leaders to conduct the affairs of government.

The schools should endeavor to teach the younger generation citizenship by impressing upon them that they are making history. The development of man in the past has been of a somewhat blind, fumbling nature. If we can convince our young generation and, in time, all citizens, that they have the positive duty of contributing their part toward man's history and development, we will be establishing a wholesome outlook contributing to the solution of present-day problems as well as toward greater understanding by the individual.

All too often each person fails to consider that he himself is a living part of man; that he can influence man's destiny for good or ill; that unconsciously he influences others just as he is influenced by them; that his acts today will have an effect upon the generations of tomorrow and all time to come.

This effect may be harmful, may be practically nil, or it may be vital. We must cause each individual to understand his responsibility, to see that his contribution is helpful. Once we can establish this understanding, this conception of duty on the part of all citizens, we will have a society creditable to us and one of which we can well be proud to be members.

The Preservation of Democracy

We have a larger task than merely saving democracy in the United States. We have the task of saving the world itself. Unless the world be saved, democracy in the United States alone will be of little avail. To save the world we must adopt emergency measures adequate to this task. This requires unity of command. Nothing less than a dictator will answer.

We have an example in some of our competitive industries, of the pernicious effect of promoting self-interest to the detriment of the industry as a whole. This has resulted in many industries establishing what substantially amounts to a czar or dictator. The primary reason for the existence of this dictator is to approach the problems of the industry with a broad viewpoint. He considers the interest of each individual firm from the broad viewpoint of the welfare of all.

It is a viewpoint of this kind that we require in both national and international affairs. It is just the opposite of this sensible policy that is in vogue today. We have strife between interest groups within our nation and in the international field practically all nations are furthering their own interests regardless of others.

We are being controlled by the same human qualities that dominate in juvenile gangs, criminal gangs, and savage tribes. All members of their tribes or gangs are worthy. All others are enemies to be exploited, enslaved, or killed. Are we civilized? No. Why do we not face the facts, admit our faults, and correct them? Instead, each person denies the existence of any fault within himself or his group. This utterly prevents their correction.

Orderly conduct is assured among the savages, the primitive-minded, and juvenile by having a firm, strong ruler. He should be so strong as to insure consistent attempts on their part to behave well in order to please him and to prevent punishment to themselves. The highly intelligent human being should be above the stage of requiring a strong ruler. He should be able to rule himself. Civilization today is in a state of transition from the prihuman state of being ruled by a strong chieftain, to the adhuman state of each individual ruling himself. Many nations today are lapsing into forms of dictatorship reminiscent of primitive chieftains. They are proving more successful than democracy. We must establish a democracy founded upon an adhuman citizenship. If we fail to do this we will be subjected to the primitive rule of dictators.

Democratic institutions dominated by vicious politics, denunciation, appeals to self-interest and grievances, tend to bring out undesirable human qualities that should be permitted to slumber. Continual agitation of this nature is permitted by the abuse of free speech. Our problem is to reform our democratic institutions so as to appeal to the finest human qualities and to avoid stirring up the bad qualities.

Our much-praised democratic institutions are unworthy when they appeal to man's poor qualities. Thoughtless worship of democracy is the very thing that will bring about its downfall. We should frankly recognize the fact that our politicians today are appealing to human desires and feelings that are incompatible with high standards of citizenship. Either we must reform our institutions or they will collapse as a result of their own viciousness.

To reform our governmental institutions will require drastic action. It will demand economical measures. Of necessity, this will require reduction of government activity and expenditures. So many interest groups and individuals must be deprived of the benefits they are now receiving that they will oppose the drastic measures required to improve conditions. Politicians will never be able to overcome this opposition. It will require a strong, ruthless dictatorship, considering not the interest of individuals and interest groups, but the interest of the nation as a whole.

It will require a man who will ruthlessly brush aside the opposition of those selfish groups unwilling to sacrifice their present benefits for the future good of all. Here is where our democratic institutions will be overthrown. As the result of a vicious political system, we have brought about a condition of affairs that democracy cannot correct. We will have to employ the most ruthless dictatorship to re-establish the freedom of our democratic institutions.

THE END

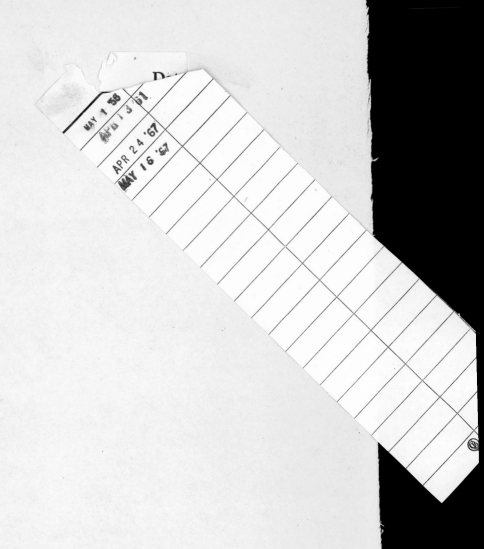